D1317046

Visual Basic™
for Windows™
INSIDER

THE WILEY INSIDER SERIES

If you think this book is just another computer book, stop right there. I am proud to tell you that it is part of an innovative series created by the Coriolis Group and published by John Wiley & Sons.

What you're holding is a "tour-de-force" of Visual Basic insider tips, secrets, undocumented features, shortcuts, and technical advice that has never been available in a book format like this.

Peter Aitken, Visual Basic expert and author, has gathered together his best tips and techniques based on his many years of programming experience to create this newest book in the INSIDER series. The book is jam-packed with innovative ideas for programming Visual Basic in ways you never thought possible. But the real kicker is that the unique format of this book will help you understand and use the tips and techniques presented as if a friendly expert were at your side, ready to answer any question you might have.

In creating the INSIDER series, we wanted to break with tradition and develop books that go way beyond the typical "documentation approach" of most computer books. In each INSIDER book, we'll show you how to customize your software, put new features to work right away, work smarter and faster, and solve difficult problems.

What you're holding represents an innovative and highly practical guide that was developed by some of the best minds in computer book publishing. We hope you enjoy each and every INSIDER guide.

—Keith Weiskamp
INSIDER Series Editor

CORIOLIS GROUP BOOK

Visual Basic™
for Windows™
INSIDER

Peter Aitken

Keith Weiskamp, Series Editor

John Wiley & Sons, Inc.
New York • Chichester • Brisbane • Toronto • Singapore

Trademarks: Microsoft is a registered trademark and Windows and Visual Basic are trademarks of Microsoft Corporation. All other brand names and product names included in this book are trademarks, registered trademarks, or trade names of their respective holders.

This text is printed on acid-free paper.

Copyright © 1993 by John Wiley & Sons, Inc.

All rights reserved. Published simultaneously in Canada.

Reproduction or translation of any part of this work beyond that permitted by section 107 or 108 of the 1976 United States Copyright Act without the written permission of the copyright owner is unlawful. Requests for permission or further information should be addressed to the Permissions Department, John Wiley & Sons, Inc.

Library of Congress Cataloging-in-Publication Data

Aitken, Peter G.
    Visual Basic for Windows insider with disk / by Peter Aitken.
        p.   cm.
    Includes index.
    ISBN 0-471-59092-4 (pbk. : alk. paper)
    1. BASIC (Computer program language)   2. Microsoft Visual BASIC
3. Windows (Computer programs). 4. Application software. I. Title.
II. Title: Visual Basic insider with disk.
    QA76.73.B3A383   1993
    005.4'3--dc20   93-12518
                                                 CIP

Printed in the United States of America

10 9 8 7 6 5 4 3 2

Contents

Chapter 3 Adding Functionality to Your Visual Basic Programs

Chapter 4 Masterful Menus

Chapter 5 Using Dynamic Data Exchange   119

Chapter 6 Object Linking and Embedding   145

Introduction

When Microsoft introduced the Visual Basic programming system, it took the world of Windows application development by storm. At least, it took my office by storm! Never had it been so easy to create attractive, robust, and full-featured Windows applications. What started out as a great product became even better with the release of Version 2.0 in 1992 and Version 3.0 in 1993. Few if any programmers were sorry to relegate their C compiler and Windows SDK to a dusty shelf.

As I worked with Visual Basic, it became clear that, like any programming environment, it has limitations. And, like any self-respecting programmer, I did my best to work around these limitations. By making the best possible use of Visual Basic's own features, and when necessary going outside to access capabilities of the Windows operating environment, I found I could significantly enhance the power and flexibility of Visual Basic. And that's where the idea for this book originated. It seemed that there must be many other Visual Basic programmers who would find these techniques useful. I suspect that you are one of them!

About this Book

My goal in writing this book is to provide a variety of advanced programming tips, tricks, and techniques that you can use in your own Visual Basic programs. The book is not a guide to the "basics" of Visual Basic. To use an automotive analogy, I will not teach you how to drive—I assume you already know that—but rather I will show you how to get some extra horsepower from your engine. To use this book, you should already be fairly comfortable with the Visual Basic programming environment and language. For the most part, I do not cover any material that is in the Visual Basic manuals or Help system. The few exceptions are for topics that are complex and which I feel are covered poorly in the product documentation.

The book's material is divided into chapters based on programming area. Within each chapter, the main topic is further divided into two or more sections. Each section contains a number of *scenarios*, which are the actual heart of the book. Each scenario presents a problem, task, or question and shows you how to solve it. Relatively simple topics are covered completely in a single scenario, while more complex topics may be subdivided among two or more scenarios.

There is no need to read the chapters in order, from start to finish. You can skip around at will, concentrating on those areas that interest you. I have intentionally written the book so that later scenarios do not depend on earlier ones. To avoid too much duplication of material, it has occasionally been necessary to refer you to another section of the book, but I have tried to keep such cross-references to a minimum.

The book incorporates a number of features that are intended to make it easier to use. Hot Tips scattered throughout the book present important suggestions, ideas, and warnings. On Disk boxes list the names of the source code and project files that are on the book's companion disk. Screen shots show you the appearance of various forms and other program elements.

On the Disk

The diskette that accompanies the book includes source code and project files for all of the listings in the book. You are free to use, modify, and distribute these listings without restrictions. Please note, however, that all code is supplied on an "as-is" basis. While I have made every effort to provide bug-free code, neither I nor the publishers can be responsible for any problems that may arise from using it.

Acknowledgments

First, I thank Keith Weiskamp, the INSIDER series editor, who first approached me with the idea for a *Visual Basic Insider* and then provided support and guidance throughout the writing process. I am also indebted to Jenni Aloi-Wolfson, the talented and persevering editor and reviewer whose sharp pencil has excised a large number of errors, inconsistencies, and dangling participles from the original manuscript. I also thank "the gang" on the CompuServe Basic Programming Forum, a seemingly endless source of ideas, suggestions, and good conversation. Finally, many thanks to my wife, Maxine, for her unflagging support and encouragement, and also for the occasional neck massage after a long programming session!

The Windows API

T he first chapter of this book introduces you to and covers the methods you use to access the Windows API, or Applications Program Interface. The API is the most important tool you have for extending the power of Visual Basic, so it is necessary that you understand what the API is and how it is used.

Introducing the Windows API

This section explains what the API is, and gives you an idea of what it can do for your programs.

What Is It?

The Windows API is a set of powerful procedures that is a part of Windows itself.

Whenever you run Windows or any Windows application, you are seeing the API in action. In fact, it's fairly accurate to say that the API is the heart of Windows. Many of the actions that Windows or a Windows program takes are accomplished by invoking an API procedure. Creating and manipulating screen windows, drawing graphics objects, working with fonts, displaying menus and dialog boxes—all these and more are handled by the API. All a program need do is call the proper API procedure and pass the appropriate arguments.

The Windows API procedures are located in files called *dynamic link libraries*, or DLLs. These files are installed on your disk when you install Windows, and are loaded into memory whenever Windows is running. There is only one copy of each API procedure, that is shared by all programs that need it (this is called *dynamic linking*). This linking process is quite different from the process used by non-Windows programs, in which every program's executable file contains copies of all the procedures the program uses. There are two major advantages to dynamic linking. The first is space savings, because disk space and memory storage are needed for only a single copy of each procedure. The second advantage is consistency, because all programs utilize the same set of API procedures.

Programs that you create with Visual Basic use API calls, just like any other Windows program. For capabilities that are built into Visual Basic, such as creating windows (forms), the API calls are hidden from you— they are placed in the program by Visual Basic in response to the program elements and features you specify. However, Visual Basic's built-in programming tools do not provide access to all of the capabilities of the Windows operating environment. You can, however, use most of those capabilities by directly calling API procedures from your Visual Basic program. As you'll see, most of the Visual Basic enhancements presented in this book involve API calls.

What's Available in the API?

The Windows API contains hundreds of different procedures that perform a wide variety of tasks.

With so many different procedures, it's clearly not practical to provide any sort of detailed information on the contents of the API. There are procedures for window management, file manipulation, printer control, menus and dialog boxes, memory management, graphics drawing, string manipulation—I could go on and on! Suffice it to say that if you want it, it's probably in there (and if it's not in there, Windows probably can't do it anyway)!

I will provide information on some of the most useful API functions in the remainder of this book. However, if you want to further explore the API you will need additional reference information. Several guides to the Windows API have been published. Two that I have found useful are *The API Bible*, published by The Waite Group and *Microsoft Windows 3.1 Programmer's Reference*, a multi-volume set published by Microsoft Press. If you have the Professional Edition of Visual Basic, online API information can be accessed by clicking the Win 3.1 SDK icon in the Visual Basic group. Whatever source of API information you choose, I suggest that you take some time to browse through it. You will probably find procedures that provide capabilities you had not even imagined!

Accessing the Windows API

Now that you know the power that the API can bring to your programs, you're probably ready to try it out! The remainder of this chapter shows you the techniques you'll need to access API procedures from your Visual Basic programs.

Calling API Procedures in Your Visual Basic Program

Calling an API procedure is not much different from calling a regular Basic subprocedure or function.

The method you use to call an API procedure is essentially identical to that used for calling a general function or subprocedure in Visual Basic. The method depends on whether the API procedure is a function (that is, returns a value to the calling program) or a subprocedure (does not return a value). For an API function, you use the function name on the right side of an assignment statement, assigning its return value to a variable of the appropriate type. For an API subprocedure, use the **Call** statement. In both cases, of course, you must pass the correct number and types of arguments to the procedure.

If you'll bear with me for a moment, I'll risk boring you with an example. Assume that **SuperAPISub** is an API subprocedure, and **SuperAPIFunc** is an API function that returns an integer. You would access them as shown here (ignoring arguments for now):

```
Call SuperAPISub()
x% = SuperAPIFunc()
```

That's all there is to it! Well, almost...there's one more thing. Every API procedure that a program uses must be declared in the program using the **Declare** statement. The **Declare** statement serves to inform the Visual Basic program about the name, arguments, and (for functions) return type of external procedures. *External* means that the procedure exists outside the Visual Basic program—and this is certainly the case for API functions, which reside in Windows dynamic link libraries! The **Declare** statement takes one of the following forms depending on whether it is a sub or a function:

```
Declare Sub globalname Lib libname [([argumentlist])]
Declare Function globalname Lib libname [([argumentlist])] [As type]
```

Here, *globalname* is the name of the API **Sub** or **Function** procedure, and *libname* is a string literal that gives the name of the DLL that contains the declared procedure. The *argumentlist* is a list of variables representing arguments that are passed to the **Sub** or **Function** procedure when it is called. Most arguments to API procedures must be passed with the **ByVal** keyword. The list has the following syntax:

```
ByVal varname1 [As type] [,ByVal varname2 [As type]]...
```

In this case, the *type* at the end of the function declaration declares the data type of the value returned by a **Function** procedure. Alternatively you can specify the return type of an API function by appending the appropriate type declaration character at the end of *globalname*.

For Windows API procedures, the required components of the **Declare** statement are strictly defined; the *globalname, libname,* and *argumentlist* must be specified exactly or the **Declare** statement won't work. When you try to run the program, Visual Basic reports a "Reference to undefined function or array." Unfortunately, the **Declare** statement required by most API procedures is rather long and involved. Here's a real example:

```
Declare Function SendDlgItemMessage Lib "User" (ByVal hDlg As Integer,
   ByVal nIDDlgItem As Integer, ByVal wMsg As Integer, ByVal wParam As
   Integer, lParam As Any) As Long
```

Don't worry about what this API function does—the point here is simply to impress you with how complex API procedure **Declare** statements can be! Fortunately, you will rarely if ever need to type them yourself. If you have the Professional Edition, a complete list of API declarations is installed along with Visual Basic; click on the Win3.1 API Help icon in the Visual Basic group, then click on Declare Statements from the contents. You can copy the **Declare** statements that you need and paste them into your programs. If you don't have the Professional Edition you can copy the **Declare** statements from the code examples provided on this book's companion disk—at least you can for the API procedures used in the book!

You may be wondering where in your program you should place API procedure **Declare** statements. That's a simple one! Place them in the general declarations section of the code or form module that calls the procedures.

Using Windows' Global Constants

Using Windows' global constants when working with API procedures can make your code easier to understand.

Working with API procedures will be simpler, and your program will be easier to understand and modify, if you use Windows' global constants to pass arguments to API procedures. The global constants include hundreds of mnemonic symbols whose names provide information about their action. For example, the API procedure **SetWindowPos** takes an argument that specifies the window's Z-order (its position in the top-to-bottom stack of screen windows). If the argument is 0, the window is moved to the top of the Z-order; if the argument is 1, the window is moved to the bottom. You could pass the literal constant 0 or 1, of course, and the function would work perfectly well. If, however, you use the constants **HWND_TOP** (which is defined as 0) and **HWND_BOTTOM** (which is defined as 1), the code will be easier to understand because the constant name in the function call makes it clear what the function is being asked to do.

The Windows global constants are not automatically defined for you— you must do so in your program using the **Global Const** statement. In most cases, global constants should be defined in the global declarations section of a code module, so they will be available in all parts of the program.

If you are using the Professional Edition of Visual Basic, you can access a list of all Windows global constants by clicking on the Win3.1 API Help icon in the Visual Basic group, then clicking on Global Constants from the contents. You can copy the needed constant definitions and paste them into your source code. When using the constants be careful of spelling errors—a misspelled constant name in a function call can cause hard-to-find bugs, as Visual Basic will interpret it as a new variable with a value of 0. Such problems can be avoided by using the **Option Explicit** statement in all your programs, which forces you to explicitly declare all variables used in a program. (I highly recommend the addition of this statement to your programs!) You can automatically include an **Option Explicit** statement in your code by clicking on the Environment menu item from the Options menu and changing the Require Variable Declaration option to Yes. Do this now, before you forget!

Declaring API Functions as Subprocedures

If your program does not need the return value of an API procedure, you can declare and use it like a subprocedure.

Most of the procedures in the API are functions that return a value to the calling program. Many times you need this return value, particularly when it indicates whether the API call has succeeded or failed. Other times, however, the return value is not needed. In this situation you can declare and use the API procedure as a sub, simplifying its use in the program.

Here's an example. The **SetTextAlign** API procedure is a function that specifies the way Windows aligns text that is printed on the screen. Its official declaration is

```
Declare Function SetTextAlign Lib "GDI" (ByVal hDC As Integer, ByVal
    wFlags As Integer) As Integer
```

In a VB program you would call it as shown here:

```
RetValue% = SetTextAlign(...)
```

The value returned by this API function is the previous text alignment setting—something most programs will not be too interested in! To use it as a subprocedure, you would modify its declaration as shown here:

```
Declare Sub SetTextAlign Lib "GDI" (ByVal hDC As Integer, ByVal wFlags
  As Integer)
```

Then, the program would call it using the normal calling method:

```
Call SetTextAlign(...)
```

Note that you cannot define the same API procedure as both a function and a subprocedure in the same program with the same name—it must be one or the other.

If you do need to use an API procedure both ways, you can declare it with an *Alias* name:

```
Declare Sub SetTextAlign Lib "GDI" (…)
Declare Function SetTextAlignFunction Lib "GDI"
  Alias "SetTextAlign" (…) As Integer
```

You may then call it using whichever declaration fits the situation at hand:

```
Call SetTextAlign (…)
```

or

```
RetValue% = SetTextAlign (…)
```

The programs in this book frequently declare and use API functions as subprocedures.

CHAPTER 2

Enhancing the Look of Your Visual Basic Programs

T he default appearance of Visual Basic applications is quite attractive, and has the advantage of being similar to the appearance of many other Windows applications. However, there are many ways that you can enhance the appearance of your programs, providing a clearer way to present specialized information or simply creating a unique look.

Creating a Graphical Toolbar

A toolbar, or button bar, is a group of small graphical symbols on the screen that the user can click to perform commonly needed actions. Visual Basic uses a toolbar, as do many Windows applications. In this section, you will learn how to add a toolbar to your Visual Basic programs.

Designing the Toolbar

On the ideal toolbar, each button displays a graphical image that represents the button's action—for example a pair of scissors on the "Cut" button.

Since we want to display a graphic on the toolbar buttons, we are limited to the two types of controls that can display graphics: Picture Box and Image. The latter is preferable for two reasons. First, an Image control displays its image faster than a Picture Box control. Second, Image controls have a Stretch property which, when set to True, causes the graphic displayed in the Image control to automatically stretch to fit the size of the control (if this property is False, the Image control automatically resizes to fit the original size of the graphic).

In principle, then, creating a graphical toolbar is simple. Create a control array of Image controls, each of which is loaded with the desired graphic. Then, position the Image controls in the desired position on a form, usually in a row along the upper edge. You can use the **Image_Click** event procedure to detect and respond to user selection from the bar.

Unfortunately, it's not quite this simple. The fact that Image controls (and their contents) can be resized suggests that you can create a toolbar that automatically changes size as its parent form is resized. You can, in fact, do so (see *Adjusting the Position and Size of Controls Automatically* in Chapter 2). However, the resizing of an Image control's graphic is a relatively slow process. In my experience, a resizable toolbar containing 10 Image controls can requires several seconds to display when its parent window is resized. This is unacceptably slow.

The only alternative is to create a fixed-size toolbar when you design your program. The Stretch property operates during design too, so if you load a graphic into an Image control then resize the control, the graphic will resize to fit. Because the resizing operation was done during program design, it does not need to be done during execution, therefore the toolbar will display quickly.

This approach requires that the individual Image controls be precisely sized and positioned during program design. If you have a fine eye and a steady hand you can do so visually. For assured accuracy, you can set the size and position properties manually based on the size of the parent Picture Box. Assuming a toolbar that contains N buttons (i.e., N Image controls) and a Picture Box with ScaleWidth equal to W and ScaleHeight equal to H, we can calculate the Height, Width, and Top for all Image controls as follows:

```
Height = H
Width = W/N
Top = 0
```

And for the Nth Image control we calculate Left as shown here:

```
Left = (N-1) * (W/N) + 1
```

Of course, a fixed-size toolbar must be associated with a fixed-size form. Typically this will be a full-screen MDI form, which serves as the container for most complex Visual Basic applications. You cannot place Image controls directly on an MDI form, however. The solution is to first place a Picture box on the MDI form, then draw the Image controls on the Picture Box.

Graphical Images for Toolbar Buttons

You can draw your own graphics, or use the icons supplied with Visual Basic.

Where can you get the graphics for your buttons? An Image control can display bitmap files (*.BMP, *.DIB), Windows metafiles (*.WMF), and icon files (*.ICO). You can use the icon files supplied in the Visual Basic icon library. If you have the Professional Edition you can use the Toolbar Bitmaps or other graphics images that are provided. You can also use an icon editor to create icons from scratch or modify existing icons for your needs. Visual Basic comes with an icon editor, ICONWRKS (ICONWRKS is a Visual Basic program, located in the \VB\SAMPLES\ICONWRKS subdirectory).

Create Your Own 3-D Icons

See the section *Designing Your Own 3-D Icon Buttons* for tips on how to draw icons with a three-dimensional appearance.

Add Animation to Your Toolbar Buttons

Add a professional touch to your toolbar by designing the buttons to appear depressed when clicked.

One additional nice touch can be added to a toolbar. In most commercial applications, the buttons appear depressed when the user clicks on them. You can obtain a similar effect by manipulating the BorderStyle property of the Image controls. When you create the toolbar, set the BorderStyle property to 0-None. In the control's **MouseDown** event procedure, set the BorderStyle property to 1-Fixed Single, then in the **MouseUp** event procedure set it back to 0. An Image control with a border appears smaller and "lower" than one without a border, so the button appears depressed while the mouse button is down. You should also place code that branches based on which button was clicked in the **MouseUp** procedure.

Always Provide Keyboard Equivalents

Remember, some users prefer to use the keyboard. Your programs should always provide a keyboard alternative to toolbar commands.

Designing Your Own 3-D Icon Buttons

With an icon editor you can create icons that appear three dimensional.

You have learned how to create a toolbar containing buttons with graphical images. If the icons in the Visual Basic icon library do not meet your needs, you can use an icon editor to create your own. By following a few simple design techniques, you can create icons that appear to be three dimensional. The icons on the Visual Basic toolbar use these techniques, and I think you'll agree that they are quite attractive.

An icon is a special type of bitmap, and is usually stored on disk in a file with the .ICO extension. It is easiest to create and modify icons with a specialized icon editor. Visual Basic's icon editor is ICONWRKS, is actually a Visual Basic demonstration program, which is found in the \VB\SAMPLES\ICONWRKS subdirectory. You may have access to another icon editor; I use the one that is provided with the Norton Desktop for Windows.

The goal is to make the icon button appear as if it is protruding from the screen surface. The trick is to use shadows. In Windows, the convention is that the "lighting" is coming from above and to the left. Therefore a square button that is raised from the surface would appear with its upper and left edges brighter (because they are exposed directly to the light) and with its right and lower edges darker (because they are in shadow). The surface of the icon should be somewhere in between— a medium gray.

You can also make the image on the icon appear three dimensional, as if it were incised into the surface of the button. Again, using shadows is the trick. This time, however, you use the reverse of the scheme used for the edges of the button: the top and left edges of incised lines should be dark, mimicking shadow, while the right and lower edges of lines should be brighter because they face the light.

Figure 2.1 illustrates the design principles that were used to shade the edges of the button and the lines forming the image on the icon. In this figure, and when viewed in an icon editor, it doesn't appear three dimensional because the elements are too large. When viewed at its "real" size, however, these techniques are quite effective.

Using the Icon File

Throughout this book the "On Disk" graphic will be used to indicate that the information presented is available on the provided diskl. In this case, the icon shown in Figure 2.1 is stored on disk as THREE-D.ICO.

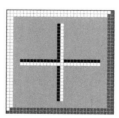

Figure 2.1 Designing a three-dimensional icon.

Figure 2.2   A graphical toolbar created using Image controls.

A Toolbar Demonstration

The program in this section demonstrates the techniques discussed in the previous scenario.

The program BTN_BAR.MAK demonstrates how to use these techniques to create a graphical button bar. This program places a toolbar with 10 buttons on an MDI form, as shown in Figure 2.2. The buttons were made relatively large for this demonstration; you would probably want them smaller in a real program. The graphics for the first nine buttons were taken from the Visual Basic icon library. The last button (which exits the program) was created from scratch using an icon editor. Properties and code for this program are presented in Listings 2.1 and 2.2.

Using BTN_BAR.MAK

This demonstration program, presented in Listings 2.1 and 2.2, are stored on disk as BTN_BAR.MAK and BTN_BAR.FRM.

Listing 2.1   Object Properties in BTN_BAR.FRM

```
Begin MDIForm frmButtonBar
   Caption        =   "MDIForm1"
   WindowState    =   2  'Maximized
      Begin PictureBox Picture1
         Align          =   1   'Align Top
         Left           =   0
         ScaleHeight    =   825
         ScaleWidth     =   9570
         Top            =   0
      Begin Image Button
         Height         =   825
         Index          =   9
         Left           =   8613
         Picture        =   (see text)
         Stretch        =   -1   'True
         Top            =   0
         Width          =   957
      End
```

```
Begin Image Button
    Height        =    825
    Index         =    8
    Left          =    7656
    Picture       =    (see text)
    Stretch       =    -1   'True
    Top           =    0
    Width         =    957
End
Begin Image Button
    Height        =    825
    Index         =    7
    Left          =    6699
    Picture       =    (see text)
    Stretch       =    -1   'True
    Top           =    0
    Width         =    957
End
Begin Image Button
    Height        =    825
    Index         =    6
    Left          =    5742
    Picture       =    (see text)
    Stretch       =    -1   'True
    Top           =    0
    Width         =    957
End
Begin Image Button
    Height        =    825
    Index         =    5
    Left          =    4785
    Picture       =    (see text)
    Stretch       =    -1   'True
    Top           =    0
    Width         =    957
End
Begin Image Button
    Height        =    825
    Index         =    4
    Left          =    3828
    Picture       =    (see text)
    Stretch       =    -1   'True
    Top           =    0
    Width         =    957
End
Begin Image Button
    Height        =    825
    Index         =    3
    Left          =    2871
```

```
            Picture          =    (see text)
            Stretch          =    -1   'True
            Top              =    0
            Width            =    957
         End
         Begin Image Button
            Height           =    825
            Index            =    2
            Left             =    1914
            Picture          =    (see text)
            Stretch          =    -1   'True
            Top              =    0
            Width            =    957
         End
         Begin Image Button
            Height           =    825
            Index            =    1
            Left             =    957
            Picture          =    (see text)
            Stretch          =    -1   'True
            Top              =    0
            Width            =    957
         End
         Begin Image Button
            Height           =    825
            Index            =    0
            Left             =    0
            Picture          =    (see text)
            Stretch          =    -1   'True
            Top              =    0
            Width            =    957
         End
      End
   End
End
```

Listing 2.2   Code in BTN_BAR.FRM

```
Option Explicit

Sub Button_MouseDown (Index As Integer, Button As Integer, Shift As
   Integer, x As Single, Y As Single)

' Change the BorderStyle so the button appears depressed.
frmButtonBar.Button(Index).BorderStyle = 1

End Sub

Sub Button_MouseUp (Index As Integer, Button As Integer, Shift As
```

```
    Integer, x As Single, Y As Single)

Dim msg As String

' Return the BorderStyle to the "raised" appearance.
frmButtonBar.Button(Index).BorderStyle = 0

' Exit if the last button was selected. Otherwise display
' a message indicating which button was clicked.
If Index = 9 Then End

msg = "You selected button " + Str$(Index + 1)
MsgBox msg

End Sub
```

Window Wonders

Every part of every Visual Basic program appears in a window, or form. Clearly, the manner in which your programs use windows is important. The techniques presented in this section show you how to enhance the appearance and functionality of your program's windows.

Creating Floating Windows

Windows lets you run and view multiple programs at once. It often happens, however, that an inactive window you need to view is hidden by other windows. You can prevent this by creating a floating window that will always be displayed on top of the desktop.

When you are running multiple Windows applications, the windows, or *forms* in Visual Basic, overlap and hide each other in the order they are displayed. While one application is active, crucial information displayed in another application's window may be hidden from view. You can designate any window as a *floating* window so that it will always remain visible, on top of the heap. It must be a partial screen window, of course, or it would hide all other windows!

To float a window, you use the API function **SetWindowPos** function. Its declaration is:

```
Declare Function SetWindowPos Lib "User" (ByVal hWnd As Integer, ByVal
    hWndInsertAfter As Integer, ByVal X As Integer, ByVal Y As Integer, ByVal
    Cx As Integer, ByVal Cy As Integer, ByVal wFlags As Integer) As Integer
```

Table 2.1   The SetWindowsPos Function Parameters

Parameter	Description
hWnd	The hWnd handle of the form
hWndInsertAfter	Specifies form status
X	X coordinate of form's left edge
Y	Y coordinate of form's top edge
Cx	Width of form
Cy	Height of form
wFlags	Function control flags

This function returns a non-zero value on success, a zero value otherwise. As you might guess from its parameters, the **SetWindowPos** function does more than create floating windows! The function parameters are described in Table 2.1.

This function can also be used to control a window's size and position. However, those capabilities are not of interest to us because Visual Basic can control windows size and position directly. To simply make a window float without changing its size or position, you pass the proper value in **hWndInsertAfter** to specify a floating form, and pass flags in **wFlags** that instruct **SetWindowPos** to ignore the size and position arguments. To unfloat, or *sink*, a form you follow the same procedure, passing a different value in **hWndInsertAfter**.

The program in Listings 2.3 and 2.4 demonstrates a floating window. The interesting parts are in FLOATWIN.BAS. The general declarations part of this module includes the declaration of **SetWindowPos** as well as several global constants that the program uses. The first four constants are Windows API global constants, the others are program specific. The **Sub FloatWindow** does the real work. The calling program passes the **Sub** two arguments: the **hWnd** property of the form to be affected and a second argument specifying whether the form is to be floated or sunk (hence the global constants **FLOAT** and **SINK**). The **SINK** constant does not actually remove the form from the top of the display, but removes its "topmost" status so that other windows can cover it if they are activated.

Listing 2.3   Code in FLOATWIN.BAS

```
' FLOATWIN.BAS
' Global definitions and declares for floating window demo.
Option Explicit

Global Const SWP_NOMOVE = 2
Global Const SWP_NOSIZE = 1
```

```
Global Const HWND_TOPMOST = -1
Global Const HWND_NOTOPMOST = -2
Global Const FLOAT = 1, SINK = 0

Declare Sub SetWindowPos Lib "User" (ByVal hWnd As Integer, ByVal
  hWndInsertAfter As Integer, ByVal x As Integer, ByVal Y As Integer,
  ByVal cx As Integer, ByVal cy As Integer, ByVal wFlags As Integer)

Sub FloatWindow (x As Integer, action As Integer)

' When called by a form:
'
' If action <> 0 makes the form float (always on top)
' If action = 0 "unfloats" the window.
'
Dim wFlags As Integer

wFlags = SWP_NOMOVE Or SWP_NOSIZE

If action <> 0 Then      ' Float
    result = SetWindowPos(x, HWND_TOPMOST, 0, 0, 0, 0, wFlags)
Else                     ' Sink
    result = SetWindowPos(x, HWND_NOTOPMOST, 0, 0, 0, 0, wFlags)
End If

End Sub
```

The remainder of the program serves to demonstrate these techniques. Create a single form containing three Command Buttons with Caption properties **&Float**, **&Sink**, and **E&xit**, and Name properties **cmdFloat**, **cmdSink**, and **cmdExit**, respectively. Then, add the event procedure code shown in Listing 2.4. Note that the demonstration program does not check the return value of **FloatWindow** for a non-zero value indicating that the call to **SetWindowPos** was successful. A real program should do so, of course.

When the program starts, the form is a regular non-floating form. Select **Float** to make it float, then activate another window to see how the floating form remains on top. Figure 2.3 shows the form floating over an Excel worksheet. It may not be obvious from the figure, but the worksheet window was active at the time the screen shot was made.

Using FLOATWIN.MAK

This program, presented in Listing 2.4, is stored on disk as FLOATWIN.MAK, FLOATWIN.FRM, and FLOATWIN.BAS.

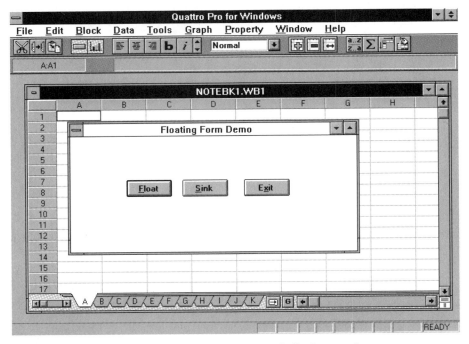

Figure 2.3 A floating form is displayed on top of all other windows.

Listing 2.4 Code in FLOATWIN.FRM

```
' FLOATWIN.FRM
' Demonstration of floating window.

Sub cmdExit_Click ()

End

End Sub

Sub cmdFloat_Click ()

' Float the active form.
Dim x As Integer

x = SCREEN.ActiveForm.hWnd

CALL FloatWindow(x, FLOAT)

End Sub
```

```
Sub cmdSink_Click ()

' Sink the active form.
Dim x As Integer

x = SCREEN.ActiveForm.hWnd

CALL FloatWindow(x, SINK)

End Sub
```

To enable selection of floating forms in your programs, add the module FLOATWIN.BAS to the project, then call **FloatWindow** as needed.

Centering Forms on the Screen

You can create a simple routine that will automatically center a form on the screen, independent of the video hardware and the form's size.

You can manually center a form on the screen during the design process, but what if you want the form to be displayed centered whenever it is displayed during program execution? You can do so by placing the following code in the form's **Resize** event procedure:

```
Sub Form_Resize ()

' Whenever the form is displayed or resized, center it
' on the screen. Exit if the form is minimized or maximized.
If WindowState > 0 Then Exit Sub

Move (Screen.Width - Width) / 2, (Screen.Height - Height) / 2

End Sub
```

This method will cause the form the be automatically centered when it is first displayed and whenever the user resizes it. The form can still be moved off center by the user, however, as long as its size is not changed.

Using Centering Forms

A program that demonstrates automatic centering of forms is on disk as CENTERED.MAK and CENTERED.FRM.

Displaying "Exploding" Forms

An exploding form is not a terrorist device! It's a form that, when first displayed, starts out small then quickly expands to its full size. By using exploding forms you can give your Visual Basic applications that extra edge in visual impact.

An exploding form is really a visual illusion. It is not the form itself that explodes, but an ordinary rectangle that has the same color as the form's background. When the rectangle reaches the full form size, the form is displayed over the rectangle. This method can be quite effective, and is relatively easy to do using Windows API calls. By bypassing Visual Basic's window management functions, you can draw the rectangles directly on the screen. Normally this would be strictly forbidden by the rules of good Windows programming practice—drawing on a screen region not owned by your application can lead to trouble. But in this case, the screen area covered by the rectangles is exactly the area that the program's form will occupy, so there's no problem.

The first API call we need is **GetWindowRect**, which returns the coordinates of a window. We need the dimensions of the Visual Basic window so we can make the exploding rectangles the proper size. The declaration is:

```
Declare Sub GetWindowRect Lib "User" (ByVal hWnd As Integer, lpRect As RECT)
```

Here, **hWnd** is the handle of the window whose size you are interested in—in our case, this is the Visual Basic form that is about to be exploded—and **lpRect** is a type **RECT** structure where the window's coordinates are placed by the procedure. **RECT** is a Windows structure that contains four integer members that hold the X,Y cordinates of the window's top-left and bottom-right corners (see Listing 2.5 for more details on the type **RECT** structure). The next API procedure we need is **GetDC**. Its declaration is:

```
Declare Function GetDC Lib "User" (ByVal hWnd As Integer) As Integer
```

This function returns a handle to the device context of a screen window. The device context is required to perform drawing operations on the screen—it identifies where the drawing operations are to take place.The argument **hWnd** is the handle of the window whose device context you want. If a handle of NULL (zero) is passed, **GetDC** returns the device context of the entire screen (which is what we do in this example).

Next, the function **CreateSolidBrush** is used to create a brush for drawing the exploding rectangles. The declaration is:

```
Declare Function CreateSolidBrush Lib "GDI" (ByVal crColor As Long) As
   Integer
```

In Windows' graphics terms, *brush* refers to a type of object that is used for drawing on the screen. As you might expect, a "solid" brush is used to draw screen images that are solid, or filled with a particular color. The argument **crColor** specifies the brush's color. For the exploding windows we'll set the brush color to the form's background color. This function returns the brush's handle.

Once we have obtained the screen's device context and have created the desired brush, the next step is to associate the brush with the screen—in other words, specify that the brush is to be used for subsequent drawing operations on the screen. This is done with the **SelectObject** API procedure:

```
Declare Sub SelectObject Lib "GDI" (ByVal hDC As Integer, ByVal
   hObject As Integer)
```

Here, the argument **hDC** is the handle, or device context, of the screen, and **hObject** is the handle of the object to be associated with it. Once the brush has been associated with the screen, we are ready to draw. This is done with the **Rectangle** API procedure:

```
Declare Sub Rectangle Lib "GDI" (ByVal hDC As Integer, ByVal X1 As
   Integer, ByVal Y1 As Integer, ByVal X2 As Integer, ByVal Y2 As Integer)
```

The argument **hDC** is the device context of the screen window that is to have a rectangle drawn on it. **X1,Y1** and **X2,Y2** are the coordinates of the upper-left and lower-right corners of the rectangle. The rectangle is drawn with whatever brush is currently associated with the **hDC** context. The exploding form code given below creates the exploding effect by drawing successively larger rectangles starting at the center of the form and expanding until the form size if reached. The number of size increments is controlled by the constant **STEPS**.

The final two API calls are for "cleanup" purposes. First, we call **ReleaseDC** in order to release the screen's device context so that other applications can use it. The procedure declaration is:

```
Declare Sub ReleaseDC Lib "User" (ByVal hWnd As Integer, ByVal hDC As
   Integer)
```

The argument **hWnd** is the handle of the window whose device context is to be released—in our case, a value of 0 specifies the screen—meaning that **hDC** is the device context being freed.

Lastly, we need to delete the brush object that was created to draw the rectangles, freeing up memory. The procedure declaration is as follows:

```
Declare Sub DeleteObject Lib "GDI" (ByVal hObject As Integer)
```

The argument **hObject** is the handle of the object being deleted.

Don't Overdo Exploding Forms

Exploding forms can add a nice touch to your programs. But use them sparingly, only where they will be most effective. Too many exploding forms can be distracting!

Now we can finally get to the demonstration program! The work of exploding a form is performed by code in the procedure FormExplode in the module EXPLODE.BAS, as shown in Listing 2.5. The procedure is passed the form's handle, then it does all the rest, including displaying the actual form after the exploding rectangles have all been drawn. To use exploding forms is your own programs, all you need to do in add the module EXPLODE.BAS to your program.

The demonstration uses a form named EXPLODE.FRM (what else!). When you create the form you can make it any size you desire, as the exploding procedure automatically adjusts for the form's size. The form contains only two command buttons, one to exit and one to hide then redisplay the form so you can see the explosion in action again without quitting and restarting the program. Objects and code in EXPLODE.FRM are given in Listings 2.6 and 2.7.

Using EXPLODE.MAK

This project, presented in Listings 2.5, 2.6, and 2.7, is stored on disk as EXPLODE.MAK, EXPLODE.FRM, and EXPLODE.BAS.

Listing 2.5   The Code in EXPLODE.BAS

```
Option Explicit

' Define the RECT type (This is a Windows type).
Type RECT
```

```
        Left As Integer
        Top As Integer
        Right As Integer
        Bottom As Integer
End Type

' API call declarations.
Declare Function CreateSolidBrush Lib "GDI" (ByVal crColor As Long) As
    Integer

Declare Sub DeleteObject Lib "GDI" (ByVal hObject As Integer)

Declare Function GetDC Lib "User" (ByVal hWnd As Integer) As Integer

Declare Sub GetWindowRect Lib "User" (ByVal hWnd As Integer, lpRect As
    RECT)

Declare Sub Rectangle Lib "GDI" (ByVal hDC As Integer, ByVal X1 As
    Integer, ByVal Y1 As Integer, ByVal X2 As Integer, ByVal Y2 As
    Integer)

Declare Sub ReleaseDC Lib "User" (ByVal hWnd As Integer, ByVal hDC As
    Integer)

Declare Sub SelectObject Lib "GDI" (ByVal hDC As Integer, ByVal
    hObject As Integer)

Sub FormExplode (Target As Form)

' "explodes" a form by drawing successively larger
' rectangles, using the form's background color, to
' fill the form area. Should be called from the
' Form_Load event procedure.

' Number of steps to use in expanding the rectangle. More
' steps result in a slower but smoother "explosion."
Const STEPS = 40

Dim FormWidth As Integer, FormHeight As Integer
Dim Count As Integer, X As Integer, Y As Integer
Dim XStep As Integer, YStep As Integer
Dim hDCScreen As Integer, hBrush As Integer
Dim MyRect As RECT

' Get the form's coordinates and detemine its
' height and width.
Call GetWindowRect(Target.hWnd, MyRect)

FormWidth = MyRect.Right - MyRect.Left
```

```
FormHeight = MyRect.Bottom - MyRect.Top

' Get the screen's device context.
hDCScreen = GetDC(0)

' Create a solid brush that uses the form's
' background color.
hBrush = CreateSolidBrush(Target.BackColor)
Call SelectObject(hDCScreen, hBrush)

' Draw successively larger rectangles until the form's
' entire area is filled.
For Count = 1 To STEPS
    XStep = FormWidth * (Count / STEPS)
    YStep = FormHeight * (Count / STEPS)
    X = MyRect.Left + (FormWidth - XStep) / 2
    Y = MyRect.Top + (FormHeight - YStep) / 2
    Call Rectangle(hDCScreen, X, Y, X + XStep, Y + YStep)
Next Count

' Release the device context and brush, and display
' the form.
Call ReleaseDC(0, hDCScreen)
Call DeleteObject(hBrush)
Target.Visible = True

End Sub
```

Listing 2.6 Objects and Properties in EXPLODE.FRM

```
Begin Form Form1
    BackColor       =    &H00C0C0C0&
    Caption         =    "Exploding form!"
    Begin CommandButton cmdDisplay
        Caption         =    "&Redisplay"
    End
    Begin CommandButton cmdExit
        Caption         =    "E&xit"
    End
End
```

Listing 2.7 The Code in EXPLODE.FRM

```
Option Explicit

Sub cmdDisplay_Click ()

Unload Form1
Load Form1
```

```
End Sub

Sub cmdExit_Click ()

End

End Sub

Sub Form_Load ()

Call FormExplode(Form1)

End Sub
```

Blinking a Form's Title Bar

A blinking title bar can be used to call the user's attention to a form.

The API procedure **FlashWindow** allows you to readily create a blinking title bar for a form. This procedure changes the appearance of a form's title bar from active to inactive or vice versa. The procedure declaration is:

```
Declare Sub FlashWindow Lib "User" (ByVal hWnd As Integer, ByVal
   bInvert As Integer)
```

Here, the argument **hWnd** identifies the form to be flashed. The window can be either open or minimized. **bInvert** specifies whether to flash the window or return it to its original state (its appearance before any calls to **FlashWindow**). If this parameter is **True**, the window's title bar is flashed from one state to the other (active to inactive or inactive to active). If the parameter is **False**, the window's title bar is returned to its original state. Each call to **FlashWindow** causes only a single change in a form's title bar. For a form's title bar to blink, we must use a Timer control, with the call to **FlashWindow** located in the **Timer** event procedure. Every time the timer counts down, the procedure will be called and the form's title bar will change appearance. By modifying the Timer.Interval property you can control the blink rate.

Sound the Alarm!

Blinking title bars are a nice touch, but cannot be guaranteed to be noticed. When it's crucial to catch the user's attention, you should use some sort of sound alarm as well.

The project BLINK.MAK demonstrates how to blink a form's title bar. The project's form is shown in Figure 2.4. When the program runs, the form blinks at the rate of twice per second (timer interval of 500 milliseconds). Selecting the Rate command button lets you modify the timer interval, with a minimum value of 100 milliseconds (which gives a blink rate of ten per second).

The objects and code in BLINK.FRM are given in Listings 2.8 and 2.9. To include the ability to blink forms in your own programs, include the declaration of the **FlashWindow** API procedure, then add a Timer control to each form that you may want to blink. Place the call to **FlashWindow** in the **Timer** event procedure for each form. To blink a form, enable the timer; to stop blinking, disable the timer. When you stop a form's blinking, you should make a final call to **FlashWindow** with the **bInvert** argument set to **False**, to ensure that the appearance of the title bar is reset to its original value. Note that a real program will usually not allow the user to specify the blink rate—this will be set at design time.

Using BLINK.MAK

This demonstration program, presented in Listings 2.8 and 2.9, is stored on disk as BLINK.MAK and BLINK.FRM.

Listing 2.8   Objects and Properties in BLINK.FRM

```
Begin Form Form1
    Caption         =   "Blinking"
    Begin Timer Timer1
        Interval     =   500
    End
    Begin CommandButton cmdRate
        Caption      =   "&Rate"
    End
    Begin CommandButton cmdExit
        Caption      =   "E&xit"
    End
End
```

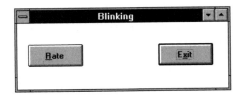

Figure 2.4   The blinking form demonstration.

Listing 2.9   Code in BLINK.FRM

```
Option Explicit

Declare Sub FlashWindow Lib "User" (ByVal hWnd As Integer, ByVal
   bInvert As Integer)

Sub cmdExit_Click ()

End

End Sub

Sub cmdRate_Click ()

Dim BlinkRate As String

BlinkRate = InputBox$("Enter blink period in milliseconds (minimum =
   100)", "Rate")

If Val(BlinkRate) < 100 Then
    Beep
Else
    Timer1.Interval = Val(BlinkRate)
End If

End Sub

Sub Timer1_Timer ()

Call FlashWindow(Form1.hWnd, True)

End Sub
```

Starting Your Programs with a Splash Screen

A splash screen is displayed when a program first starts.

Many programs display a *splash screen* when they start. A splash screen typically presents a visually attractive image, and can also display information such as the program's version number and copyright notice. A splash screen can also serve to distract the user if the program takes a while to load and initialize. Microsoft Windows uses a splash screen, and you can add a splash screen to your Visual Basic programs.

The first step to adding a splash screen to a program is to create the splash screen form:

1. Create the splash screen form. Set its BorderStyle property to 3-Fixed Double so that Min and Max buttons are not displayed on the form.

2. Set the form to the desired size, or for a full-screen form set the WindowState property to 2-Maximized.

3. Place one or more Picture Box controls on the form, and size them as desired. These will be used to display the splash screen's graphical elements (see below). Save the splash screen form to disk.

There are two possible approaches that you can use for adding graphical elements to the splash screen. One is to use the **Print** method in the program's code to display text in the Picture Box control on the splash screen form. The other is to load a graphical image into the Picture Box at design time. I used the latter approach in the demonstration. I used the Windows PaintBrush program to draw the splash screen image, then saved it to disk. Back in Visual Basic, I then selected the Picture Box's Image property and specified the PaintBrush file. You could also use the **LoadPicture** function to load a graphic into the Picture Box at run-time.

All that remains is to integrate the splash screen into your application. Normally, a project's startup form is the first to be displayed when the program executes. To have the splash screen display first, you must create a **Sub Main** procedure and specify that execution is to begin there. Here's how:

1. Load the project to which you want to add the splash screen.

2. Use the Add File command to add the splash screen form module to the project.

3. The **Sub Main** procedure must be in a Basic module. If the project already has a Basic module, display its code. If not, use the New Module command to create a new Basic module.

4. Use the New Procedure command to add a **Sub** procedure named **Main**. Add code to **Main** that performs the following tasks (in this order):

   - Loads and displays the splash screen form. If the form does not have a pre-loaded graphic, code here can use Print or LoadPicture to create the splash screen display.

   - Delays, if necessary, so the splash screen is displayed for a sufficient time.

   - Performs required program initialization, such as loading (but not displaying) other program forms.

- Unloads the splash screen form.
- Displays the program's "real" startup form.

5. Select Options Project, then specify Sub Main as the startup form.

The demonstration program SPLASH.MAK shows how this is done. The splash screen that this program displays is shown in Figure 2.5.

The splash screen form SPLASH.FRM, described in Listing 2.10, contains only a single Picture Box with a pre-loaded picture (as described above). There is no code in this form. The Basic module SPLASH.BAS, in Listing 2.11, contains the **Sub Main** procedure. There is also another form, SPLASH1.FRM, in Listing 2.12, that is simply a "dummy" form representing the real program. The only code in SPLASH1.FRM is an **End** statement in the **cmdExit_Click** event procedure.

If you look at the code in **Sub Main** you'll see an additional feature that I have added. If the program is started with the command line argument **:** (colon) the splash screen display is suppressed. This is the same way Windows works: if you start Windows by entering WIN : at the DOS prompt, the Windows splash screen is not displayed. Remember, to specify a command line argument from within the Visual Basic programming environment, select Options Project.

Using SPLASH.MAK

This demonstration program, presented in Listings 2.10, 2.11 and 2.12, is stored on disk as SPLASH.MAK, SPLASH.FRM, SPLASH.BAS, and SPLASH1.FRM.

Figure 2.5 The splash screen displayed by SPLASH.MAK.

Listing 2.10 Objects and Properties in SPLASH.FRM

```
Begin Form frmSplash
    BorderStyle      =   3  'Fixed Double
    Begin PictureBox Picture1
        Picture          =   (see text)
    End
End
```

Listing 2.11 Code in SPLASH.BAS

```
Option Explicit

Sub Main ()

Dim i As Long

If (Command$ <> ":") Then

frmSplash.Show

' The loop provides
' a delay during which the splash screen is displayed.
For i = 0 To 200000
Next i

Unload frmSplash

End If

' Load the program's main form. Other initialization
' code would go here as well.
Load frmMain

' Display the main form.
frmMain.Show

End Sub
```

Listing 2.12 Objects and Properties in SPLASH1.FRM

```
Begin Form frmMain
    Caption          =   "Dummy main program"
    Begin CommandButton cmdExit
        Caption          =   "E&xit"
    End
End
```

Controls and Text

Controls are central to any Visual Basic application, and text usually plays an important role as well. This section shows you some nifty techniques to enhance the use of controls and text in your programs.

Adjusting the Position and Size of Controls Automatically

For a form that can be resized, it is sometimes desirable to have the controls on the form automatically adjust their individual sizes and positions to fit the new form size.

The controls on a form automatically move when the form is moved, but they do not automatically adjust when the form's size is changed—each control stays the same size and in its original position with respect to the upper-left corner of the form. Some applications would benefit from the ability to have all a form's controls automatically adjust their sizes and position whenever the form is resized. To see an example of this, take a look at Windows' Paintbrush program. All of Paintbrush's icons and other screen items adjust automatically whenever the main program window is resized so that they retain the same relative sizes and positions.

A Visual Basic program can do the same thing. You will see a simple example in Chapter 3 (see *Creating a Baby Text Editor*). That program contains code that automatically resizes a Text Box control to fill the entire form. More sophisticated effects are possible, as you'll see in this section.

The size and position of controls are, of course, relative to the size of the form they are displayed on. If a Command Button starts out with a width equal to 1/6 the form's width and a height equal to 1/10 the form's height, then these ratios must be maintained whenever the form is resized. For example, you could put the following code in the form's **Resize** event procedure:

```
Command1.Height = Form1.ScaleHeight / 10
Command1.Width = Form1.ScaleWidth / 6
```

A similar procedure is used to set the position of controls. A Frame, for example, might be displayed in the upper-left corner of the form, separated from the top and left edges of the form by a space equal to 1/20 of the form's height and width, respectively. The following code, in the form's **Resize** event procedure, would keep the Frame in the same relative position:

```
Frame1.Top = Form1.ScaleHeight / 20
Frame1.Left = Form1.ScaleWidth / 20
```

If you want the control's position specified with respect to the right and/or lower edge of the form, you must take the control's width and height into account when setting its new position. For example, to position the Frame with the same position relative to the lower-right corner of the form, you would use code like this:

```
Frame1.Left = (Form1.ScaleWidth * .95) - Frame1.Width
Frame1.Top = (Form1.ScaleHeight * .95) - Frame1.Height
```

When developing code to automatically adjust controls, there are two approaches you can take. One is to decide ahead of time the relative sizes and positions of the controls. For example, "This text box will be 2/3 the width of the form." Then, write the adjustment code (as in the above examples) using the relative sizes and positions you have decided on. This approach can work relatively well for forms with only a few controls, but sometimes the final form does not have exactly the appearance you were hoping for.

The second approach is more in line with the visual design philosophy of Visual Basic. You start by using Visual Basic to design the form visually, adjusting the size and position of controls until the form appears exactly as you want it. Then, examine the size and position properties of the controls, and use these values and the form size to derive the scaling factors that the code will use to adjust control size and position.

Let's look at an example for a single Picture Box control. You have designed a form, and given the Picture Box the relative size and position that you want. The values of the relevant properties are as follows:

```
Picture box:  Top = 360
              Left = 480
              Height = 1572
              Width = 1452
Form:         ScaleHeight = 3156
              ScaleWidth = 3960
```

Using your trusty calculator you can derive the following factors:

```
PBTopFactor = PB.Top/Form.ScaleHeight = 360/3156 = 0.1141
PBLeftFactor = PB.Left/Form.ScaleWidth = 480/3960 = 0.1212
PBHeightFactor = PB.Height/Form.ScaleHeight = 1572/3156 = 0.4981
PBWidthFactor = PB.Width/Form.ScaleWidth = 1452/3960 = 0.3667
```

Then, in the form's **Resize** event procedure, the following code will adjust the Picture Box to the same relative size and position it had when you designed the form:

```
Picture1.Height = Form1.ScaleHeight * 0.4981      'PBHeightFactor
Picture1.Width = Form1.ScaleWidth * 0.3677        'PBWidthFactor
Picture1.Left = Form1.ScaleWidth * 0.1212         'PBLeftFactor
Picture1.Top = Form1.ScaleHeight * 0.1142         'PBTopFactor
```

You can calculate the various factors and enter them in the program as literal constants, as in the example immdiately above. Another approach is to let the program calculate the factors for you. Put the code to calculate the factors and assign them to global variables in the **Form_Load** event procedure. The code in the **Form_Resize** procedure can then use these variables in its calculations. Because when the program starts the **Load** event occurs before the **Resize** event, the factors will be calculated based on the form and control properties that you set during design.

When resizing controls, a problem can sometimes arise with the text that is displayed as part of some controls—for example, the captions on Frames, Command Buttons, and so on. If the control becomes very small, the text may be too large to display completely. Likewise, if the control becomes very large, the original text size may now appear out of proportion. There's no easy solution to this problem. Because font size is specified in points, and not in Twips, you cannot use the same techniques to scale font size as can be used for scaling control size. You can, however, experiment to determine which font sizes best suit certain ranges of control size, then place code in the **Resize** event procedure to set each control's **FontSize** property to a value appropriate for the new control size. Another approach is to include code that prevents the user from making the form so small that text size becomes a problem.

The demonstration program AUTOSIZE demonstrates the techniques discussed above; its properties and code are presented in Listings 2.13 and 2.14. It consists of a single form containing a Picture Box and a Command button. When you run the program, you'll see that both controls retain the same relative sizes and positions when the form is resized. You can also load the program into Visual Basic and modify the original size and/or position of the controls. Run the program again and you'll see that the new control positions and sizes are in effect.

On Disk

Using AUTOSIZE.MAK

This demonstration program, presented in Listings 2.13 and 2.14, is stored on disk as AUTOSIZE.MAK and AUTOSIZE.FRM.

Listing 2.13   Objects and Properties in AUTOSIZE.FRM

```
Begin Form Form1
    Caption          =    "Resize me!"
    Begin CommandButton Command1
      Caption        =    "E&xit"
    End
    Begin PictureBox Picture1
      BackColor      =    &H000000C0&
    End
End
```

Listing 2.14   Code in AUTOSIZE.FRM

```
Option Explicit

' Declare global variables for use in control scaling.
Dim PBTopFactor As Single, PBLeftFactor As Single
Dim PBHeightFactor As Single, PBWidthFactor As Single
Dim CBTopFactor As Single, CBLeftFactor As Single
Dim CBHeightFactor As Single, CBWidthFactor As Single

Sub Command1_Click ()

End

End Sub

Sub Form_Load ()

' Calculate control scaling factors based on the
' form size and control size and position set at
' design time.

' For the Picture Box
PBTopFactor = Picture1.Top / Form1.ScaleHeight
PBLeftFactor = Picture1.Left / Form1.ScaleWidth
PBHeightFactor = Picture1.Height / Form1.ScaleHeight
PBWidthFactor = Picture1.Width / Form1.ScaleWidth

' For the Command Button
CBTopFactor = Command1.Top / Form1.ScaleHeight
CBLeftFactor = Command1.Left / Form1.ScaleWidth
CBHeightFactor = Command1.Height / Form1.ScaleHeight
CBWidthFactor = Command1.Width / Form1.ScaleWidth

End Sub

Sub Form_Resize ()
```

```
' Give the controls the same size and position relative
' to the new form size.
Picture1.Height = Form1.ScaleHeight * PBHeightFactor
Picture1.Width = Form1.ScaleWidth * PBWidthFactor
Picture1.Left = Form1.ScaleWidth * PBLeftFactor
Picture1.Top = Form1.ScaleHeight * PBTopFactor

Command1.Height = Form1.ScaleHeight * CBHeightFactor
Command1.Width = Form1.ScaleWidth * CBWidthFactor
Command1.Left = Form1.ScaleWidth * CBLeftFactor
Command1.Top = Form1.ScaleHeight * CBTopFactor

End Sub
```

Aligning Text Automatically

When you use the Print method, the text is left-aligned by default. You can use a Windows API call to obtain different types of text alignment.

The API procedure **SetTextAlign** permits a program to control both the vertical and horizontal alignment of text. The procedure's declaration is

```
Declare Sub SetTextAlign Lib "GDI" (ByVal hDC As Integer, ByVal wFlags
   As Integer)
```

Here, the argument **hDC** is the hDC property of the object you are printing to, and **wFlags** contains the text-alignment flags. The flags specify how the text is justified with relation to a point on the object it is printed on. It can specify vertical and/or horizontal alignment. Possible values for horizontal alignment are (these are Windows global constants):

```
TA_CENTER: Centers the text.
TA_LEFT: Left-aligns the text (the default).
TA_RIGHT: Right-aligns the text.
```

To understand vertical alignment, think of the total vertical extent that characters in a given font can span. The *bottom* is the lowest any character extends, such as the descenders on characters such as g and y. The *top* is the highest any character extends, such as tall uppercase letters or diacritical marks such as Ä and é. The *baseline* is the bottom of characters without descenders, such as m and o. Now, the vertical alignment options will make sense (these too are Windows global constants):

```
TA_BASELINE: Aligns the point with the font base line.
TA_BOTTOM: Aligns the point with the font bottom.
TA_TOP: Aligns the point with the font top (the default).
```

It's important to remember that all these alignments are with respect to a specific point on the object (a Picture Box or a non-MDI form). The point is defined by the object's CurrentX and CurrentY properties. In other words, the **SetTextAlignment** procedure does not automatically align text with respect to the edges of the print area. For example, to right-align text in a Picture Box so that the right edge of the text lines up with the right edge of the Picture Box, you must follow three steps:

1. Set the Picture Box's CurrentX property to the right edge (i.e., set it equal to the ScaleWidth property.

2. Use **SetTextAlignment** to specify **TA_RIGHT** alignment.

3. Display the text with the Print method.

Likewise, to center text in a Picture Box you would set CurrentX to the center of the box (ScaleWidth / 2), then use **SetTextAlignment** to specify **TA_CENTER** alignment.

This will all become clearer when you run the demonstration program. To create the form, draw a Picture Box, a Command Button, and two Frame controls. On each Frame create a control array of three Option Buttons. The object properties are shown in Listing 2.15, and the form's code in Listing 2.16. The form is shown in Figure 2.6.

The alignment that you set with **SetTextAlign** is guaranteed to be in effect for only a single **Print** method. Therefore, if you call **SetTextAlign** then execute these statements:

```
PictureBox.Print "Message1"
PictureBox.Print "Message2"
```

the specified alignment may not be used for the second message. You need to call **SetTextAlign** before each execution of a **Print** method. Note that Visual Basic treats multiple arguments to a **Print** method, as in

```
PictureBox.Print "Message1";"Message2"
```

as two distinct **Print** methods, and the same alignment problems may arise for Message2. You can avoid the problem by concatenating the strings:

```
PictureBox.Print "Message1" + "Message2"
```

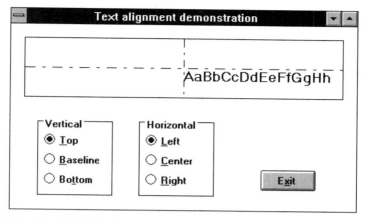

Figure 2.6 The TXTALIGN demonstration form.

Call SetTextAlign in Every Procedure that Needs to Align Text

The **hDC** property can change whenever Visual Basic calls the **DoEvent** function to process events, or whenever execution exits a procedure. Therefore **SetTextAlign** should be called in every procedure that needs it, preferably just before execution of the **Print** method.

Listing 2.15   Objects and Properties in TXTALIGN.FRM

```
Begin Form frmTxtAlign
   BorderStyle      =   1  'Fixed Single
   Caption          =   "Text alignment demonstration"
   Begin CommandButton cmdExit
      Caption       =   "E&xit"
   End
   Begin PictureBox Picture1
      DrawStyle     =   3  'Dot
      FontSize      =   12
   End
   Begin Frame Frame2
      Caption       =   "Horizontal"
      Begin OptionButton HorizAlign
         Caption    =   "&Left"
         Index      =   0
      End
      Begin OptionButton HorizAlign
         Caption    =   "&Center"
         Index      =   1
      End
```

```
       Begin OptionButton HorizAlign
          Caption          =    "&Right"
          Index            =    2
       End
    End
    Begin Frame Frame1
       Caption          =    "Vertical"
       Begin OptionButton VertAlign
          Caption          =    "&Top"
          Index            =    0
       End
       Begin OptionButton VertAlign
          Caption          =    "&Baseline"
          Index            =    1
       End
       Begin OptionButton VertAlign
          Caption          =    "Bo&ttom"
          Index            =    2
       End
    End
 End
End
```

Listing 2.16   Code in TXTALIGN.FRM

```
' TXTALIGN.FRM
' Demonstrates using API calls to set text alignment.

Option Explicit

' In a real program you would make these constants
' global and put them in a BAS module.
Const TA_LEFT = 0
Const TA_RIGHT = 2
Const TA_CENTER = 6
Const TA_TOP = 0
Const TA_BOTTOM = 8
Const TA_BASELINE = 24

' API procedure declaration. This too would go in a global module.
Declare Sub SetTextAlign Lib "GDI" (ByVal hDC As Integer, ByVal
  wFlags As Integer)


Sub cmdExit_Click ()

End

End Sub
```

```vb
Sub cmdPrint_Click ()

Picture1_Paint

End Sub

Sub Form_Load ()

' Establish the default option button settings.
HorizAlign(0).Value = True
VertAlign(0).Value = True

End Sub

Sub HorizAlign_Click (Index As Integer)

' If alignment option changed, repaint the Picture Box.
Picture1_Paint

End Sub

Sub Picture1_Paint ()

Dim wFlags As Integer

' Clear the picture box and draw centered vertical
' and horizontal lines.
Picture1.Cls
Picture1.Line (0, Picture1.ScaleHeight / 2)-Step(Picture1.ScaleWidth, 0)
Picture1.Line (Picture1.ScaleWidth / 2, 0)-Step(0, Picture1.ScaleHeight)

' Move the reference point to the intersection of the lines.
Picture1.CurrentY = Picture1.ScaleHeight / 2
Picture1.CurrentX = Picture1.ScaleWidth / 2

' Set wFlags to reflect the alignment options selected.
If HorizAlign(0).Value Then wFlags = TA_LEFT
If HorizAlign(1).Value Then wFlags = TA_CENTER
If HorizAlign(2).Value Then wFlags = TA_RIGHT

If VertAlign(0).Value Then wFlags = wFlags Or TA_TOP
If VertAlign(1).Value Then wFlags = wFlags Or TA_BASELINE
If VertAlign(2).Value Then wFlags = wFlags Or TA_BOTTOM

Call SetTextAlign(Picture1.hDC, wFlags)

Picture1.Print "AaBbCcDdEeFfGgHh"

End Sub
```

```
Sub VertAlign_Click (Index As Integer)

' If alignment option changed, repaint the picture box.
Picture1_Paint

End Sub
```

Using TXTALIGN.MAK

This demonstration program, presented in Listings 2.15 and 2.16, is stored on disk as TXTALIGN.MAK and TXTALIGN.FRM.

Create a Custom Check Box

Your programs can use a check box that displays a real check mark!

Visual Basic's CheckBox controls function perfectly well, but they display an "X," not a check mark, when they are selected. You can create a custom check box that displays a check mark or any other symbol you desire.

The technique is relatively simple. For each check box, place two Image controls on the form; they must be in a control array. One of the Image controls represents the "on" check box, and the other represents the "off" check box. The two Image controls must have the exact same size and position so that they overlap completely. Both should have the Stretch property set to True and the BorderStyle property set to 1–Fixed Single. The Visible property should be True for one and False for the other.

Next, use the Picture property to load the "on" Image control with the desired graphic. For the program below I used the icon file CHECKMRK.ICO from the Visual Basic icon library, but you can use anything you like. Because the Image control's Stretch property is True, whatever image you place in it will automatically expand or shrink to fit the size of the Image control. Typically the "off" state is indicated by an empty check box. Therefore, you would not load a Picture property for the "off" Image control.

The code is equally straightforward. In the Click event procedure, test the Visible property of one of the Image controls. If it is True, set it to False and set the Visible property of the other Image control to True. If it is False, set it to True and set the Visible property of the other Image control to False. Code in other parts of the program can query the Visible property of the "on" Image box to determine if the corresponding program option is currently on or off.

A custom check box is demonstrated by CHECKBOX.MAK. The program's display is shown in Figure 2.7. Its objects and Properties are in Listing 2.17, and its code is in Listing 2.18.

Using CHECKBOX.MAK

This demonstration program, presented in Listings 2.17 and 2.18, is stored on disk as CHECKBOX.MAK and CHECKBOX.FRM.

Listing 2.17 Objects and Properties in CHECKBOX.FRM

```
Begin Form Form1
    Caption          =    "Custom Check Box"
    Begin Label Label1
       Caption        =     "Confirm changes"
    End
    Begin Image imgCheck
       BorderStyle    =    1    'Fixed Single
       Index          =    1
       Picture        =    (none)
       Stretch        =    -1   'True
       Visible        =    0    'False
    End
    Begin Image imgCheck
       BorderStyle    =    1    'Fixed Single
       Index          =    0
       Picture        =    (see text)
       Stretch        =    -1   'True
       Visible        =    -1   'True
    End
End
```

Listing 2.18 Code in CHECKBOX.FRM

```
Option Explicit

Sub imgCheck_Click (Index As Integer)

If imgCheck(0).Visible = False Then
    imgCheck(0).Visible = True
    imgCheck(1).Visible = False
Else
    imgCheck(1).Visible = True
    imgCheck(0).Visible = False
End If

End Sub
```

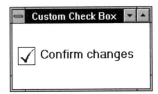

Figure 2.7   A custom check box.

Multiline Command Buttons

Create Command Buttons that display more than one line of text.

The default Command Buttons in Visual Basic are limited to displaying a single line of text. That's fine for most situations, but there may be times when you want do display a longer message on your button. You can create a multi-line "Command Button" using a Picture Box control. An example of this is shown in Figure 2.8.

At its simplest, a multi-line Command Button can be created by placing a Picture Box on the form, then placing code in the Picture Box's **Paint** event procedure to display the desired text on the "button" using the Print method. You can get a bit fancier, if you like, creating a more professional appearance. You can use the TextWidth property to set the Picture Box's CurrentX so that each line of text is centered. You can also simulate the visual appearance of a depressed button by setting the BackColor to light gray at design time, changing it to dark gray in the **MouseDown** procedure, then back to light gray in the **MouseUp** procedure. If you do this, both the **MouseDown** and **MouseUp** procedures must call the **Paint** procedure to redisplay the text in the Picture Box.

The demonstration program CMD_BTN.MAK, which created the form in Figure 2.8 illustrates these techniques. The program's Objects, Properties, and code are given in Listings 2.19 and 2.20. Note that the program is coded so that a double click is required to exit. This permits you to single click the "Command Button" to observe the visual effects.

Using CMD_BTN.MAK

This program, presented in Listings 2.19 and 2.20, is stored on disk as CMD_BTN.MAK and CMD_BTN.FRM.

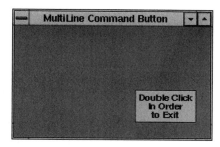

Figure 2.8   A multi-line "Command Button" created from a Picture Box.

Listing 2.19   Objects and Properties in CMD_BTN.FRM

```
Begin Form Form1
    Caption         =     "MultiLine Command Button"
    Begin PictureBox pbBtn
        BackColor     =     &H00C0C0C0&
        FontName      =     "MS Sans Serif"
        FontSize      =     9.6
    End
End
```

Listing 2.20   Code in CMD_BTN.FRM

```
Option Explicit

Sub pbBtn_DblClick ()

End

End Sub

Sub pbBtn_MouseDown (Button As Integer, Shift As Integer, X As Single,
  Y As Single)

' Set BackColor to dark gray when MouseDown
' to simulate depressed button.
pbBtn.BackColor = &H808080

' Call Paint procedure to re-display text.
pbBtn_Paint

End Sub

Sub pbBtn_MouseUp (Button As Integer, Shift As Integer, X As Single, Y
  As Single)
```

```
' Return to light gray BackColor when MouseUp occurs.
pbBtn.BackColor = &HC0C0C0

' Call Paint procedure to redisplay text.
pbBtn_Paint

End Sub

Sub pbBtn_Paint ()

Dim Msg As String

' Start at the top of the Picture Box.
pbBtn.CurrentY = 0

' Center each line of text.
Msg = "Double Click"
pbBtn.CurrentX = (pbBtn.ScaleWidth - pbBtn.TextWidth(Msg)) / 2
pbBtn.Print Msg

Msg = "in Order"
pbBtn.CurrentX = (pbBtn.ScaleWidth - pbBtn.TextWidth(Msg)) / 2
pbBtn.Print Msg

Msg = "to Exit"
pbBtn.CurrentX = (pbBtn.ScaleWidth - pbBtn.TextWidth(Msg)) / 2
pbBtn.Print Msg

End Sub
```

3

Adding Functionality to Your Visual Basic Programs

V isual Basic has brought new levels of ease and power to Windows programming, making it relatively simple to provide a wide range of abilities in your programs. Programmers, however, are always trying to stretch the envelope, adding to their programs new capabilities that are not directly supported by the programming language. In this chapter, I present a number of useful capabilities, that can be included in your Visual Basic programs.

Saving Program Configuration between Sessions

Most programs use various types of configuration settings, such as screen colors, the letter of the default data drive, and the sizes and positions of program windows. You can modify these settings to suit your preference. However, it is your responsibility to make sure that the program "remembers" any new settings so they will be in effect the next time the program is executed. How and where can you store this information?

Use an .INI File to Save Program Information

You should store program configuration information in an .INI file.

To save configuration information between work sessions you must store the information on disk. The question is, where and how? For Visual Basic programs (and other Windows applications as well), the answer is clear: use an initialization file (often called an .INI file because .INI is the standard initialization file extension).

What Is the Format of an .INI File?

.INI files are standard ASCII text files that follow certain rules of organization.

All Windows .INI files follow the same rules. An .INI file is a standard text file that uses the Windows character set. Within an .INI file, information is contained in sections that are delimited by headings enclosed in brackets. Within each section are one or more setting names, each followed by an equal sign and the value of the setting The format is shown here:

```
[section]
entry1=value1
entry2=value2
```

Now, for a real example:

```
[colors]
Background=blue
Foreground=white
Highlight=yellow
[paths]
Data=c:\data
Backup=c:\data\backup
[keyboard]
Repeat=20
Delay=200
```

Which .INI File Should I Use?

You have two choices when deciding on which .INI file to use.

When storing program information in an .INI file there are two options. You can use WIN.INI, the main Windows initialization file, which holds configuration information for Windows itself, as well as selected configuration information for Windows applications. Or, you can use a private initialization file, which holds configuration information specific to one application. Private initialization files are usually given a name identical or similar to the application they belong to. For example, Visual Basic's private .INI file is named VB.INI. Private initialization files are usually stored in the main Windows directory, although some applications keep them in the application directory. The internal format is the same for both types of .INI files.

Use a Private .INI File for Application-Specific Information

When deciding whether to use WIN.INI or a private .INI file, the general rule you should follow is to use WIN.INI only for information that affects more than one application. For example, use WIN.INI if you want to specify the same default background color for all Visual Basic applications. You would use a private .INI file to hold initialization information that affects only a single application. This approach improves the performance of both Windows and your applications by minimizing the amount of information that must be read when the WIN.INI file is accessed. It also makes it easier to keep track of .INI files, to delete those that are no longer needed, and to determine which information goes with which application.

Reading and Writing .INI Files

You use API calls to read and write .INI files.

The task of reading and writing .INI files is made relatively simple by a group of Windows API functions that do most of the work for you. You can read and write both WIN.INI and private .INI files. There are two API functions for reading strings from .INI files. Their declarations in a Visual Basic program are as follows:

```
Declare Function GetProfileString Lib "Kernel" (ByVal lpAppName As
    String, ByVal lpKeyName As String, ByVal lpDefault As String, ByVal
    lpReturnedString As String, ByVal nSize As Integer) As Integer

Declare Function GetPrivateProfileString Lib "Kernel" (ByVal lpAppName
    As String, ByVal lpKeyName As String, ByVal lpDefault As String,
    ByVal lpReturnedString As String, ByVal nSize As Integer, ByVal
    lpFileName As String) As Integer
```

The return value of both functions is the number of bytes read; usually this value is ignored by the program. Note that these two declarations are the same except for the **lpFileName** argument found in the **GetPrivateProfileString()** function. **GetProfileString()** always reads from WIN.INI, whereas the **GetPrivateProfileString()** function reads from the file specified by **lpFileName**. The argument **lpFilename** can include a path. If path information is not included, the function looks for the file in the Windows directory. The remainder of the function arguments are as follows:

- **lpAppName** specifies which .INI file section contains the information to be read; this argument is not case sensitive.

- **lpKeyName** specifies the specific entry whose value is to be read; this argument is not case sensitive.

- **lpReturnedString** is the string variable where the data read from the file will be placed.

- **lpDefault** specifies the string that will be placed in **lpReturnedString** if **lpAppName** or **lpKeyName** cannot be found in the .INI file (or, in the case of the **GetPrivateProfileString()** function, if the file specified by **lpFileName** cannot be found).

- **nSize** is the size, in characters, of **lpReturnedString**.

You can see that these functions are designed to be fail-safe. Since the programmer specifies a default value for the configuration item, the program is guaranteed to receive configuration data even if the file, section, or entry is not found, if there is a disk read error, or any other problem occurs.

There are two additional API functions that read integer values from .INI files: **GetProfileInt()** and **GetPrivateProfileInt()**. Remember, however, that all .INI file data, including numbers, is stored as text. The **Get...Int()** functions read the text and convert it to an integer before passing it to the calling program. You can accomplish the same thing by using either **Get...String()** function, and then using the **Val()** function to convert the string to a value. In fact, this latter method is more flexible when dealing with numbers because it can input floating point values, as well as integer values from .INI files. I will not cover the **Get...Int()** functions further; if you're interested please refer to a Windows API reference.

There are two API functions that write data to an .INI file. The first function always writes to WIN.INI, and the second function writes to the file specified by the **lpFileName** argument:

```
Declare Function WriteProfileString Lib "Kernel" (ByVal lpAppName As
    String, ByVal lpKeyName As String, ByVal lpString As String) As
    Integer

Declare Function WritePrivateProfileString Lib "Kernel" (ByVal
    lpAppName As String, ByVal lpKeyName As String, ByVal lpString As
    String, ByVal lpFileName As String) As Integer
```

Here, the **lpAppName** and **lpKeyName** arguments specify the .INI file section and entry, respectively, where the data is to be written, and **lpString** contains the string to be written.

Both functions return a non-zero value on success, and return zero if an error, such as a disk write error, occurs. If **lpFileName** does not specify a path, the Windows directory is used. Both functions follow these rules:

- If **lpFileName** does not exist, it is created.

- If the entry specified by **lpKeyName** does not exist in the specified section, it is created. If the entry does exist, the current data is replaced with the new data.

- If the entry specified by **lpKeyName** is an empty string, the entire section (between the heading specified by **lpAppName** and the next heading) is deleted from the .INI file.

- If the **lpString** argument is an empty string, the entry specified by the **lpKeyName** argument is deleted from the section.

Data is always written to .INI files as strings. When you need to store a numerical value, use the **Str$()** function to convert it to text before writing it to the file.

The specific procedure for using .INI files will depend on the needs of your program. Most commonly, code in a **Form_Load** procedure is used to read data from an .INI file. You can use the startup form's **Form_Load** procedure to read all of the program configuration information. In a multiform project, you can also use individual forms' **Form_Load** procedures to read .INI information pertinent to each form. Saving information can likewise be done all at once in the startup form's **Form_Unload** procedure, or bit by bit in individual forms' Unload procedures. Saving configuration information can also be made optional, in response to a user command.

An .INI File Demonstration

The program in this section demonstrates using a private .INI file to store program information

The program in the listing consists of nothing more than a single form containing one command button. When the form is loaded, code in the **Form_Load** event procedure reads values for the form's size and position properties from an initialization file named XXYYZZ.INI (I used this weird name to avoid possible conflict with real .INI files on your disk!). If XXYYZZ.INI is not found, the program uses default values for the form's size and position. While the form is displayed, you can move and resize it as desired. When the form is unloaded (when you quit the program), code in the **Unload** event procedure writes the current form size and position properties back to XXYYZZ.INI. Note that this program does not test the return value of **WritePrivateProfileString** to determine if a disk write error has occurred. A real-world application would, of course, perform such error checking.

To run the project, create one form with a single command button in the upper-left corner of the form. Change the Caption property of the command button to E&xit and the Caption property of the form to .INI File Demonstration; leave all other Form and Command Button properties at their default values. Add the code from Listing 3.1 to the form's event procedures, and you are ready to go.

Using INI_FILE.MAK

This example program, presented in Listing 3.1, is stored on disk as
INI_FILE.MAK and INI_FILE.FRM.

Listing 3.1   Code in INI_FILE.FRM

```
' INI_FILE.FRM

' Demonstrates using API functions to read and write program
' configuration information.
Declare Function GetPrivateProfileString Lib "Kernel" (ByVal lpAppName
   As String, ByVal lpKeyName As String, ByVal lpDefault As String,
   ByVal lpReturnedString As String, ByVal nSize As Integer, ByVal
   lpFileName As String) As Integer

Declare Function WritePrivateProfileString Lib "Kernel" (ByVal lpAppName
   As String, ByVal lpKeyName As String, ByVal lpString As String, ByVal
   lplFileName As String) As Integer

Sub Command1_Click ()

' Quit the program.
Unload Form1
End

End Sub

Sub Form_Load ()

' Read form size and position from .INI file. If the file doesn't
' exist use default values.
Dim FileName As String, lpAppName As String, lpKeyName As String
Dim lpDefault As String, Temp As String * 20, x As Integer

FileName = "XXYYZZ.INI"
lpAppName = "INI_FILE"

' Get width.
lpKeyName = "Width"
lpDefault = "7000"
x = GetPrivateProfileString(lpAppName, lpKeyName, lpDefault, Temp,
   Len(Temp), FileName)
Form1.Width = Val(Temp)

' Get height.
lpKeyName = "Height"
lpDefault = "4000"
```

```
x = GetPrivateProfileString(lpAppName, lpKeyName, lpDefault, Temp,
  Len(Temp), FileName)
Form1.Height = Val(Temp)

' Get X position.
lpKeyName = "Left"
lpDefault = "400"
x = GetPrivateProfileString(lpAppName, lpKeyName, lpDefault, Temp,
  Len(Temp), FileName)
Form1.Left = Val(Temp)

' Get Y position.
lpKeyName = "Top"
lpDefault = "400"
x = GetPrivateProfileString(lpAppName, lpKeyName, lpDefault, Temp,
  Len(Temp), FileName)
Form1.Top = Val(Temp)

End Sub

Sub Form_Unload (Cancel As Integer)

' Save form size and position in .INI file.
Dim FileName As String, lpAppName As String, lpKeyName As String
Dim Temp As String * 20, x As Integer

FileName = "XXYYZZ.INI"
lpAppName = "INI_FILE"

' Save width.
lpKeyName = "Width"
Temp = Str$(Form1.Width)
x = WritePrivateProfileString(lpAppName, lpKeyName, Temp, FileName)

' Save height.
lpKeyName = "Height"
Temp = Str$(Form1.Height)
x = WritePrivateProfileString(lpAppName, lpKeyName, Temp, FileName)

' Save X position.
lpKeyName = "Left"
Temp = Str$(Form1.Left)
x = WritePrivateProfileString(lpAppName, lpKeyName, Temp, FileName)

' Save Y position.
lpKeyName = "Top"
Tept = Str$(Form1.Top)
x = WritePrivateProfileString(lpAppName, lpKeyName, Temp, FileName)

End Sub
```

In the code, note that the **Command1_Click** procedure includes an explicit **Unload** statement for the form prior to the **End** statement that terminates the program. This is necessary because **End** by itself does not generate an **Unload** event for the form. Ending the program using the Control-menu box does generate an **Unload** event.

Working with Controls

Controls are central to the operation of Visual Basic programs. This section presents some enhancements that you may find useful.

Assigning Access Keys to Controls without a Caption Property

Access keys permit you to move the focus to a particular control by pressing Alt plus a character key. To specify an access key for a control, you place an ampersand (&) in front of the desired character in the control's Caption property; this character will be displayed underlined in the control's caption at run time. You cannot directly assign an access key to a control that does not have a Caption property, such as a Text Box. However, you can do so indirectly.

The technique we will use here is based on features of Visual Basic's Label control. A Label control has a Caption property, so you can assign an access key. However, a Label control cannot receive the focus. What happens, then, if the user presses a Label's access key? The focus will be set to the next control in the TabIndex order—in other words, to the control whose TabIndex property is one greater than the Label's TabIndex property. This assumes, of course, that the next control in the TabIndex order can receive the focus and has its TabStop property set to True.

To assign an access key to a Text Box control, it must have a label associated with it. This is no problem, as most Text Box controls have identifying Label controls placed next to them anyway. Assign the desired access key to the Label control, then assign the Text Box a TabIndex property one greater than the that of the Label control. Remember, the Text Box's TabStop property must remain at its default value of True.

Figure 3.1 shows a simple example. The form is a data entry form for a database application that keeps track of a compact disk music collection. There are four Text Box controls with four corresponding Label controls, each of which has a an access key assigned to it. TabIndex

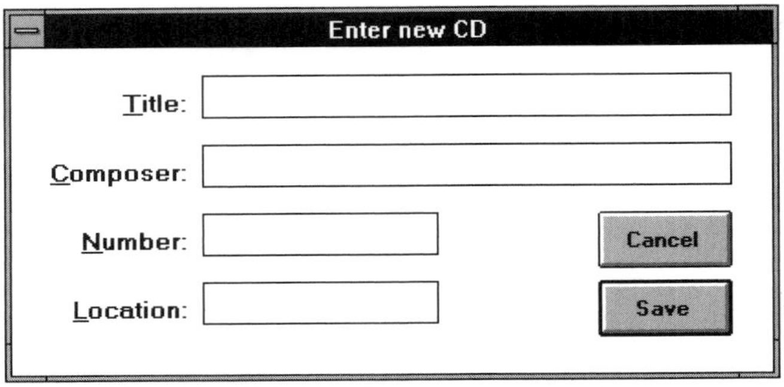

Figure 3.1   Using Label controls to assign access keys to Text Box controls.

properties are assigned so that the "Title" label has a TabIndex of 0, the Text Box next to it has a TabIndex of 1, the "Composer" label has a TabIndex of 2, and so on.

There's no code in this demonstration form, so no listing is presented for it. If you run the program all you will be able to do is move the focus to various Text Box controls using the indicated access keys. Quit the program using the Control-menu box.

Using ACCSKEYS.MAK

This demonstration program is stored on disk as ACCSKEYS.MAK and ACCSKEYS.FRM.

Use the Enter Key to Move between Controls

You can program a form so the Enter key, or the Tab key, moves the focus between controls.

Visual Basic's normal operation is for the Tab key to move the focus to the next control in the tab order. Some users, however, may prefer to use the Enter key for this purpose. This is particularly true during high-speed data entry on a form with many Text Box controls—many people find it more natural to press Enter at the end of a data field to move to the next field. You can make Enter serve the same function as Tab by following these steps. In the control's **KeyDown** event, examine the **KeyAscii** argument to see if the user pressed Enter. If so, use the **SendKeys** statement to send a Tab. You may also want to set **KeyAscii** to 0 to prevent the Enter keystroke from being passed through, since it will cause the computer to beep if the focus is on a single-line Text Box.

The code to trap Enter as described in the previous paragraph must be placed in the **KeyPress** event procedure for every control for which you want Enter to substitute for Tab. Note that Tab and Shift+Tab will function in the normal manner—the user is merely given the choice of using either Enter or Tab to move the focus to the next control. Note also that the form cannot contain a Command Button with the Default property set to True, because the Command Button would trap the Enter before it could be processed by your code.

The program ENTR_TAB.MAK, in Listings 3.2 and 3.3, demonstrates this technique. The program's form, shown in Figure 3.2, contains three Text Box controls to simulate a data entry form. The form also has a Command Button captioned Record; when selected, it simulates "recording" of the data by clearing the Text Box controls and moving the focus to the first text box in preparation for entry of more data. The form is designed so that a user can enter repeated records of data using only the Enter key. Note that the Exit Command Button has both its TabStop and Default properties set to False so the only way the user can select it is with the access key or the mouse.

Using ENTR_TAB.MAK

This demostration program, presented in Listings 3.2 and 3.3, is stored on disk as ENTR_TAB.MAK, ENTR_TAB.FRM.

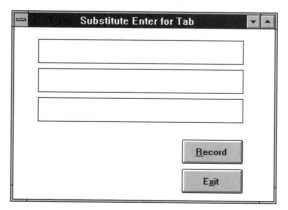

Figure 3.2 The form created by ENTR_TAB.MAK.

Listing 3.2   Objects and Properties in ENTR_TAB.FRM

```
Begin Form Form1
    Caption          =    "Substitute Enter for Tab"
    Begin CommandButton cmdExit
        Caption      =    "E&xit"
        TabStop      =    0    'False
    End
    Begin CommandButton cmdRecord
        Caption      =    "&Record"
        TabIndex     =    3
    End
    Begin TextBox Text3
        TabIndex     =    2
    End
    Begin TextBox Text2
        TabIndex     =    1
    End
    Begin TextBox Text1
        TabIndex     =    0
    End
End
```

Listing 3.3   Code in ENTR_TAB.FRM

```
Option Explicit

' ASCII value of Enter.
Const KEY_ENTER = 13

Sub cmdExit_Click ()

End

End Sub

Sub cmdRecord_Click ()

' Empty the Text Box controls (Simulates
' recording of real data).
Text1.Text = ""
Text2.Text = ""
Text3.Text = ""

' Set focus to first Text Box.
Text1.SetFocus

End Sub
```

```
Sub Text1_KeyPress (KeyAscii As Integer)

' If user presses Enter, send a Tab instead.
' Set KeyAscii to 0 to prevent beep.
If KeyAscii = KEY_ENTER Then
    SendKeys "{Tab}"
    KeyAscii = 0
End If

End Sub

Sub Text2_KeyPress (KeyAscii As Integer)

If KeyAscii = KEY_ENTER Then
    SendKeys "{Tab}"
    KeyAscii = 0
End If

End Sub

Sub Text3_KeyPress (KeyAscii As Integer)

If KeyAscii = KEY_ENTER Then
    SendKeys "{Tab}"
    KeyAscii = 0
End If

End Sub
```

Sending a Windows Message to a Control

By using Windows messages you can give your controls capabilities not provided by Visual Basic.

Windows makes extensive use of a technique called messaging. This means that much of what goes on in Windows, and in Windows programs, is meadiated by means of information passed back and forth between objects by means of messages. Much of what you can do in Visual Basic is accomplished with messages. For example, when you use the Clear method to empty a List Box, Visual Basic is actually sending the List Box a message that says, in effect, "Clear Yourself."

As you are aware, Visual Basic does not provide direct access to all of Windows' capabilities. Many of these untapped features can be accessed by sending the appropriate message to a Visual Basic control. Messages are sent using the **SendMessgage** API procedure. The declaration is:

```
Declare Function SendMessage Lib "User" (ByVal hWnd As Integer, ByVal
   wMsg As Integer, ByVal wParam As Integer, lParam As Any) As Long
```

The **hWnd** argument specifies the handle of the message destination. The **wMsg** argument is the message to be sent. The final two arguments specify 16 bits (**wParam**) and 32 bits (**lParam**) of additional message-dependent information. These two arguments, as well as the return value of the function, are dependent on the specific message being sent and the recipient.

A program can call **SendMessage** directly every time it needs to send a message to a control. At times it's preferable to hide the API call inside a Basic procedure, and that's what we'll do in the demonstration shown next. We will also need another API call, **GetFocus**; its declaration is:

```
Declare Function GetFocus Lib "User" () As Integer
```

GetFocus returns the **hWnd** of the object that currently has the focus. We will use it to obtain the **hWnd** of the control to which we want to send a message. To do so the focus must first be set to the target control. After sending the message, however, it's a good idea to return the focus to wherever it was originally (which may or may not have been the target control). This is done with the following API call:

```
Declare Sub SetFocusAPI Lib "User" Alias "SetFocus" (ByVal hWnd As Integer)
```

The argument **hWnd** is the handle of the object to receive the focus. You'll note that this procedure declaration uses the **Alias** keyword. The actual API procedure is called **SetFocus**. However, there's a Visual Basic method of the same name, so using the procedure name **SetFocus** would cause a conflict. The **Alias** keyword does just what it sounds like—it establishes an alias, or alternate name, for the procedure. In the Visual Basic program you call the procedure with the name **SetFocusAPI**, and no conflicts arise.

Now we have the tools to create a Basic function to send a message to a control. Listing 3.4 gives the code in SEND_MSG.BAS. The Basic function **MessageToControl** takes four arguments: The name of the control to receive the message, the message itself, and the two parameters **wParam** and **lParam**. Code in the function sets the focus to the target control, sends the message, then returns the focus to its original location. The return value of the function is the value returned by the **SendMessage** API function. You can use the **MessageToControl** function in your own programs by adding this module to your project (as I'll demonstrate in the next scenario).

Using SEND_MSG.BAS

This demonstration code, presented in Listing 3.4, is stored on disk as SEND_MSG.BAS.

Listing 3.4   Code in SEND_MSG.BAS

```
Option Explicit

Declare Function GetFocus Lib "User" () As Integer

Declare Function SendMessage Lib "User" (ByVal hWnd As Integer, ByVal
    WMsg As Integer, ByVal wParam As Integer, ByVal lParam As Long) As
    Integer

Declare Sub SetFocusAPI Lib "User" Alias "SetFocus" (ByVal hWnd As
    Integer)

Function MessageToControl (Target As Control, WMsg As Integer, wParam
    As Integer, lParam As Long) As Integer

Dim OldFocus As Integer, TargetHWnd As Integer, X As Integer

' Sends the specified message and parameters to the
' control specified by Target.

' Get the handle of the object with the focus.
OldFocus = GetFocus()

' Get the handle of the target control.
Target.SetFocus
TargetHWnd = GetFocus()

X = SendMessage(TargetHWnd, WMsg, wParam, lParam)
MessageToControl = X

' Return the focus to its original location.
Call SetFocusAPI(OldFocus)

End Function
```

To Receive a Message, a Control Must Be Visible

A control cannot receive a Windows message unless it is visible. If you want to send a message in a **Form_Load** event procedure, be sure to display the form before sending the message.

Scrolling a Text Box under Program Control

You can scroll the contents of a Text Box control under program control by sending it a Windows message.

A multiline Text Box has scrolling capabilities built into it, but they require user action—pressing a direction key or clicking a scroll bar. By sending a Windows message to the Text Box, however, you can scroll it under program control.

The details of sending a message to a control were presented in the previous scenario *Sending a Windows Message to a Control.* The demonstration program for this scenario will use the Basic procedure presented in that section, so you might want to review it.

To instruct a Text Box to scroll, you send it the message **EM_LINESCROLL**, a Windows global constant with the value **WM_USER+6**, with the constant **WM_USER** equal to &H400. Information on the amount and direction to scroll are passed in the **lParam** argument to the API **SendMessage** function. You'll remember that this argument is a type **Long**; the number of lines to scroll vertically are passed in the low order word of **lParam**, and the number of columns to scroll horizontally are passed in the high-order word. You can pass negative or positive values to scroll up or down vertically, left or right horizontally. If **dv** is the number of rows to scroll vertically, and **dh** is the number of columns to scroll horizontally, you can calculate **lParam** as follows:

```
lParam = (65536 * dh) + dv
```

Use negative values to scroll left or up—that is, to have the contents of the Text Box move to the left or upward with respect to the Text Box borders.

We can now demonstrate the technique of scrolling a Text Box under program control. The program SCROLL1.MAK (Listings 3.5 and 3.6) displays the form shown in Figure 3.3. The form contains a multiline Text Box that is sized to fill the left portion of the form; the exact size is not critical. There's a single Exit Command Button, as well as a control array of four Command Buttons labelled Up, Left, Down, and Right. The code in the Command Button array's Click event procedure calls the **MessageToControl** function, passing the message and appropriate arguments that instruct the Text Box to scroll in the proper direction. Remember, you must add the module SEND_MSG.BAS to the project to make the **MessageToControl** function available.

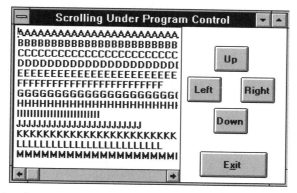

Figure 3.3   Scrolling a Text Box under program control.

Using SCROLL1.MAK

This demonstration program, presented in Listings 3.5 and 3.6, is stored on disk as SCROLL1.MAK, SCROLL1.FRM, SEND_MSG.BAS.

Listing 3.5   Objects and Properties in SCROLL1.FRM

```
Begin Form Form1
    Caption          =    "Scrolling Under Program Control"
    Begin CommandButton cmdExit
        Caption          =    "E&xit"
    End
    Begin CommandButton Command1
        Caption          =    "Down"
        Index            =    3
    End
    Begin CommandButton Command1
        Caption          =    "Right"
        Index            =    2
    End
    Begin CommandButton Command1
        Caption          =    "Left"
        Index            =    1
    End
    Begin CommandButton Command1
        Caption          =    "Up"
        Index            =    0
    End
    Begin TextBox Text1
        MultiLine        =    -1   'True
        ScrollBars       =    1    'Horizontal
    End
End
```

Listing 3.6   Code in SCROLL1.FRM

```
Option Explicit

Const WM_USER = &H400
Const EM_LINESCROLL = WM_USER + 6

Sub cmdExit_Click ()

End

End Sub

Sub Command1_Click (Index As Integer)

Dim lParam As Long, x As Integer

' Depending on the scroll button selected, construct the
' appropriate message to send to the Text Box.
Select Case Index
    Case 0          ' Down
        lParam = 1
    Case 1          ' Right
        lParam = 65536
    Case 2          ' Left
        lParam = -65536
    Case 3          ' Up
        lParam = -1
End Select

x = MessageToControl(Text1, EM_LINESCROLL, 0, lParam)

End Sub

Sub Form_Load ()

Dim i As Integer, j As Integer
Dim Msg As String

' Put some text in the Text Box.
For i = 65 To 90
    Msg = ""
    For j = 1 To 25
        Msg = Msg + Chr$(i)
    Next j
    Msg = Msg + Chr$(13) + Chr$(10)
    Text1.Text = Text1.Text + Msg
Next i

End Sub
```

Filtering User Input

Visual Basic has the capability to filter input from the keyboard, accepting certain characters, while rejecting others. This technique can be very useful in preventing erroneous data entry caused by careless typing.

Data entry in a Visual Basic program is usually done by means of Text Box controls. Depending on the nature of the data being entered, you may want to restrict entry to certain characters. For example, a Text Box for entry of a ZIP code should accept only the digits 0 through 9, with no more or less than five digits accepted. Entry of financial figures could accept the digits 0 through 9, a single decimal point, and a leading minus sign. A person's name could be restricted to the twenty six letters. There are many other examples, all of which can be implemented in Visual Basic.

The key (pardon the pun!) to these techniques is the **KeyPress** event procedure. Visual Basic automatically passes the ASCII value of the key that was pressed to this procedure, in the argument **Keyascii**. Code in the procedure can examine this value and determine whether it's one of the acceptable characters. If it's not acceptable, setting **Keyascii** to 0 prevents the keystroke from reaching the underlying control. For example, the following **KeyPress** event procedure would permit a text Box to accept only the digits 0 through 9:

```
Sub Text1_KeyPress (Keyascii As Integer)

Dim k As String * 1

k = Chr$(Keyascii)

Select Case k
    Case "0" To "9"    ' Do nothing - pass key through.
    Case Else          ' Beep and cancel key.
        Keyascii = 0
        Beep
End Select

End Sub
```

The code in the next example is considerably more sophisticated. Depending on the settings of several constants, it can accept letters, digits, a single decimal point, and/or a leading minus sign. (It always passes through **CHR$(8)**, the Backspace character.) You can incorporate this procedure into your own programs and tailor it to suit your needs by setting the appropriate constants to **TRUE** or **FALSE**. You can select one or more of the following choices:

- Uppercase letters
- Lowercase letters
- Digits
- A leading minus sign
- A single decimal point

Operation of the code for letters and digits is straightforward. To accept a single decimal point, the code must first verify that a decimal point has not already been entered; it does so using the **INSTR** function. For a leading minus sign, the code must verify not only that a minus sign has not already been entered (again using the **INSTR** function), but also that the insertion point is at the first position (otherwise, it wouldn't be a leading minus sign!). It does this using the **SelStart** property.

To try the procedure out, create a form that contains a single Text Box control, then add the code from Listing 3.7 to the Text Box's **KeyPress** event procedure. To use the code in your own programs, simply use the Visual Basic editor to copy the **Text1_KeyPress** event procedure from the demonstration program and paste it into your own program.

Using FILTER.MAK

This demonstration program, presented in Listing 3.7, is stored on disk as FILTER.MAK and FILTER.FRM.

Listing 3.7   Code in FILTER.FRM

```
Sub Text1_KeyPress (Keyascii As Integer)

' Constants that control which characters the Text
' Box will accept.
Const LOWERCASE_LETTERS_OK = False
Const UPPERCASE_LETTERS_OK = True
Const DIGITS_OK = True
Const LEADING_MINUS_OK = True
Const SINGLE_DECIMAL_OK = True

' Controls beep if unacceptable character entered.
Const BEEP_ON_BAD_CHAR = True

Dim k As String * 1

k = Chr$(Keyascii)
```

```
' Pass through Backspace.
If k = Chr$(8) Then Exit Sub

If LOWERCASE_LETTERS_OK Then
    Select Case k
        Case "a" To "z"
        Exit Sub
    End Select
End If

If UPPERCASE_LETTERS_OK Then
    Select Case k
        Case "A" To "Z"
        Exit Sub
    End Select
End If

If DIGITS_OK Then
    Select Case k
        Case "0" To "9"
        Exit Sub
    End Select
End If

If LEADING_MINUS_OK And (k = "-") Then
    If (ActiveControl.SelStart = 0) Then
        If InStr(ActiveControl.Text, "-") = 0) Then Exit Sub
    End If
End If

If SINGLE_DECIMAL_OK And k = "." Then
    If InStr(ActiveControl.Text, ".") = 0 Then
        Exit Sub
    End If
End If

' The character was not accepted, so don't pass it through.
If BEEP_ON_BAD_CHAR Then Beep
Keyascii = 0

End Sub
```

Creating a Macintosh-Style Trash Can

The Apple Macintosh first popularized the use of icons, and one of the best known is the "trash can." You use this icon to throw away, or delete, unecessary files by dragging the items onto the icon and dropping them.

For people who like to use a mouse, dragging and dropping is a very intuitive way to do things. When you want to get rid of an item, dragging it to a trash can makes perfect sense—after all, we do it in everyday life so why not with our computer as well! It's not too difficult to add a trash can to your Visual Basic programs.

What Do You Use for the Trash Can?

The Visual Basic icon library contains several trash can icons.

Since an attractive visual interface is an important part of Visual Basic programs, we want a trash can that looks like—well, a trash can! Fortunately, the Visual Basic icon library includes a number of trash can icons; you'll find them in files named TRASH??.ICO in the subdirectory VB\ICONS\COMPUTER. For the demonstration below, I have used TRASH01.ICO, but you can try the others to see which you prefer.

How Do You Drag Items to the Trash Can?

Use Visual Basic's MouseDown event to initiate dragging, and the DragDrop event to detect when an item is dropped in the trash can.

The drag-and-drop operation is implemented in the standard manner. The **MouseDown** event procedure for the source control initiates the Drag method; the source control can be almost any of Visual Basic's controls. You can set the source control's DragIcon property to a special symbol to indicate that a dragging operation is in progress. If the item being dragged is dropped on the trash can (which is displayed in a Picture Box), the Picture Box's **DragDrop** event procedure performs any required verification and the actual delete operation. This will all be clearer after you examine the demonstration program.

A Trash Can Demonstration

This section demonstrates a dialog box that lets you delete files by dropping them in the trash.

The trash can is implemented in a separate File Delete form, shown in Figure 3.4. The trash can is contained in a Picture Box control that has its BackColor property set to Light Gray (&H00C0C0C0&) and its size adjusted to be 492 x 492 twips, slightly larger than the icon displayed in it. In addition to the trash can icon, the form includes Visual Basic's

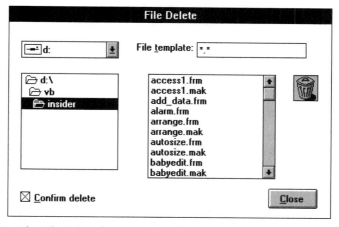

Figure 3.4 The File Delete form uses a trash can with drag-and-drop operation.

standard file manipulation controls: a File list box, a Directory list box, and a Drive list box. There's also a File Template text box, which specifies the files displayed in the File list box, and a Confirm delete check box, which determines whether the user must confirm each deletion.

Here's how the form works: if you want to restrict the filenames displayed, you enter the desired template in the File Template text box. The Drive list and Directory list controls are used to display the desired directory. Then, you point at the name of the file to be deleted and drag it to the trash can icon. If the Confirm delete check box is checked (the default), the program asks for confirmation before deleting the file.

The drag-and-drop operation is implemented as outlined above. Before initiating dragging with the Drag method, the **MouseDown** event procedure for the File List box verifies that the File List box is not empty and that it is the left mouse button that was depressed. The File List box's DragIcon property is set to the icon file DRAG3PG.ICO (this too is provided with Visual Basic, and will be found in the VB\ICONS\DRAGDROP subdirectory). This icon displays several sheets of paper with an arrow; you can substitute any other icon for the drag icon, if you desire.

If the item being dragged is dropped on the Picture Box (i.e., the trash can), the **Picture1_DragDrop** procedure does the rest. It first verifies that that dragged item originated from the File List box by verifying the Tag property of the Source. (The Tag property of the File list box should be set to "FileList" at design time.) If so, the full filename of the to-be-deleted file is constructed, and the file is then deleted with the **Kill** statement (after confirmation, if the Confirm delete check box is checked). Finally, the File List box is refreshed.

Properties and code for this form are presented in Listings 3.8 and 3.9. Please note that the TabIndex property of the Text Box control must be one greater than that of the Label control, permitting the focus to be moved to the Text Box with the Label's access key. This program will *really* delete files, so use care. Don't call me if you delete your tax records or Christmas list!

The code takes into account the possibility of two types of errors. One error would occur of the user selects a diskette drive that is not ready. In this case, the error handler in the **Drive1_Change** procedure resets the path to its old setting. The other error could occur when the program attempts to delete a file—the file could be read-only, for example, or the user might not have proper access rights. If this occurs, the error handler in the **Picture1_DragDrop** procedure displays an error message.

Using TRASHCAN.MAK

This demonstration program, presented in Listings 3.8 and 3.9, is stored on disk as TRASHCAN.MAK and TRASHCAN.FRM.

You can incorporate the File Delete form into your own programs essentially as is. The only required change is to code in the **Command1_Click** procedure. Rather than ending the program, this procedure should return execution to wherever in the program is appropriate. It's also a good idea to make the form modal (FileDelete.Show 1) so that the user must select Close to exit the form.

Listing 3.8   Objects and Properties in TRASHCAN.FRM

```
Begin Form FileDelete
    BorderStyle     =   1  'Fixed Single
    Caption         =   "File Delete"
    ControlBox      =   0  'False
    MaxButton       =   0  'False
    MinButton       =   0  'False
    Begin CommandButton Command1
       Caption       =    "&Close"
    End
    Begin CheckBox Check1
       Caption       =    "&Confirm delete"
       Value         =   1  'Checked
    End
    Begin TextBox Text1
       TabIndex      =   6
       Text          =    "*.*"
    End
```

```
      Begin FileListBox File1
         DragIcon        =    (see text)
         Tag             =    "FileList"
      End
      Begin DirListBox Dir1
      End
      Begin DriveListBox Drive1
      End
      Begin PictureBox Picture1
         BackColor       =    &H00C0C0C0&
         Picture         =    (see text)
      End
      Begin Label Label1
         Caption         =    "File &template:"
         TabIndex        =    5
      End
   End
End
```

Listing 3.9   Code in TRASHCAN.FRM

```
' TRASHCAN.FRM
' Macintosh-style trash can for deleting files.

Option Explicit

Sub Command1_Click ()

End

End Sub

Sub Dir1_Change ()

File1.Path = Dir1.Path

End Sub

Sub Drive1_Change ()

' When the user changes the drive, update the
' directory list's path. If there's an error, such
' as changing to a diskette drive that has no
' diskette in it, the error handler resets the
' drive to the original setting.
On Error GoTo DriveHandler

Dir1.Path = Drive1.Drive
Exit Sub

DriveHandler:
```

```vb
Drive1.Drive = Dir1.Path
Resume Next

End Sub

Sub File1_MouseDown (button As Integer, Shift As Integer, X As Single,
  Y As Single)

' If the user depresses the left mouse button while
' pointing at an item in a non-empty File List,
' initiate dragging.
If File1.ListCount > 0 Then
    If button = 1 Then
        File1.Drag 1
    End If
End If

End Sub

Sub Form_Load ()

' Set the File List's pattern to that specified
' in the Text Box's default text.
File1.Pattern = text1.Text

End Sub

Sub Picture1_DragDrop (source As Control, x As Single, Y As Single)

' If the user drops a filename on the trash can.
Dim reply As Integer, FileName As String

On Error GoTo DeleteHandler

' Exit if DragDrop did not originate with File List box.
If source.Tag <> "FileList" Then Exit Sub

' Construct full filename.
If Right(Dir1.Path, 1) = "\" Then
    FileName = Dir1.Path + File1.List(File1.ListIndex)
Else
    FileName = Dir1.Path + "\" + File1.List(File1.ListIndex)
End If

If Check1.Value = 0 Then
    Kill FileName
Else
    reply = MsgBox("Delete " + FileName + "?", 1)
    If reply = 1 Then Kill FileName
```

```
End If

File1.Refresh

Exit Sub

' Execution comes here if there's any error deleting
' the file, such as trying to delete a read-only file.
DeleteHandler:

MsgBox "Error deleting " + FileName
Resume Next

End Sub

Sub Text1_GotFocus ()

' When the File Template Text Box gets the focus, select
' all of its text so that user input replaces it.
text1.SelLength = Len(text1.Text)

End Sub

Sub Text1_KeyUp (KeyCode As Integer, Shift As Integer)

' If the user presses Enter while the text box has
' the focus, generate a LostFocus event to update
' the File List's Pattern property.
If KeyCode = 13 Then
    Text1_LostFocus
    KeyCode = 0
End If

End Sub

Sub Text1_LostFocus ()

' If the user enters a new file template, set the
' File List's Pattern property to it.
File1.Pattern = text1.Text

End Sub
```

Creating a "Baby" Text Editor

What can you do if you need to edit a text file while working in a Visual Basic application? You can, of course, return to the Program Manager and open an editor, such as Notepad. In some cases, however, it would be better to have the ability to edit text files built right into the Visual Basic application. In this section, I'll show you how to create a basic text editor that you can incorporate into your own programs.

What's a Baby Editor?

A Baby Editor is an editor that provides only the most basic editing functions, but is quick and simple to use.

The following features are the bare minimum I would want in any editor:

- Inserting and deleting text
- Cursor movement
- Selecting text
- Cut, copy, and paste text
- Open any file that the user specifies
- Save a file under its original name or a new name
- Never lose unsaved changes without warning the user

These are the features that are included in the demonstration to follow. You may have a different list of "must have" features. But that's one of the beauties of the baby editor—you can easily customize it to your heart's desire!

For a Fully Functional Text Editor Use NOTEPAD.FRM

Visual Basic comes with a text editor form called NOTEPAD.FRM. This is a rather fancy editor, with many capabilities not provided in the "baby" editor. If you need these features, then by all means use it. However, the editor presented here is simpler, requires less memory, and can be easily customized.

Programming the Editor

Creating a basic editor is easier than you may think!

At the heart of the editor is a Text Box control, which has many of the text handling capabilities we need: cursor movement, selecting text, inserting and deleting characters—all these are automatically available within a Text Box control. All we need to add is the ability to cut, copy, and paste text (using the Clipboard) and the editing part of the project is complete.

The Baby Editor Project

This section demonstrates how to include a baby editor in your own projects.

All of the desired editing capabilities can be implemented in a single form with a moderate amount of code. The baby editor, shown executing in Figure 3.5, consists of a form with only a single control, a Text Box. Code in the form's **Resize** event procedure adjusts the size of the Text Box so it always fills the form. You can see that the Text Box has its ScrollBars property set to Both so that horizontal and vertical scroll bars are displayed. When a horizontal scroll bar is present, long lines of text are not wrapped, rather, they extend past the right edge of the editing window—you must scroll to view the entire line. If you prefer, you can set the ScrollBars property to Vertical so that long lines will automatically wrap within the Text Box.

As written, the editor does not use dialog boxes for the File Open or File Save As commands—it simply prompts the user to enter a filename. You could enhance the editor by creating dialog boxes for these functions, using the File, Directory, and Drive list box controls. If you have the Professional Edition, you can use the Common Dialog custom control for this purpose.

Listings 3.10 and 3.11 present the properties and code for the baby editor. When designing the form don't worry about the exact size of the Text Box, since the size is adjusted in code during execution. You can use this editor for files up to about 32Kb in length—that's the maximum

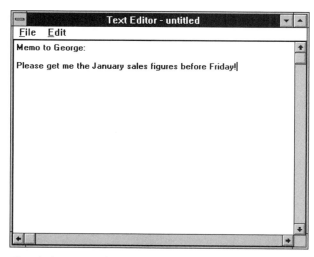

Figure 3.5 The "baby" text editor in operation.

capacity of a multiline Text Box. The editor has no way of distinguishing between text and non-text (e.g., program) files.

Using BABYEDIT.MAK

This demonstration program, presented in Listings 3.10 and 3.11, is stored on disk as BABYEDIT.MAK and BABYEDIT.FRM.

You can incorporate the baby editor into your own programs as is, by adding the file BABYEDIT.FRM.

Listing 3.10 Objects and Properties in BABYEDIT.FRM

```
Begin Form frmBabyEditor
    Caption         =   "Text Editor - Untitled"
    Begin TextBox Text1
        MultiLine       =   -1  'True
        ScrollBars      =   3   'Both
    End
    Begin Menu mnuFile
        Caption         =   "&File"
        Begin Menu mnuFileNew
            Caption         =   "&New"
        End
        Begin Menu mnuFileOpen
            Caption         =   "&Open"
        End
        Begin Menu mnuFileSave
            Caption         =   "&Save File"
        End
        Begin Menu mnuFileSaveAs
            Caption         =   "Save File &As"
        End
        Begin Menu mnuFileSeparator
            Caption         =   "-"
        End
        Begin Menu mnuFileExit
            Caption         =   "E&xit"
        End
    End
    Begin Menu mnuEdit
        Caption         =   "&Edit"
        Begin Menu mnuEditCopy
            Caption         =   "&Copy"
            Shortcut        =   ^F
        End
        Begin Menu mnuEditCut
```

```
            Caption          =    "Cu&t"
            Shortcut         =    ^X
        End
         Begin Menu mnuEditPaste
            Caption          =    "&Paste"
            Shortcut         =    ^V
        End
    End
  End
End
```

Listing 3.11   Code in BABYEDIT.FRM

```
Option Explicit

' Global variables
Dim TextChanged As Integer
Dim FileName As String, OldName As String

' Constants for use with message boxes.
Const MB_YESNOCANCEL = 3
Const MB_RETRYCANCEL = 5
Const MB_ICONQUESTION = 32
Const MB_YES = 6
Const MB_CANCEL = 2


Sub Form_Load ()

' On Form Load set TextChanged to False
TextChanged = False

End Sub

Sub Form_Resize ()

' Size the Text Box to fill the form.
Text1.Top = 0
Text1.Left = 0
Text1.Width = ScaleWidth
Text1.Height = ScaleHeight

End Sub

Sub Form_Unload (Cancel As Integer)

' Verify that changes are saved, if user desires.
Dim Reply As Integer

Reply = SaveChanges()
```

```
If Reply = False Then Cancel = True

End Sub

Function GetFileName () As String

' Loop until the name of an existing file is entered.
' Returns the name or an empty string if the user
' has canceled.
Dim fn As String, FileExist As String
Dim Title As String, Msg As String
Dim Reply As Integer, Flags As Integer

Do While 1

fn = InputBox$("Name of file to edit:")
FileExist = Dir$(fn)

If FileExist = "" Then
    Title = "File not found"
    Msg = fn + " not found."
    Flags = MB_RETRYCANCEL
    Reply = MsgBox(Msg, Flags, Title)
    If Reply = MB_CANCEL Then
        GetFileName = ""
        Exit Function
    End If
Else
    Exit Do
End If

Loop

GetFileName = fn

End Function

Sub mnuEdit_Click ()

' Enable Paste command only if there is text on
' the Clipboard.
Dim x As String

x = Clipboard.GetText()

If x = "" Then
    mnuEditPaste.Enabled = False
Else
    mnuEditPaste.Enabled = True
```

```
   End If

   End Sub

   Sub mnuEditCopy_Click ()

   ' If any text is selected copy it to the Clipboard.
   If Text1.SelLength = 0 Then
       Beep
       Exit Sub
   End If

   Clipboard.SetText  Text1.SelText

   End Sub

   Sub mnuEditCut_Click ()

   ' If any text is selected copy it to the Clipboard,
   ' then delete it.
   If Text1.SelLength = 0 Then
       Beep
       Exit Sub
   End If

   Clipboard.SetText  Text1.SelText
   Text1.SelText = ""

   End Sub

   Sub mnuEditPaste_Click ()

   ' Paste Clipboard text.
   Text1.SelText = Clipboard.GetText()

   End Sub

   Sub mnuFileExit_Click ()

   Unload  frmBabyEditor

   End Sub

   Sub mnuFileNew_Click ()

   ' Verify that changes are saved, if user desires.
   Dim Reply As Integer

   Reply = SaveChanges()
```

```
If Reply = False Then Exit Sub

Text1.Text = ""
FileName = ""
frmBabyEditor.Caption = "Text Editor - Untitled"
TextChanged = False

End Sub

Sub mnuFileOpen_Click ()

Dim Buffer1 As String, Buffer2 As String, CRLF As String
Dim Reply As Integer, Flags As Integer, FileNum As Integer

CRLF = Chr$(13) + Chr$(10)

' Verify that changes are saved, if user desires.
Reply = SaveChanges()
If Reply = False Then Exit Sub

' Get a filename from the user.
FileName = GetFileName()

If FileName = "" Then Exit Sub

FileNum = FreeFile

Open FileName For Input As FileNum

Do While Not EOF(FileNum)
    Line Input #1, Buffer1
    Buffer2 = Buffer2 + Buffer1 + CRLF
Loop

Close FileNum

Text1.Text = Buffer2
frmBabyEditor.Caption = "Text Editor - " + FileName

End Sub

Sub mnuFileSave_Click ()

Call SaveFile

End Sub

Sub mnuFileSaveAs_Click ()

OldName = FileName
```

```
FileName = ""
Call SaveFile

End Sub

Function SaveChanges ()

' Determines if the text being edited has changed since the
' last File Save. If so, offers the user the option of saving it.
' Function returns True if there have been no changes OR if
' the user saves the changes. Returns False if the user
' selects Cancel.
Dim Title As String, Msg As String
Dim Reply As Integer, Flags As Integer

If TextChanged = True Then
    Title = "Text has changed"
    Msg = "Save changes to text?"
    Flags = MB_YESNOCANCEL + MB_ICONQUESTION
    Reply = MsgBox(Msg, Flags, Title)

    If Reply = MB_YES Then
        Call SaveFile
    ElseIf Reply = MB_CANCEL Then
        SaveChanges = False
        Exit Function
    End If
End If

SaveChanges = True

End Function

Sub SaveFile ()

' Saves current text under original filename.
' If no filename, prompts for one.
Dim FileNum As Integer, Buffer As String

Buffer = Text1.Text

Do While FileName = ""
    FileName = InputBox("Enter name for file:", , OldName)
Loop

frmBabyEditor.Caption = "Text Editor - " + FileName

FileNum = FreeFile

Open FileName For Output As FileNum
```

```
Print #FileNum, Buffer
Close FileNum

TextChanged = False

End Sub

Sub Text1_Change ()

' If the Text Box's contents change, set global
' variable TextChanged to True.
TextChanged = True

End Sub
```

Using Passwords for Security

You may find yourself writing programs that deal with sensitive data. If so, you'll want to use some sort of password system to prevent unauthorized access to the programs and their data.

Implementing a Password Entry System

When a user enters a password to start a password-protected program, you want to provide a couple of chances to get it right.

When a user enters a password, the characters should not be echoed on the screen. You can readily achieve this by setting the password entry Text Box's PasswordChar property to the single character, such as an asterisk, that you want echoed instead. In addition, you need to take into account that users often make errors when entering their password, so they should be given two or three chances. The form presented below does just this. When used as an application's startup form, it gives the user a specified number of chances to enter the correct password. The password itself is assumed to be stored in the constant **USER_PASSWORD**. The number of tries allowed is set by the constant **NUM_TRIES**.

The password entry form is shown in Figure 3.6, and the form's properties and code are presented in Listings 3.12 and 3.13. In the demonstration program, the "program" being accessed is represented by the dummy form frmMain. This module consists of only a form with no controls; its code is given in Listing 3.14.

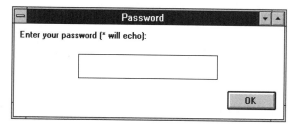

Figure 3.6 The password entry form.

Using PASSWORD.MAK

This demonstration program, presented in Listings 3.12, 3.13, and 3.14, is stored on disk as PASSWORD.MAK, PASSWORD.FRM, and FRMMAIN.FRM.

To use the password form in your program, add PASSWORD.FRM to your project and specify it as the startup form. Change the line of code in the **Command1_Click** procedure to show the appropriate form. Don't forget to change the **USER_PASSWORD** and **NUM_TRIES** constants!

This password system is functional, but limited. See the next section for a more capable implementation.

Listing 3.12 Objects and Properties in PASSWORD.FRM

```
Begin Form frmPassWord
    Caption        =   "Password"
    Begin CommandButton Command1
        Caption      =   "OK"
        Default      =   -1   'True
    End
    Begin TextBox Text1
        PasswordChar    =   "*"
    End
    Begin Label Label1
        Caption        =   "Enter your password (* will echo):"
    End
End
```

Listing 3.13 Code in PASSWORD.FRM

```
Option Explicit

' Number of tries permitted.
Const NUM_TRIES = 3
Const USER_PASSWORD = "Visual Basic"
```

```
Sub Command1_Click ()

' Assume actual password is stored in the constant
' USER_PASSWORD, in all uppercase.
Static Tries As Integer

Tries = Tries + 1

If UCase$(Text1.Text) = USER_PASSWORD Then
    Unload frmPassWord
    frmMain.Show   ' Change this to show your program's form.
ElseIf Tries >= NUM_TRIES Then
    MsgBox "ACCESS DENIED"
    End
End If

MsgBox "Invalid password - please try again"
Text1.Text = ""
Text1.SetFocus

End Sub
```

Listing 3.14   Code in FRMMAIN.FRM

```
Sub Form_Load ()

' This is the dummy main program form. Execution
' comes here only if the password is entered properly.
Show
MsgBox "Program accessed successfully."
End

End Sub
```

A More Sophisticated Password System

It is often desirable to allow users to change their password when desired. In addition, the password must be stored in an encoded form to prevent unauthorized access.

The password system shown in the previous section is functional, but rather basic. You will probably prefer a system that permits the user to change their password. The ability to change a password is crucial if there is reason to believe that the old one is no longer secure, or if a former password is difficult to remember. To be changeable, a password must be stored in a disk file, not coded as part of the program's source code (as in the previous example). However, the stored password should be encrypted in some manner, to prevent an unauthorized person from reading the password from the file and then using it to access the program.

The program below provides these functions. The program password is stored in a small disk file that is given the arbitrary and unobvious name {555}.@@@; you can, of course, use any name you wish as long as you use something that is not likely to conflict with other filenames. When the program starts, it looks for this file. If it is found, the program reads in and decodes the password (explained below). If the file is not found the program defaults to the password "Visual Basic."

Prompting the user for the password and verifying it are done in the same manner as for the previous example. Once the user has successfully accessed the program (again, a "dummy" program is used for demonstration purposes), they have the option of changing the password. This is done by the form frmNewPassword, which provides two safety features: first, the new password must be at least a certain length, as specified by the constant **MINIMUM_PASSWORD_LENGTH**; second, the user must enter the new password twice, to prevent typing errors.

After an acceptable new password has been entered, it is stored in the file {555}.@@@. A simple encryption method is used to prevent the file from being easily read. Each character in the password is stored as an integer value that equals the character's ASCII value minus a value n, where n is the character's position in the password (all letters are converted to uppercase first). For example, the password MICROSOFT would be stored as follows:

M: ASCII value = 77, position = 1, value stored = 76

I: ASCII value = 73, position = 2, value stored = 71

C: ASCII value = 67, position = 3, value stored = 64

And so on. You can come up with other encryption schemes, of course. Please note that this is a fairly simply code, and will not keep the CIA or FBI out of your program! It is perfectly effective, however, at foiling casual unauthorized users.

What if a Password Is Forgotten?

If a user forgets the password, the user or system administrator can simply delete the password file, and the program will revert to the default password "Visual Basic."

The demonstration program PASSWRD1 shows how to use these techniques. There are two essential forms: PASSWRD1.FRM is for entering the password at program startup (it's essentially identical to the form from the previous password demonstration), and NEW_PW.FRM is for entering a new password. The third form, FRMMAIN1.FRM, represents the "dummy" application. Properties and code for these forms are shown in Listings 3.15 through 3.20.

Using PASSWRD1.MAK

This demonstration program, presented in Listings 3.15, 3.16, 3.17, 3.18, 3.19, and 3.20, is stored on disk as PASSWRD1.MAK, PSSWRD1.FRM, NEW_PW.FRM, and FRMMAIN1.FRM.

To use this code in your own programs, use the Add File command to add the PASSWRD1.FRM and NEW_PW.FRM modules to your program; PASSWRD1.FRM must be the startup module. In both modules' code, change references to frmMain as required so that execution passes to your program's form. In your program, include a menu command or other means to display the new password form.

Listing 3.15   Objects and Properties in PASSWRD1.FRM

```
Begin Form frmPassWord
   Caption        =    "Password"
   Begin CommandButton cmdOK
      Caption        =    "OK"
      Default        =    -1   'True
   End
   Begin TextBox Text1
      PasswordChar   =    "*"
   End
   Begin Label Label1
      Caption        =    "Enter your password (* will echo):"
   End
End
```

Listing 3.16   Code in PASSWRD1.FRM

```
Option Explicit

Const MB_ICONSTOP = 16
Const MB_ICONEXCLAMATION = 48
Const NUM_TRIES = 3

' Password filename.
```

```
Const PASSWORD_FILE = "{555}.@@@"

' Global variable for password.
Dim PassWord As String

Sub cmdOK_Click ()

' Assume actual password is stored in the
' global variable PassWord.

' Number of times user has tried to enter password.
Static Tries As Integer
Tries = Tries + 1

If UCase$(Text1.Text) = PassWord Then
    Unload frmPassWord
    frmMain.Show
    Exit Sub
ElseIf Tries >= NUM_TRIES Then
    MsgBox "ACCESS DENIED", MB_ICONSTOP, "Password"
    End
End If

MsgBox "Invalid password - please try again", MB_ICONEXCLAMATION,
  "Password"
Text1.Text = ""
Text1.SetFocus

End Sub

Sub Form_Load ()

' Look for the encrypted password file. If not found,
' set the PassWord to the default "Visual Basic."
Dim x As String, FileNum As Integer
Dim y As Integer, z As Integer

x = Dir$(PASSWORD_FILE)

If x = "" Then
    PassWord = "Visual Basic"
    Exit Sub
End If

FileNum = FreeFile
Open PASSWORD_FILE For Binary As FileNum
PassWord = ""

z = 1
While Not EOF(FileNum)
```

```
      Get #FileNum, , y
      PassWord = PassWord + Chr$(y + z)
      z = z + 1
Wend

' Discard EOF character.
PassWord = Left$(PassWord, Len(PassWord) - 1)

End Sub
```

Listing 3.17   Objects and Properties in NEW_PW.FRM

```
Begin Form frmNewPassword
    Caption         =   "Change Password"
    Begin CommandButton cmdCancel
        Cancel          =   -1  'True
        Caption         =   "Cancel"
    End
    Begin CommandButton cmdOK
        Caption         =   "OK"
        Default         =   -1  'True
    End
    Begin TextBox Text1
        PasswordChar    =   "*"
    End
    Begin Label Label1
    End
End
```

Listing 3.18   Code in NEW_PW.FRM

```
Option Explicit

Dim Tries As Integer

Const MINIMUM_PASSWORD_LENGTH = 6
Const PASSWORD_FILE = "{555}.@@@"
Const MB_ICONEXCLAMATION = 48

Sub cmdCancel_Click ()

Unload frmNewPassword
frmMain.Show

End Sub

Sub cmdOK_Click ()

' If user enters a new password.
Static Try1 As String, Try2 As String
```

```
Dim c As String * 1, msg As String
Dim FileNum As Integer, x As Integer, y As Integer

' Don't accept passwords under the minimum length.
If Len(Text1.Text) < MINIMUM_PASSWORD_LENGTH Then
    msg = "Too short - minimum is "
    msg = msg + Str$(MINIMUM_PASSWORD_LENGTH) + " characters."
    MsgBox msg, MB_ICONEXCLAMATION, "Password"
    Text1.Text = ""
    Text1.SetFocus
    Exit Sub
End If

Tries = Tries + 1

If Tries = 1 Then
    Try1 = UCase$(Text1.Text)
    Text1.Text = ""
    Label1.Caption = "Please enter new password again to verify:"
    Text1.SetFocus
    Exit Sub
Else
    Try2 = UCase$(Text1.Text)
    If Try1 <> Try2 Then
        MsgBox "Sorry - entries do not match"
        frmNewPassword.Hide
        frmMain.Show
        Unload frmNewPassword
        Exit Sub
    End If
End If

' Execution reaches here only if the two
' enties match.
FileNum = FreeFile

Open PASSWORD_FILE For Binary As #FileNum

For x = 1 To Len(Try1)
    c = Mid$(Try1, x, 1)
    y = Asc(c) - x
    Put #FileNum, , y
Next x

MsgBox "Password changed."
Close #FileNum
Tries = 0

Unload frmNewPassword
frmMain.Show
```

```
End Sub

Sub Form_Load ()

Label1.Caption = "Enter new password:"
Tries = 0

End Sub

Sub Form_Paint ()
Text1.SetFocus
End Sub
```

Listing 3.19   Objects and Properties in FRMMAIN1.FRM

```
Begin Form frmMain
    Caption           =    "Password demo #2"
    Begin CommandButton cmdExit
        Caption       =     "E&xit"
    End
    Begin CommandButton cmdChange
        Caption       =     "Change &Password"
    End
End
```

Listing 3.20   Code in FRMMAIN1.FRM

```
Option Explicit

Sub cmdChange_Click ()

' Show the form for entering a new password.
frmNewPassword.Show

End Sub

Sub cmdExit_Click ()

End

End Sub

Sub Form_Load ()

' This is the dummy main program form. Execution
' comes here only if the password is entered properly.
Show
MsgBox "Program accessed successfully."

End Sub
```

Masterful Menus

isual Basic makes it easy to create professional looking menus. With the techniques presented in this chapter you can further improve the appearance and usefulness of your applications' menus.

Using Floating Menus in Your Programs

Visual Basic menus are great, but they are limited to appearing at the top of a form. At times you might like to have a menu apprear at other screen locations. As its name implies, a floating menu pops up, or floats, at different screen locations. Visual Basic 3 now supports floating menus with its new PopupMenu method, but we can do the same thing in VB2 with the help of the Windows API.

Why Use Floating Menus?

A floating menu can increase your program's ease of use. For example, a drawing program's color selection menu could pop up near the current mouse position, making it easier for the user to "point and shoot" to select a color.

By default, Visual Basic's menus display at the top of the form. For mouse users, this means repeatedly moving the mouse pointer to the top of the form to make selections. If the menu were to pop up at the current mouse pointer location, mouse movement would be minimized.

Creating Floating Menus

The API has procedures for creating floating menus.

To create a floating, or pop-up, menu, you begin by using Visual Basic's standard menu design techniques to create a normal menu. The program code then uses API calls to manipulate the menu position, causing it to appear in an unexpected location.

The first API call we'll use is **GetMenu**; the declaration for this function is:

```
Declare Function GetMenu Lib "User" (ByVal hWnd As Integer) As Integer
```

This function returns the handle of the menu associated with the form indentified by the **hWnd** argument. it returns Null if the form has no menu, and its return value is undefined if the form is a child form.

The next API call we need is **GetSubMenu**. The declaration for this function is:

```
Declare Function GetSubMenu Lib "User" (ByVal hMenu As Integer, ByVal
   nPos As Integer) As Integer
```

This function returns the handle of a submenu—that is, the pull-down menu associated with an item on a form's main menu. The argument **hMenu** is the handle of the menu, and the argument **nPos** identifies the position of the submenu whose handle you want. Position values start at 0 for the left-most submenu. The return value is the handle of the given submenu; if no submenu menu exists at the given position, the function returns Null.

The final API call we need is **TrackPopupMenu**. The declaration for this function is:

```
Declare Function TrackPopupMenu Lib "User" (ByVal hMenu As Integer,
   ByVal wFlags As Integer, ByVal x As Integer, ByVal y As Integer,
   ByVal nReserved As Integer, ByVal hWnd As Integer, lpReserved As
   Any) As Integer
```

This function displays the submenu specified by the **hMenu** argument at a specified location. A floating menu can appear anywhere on the screen. No matter what the menu's location, the **TrackPopupMenu** function automatically detects when the user makes a menu selection, and passes it to the program in the normal fashion. The function's arguments are explained here:

The **wFlags** argument specifies both the menu's screen-position and mouse-button flags. The screen-position flag can be one of the following:

- **TPM_CENTERALIGN** (value = 4) centers the menu horizontally relative to the coordinate specified by the x parameter.
- **TPM_LEFTALIGN** (value = 0) aligns the left side of the menu at the coordinate specified by the x parameter.
- **TPM_RIGHTALIGN** (value = 8) aligns the right side of the menu at the coordinate specified by the x parameter.

The mouse-button flag can be one of the following:

- **TPM_LEFTBUTTON** (value = 0) causes the pop-up menu to track the left mouse button.
- **TPM_RIGHTBUTTON** (value = 2) causes the pop-up menu to track the right mouse button.

Additional arguments in the **TrackPopupMenu** function are described here:

- **x** specifies the horizontal position, in screen coordinates, of the menu.
- **y** specifies the vertical position, in screen coordinates, of the top of the menu.

- **hWnd** identifies the window that owns the menu. This window receives all messages from the menu.
- **lpReserved** and **nReserved** are reserved and must both be zero.

The function's return value is non-zero if the function is successful. Otherwise, it is zero.

A Floating Menu Demonstration

This section presents a program that demonstrates floating menus.

Now let's put it all together. The program FLOATMNU.MAK demonstrates floating menus; it also demonstrates some other useful techniques. The program consists of a single full-screen form with a single Command Button control. When this button is clicked a sample message is displayed on the form, using the Form's FontName and ForeColor properties. The form has two menus; the Color menu lets you change the form's ForeColor property, and the Fonts menu lets you change the form's FontName property. When you click the Display button again, the message is redisplayed using the new color and font. So far, everything is quite straightforward.

The difference is the program's floating menus. The floating menus are implemented by code in the form's **MouseDown** event procedure. The Color menu is displayed if the left button is pressed, and the Font menu is displayed if the right mouse button is pressed. In both cases, the menu displays at the mouse pointer position.

Before the menu can be displayed, some calculations are necessary; the API call **TrackPopupMenu** requires that the menu position coordinates be passed in terms of pixels, not twips. The calculations first determine the twips per pixel ratio for the form, and then use this value to convert the mouse pointer position to pixel coordinates. Then, the API calls described above are used to pop-up the appropriate menu.

Note that the selection made from a floating menu is automatically passed to the Visual Basic application and can be trapped by the menu's **Click** event procedure in the normal fashion. Note also that the menus remain available at their normal positions as well. In VB3 we could hide the menus by setting their visible properties to **False**. The PopupMenu method in VB3 would still be able to display them. Figure 4.1 shows the program with the Fonts menu popped up. When a floating menu is displayed, clicking anywhere outside the menu hides it.

A couple of other useful techniques used in this demonstration bear mentioning. The selections on the Color menu are implemented as a control

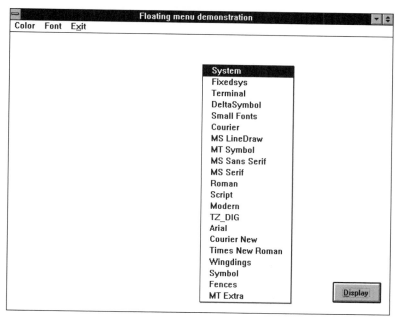

Figure 4.1 A floating font selection menu.

array so that each color's Index is the same as its "old" Quick Basic color value. When a selection is made, it's easy to use the selection's Index value and the **QBColor** function to obtain the desired ForeColor property setting.

The other technique is loading a menu with the font names. The available fonts can differ from system to system, so these names cannot be coded into the menu at design time. Rather, the Font menu is designed with a control array that contains only a single dummy item. Then, at run time code in the **Form_Load** event procedure uses the SCREEN object's FontCount and Fonts() properties to load the control array with the names of all the screen fonts that are available on the system.

To reiterate, the steps to create floating menus in your own programs are:

1. Design the menus and write the menu event processing code in the usual manner.

2. Decide on the event(s) that will trigger display of the floating menu(s).

3. In the appropriate event procedures, calculate the menu position in terms of pixels and use the API calls to display the menu.

Unfortunately, in VB2 there's no way to design a menu then have it appear only as a floating menu, without it also appearing in the normal position at the top of the form. If you set the menu item's Visible property to False you will not be able to pop it up.

The techniques for creating a floating menu are demoinstrated in FLOATMNU.MAK. The objects and properties for this project are presented in Listintg 4.1, and the code is in Listing 4.2.

Using FLOATMNU.MAK

This demonstration program, presented in Listings 4.1 and 4.2, is stored on disk as FLOATMNU.MAK and FLOATMNU.FRM.

Listing 4.1   Objects and Properties in FLOATMNU.FRM

```
Begin Form frmFloatMenu
    AutoRedraw      =   -1  'True
    Caption         =   "Floating menu demonstration"
    WindowState     =   2   'Maximized
    Begin CommandButton cmdDisplay
        Caption         =   "&Display"
    End
    Begin Menu mnuColors
        Caption         =   "Color"
        Begin Menu mnuColor
            Caption         =   "Black"
            Index           =   0
        End
        Begin Menu mnuColor
            Caption         =   "Blue"
            Index           =   1
        End
        Begin Menu mnuColor
            Caption         =   "Green"
            Index           =   2
        End
        Begin Menu mnuColor
            Caption         =   "Cyan"
            Index           =   3
        End
        Begin Menu mnuColor
            Caption         =   "Red"
            Index           =   4
        End
        Begin Menu mnuColor
            Caption         =   "Magenta"
            Index           =   5
        End
        Begin Menu mnuColor
            Caption         =   "Yellow"
            Index           =   6
```

```
               End
            Begin Menu mnuColor
               Caption          =     "White"
               Index            =     7
            End
         End
         Begin Menu mnuFonts
            Caption          =     "Font"
            Begin Menu mnuFont
               Caption          =     "Dummy"
               Index            =     0
            End
         End
         Begin Menu mnuExit
            Caption          =     "E&xit"
         End
      End
End
```

Listing 4.2   Code in FLOATMNU.FRM

```
Option Explicit

Declare Function GetMenu Lib "User" (ByVal hWnd As Integer) As Integer

Declare Function GetSubMenu Lib "User" (ByVal hMenu As Integer, ByVal
   nPos As Integer) As Integer

Declare Sub TrackPopupMenu Lib "User" (ByVal hMenu As Integer, ByVal
   wFlags As Integer, ByVal X As Integer, ByVal Y As Integer, ByVal
   nReserved As Integer, ByVal hWnd As Integer, lpReserved As Any)

Sub cmdDisplay_Click ()

Dim temp As String, msg As String

temp = frmFloatMenu.FontName

msg = "Message displayed in " + temp + " font"
frmFloatMenu.Print msg

End Sub

Sub cmdExit_Click ()

End

End Sub

Sub Form_Load ()
```

```
Dim i As Integer

' Load the fonts menu
'  with the available screen fonts.
mnuFont(0).Caption = SCREEN.Fonts(0)

For i = 1 To SCREEN.FontCount - 1
    Load frmFloatMenu.mnuFont(i)
    frmFloatMenu.mnuFont(i).Caption = SCREEN.Fonts(i)
Next i

' Set a larger font size for the form.
frmFloatMenu.FontSize = 16

End Sub

Sub Form_MouseDown (button As Integer, Shift As Integer, X As Single,
  Y As Single)

Dim TwipsPerPixel As Integer, WidthInPixels As Integer
Dim MenuX As Integer, MenuY As Integer
Dim hMenu As Integer, hSubMenu As Integer

' Calculate the relationship between twips and pixels.
ScaleMode = 3
WidthInPixels = ScaleWidth
ScaleMode = 1
TwipsPerPixel = ScaleWidth / WidthInPixels

' Calculate the menu position.
MenuX = (X + Left) / TwipsPerPixel
MenuY = (Y + Top) / TwipsPerPixel

' Pop up the color or font menu depending on
' which mouse button was clicked.
hMenu = GetMenu(hWnd)

If button = 1 Then        ' Left button = color menu
    hSubMenu = GetSubMenu(hMenu, 0)
    Call TrackPopupMenu(hSubMenu, 0, MenuX, MenuY, 0, hWnd, 0)
ElseIf button = 2 Then    ' Right button = font menu
    hSubMenu = GetSubMenu(hMenu, 1)
    Call TrackPopupMenu(hSubMenu, 0, MenuX, MenuY, 0, hWnd, 0)
End If

End Sub

Sub mnuColor_Click (Index As Integer)
```

```
' Set the form's foreground color to the color
' corresponding to the menu index.
frmFloatMenu.ForeColor = QBColor(Index)

End Sub

Sub mnuExit_Click ()

End

End Sub

Sub mnuFont_Click (Index As Integer)

' Set the form's font name to the selected font.
frmFloatMenu.FontName = SCREEN.Fonts(Index)

End Sub
```

The Control Menu

Every Visual Basic form—and indeed every window in Windows—has a Control menu. You display the Control menu (also called the system menu) by clicking the Control-menu box at the top left of the form, or by pressing Alt+Spacebar while the form is active. You can create a form without a Control menu by setting the ControlBox property to False. For more flexibility, you can modify the Control menu.

Modifying a Form's Control Menu

You can use API calls to modify a form's Control menu.

The default Control menu on Visual Basic forms has commands for restoring, resizing, and moving the form, exiting the application, and displaying the Task Manager. The Task Manager enables you to switch among other running Windows applications. If this complement of Control menu selections doesn't suit you, you can use API calls to modify the menu. You can't add new items but you can modify the text displayed for existing items, or delete then completely.

The first API call you'll need is **GetSystemMenu**. The declaration for this function is:

```
Declare Function GetSystemMenu Lib "User" (ByVal hWnd As Integer,
  ByVal bRevert As Integer) As Integer
```

If the **bRevert** argument is False, the function simply returns the handle of the Control menu belonging to the form identified by the argument **hWnd**. If the **bRevert** argument is True, the function resets the form's Control menu to its default state; in this case the return value is undefined.

To change the text displayed for a Control-menu item, you'll need the **ModifyMenu** function. The declaration for this function is:

```
Declare Function ModifyMenu Lib "User" (ByVal hMenu As Integer, ByVal
    nPosition As Integer, ByVal wFlags As Integer, ByVal wIDNewItem As
    Integer, ByVal lpString As Any) As Integer
```

The **ModifyMenu** function arguments are described below:

- **hMenu** is the handle of the menu to change.

- **nPosition** specifies the menu item to change. The way that **nPosition** is interpreted depends on the **wFlags** argument: when **wFlags** is set to **MF_BYCOMMAND** (value = 0), the **nPosition** argument specifies the menu-item identifier (described following this list). When **wFlags** is set to **MF_BYPOSITION** (value = &H400), the **nPosition** argument specifies the position of the menu item (the first item has position 0).

- **wIDNewItem** specifies the identifier of the menu item.

- **lpString** specifies the text of the menu item. If **wFlags** is set to **MF_STRING** (value = 0; the default), **lpString** is a long pointer to a null-terminated string (when you pass a string using the **ByVal** keyword, Visual Basic automatically provides the necessary conversion).

The return value is non-zero if the function is successful. Otherwise, it is zero.

So what is a menu-item identifier anyway? Each item on the Control menu has a numerical identifier associated with it. This number is the message that is sent to Windows when the menu item is selected. The message tells Windows what to do. Below is a list of the identifiers for the default Control menu commands and their Windows constants:

```
SC_RESTORE = &HF120
SC_MOVE = &HF010
SC_SIZE = &HF000
SC_MINIMIZE = &HF020
SC_MAXIMIZE = &HF030
SC_CLOSE = &HF060
SC_TASKLIST = &HF130 ' The "Switch To" command
```

A Control Menu Demonstration

The program in this section shows how to modify a form's Control menu.

Let's see how these procedures work. CTRLMENU.MAK (Listings 4.3 and 4.4) starts execution with the form's Control menu in its default state. Click the Modify button to remove the Restore, Size, and Move items and to change the text for the Switch To item. Figure 4.2 shows the form with the modified Control menu displayed.

Using CTRLMENU.MAK

This demonstration program, presented in Listings 4.3 and 4.4, is stored on disk as CTRLMENU.MAK and CTRLMENU.FRM.

Listing 4.3   Objects and Properties in CTRLMENU.FRM

```
Begin Form frmCtrlMenu
   Caption        =    "Modify Control Menu Demo"
   Begin CommandButton cmdRestore
      Caption        =    "&Restore Control Menu"
   End
   Begin CommandButton cmdModify
      Caption        =    "&Modify Control Menu"
   End
   Begin CommandButton cmdExit
      Caption        =    "E&xit"
   End
End
```

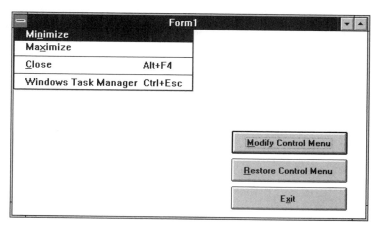

Figure 4.2   CTRLMENU.MAK demonstrates modifying a form's Control menu.

Listing 4.4   Code in CTRLMENU.FRM

```
Option Explicit

Declare Function GetSystemMenu Lib "User" (ByVal hWnd As Integer,
  ByVal bRevert As Integer) As Integer

Declare Function ModifyMenu Lib "User" (ByVal hMenu As Integer, ByVal
  nPosition As Integer, ByVal wFlags As Integer, ByVal wIDNewItem As
  Integer, ByVal lpString As Any) As Integer

Declare Function DeleteMenu Lib "User" (ByVal hMenu As Integer, ByVal
  nPosition As Integer, ByVal wFlags As Integer) As Integer

Sub cmdExit_Click ()

End

End Sub

Sub cmdModify_Click ()

Const MF_BYCOMMAND = 0
Const MF_BYPOSITION = &H400
Const SC_TASKLIST = &HF130
Const ICON_STOP = 16

Dim hSystemMenu As Integer, X As Integer, I As Integer
Dim ItemToAdd As String

' Get the Control menu's handle.
hSystemMenu = GetSystemMenu(hWnd, False)

' Change the text for the "Switch To" entry, which
' displays the Windows Task Manager.
ItemToAdd = "Windows Task Manager" + Chr$(9) + "Ctrl+Esc"

X = ModifyMenu(hSystemMenu, SC_TASKLIST, MF_BYCOMMAND, SC_TASKLIST,
  ItemToAdd)

' Display error message if call failed.
If X = 0 Then
    MsgBox "Unable to modify menu item.", ICON_STOP
End If

' Remove the "Restore", "Move", and "Size"
' choices from the Control menu.
```

```
For I = 0 To 2
    X = DeleteMenu(hSystemMenu, 0, MF_BYPOSITION)
    If X = 0 Then
        MsgBox "Unable to delete menu item.", ICON_STOP
    End If
Next I

End Sub


Sub cmdRestore_Click ()


' Restores the Control menu to its default state.
Dim hSystemMenu As Integer

hSystemMenu = GetSystemMenu(hWnd, True)

End Sub
```

Menus and Fonts

For many programmers, Visual Basic's easy access to different screen and printer fonts is a very important feature. A menu is one way that the program can provide for the user to select among fonts. This section provides some techniques for creating font selection menus.

Coordinating Screen and Printer Fonts on a Menu

When offering the user a selection of fonts to choose from, you usually want to limit the selections to those fonts that are available for both the screen and printer objects.

In many Windows applications, selection of a font relates to both the screen display of text and to printer output. The number and types of fonts available depend, of course, on your specific Windows setup. However, it's a sure bet that there's only a partial overlap between the fonts available for printing and those available for screen display. Clearly, you want to offer the user only that subset of fonts common to both.

It's easy to do so using the Fonts property. This property is available for both the PRINTER and SCREEN objects, and provides an indexed list of the names of all the fonts available for the specified object. The FontCount property tells you the number of fonts for each item; they are indexed from 0 to (FontCount–1). By simply going through both lists comparing font names and extracting only those names that appear on both lists, it's an easy matter to create a list of fonts that are available on both the screen and the printer. The font names can then be displayed on a Fonts menu (or, if you prefer, in a List Box or Combo Box).

A nice touch would be to have the font names appear on the menu in alphabetical order. You couild write your own sorting routine, but it is easier to let Visual Basic do the work for you! At design time, create a List Box control with the Sorted property set to True and the Visible property set to False. At run time, load the font names into the List Box, which will automatically sort them. Finally, copy the now-sorted font names into the menu.

The demonstration program FONTLIST.MAK shows how this is done. The program's objects and properties are given in Listing 4.5, and its code in Listing 4.6. The resulting menu is shown in Figure 4.3. The fonts available on your system may well be different.

Using FONTLIST.MAK

This demonstration program, presented in Listings 4.5 and 4.6, is stored on disk as FONTLIST.MAK and FONTLIST.FRM.

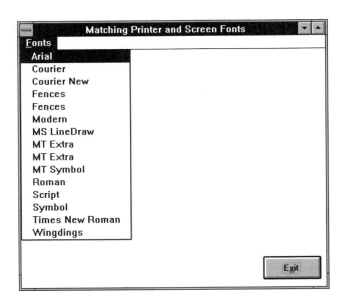

Figure 4.3 A menu displaying fonts available for both the SCREEN and PRINTER objects.

Listing 4.5   Objects and Properties in FONTLIST.FRM

```
Begin Form frmFontList
    Caption          =    "Matching Printer and Screen Fonts"
    Begin CommandButton cmdExit
        Caption          =    "E&xit"
    End
    Begin ListBox lstFonts
        Sorted           =    -1   'True
        Visible          =    0    'False
    End
    Begin Menu mnuFonts
        Caption          =    "&Fonts"
        Begin Menu mnuFontList
            Caption          =    "Dummy"
            Index            =    0
        End
    End
End
End
```

Listing 4.6   Code in FONTLIST.FRM

```
Option Explicit

Sub cmdExit_Click ()

End

End Sub

Sub Form_Load ()

Dim i As Integer, j As Integer

' Display hourglass mouse pointer.
MousePointer = 11

' Go through the lists of screen and printer fonts. Add
' to the List Box those fonts present in both lists.
For i = 0 To SCREEN.FontCount - 1
    For j = 0 To PRINTER.FontCount - 1
        If SCREEN.Fonts(i) = PRINTER.Fonts(j) Then
            lstFonts.AddItem PRINTER.Fonts(j)
        End If
    Next j
Next i

' Load new entries onto the Font List menu array.
For i = 1 To lstFonts.ListCount - 1
```

```
      Load mnuFontList(i)
Next i

' Copy the sorted items from the List Box
' to the menu.
For i = 0 To lstFonts.ListCount - 1
      mnuFontList(i).Caption = lstFonts.List(i)
Next i

' Clear the List Box to release memory.
lstFonts.Clear

' Display default mouse pointer.
MousePointer = 0


End Sub
```

Displaying Different Fonts on a Menu

On a font selection menu you can display not only the font names, but the actual typefaces as well.

When you are offering the user a menu of fonts from which to select, it is preferable to provide not only the names of the fonts but also an indication of what they look like. Normally, Visual Basic menu items are all displayed in the same system font. We can, however, take advantage of Windows' ability to display bitmaps in a menu to display different typefaces.

To display typefaces in a menu we will use the API procedure **ModifyMenu**. One of the many things that this procedure can do is to replace the menu item's caption with a bitmap. **ModifyMenu** is a function, but for the present purposes we will declare it as a subprocedure:

```
Declare Sub ModifyMenu Lib "User" (ByVal hMenu As Integer, ByVal
      nPosition As Integer, ByVal wFlags As Integer, ByVal wIDNewItem As
      Integer, ByVal lpString As Any)
```

The **ModifyMenu** subprocedure arguments are described below:

- **hMenu** is the handle of the menu to change.

- **nPosition** specifies the menu item to change. The way that **nPosition** is interpreted depends on the **wFlags** argument: **wFlags** can be set to **MF_BYCOMMAND** (value = 0), in which case the **nPosition** argument specifies the menu-item identifier (see *Modifying a Form's Control Menu,* earlier in this chapter, for a definition of menu-item identifier). To place a bitmap in the menu, set **wFlags** to **MF_BITMAP** (value = 4).

- **wIDNewItem** specifies the identifier of the menu item.
- **lpString** specifies the content of the menu item. When placing a bitmap in the menu (**wFlags = MF_BITMAP**), **lpString** is the handle of the bitmap to be placed in the menu.

Note that in the arguments to **ModifyMenu** there are two that refer to the menu-item identifier. The first identifier argument, **nPosition**, specifies the menu item that **ModifyMenu** is going to affect (when **wFlags = MF_BYCOMMAND**). The second identifier argument, **wIDNewItem**, specifies the new identifier for the menu item. Since we do not want to change what the menu item does, we will pass the same value for both **nPosition** and **wIDNewItem** when we call **ModifyMenu**.

The next API call we will need is **GetMenu**. The declaration for this function is:

```
Declare Function GetMenu Lib "User" (ByVal hWnd As Integer) As Integer
```

This function returns the handle of the menu associated with the form indentified by the argument **hWnd**. It returns Null if the form has no menu.

We will also use the API call **GetSubMenu**. Its declaration is:

```
Declare Function GetSubMenu Lib "User" (ByVal hMenu As Integer, ByVal
   nPos As Integer) As Integer
```

This function returns the handle of a submenu—that is, the pull-down menu associated with an item on a form's main menu. The argument **hMenu** is the handle of the menu, and the argument **nPos** identifies the position of the submenu whose handle you want. Position values start at 0 for the left-most submenu. The return value is the handle of the given submenu; if no submenu menu exists at the given position, the function returns Null.

The final API procedure that we will use is **GetMenuItemID**, which returns the identifier of a particular menu item. The declaration for this function is:

```
Declare Function GetMenuItemID Lib "User" (ByVal hMenu As Integer,
   ByVal nPos As Integer) As Integer
```

The argument **hMenu** is the handle of the submenu, and **nPos** is the zero-based position of the menu item whose identifier is needed.

We now have all the tools needed. The first steps required are at design time. Create a Fonts menu with a single "dummy" item with Index = 0; this will serve as the basis for an array of menu items. Also create a single

Picture Box with Index = 0. Set the Picture Box's AutoRedraw property to True and the Visible property to False. Set the FontSize property to the size that you want used for menu items; 12 is a good value to use. The exact Picture Box size doesn't matter, as it will be sized in code. However, I have found that it's necessary to make it quite small because the resizing procedure seems only able to make it larger than its design size, not smaller.

Next, decide on the list of fonts to be displayed. This can be obtained from the Fonts property of the SCREEN object, or you can use a List Box to construct a sorted list of fonts common to both the SCREEN and PRINTER objects (see *Coordinating Screen and Printer Fonts on a Menu,* earlier in this chapter). This latter technique will be used in the demonstration program.

The remainder of the action takes place in code, preferably in the **Form_Load** procedure. Add sufficient members to the Picture Box and menu arrays to hold all the fonts in the list. Then, for each font:

1.   Set the FontName property of a Picture Box to the corresponding font from your list.
2.   Use the Print method to print the font name to the Picture Box.
3.   Use the TextHeight and TextWidth properties to set the Picture Box's size to fit the text.
4.   Get the menu-itemidentifier for the corresponding menu item.
5.   Call **ModifyMenu** to load the Picture Box bitmap into the menu.

That's all there is to it! The above processing can take a few seconds, so you might want to display a "Please wait—fonts loading" message or an hourglass mouse pointer in the meanwhile. The demonstration program FONTMENU.MAK demonstrates these techniques; objects and properties are give in Listing 4.7, and Listing 4.8 displays the code. The program's Font menu is shown in Figure 4.4.

If you look closely at Figure 4.4 you'll notice that some of the fonts don't appear as recognizable words or letters. This is because some of Windows' fonts, such as Symbol and Wingdings, are specialized symbols sets rather than the normal alphabet and punctuation marks that we expect to see. When the font name "Wingdings," for example, is translated into the Wingdings symbols, it displays as shown on the menu. If you don't want these symbol fonts displayed on the menu, you can test for them in code then either display their names in a standard alphanumeric font, or not display them at all.

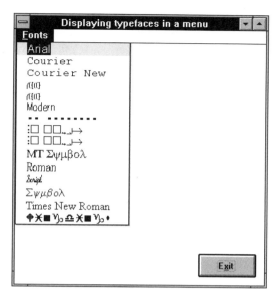

Figure 4.4 Font typefaces displayed on a menu.

Using FONTMENU.MAK

This demonstration program, presented in Listings 4.7 and 4.8, is stored on disk as FONTMENU.MAK and FONTMENU.FRM.

Listing 4.7 Objects and Properties in FONTMENU.FRM

```
Begin Form Form1
   Caption         =   "Displaying typefaces in a menu"
    Begin CommandButton cmdExit
      Caption       =   "E&xit"
   End
   Begin ListBox lstFonts
      Sorted        =   -1   'True
      Visible       =   0    'False
   End
   Begin PictureBox FontGraphic
      AutoRedraw    =   -1   'True
      FontSize      =   12
      Visible       =   0    'False
   End
   Begin Menu mnuFont
      Caption       =   "&Fonts"
       Begin Menu mnuFontList
```

```
        Caption          =    "Dummy"
        Index            =    0
      End
    End
End
```

Listing 4.8   Code in FONTMENU.FRM

```
Option Explicit

Declare Function GetMenu Lib "User" (ByVal hWnd As Integer) As Integer

Declare Function GetSubMenu Lib "User" (ByVal hMenu As Integer, ByVal
   nPos As Integer) As Integer

Declare Function GetMenuItemID Lib "User" (ByVal hMenu As Integer,
   ByVal nPos As Integer) As Integer

Declare Function ModifyMenu Lib "User" (ByVal hMenu As Integer, ByVal
   nPosition As Integer, ByVal wFlags As Integer, ByVal wIDNewItem As
   Integer, ByVal lpString As Any) As Integer

Sub cmdExit_Click ()

End

End Sub

Sub Form_Load ()

Dim hMenu As Integer, hFontMenu As Integer
Dim x As Integer, y As Integer, id As Integer, size As Single

Const MF_BITMAP = &H4

' Display the form with an hourglass mouse pointer.
Show
MousePointer = 11

' Go through the lists of screen and printer fonts. Add
' to the List Box only those fonts present in both lists.
For x = 0 To SCREEN.FontCount - 1
    For y = 0 To PRINTER.FontCount - 1
        If SCREEN.Fonts(x) = PRINTER.Fonts(y) Then
            lstFonts.AddItem SCREEN.Fonts(x)
        End If
    Next y
Next x
```

```
' Load the needed members into the menu and
' Picture Box control arrays. Element 0 already exists.
For x = 1 To lstFonts.ListCount - 1
    Load mnuFontList(x)
    Load FontGraphic(x)
Next x

' Switch to each font, then print the font name in the
' corresponding picture box. Adjust the Picture Box
' size to fit its contents, then get the bitmap handle
' from the Image property.
For x = 0 To lstFonts.ListCount - 1
    FontGraphic(x).FontName = lstFonts.List(x)
    size = FontGraphic(x).TextWidth(lstFonts.List(x))
    FontGraphic(x).Width = 1.1 * size
    size = FontGraphic(x).TextHeight(lstFonts.List(x))
    FontGraphic(x).Height = 1.1 * size
    FontGraphic(x).Print lstFonts.List(x)
    FontGraphic(x).Picture = FontGraphic(x).Image
    y = DoEvents()
Next x

' Get the handles of the form's menu and the
' Font submenu.
hMenu = GetMenu(hWnd)
hFontMenu = GetSubMenu(hMenu, 0)

' Load each menu item with the
' corresponding bitmap.
For x = 0 To lstFonts.ListCount - 1
    id = GetMenuItemID(hFontMenu, x)
    y = ModifyMenu(hMenu, id, MF_BITMAP, id,
  CLng(FontGraphic(x).Picture))
    If y = 0 Then MsgBox "Error"
Next x

' Reset default mouse pointer.
MousePointer = 0

End Sub
```

More Menu Techniques

In the final section of this chapter, I present some more techniques for enhancing your applications program menus.

Displaying Images on a Menu

You can liven up your menus by displaying graphical images instead of text.

Visual Basic is supposed to be, well, visual! And Windows is a graphical environment, right? The emphasis is on using graphical screen elements to represent tasks, data items, and so on—Visual Basic's toolbar is a good example of this. However, Visual Basic's menus are limited to text. Is there some way to apply the graphical design principles to menus? You bet!

As you know, **ModifyMenu** allows you to replace a menu item's caption with a bitmap. Again, although **ModifyMenu** is actually a function, we will declare it as a subprocedure:

```
Declare Sub ModifyMenu Lib "User" (ByVal hMenu As Integer, ByVal
   nPosition As Integer, ByVal wFlags As Integer, ByVal wIDNewItem As
   Integer, ByVal lpString As Any)
```

The **ModifyMenu** subprocedure arguments are described here:

- **hMenu** is the handle of the menu to change.

- **nPosition** specifies the menu item to change. The way that **nPosition** is interpreted depends on the wFlags argument: **wFlags** can be set to **MF_BYCOMMAND** (value = 0), in which case the **nPosition** argument specifies the menu-item identifier (see Modifying a Form's Control Menu earlier in this chapter for a description of menu-item identifiers). To place a bitmap in the menu, set **wFlags MF_BITMAP** (value = 4). As an option, set **wFlags** to **MF_CHECKED** (value = 8) to display a checkmark next to the menu item.

  Note: To pass more than one command in ***wFlags***, *combine them with the* ***OR*** *operator.*

- **wIDNewItem** specifies the identifier of the menu item.

- **lpString** specifies the content of the menu item. When placing a bitmap in the menu (**wFlags = MF_BITMAP**), **lpString** is the handle of the bitmap to be placed in the menu.

Another API call we will need is **GetMenu**. The declaration for this function is:

```
Declare Function GetMenu Lib "User" (ByVal hWnd As Integer) As Integer
```

This function returns the handle of the menu associated with the form indentified by the argument **hWnd**. It returns Null if the form has no menu, and its return value is undefined if the form is a child form.

The next API call needed is **GetSubMenu**. The declaration for this function is:

```
Declare Function GetSubMenu Lib "User" (ByVal hMenu As Integer, ByVal
    nPos As Integer) As Integer
```

This function returns the handle of a submenu—that is, the pull-down menu associated with an item on a form's main menu. The argument **hMenu** is the handle of the menu, and the argument **nPos** identifies the position of the submenu whose handle you want. Position values start at 0 for the left-most submenu. The return value is the handle of the given submenu; if no submenu menu exists at the given position, the function returns Null.

The final API procedure that we will use is **GetMenuItemID**, which returns the identifier of a particular menu item. The declaration for this function is:

```
Declare Function GetMenuItemID Lib "User" (ByVal hMenu As Integer,
    ByVal nPos As Integer) As Integer
```

The argument **hMenu** is the handle of the submenu, and **nPos** is the zero-based position of the menu item whose identifier is needed.

Now we can get to work! To place a bitmap in a menu, the menu item must first exist. The initial step, therefore, is to use the Menu Design window to create the desired menu structure. Each menu item that will receive a bitmap should be given a name, index number (if you're using a control array), and so on in the usual fashion. The caption that you assign does not matter, as it will be replaced by the bitmap.

Next, add one Picture Box control to the form for each menu bitmap. Set the Autosize property to True and the Visible property to False. Then select the Picture property and load the graphic that you want displayed in the menu. You can use any bitmap file, icon file, or Windows metafile; of course, for a menu you will probably use relatively small pictures. The example program below uses three icons from the Visual Basic icon library.

The remainder of the process is carried out by code in the **Form_Load** procedure. The first step is to retrieve the handle of the submenu. For each menu item, the program retrieves the menu-item identifier, then calls

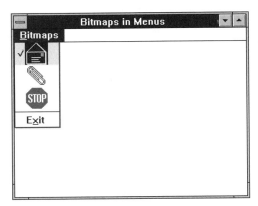

Figure 4.5   Bitmaps in a menu.

ModifyMenu to load the bitmap into the menu. That's all there is to it! The menu items can be selected in the usual manner using the keyboard or the mouse. The only restriction is that access keys and shortcut keys are not available. Figure 4.5 shows a menu containing bitmaps. Note that you can mix regular text items with bitmaps.

Don't Overuse Bitmaps in Your Menus

Using bitmaps in your menus can add a nice professional touch to your programs, but don't overdo it! In particular, be sure that the user will understand what the bitmaps stands for.

The program BIT_MENU.MAK created the display in Figure 4.5. The program's objects and properties are presented in Listing 4.9, and its code is in Listing 4.10.

Using BIT_MENU.MAK

This demonstration program, presented in Listings 4.9 and 4.10, is stored on disk as BIT_MENU.MAK and BIT_MENU.FRM

Listing 4.9   Objects and Properties in BIT_MENU.FRM

```
Begin Form Form1
   Caption          =   "Bitmaps in Menus"
   Begin PictureBox Picture3
      AutoSize       =   -1  'True
      Picture        =   (see text)
      Visible        =   0   'False
```

```
      End
      Begin PictureBox Picture2
         AutoSize         =    -1   'True
         Picture          =    (see text)
         Visible          =    0    'False
      End
      Begin PictureBox Picture1
         AutoSize         =    -1   'True
         Picture          =    (see text)
         Visible          =    0    'False
      End
      Begin Menu mnuBitmap
         Caption          =    "&Bitmaps"
         Begin Menu mnuDummy1
            Caption          =    "Dummy"
         End
         Begin Menu mnuDummy2
            Caption          =    "Dummy"
         End
         Begin Menu mnuDummy3
            Caption          =    "Dummy"
         End
         Begin Menu Separator
            Caption          =    "-"
         End
         Begin Menu mnuExit
            Caption          =    "E&xit"
         End
      End
   End
End
```

Listing 4.10   Code in BIT_MENU.FRM

```
Option Explicit

Declare Function GetMenu Lib "User" (ByVal hWnd As Integer) As Integer

Declare Function GetSubMenu Lib "User" (ByVal hMenu As Integer, ByVal
   nPos As Integer) As Integer

Declare Function GetMenuItemID Lib "User" (ByVal hMenu As Integer,
   ByVal nPos As Integer) As Integer

Declare Sub ModifyMenu Lib "User" (ByVal hMenu As Integer, ByVal
   nPosition As Integer, ByVal wFlags As Integer, ByVal wIDNewItem As
   Integer, ByVal lpString As Any)

Const MF_BITMAP = 4
Const MF_CHECKED = 8
```

```
Sub Form_Load ()

Dim hMenu As Integer, hSubMenu As Integer
Dim id As Integer, X As Integer

' Get the menu and submenu handles.
hMenu = GetMenu(hWnd)
hSubMenu = GetSubMenu(hMenu, 0)

' Put the first bitmap in the first submenu item. Display
' a checkmark next to the item.
Picture1.Picture = Picture1.Image
id = GetMenuItemID(hSubMenu, 0)
Call ModifyMenu(hMenu, id, MF_BITMAP Or MF_CHECKED, id,
  CLng(Picture1.Picture))

' Put the second bitmap in the second submenu item.
Picture2.Picture = Picture2.Image
id = GetMenuItemID(hSubMenu, 1)
Call ModifyMenu(hMenu, id, MF_BITMAP, id, CLng(Picture2.Picture))

' Put the third bitmap in the third submenu item.
Picture3.Picture = Picture3.Image
id = GetMenuItemID(hSubMenu, 2)
Call ModifyMenu(hMenu, id, MF_BITMAP, id, CLng(Picture3.Picture))

End Sub

Sub mnuExit_Click ()

End

End Sub
```

Right-Justifying Menu Items

An undocumented feature lets you right-justify items on a form's menu bar. You can, for example, display the Help menu in its traditional position at the right side of the menu bar.

The items of a Visual Basic form's top-level menu (the menu bar) are normally left-justified. You can right-justify one or more items by adding a backspace character (**CHR$(8)**) as the first character in the caption of the first menu item to be right justified. This can only be done at run time.

  The program MENUJUST.MAK demonstrates this. At design time the form was given a five-item menu bar, as shown in Listing 4.11. In the **Form_Load** event procedure (Listing 4.12) a **CHR$(8)** was added to the

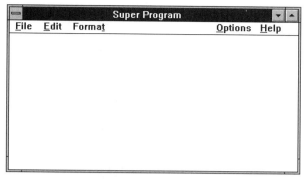

Figure 4.6 Right-justified menu items.

beginning of the fourth item's caption. The result, shown in Figure 4.6, is that the first through third menu items are in their normal left-justified position, while the fourth and fifth menu items are right-justified. Note that the code also addes a few spaces at the end of the "Help" caption to provide some space between it and the right edge of the form.

Using MENUJUST.MAK

This demonstration program, presented in Listings 4.11 and 4.12, is stored on disk as MENUJUST.MAK and MENUJUST.FRM.

Listing 4.11 Objects and Properties in MENUJUST.FRM

```
Begin Form Form1
    Caption        =    "Super Program"
    Begin Menu mnuOne
        Caption    =    "&File"
    End
    Begin Menu mnuEdit
        Caption    =    "&Edit"
    End
    Begin Menu mnuFormat
        Caption    =    "Forma&t"
    End
    Begin Menu mnuOptions
        Caption    =    "&Options"
    End
    Begin Menu mnuHelp
        Caption    =    "&Help"
    End
End
```

Listing 4.12   Code in MENUJUST.FRM

```
Option Explicit

Sub Form_Load ()

' Right-justufy the fourth and fifth menu items.
mnuOptions.Caption = Chr$(8) + mnuOptions.Caption

' Add some spacing after the final menu item.
mnuHelp.Caption = mnuHelp.Caption + "      "

End Sub
```

sing Dynamic
Data Exchange

Dynamic Data Exchange (DDE) is a Windows feature that allows you to share data between Windows applications. Visual Basic supports DDE, permitting you to create programs that can share data with other Windows applications. The first section of this chapter provides a brief introduction to DDE, which you can skip if you feel you don't need it. The remainder of the chapter presents some techniques you can use to exploit the power of DDE.

A DDE Primer

The Visual Basic documentation covers DDE in great detail—too great, it might be argued! After reading it, I felt a sudden urge to take an aspirin—and you may feel the same way. DDE is unavoidably somewhat complex, but it's essential for you to understand the fundamentals if you are to use DDE effectively in your own programs. For these reasons, I felt it was a good idea to start this chapter with a simplified explanation of DDE that I hope you will find easier to understand than the documentation. This is not intended to be a complete treatment of DDE, only a simplified coverage of the basics. For complete information on DDE, you'll have to slog through the Visual Basic manual and on-line Help.

What Is DDE?

Ordinarily, when you need to copy data from one Windows application into another, you use the Clipboard. Unfortunately, each time you update the data in the original, you must do the same for the copied data. DDE remedies this situation by automatically updating transferred (linked) data.

Data transfer between programs has always been possible using the Windows Clipboard. Imagine that you are using a word processor to write a report, and you want to include a table of numbers from a spreadsheet. First you would need to start the spreadsheet and copy the table to the Clipboard. Then, you would switch back to the word processor and paste the table into your document.

So far so good. But what happens when the numbers in the spreadsheet change? You'll have to repeat the entire process—manually copying the new numbers from the spreadsheet to the document. Here's where DDE comes in. With DDE you can establish a *link* between the spreadsheet and the document, allowing changes to the spreadsheet data to be automatically reflected in the word processing document. In other words, there's no need for manual updating—the DDE link takes care of it for you. You can establish any number of links between multiple applications. And, the linked data can be just about anything—numbers, text, or a graphical image.

I'm sure that you are beginning to see the power of DDE. With proper use of DDE, you only need to enter data once—the DDE links will automatically transfer it to any other place it is needed. The same is true of changes to existing data; manual updates are no longer necessary, saving you time and decreasing potential errors

DDE Terminology

Just to make things difficult, DDE comes with a vocabulary of its own. There are a few special DDE terms that you need to know to grasp DDE firmly.

When DDE is used to exchange data between two applications, one application is called the *source* and the other is called the *destination*. As these names indicate, the data being exchanged originates in the source and is transferred to the destination. The process of data exchange—the link—is often referred to as a *conversation*. It is always the destination application that initiates a DDE conversation.

A Change in Terminology

In Visual Basic 1.0, the DDE destination was called the client, and the source was called the server.

When a destination application initiates a conversation, it must specify the name of the source application. Every Windows application that can act as a DDE source has a unique name for this purpose. Usually, this is the executable filename, less the .EXE extension. The destination application must also specify the topic of the conversation. The topic is some unit of data that is meaningful to the source; typically it is the name of a data file.

Both the application and the topic remain constant throughout a DDE conversation. The conversation will terminate if either the source or the destination attempts to change the application or topic.

The actual chunk of data being transferred by the DDE conversation is called the *item*. The item must be identified in some manner that can be understood by the source application. For example, a spreadsheet program such as Excel recognizes row and column addresses of spreadsheet cells, and a word processor such as Word for Windows recognizes bookmark names.

Let's look at an example. If a destination application wants to establish a link to the contents of cell A1 in the Excel worksheet C:\DATA\SALES.XLS, then the conversation application will be EXCEL, the topic will be C:\DATA\SALES.XLS, and the item will be R1C1 (row 1, column 1).

When Are DDE Links Updated?

DDE links fall into three updating modes.

One of the main attractions of DDE is that data in the destination is automatically updated if the linked data in the source application changes. In actuality, it's more accurate to say that the destination data *can* be automatically updated. A DDE link can be established in one of three modes, specifying when and how updating takes place:

- With an *automatic* link, the source updates the data every time it changes.
- With a *manual* link, the source updates the data only when specifically requested by the destination.
- With a *notify* link, the source automatically notifies the destination whenever the data changes, but actually updates the data only when specifically requested by the destination.

Another Change in Terminology

In Visual Basic 1.0, automatic links were called "hot links" and manual links were called "cold links."

Visual Basic Sources and Destinations

In a Visual Basic program, only certain objects can participate in DDE conversations.

The only Visual Basic objects that can serve as the destination in a DDE conversation are Text Boxes, Picture Boxes, and Labels. Each of these controls has a LinkTopic property that specifies the application and topic of the conversation, a LinkItem property that specifies the data item, and a LinkMode property that specifies whether the link mode is automatic, manual, or notify.

Any Visual Basic form can be the source in a DDE conversation. A form has a LinkTopic property for specifying the topic name that a destination application must use to refer to the form in a DDE conversation. The item in a conversation can be a Text Box, Picture Box, or Label control on the form. In the DDE conversation, the destination application specifies the control's Name property as the item.

Using a Visual Basic Control as a DDE Destination

There are four properties that you must set for a control to act as a DDE destination.

To have a Text Box, Picture Box, or Label to serve as a DDE destination, you use the control's LinkTopic property to specify both the source application and the source topic. The property must list the application followed by a vertical pipe character (**CHR$(124)**) and the topic name. For example, to link a Text Box to data in the Excel worksheet SALES.XLS you would write

```
Text1.LinkTopic = "EXCEL|SALES.XLS"
```

or

```
Text1.LinkTopic = "EXCEL" + CHR$(124) + "SALES.XLS"
```

The LinkItem property specifies the specific data item to be linked. The content and format of the LinkItem property depend on the requirements of the source application. As I mentioned earlier, row and column coordinates are usually meaningful to a worksheet source such as Excel, whereas a bookmark name will be meaningful to a word processor such as Word for Windows.

The LinkMode property specifies the way in which the destination will be updated. The default setting is 0-None, which specifies no DDE conversation. When you want the control to be an active DDE destination there are three possible settings: 1-Automatic, 2-Manual, and 3-Notify (see *When Are DDE Links Updated* earlier in this chapter).

The final DDE destination-related property is LinkTimeout. This property specifies how long a Visual Basic DDE destination control will wait for the source application to respond to a DDE message before generating an error. LinkTimeout specifies the wait time in tenths of seconds, with a default setting of 50 (5 seconds). Set LinkTimeout to -1 to obtain the longest possible wait, 65535 tenths or approximately 1 hour, 49 minutes.

Using a Visual Basic Control as a DDE Source

Three properties determine how a Visual Basic control will respond in a DDE conversation.

Remember that all DDE conversations are initiated by the destination application. When acting as a DDE source, therefore, a Visual Basic application simply responds to the DDE messages sent by the destination. To initiate a DDE link the destination must specify three things: the application, topic, and item. Here's how this information is determined by Visual Basic.

The application is the name of the Visual Basic source application. If the application is running in the Visual Basic development environment, it is the project name without the .MAK extension. If the application is running as a stand-alone executable, it is the Visual Basic application name without the .EXE extension.

HOT TIP

Use the EXEName Property to Obtain the Application Name

In code, you can obtain the application name for DDE from the EXEName property of the App object, unless the user has renamed the EXE file. The EXEName property always returns the actual, or current, EXE file name of the application on disk, whereas DDE always requires the original EXE file name that was specified in the Make EXE dialog.

The topic is the LinkTopic property of the Visual Basic form that contains the data to be linked. The default setting for this property is in the format Form1, Form2, etc. If a form will serve as a DDE topic, you should change its LinkTopic property to an appropriate name.

The item is the Name property of the control (Text Box, Picture Box, or Label) that contains the data to be linked.

In order for a conversation to take place, the LinkMode property must be reset. If LinkMode is set to 0-None (the default), no DDE interaction is allowed. That is, no destination application can initiate a conversation with the source form as the topic. If LinkMode is set to 1-Source, then any Label, Picture Box, or Text Box on the form can serve as the source in a DDE link with any destination application that establishes a DDE conversation with the form. If a DDE link exists, Visual Basic automatically notifies the destination application whenever the contents of a control are changed. If LinkMode is 1-Source at design time, you can change it to 0-None and back at run time. If LinkMode is 0-None at design time, you cannot change it to 1-Source at run time.

Here's an example. A Visual Basic program named MYAPP.MAK (or MYAPP.EXE) has a form with its LinkTopic property set to DataEntry and its LinkMode property set to 1-Source; the form contains a Text Box with its Name property set to LastName. The destination application would establish a DDE link with that Text Box by specifying MYAPP as the application, DataEntry as the topic, and LastName as the item.

Case Does Not Matter

DDE link specifiers are not case sensitive. Thus, MYAPP, myapp, and MyApp all refer to the same application.

DDE-Related Events

Certain events associated with DDE links are recognized by Visual Basic objects.

Visual Basic's event-driven paradigm extends to DDE. Several events are associated with DDE activities, and you can put code in the event procedures to enable your program to respond appropriately. The events and their use differs slightly depending on whether the Visual Basic object is the source or the destination in a DDE conversation.

A **LinkOpen** event will occur when a destination control successfully initiates a DDE conversation. The event procedure format is:

```
Sub CtlName_LinkOpen ([Index as Integer], Cancel as Integer)
...
End Sub
```

The optional **Index** argument identifies the control if it is part of a control array. The **Cancel** argument is not used for destination **LinkOpen** events. Use the destination **LinkOpen** event procedure to perform any tasks required when a DDE link is established, such as opening files. It can also be used for debugging purposes.

A **LinkOpen** event will also occur when a destination application initiates a DDE conversation with a Visual Basic source form. In this case, the **LinkOpen** event procedure has the following structure:

```
Sub FormName_LinkOpen (Cancel as Integer)
...
End Sub
```

If the **Cancel** argument is left at its default value of False (0), the link is established. If code in the event procedure sets **Cancel** to any non-zero value, Visual Basic will not permit the link to be established. The source **LinkOpen** event procedure can be used to keep track of the number of DDE links for which the Visual Basic program is acting as source, and refusing to establish additional links if the total becomes too great for satisfactory performance.

A **LinkClose** event will occur for either a destination control or a source form if the DDE conversation is terminated. The event procedure makes no distinction as to why the conversation was terminated.

A **LinkError** event can occur for either a destination control or a source form, but only under certain special error conditions. If an error occurs while DDE-related code is executing, Visual Basic's standard error handling procedures are invoked, and you can trap and handle the error in the usual fashion. The **LinkError** event is triggered only if an error occurs while no Basic code is executing. For example, data may be transferred in a format that the destination cannot handle, or the operating environment may run out of memory (see *Dealing With DDE Errors* later in this chapter for more information).

A **LinkNotify** event occurs only for destination controls whose LinkMode property is set to 3-Notify. This event is triggered when the source data changes. Code in the **LinkNotify** event procedure can use the **LinkRequest** method to update the destination with the changed data. Alternatively, if the updated data is not required immediately, the **LinkNotify** event procedure can set a flag indicating that the destination needs to be updated at a later time.

A **LinkExecute** event occurs for a source form when the destination in the DDE conversation sends a command string to be executed. The format of a **LinkExecute** event procedure is:

```
Sub Form_Execute (Cmd As String, Cancel As Integer)
...
End Sub
```

The **Cmd** argument contains the command string sent by the DDE destination. There are no predefined rules for the content and format of **Cmd**; the way that your application responds to **Cmd** is totally up to you, the programmer.

The **Cancel** argument determines the response sent to the application that sent the command string. If **Cancel** is set to 0, the Visual Basic program sends a positive acknowledgment, which is usually taken to mean that the command string was received and acted upon. If **Cancel** is set to any non-zero value, a negative acknowledgment is sent. A negative acknowledgment is automatically sent if there is no **LinkExecute** event procedure.

Pasting DDE Links into a Visual Basic Program

If you have worked with Windows applications, you have probably noticed that most of them have a Paste Link command, usually found on the Edit menu. This command allows you to quickly establish a DDE link with any other Windows application that supports active links. The procedure for establishing links is shown here:

1. In the source application, select the data that you want linked.
2. Select Copy (usually found on the Edit menu). This places the data and required link information on the Windows Clipboard.
3. Switch to the destination application.
4. Move the focus, pointer, or insertion point to the location where you want the link placed.
5. Select Paste Link. An automatic link is established between the two applications.

Including a Paste Link command in your Visual Basic programs can greatly increase their usefulness by permitting the user to "cut and paste" DDE links with very little effort.

The Clipboard and DDE

The Clipboard is an essential ingredient of a Paste Link implementation. It serves for temporary storage of the link information.

When an application uses the Paste Link command to create a DDE link, the Windows Clipboard is the intermediate storage location where the link information is kept between the Copy action and the Paste action. You need to know a little about how the Clipboard works in order to use it effectively. In Visual Basic, of course, you access the Windows Clipboard via the Clipboard object.

The Clipboard is not just a dumb container that can hold and spit back whatever data is put there. The Clipboard has the ability to hold data in several different formats—in fact, it can hold more than one item if they are in different formats. If you ask nicely, the Clipboard will even tell you whether it currently contains a data item of a specified format. Here are the data formats that the Clipboard can work with:

- DDE link information
- Text
- Bitmap (.BMP files)
- Metafile (.WMF files)
- Device-independent bitmap (.DIB files)
- Color palette

What is meant by "DDE link information?" It is the information required to establish a DDE link to the data on the Clipboard. When you use the Copy command, most Windows applications (those that support active DDE links) place not only the selected data (text, a bitmap, etc.) on the Clipboard, but also place the application, topic, and item information required to establish a DDE link to the original data. If another application executes the Paste (*not* Paste Link) command, only the data will be copied from the Clipboard. In contrast, if an application executes the Paste Link command, the data and DDE link information will be retrieved from the Clipboard and an active DDE link will be established.

To determine if a particular data format is available on the Clipboard, use the **GetFormat** method with the Clipboard object. The syntax is shown here:

```
result = Clipboard.Getformat(type)
```

The **type** argument specifies the data format you are interested in. You can specify **type** with the Windows global constants shown in Table 5.1. The **GetFormat** method returns True if the specified type is present on the Clipboard, False if not.

For example, the statement

```
Clipboard.GetFormat(CF_TEXT)
```

returns True only if there is text format data on the Clipboard. As we will see next, we must use the **GetFormat** method to verify that there is DDE link information on the Clipboard for the Paste Link command to work properly.

Obtaining DDE Link Information from the Clipboard

The Clipboard supplies the DDE link information in a specific format.

You use the **GetText** method to retrieve the DDE link information from the Clipboard. Normally, the **GetText** method returns any text data that is on the Clipboard. If you pass the argument **CF_LINK (value &HBF00)**

Table 5.1   Windows Global Constants Used with GetFormat

Constant	Value	Data Format
CF_LINK	&HBF00	DDE conversation information
CF_TEXT	1	Text
CF_BITMAP	2	Bitmap
CF_METAFILE	3	Metafile
CF_DIB	8	Device-independent bitmap
CF_PALETTE	9	Color palette

---

then **GetText** returns DDE link information, as well (or an empty string if DDE link information is not present on the Clipboard), assuming the constant **CF_LINK** is defined elsewhere in the program:

```
link = Clipboard.GetText(CF_LINK)
```

The DDE link information is returned in a specific format. The application followed by a vertical pipe (**CHR$(124)**), then the topic followed by an exclamation point and the item:

```
application|topic!item
```

Some DDE links do not include an item, in which case only the application and topic are returned (separated by a vertical pipe).

Establishing the Link

Once the you have obtained the DDE link information from the Clipboard, you can establish the link with only a few lines of code.

Now that you have the DDE link information, you can use Visual Basic's string manipulation functions to extract strings for the application, topic, and (if present) item. Then, follow the procedure here to establish the link:

1. Set the destination control's LinkMode property to 0-None.
2. Set the LinkTopic property to the application and topic retrieved from the Clipboard.
3. If necessary, set the LinkItem property using the item obtained from the Clipboard.
4. Set the destination control's LinkMode property to 1-Automatic

That's all there is to it!

Verifying the Validity of a Paste Link Operation

Before attempting to establish a DDE link your program should verify that the operation is valid.

For a Paste Link operation to succeed, two conditions must be satisfied. First, there must be DDE link information available on the Clipboard. Second, the data available on the Clipboard must be appropriate for the destination control. In other words, you can link text data, but not a graphic, to a Text Box control. Likewise, you can link a graphic, but not text, to a Picture Box control. A program should verify that both of these conditions are met before attempting a Paste Link. The program in the next scenario accomplishes this by setting Paste Link's Enabled property to False if the conditions are not met.

A Paste Link Demonstration

This program shows how to implement a Paste Link command.

The program PASTELNK.MAK shows how to implement a Paste Link command. This is a simple program, with one form containing only a Picture Box, a Text Box, and a Command Button. The Edit menu contains only a single command, Paste Link. The program's form is shown in Figure 5.1, with the Picture Box displaying a graph linked from an Excel spreadsheet.

To try the program, you can execute it either from within the Visual Basic environment or as a stand-alone. Then, start another Windows program, preferably one that works with both text and graphics (such as Excel). In the second program, select some text or a graphics object, then copy it to the Clipboard (usually with the Edit Copy command). Switch back to the Visual Basic program, move the focus to either the Picture Box or the Text Box (by clicking it), then select Edit Paste Link. Move back to the source program and modify the data, and when you return to the Visual Basic program you'll see the changes have appeared there too. The program's objects and properties are given in Listing 5.1, and its code in Listing 5.2. You can see that the code uses the verification procedures discussed above, then either enables or disables the Paste Link command accordingly.

Using PASTELNK.MAK

This demonstration, presented in Listings 5.1 and 5.2, is stored on disk as PASTELNK.MAK and PASTELNK.FRM.

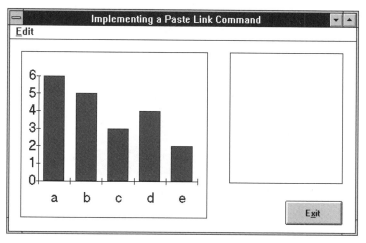

Figure 5.1 PASTELNK.MAK displaying a graph linked from an Excel spreadsheet.

Listing 5.1 Objects and Properties in PASTELNK.FRM

```
Begin Form Form1
    Caption          =    "Implementing a Paste Link Command"
    Begin CommandButton cmdExit
        Caption          =    "E&xit"
    End
    Begin TextBox Text1
        MultiLine        =    -1   'True
    End
    Begin PictureBox Picture1
    End
    Begin Menu mnuEdit
        Caption          =    "&Edit"
        Begin Menu mnuPasteLink
            Caption          =    "Paste &Link"
        End
    End
End
```

Listing 5.2 Code in PASTELNK.FRM

```
Option Explicit

' Constants for Clipboard formats.
Const CF_LINK = &HBF00
Const CF_DIB = 8, CF_BITMAP = 2, CF_TEXT = 1
Const CF_METAFILE = 3, CF_PALETTE = 9

' Constants for LinkMode property.
Const NONE = 0, AUTOMATIC = 1
```

```
Sub cmdExit_Click ()

End

End Sub

Sub mnuEdit_Click ()

Dim X As Integer

' Enable the Paste Link command only if the Clipboard
' contains data that is valid for linking to
' the active control.
mnuPasteLink.Enabled = False

' If the Clipboard does not contain valid DDE information,
' exit the sub.
If Clipboard.GetFormat(CF_LINK) = False Then Exit Sub

' If the active control is a Text Box and the Clipboard
' contains text, enable the Edit Paste command.
If Clipboard.GetFormat(CF_TEXT) Then
    If TypeOf SCREEN.ActiveControl Is TextBox Then
        mnuPasteLink.Enabled = True
        Exit Sub
    End If
End If

' See if the Clipboard contains a graphic.
X = Clipboard.GetFormat(CF_BITMAP)
X = X Or Clipboard.GetFormat(CF_METAFILE)
X = X Or Clipboard.GetFormat(CF_PALETTE)
X = X Or Clipboard.GetFormat(CF_DIB)

' If Clipboard contains a graphic and the active control
' is a Picture Box, enable the Edit Paste command.
If X Then
    If TypeOf SCREEN.ActiveControl Is PictureBox Then
        mnuPasteLink.Enabled = True
    End If
End If

End Sub

Sub mnuPasteLink_Click ()

Dim Link As String, X As Integer

' Get link information from the Clipboard
```

```
' and locate the "!".
Link = Clipboard.GetText(CF_LINK)
X = InStr(Link, "!")

' If Link contains "!" there is a link item.
If X <> 0 Then
    SCREEN.ActiveControl.LinkMode = NONE
    SCREEN.ActiveControl.LinkTopic = Left(Link, X - 1)
    SCREEN.ActiveControl.LinkItem = Mid(Link, X + 1)
    SCREEN.ActiveControl.LinkMode = AUTOMATIC

' If Link does not contain "!" there is no link item,
' only an application and topic.
ElseIf InStr(Link, "|") Then
    SCREEN.ActiveControl.LinkMode = NONE
    SCREEN.ActiveControl.LinkTopic = Link
    SCREEN.ActiveControl.LinkItem = ""
    SCREEN.ActiveControl.LinkMode = AUTOMATIC
End If

End Sub
```

Copying a DDE Link from a Visual Basic Program

Most Windows applications have a Copy command that you use to copy selected program data to the Clipboard. If the program supports active DDE links (and most do), the Copy command also places on the Clipboard, in addition to the selected data, the information that another application would need to establish a DDE link with the data. This information consists of the application name, the topic, and (in most cases) the item. Another application can then retrieve just the data (using the Paste command) or the DDE link information (using the Paste Link command). For a Visual Basic program to support active links, it must permit the user to copy DDE link information to the Windows Clipboard.

Assembling DDE Link Information

You must assemble the required link information before copying it to the Clipboard.

As you know, the link information consists of three parts. The application is the name of the Visual Basic program, the topic is the LinkTopic property of the form, and the item is the name of the control (Text Box or Picture Box) whose data you want to link.

If you're running a program from within the Visual Basic development environment, the application name is the project name (without the extension). If you're running a stand-alone Visual Basic program, the application name is the EXE filename (again, minus the extension). In either case, you can obtain the name from the EXEName property of the App object:

```
application = App.EXEName
```

This method will work for stand-alone programs only if the user has not changed the name of the EXE file. A DDE link always requires the program's original name (the name assigned to the program in the Make EXE dialog box), but the APP.EXEName property always returns the application's current EXE filename.

The LinkTopic property of the form can be set at design time or in code, but for clarity it should be something that describes the form it applies to.

The Name property is not available at run time. Therefore it is necessary, at design time, to store the control's Name in its Tag property. If the source control is part of a control array, the name stored in the Tag property must include its name followed by its array index in parentheses.

These three items must be combined in a single string with a specific format: the application name followed by a vertical pipe (**CHR$(124)**), then the LinkTopic followed by an exclamation point and the control name. An example is shown here:

```
LinkInfo = App.EXEName & "|" & LinkTopic & "!" & Screen.ActiveControl.Tag
```

Once the string containing the link information has been put together, you are ready to put it on the Clipboard.

Copying the DDE Link String and the Data to the Clipboard

The Copy command must put both the DDE link string and the selected data on the Clipboard.

To put the DDE link string on the Clipboard, you use the **SetText** method with the argument **CF_LINK**. Remember, **CF_LINK** is a Windows global constant with a value of &HBF00. For example, if the link string is stored in the variable **LinkInfo** you would write

```
Clipboard.SetText LinkInfo, CF_LINK
```

The **CF_LINK** argument tells the Clipboard to interpret **LinkInfo** as DDE link information rather than as regular text.

The second step is to copy the data to the Clipboard—that is, the contents of the source control. Remember, only two types of controls can act as DDE sources: Text Boxes and Picture Boxes. For a Text Box, you use the **SetText** method to copy its text to the Clipboard. The statement shown here assumes that the Text Box is the active control—something the program must verify before executing the **SetText** method:

```
Clipboard.SetText  SCREEN.ActiveControl.Text
```

If the source control is a Picture Box you use the **SetData** method to copy the Picture Box contents to the Clipboard. Again, your program must verify that the active control is indeed a Picture Box:

```
Clipboard.SetData  SCREEN.ActiveControl.Picture
```

Remember that your Copy command should support copying of data from all types of controls, not just Picture Boxes and Text Boxes. If the Copy command is executed when another type of control is active, your code can copy the control's data to the Clipboard—but not, of course, DDE information because only Text Boxes and Picture Boxes can act as DDE sources.

A Copy Link Demonstration

This section demonstrates how to implement an active link Copy command in your programs.

The program COPYLINK.MAK shows how a Visual Basic program can support creation of active DDE links via the Clipboard. The program's form, shown in Figure 5.2, contains a Picture Box that is loaded with a bitmap at design time. I used one of the bitmaps supplied with Visual Basic, but you can use anything you like. The figure also shows a Text Box and a Combo Box, both of which are loaded with some text at run time by code in the form's **Load** event procedure.

When you run the program, set the focus to the Picture Box, the Text Box, or the Combo Box by clicking with the mouse. Next, select Edit Copy from the menu. Then, switch to another application that has a Paste Link command; almost any Windows word processor will do. You can also use the demonstration program PASTELNK.MAK from the previous section, if you like. Select the Paste Link command, or whatever the application uses as the equivalent (for example, in Word for Windows you would

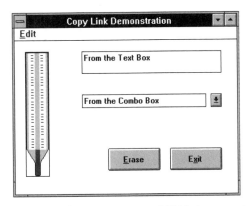

Figure 5.2   COPYLINK.MAK lets you create a DDE link to another application using either the Text Box or the Picture Box as the source control.

select Paste Special). You'll see that the data you copied appears in the destination application.

Now return to the COPYLINK program and modify the data in the Text Box and the Combo Box. Select the Erase Command Button to clear the Picture Box. Then, return to the destination application. You'll see that changes to the Text Box and Picture Box are automatically reflected in the destination, courtesy of the DDE link. Changes to the Combo Box, however, are not.

Using COPYLINK.MAK

This demonstration, presented in Listings 5.3 and 5.4, is stored on disk as COPYLINK.MAK and COPYLINK.FRM.

Listing 5.3   Objects and Properties in COPYLINK.FRM

```
Begin Form Form1
   Caption          =    "Copy Link Demonstration"
   LinkMode         =    1 'Source
   LinkTopic        =    "Form1"
   Begin CommandButton cmdErase
      Caption        =    "&Erase"
   End
   Begin CommandButton cmdExit
      Caption        =    "E&xit"
   End
   Begin ComboBox Combo1
   End
   Begin TextBox Text1
```

```
      Tag               =    "Text1"
   End
   Begin PictureBox Picture1
      AutoRedraw        =    -1    'True
      AutoSize          =    -1    'True
      Picture           =    (see text)
      Tag               =    "Picture1"
   End
   Begin Menu mnuEdit
      Caption           =    "&Edit"
      Begin Menu mnuCopy
         Caption        =    "&Copy"
      End
   End
End
```

Listing 5.4   Code in COPYLINK.FRM

```
Option Explicit

Const CF_LINK = &HBF00

Sub CmdErase_Click ()

' Clear the Picture Box.
Picture1.Picture = LoadPicture()

End Sub

Sub cmdExit_Click ()

End

End Sub

Sub Form_Load ()

' Put some text in the Text Box and Combo Box.
Text1.Text = "From the Text Box"
Combo1.Text = "From the Combo Box"

End Sub

Sub mnuCopy_Click ()

Dim LinkInfo As String

Clipboard.Clear
```

```
' If the active control is a Text Box copy its text and
' DDE information to the Clipboard.
If TypeOf Screen.ActiveControl Is TextBox Then
    LinkInfo = App.EXEName & "|" & LinkTopic
    LinkInfo = LinkInfo & "!" & Screen.ActiveControl.Tag
    Clipboard.SetText LinkInfo, CF_LINK
    Clipboard.SetText Screen.ActiveControl.Text

' If the active control is a Picture Box copy its picture and
' DDE information to the Clipboard.
ElseIf TypeOf Screen.ActiveControl Is PictureBox Then
    LinkInfo = App.EXEName & "|" & LinkTopic
    LinkInfo = LinkInfo & "!" & Screen.ActiveControl.Tag
    Clipboard.SetText LinkInfo, CF_LINK
    Clipboard.SetData Screen.ActiveControl.Picture

' If the active control is another type copy its data
' to the Clipboard.
Else
    Clipboard.SetText Screen.ActiveControl.Text
End If

End Sub
```

Creating a Visual Basic "Front End" for Data Entry into Another Program

Visual Basic makes it easy to create user friendly data entry forms. Unfortunately, not all programs are so cooperative! Spreadsheet programs in particular can present data entry problems for individuals who are not accustomed to their row and column format. With DDE, you can use Visual Basic to create a user friendly front end that automatically transfers data to the spreadsheet. You can also start the other application, if necessary, and send it commands.

Starting Another Windows Application

Before you can use DDE to transfer data to another application, the application must be running. You can start any Windows application from within your Visual Basic program.

You can start another Windows application from within a Visual Basic program using the **Shell** function. The syntax for this function is:

```
x = Shell(commandstring [, windowstyle])
```

The **commandstring** argument specifies the name of the program to execute, including any required arguments or command line switches. If the program name in **commandstring** doesn't include a .COM, .EXE, .BAT, or .PIF file extension, .EXE is assumed.

The **windowstyle** argument specifies the style of the application window. If this argument is omitted, the program is opened minimized with focus. Possible values for **windowstyle** are shown here:

1, 5, 9	Normal with focus
2	Minimized with focus (default)
3	Maximized with focus
4, 8	Normal without focus
6, 7	Minimized without focus

If the **Shell** function successfully starts the specified application, it returns the application's task identification. The task ID is a unique number that identifies the running application. If the **Shell** function can't start the named application, an error occurs.

When you use the **Shell** function, remember that it runs other applications asynchronously. That means that you cannot depend on a program started with **Shell** to have completed its start-up procedures before the code following the **Shell** function in your Visual Basic application is executed.

Sending Commands to Another Program

Your Visual Basic program can use DDE to boss around many other programs by sending commands.

Once a DDE link has been established, the destination can use the **LinkExecute** method to send a command to the source. This method is applied to the control that is maintaining the link, that is, the active destination control. However, that's just a syntax requirement. The control has nothing to do with the command sent. The syntax for the **LinkExecute** method is shown here:

```
DDEControl.LinkExecute   Command
```

DDEControl is the name of a control that is the destination in an active DDE link. The **Command** argument is a string that contains the command(s) to be sent to the DDE source application.

Different applications require different command strings. For example, Excel accepts any of its macro commands enclosed in brackets. For other applications, consult the documentation.

Sending Data to Another Program

You can use the LinkPoke method to reverse the normal DDE flow, transferring data from a destination to a source.

Once you have established a DDE link, the **LinkPoke** method can be used to "poke" data from the destination to the source. The steps to follow are shown here:

1. Put the data to be poked in a Text Box or Picture Box control.
2. Set the control's LinkMode property to 0-None.
3. Set the control's LinkTopic and LinkItem properties to identify the location where you want to poke the data.
4. Set the LinkMode property to 2-Manual
5. Execute the **LinkPoke** method.

For example, the code here will poke the label "I've been poked!" to cell A1 in the Excel spreadsheet MYDATA.XLS:

```
Text1.Text = "I've been poked!"
Text1.LinkMode = 0
Text1.LinkTopic = "EXCEL|MYDATA"
Text1.LinkItem = "R1C1"
Text1.LinkMode = 2
Text1.LinkPoke
```

A Front End Demonstration

The program presented here shows how a Visual Basic program can serve as a data entry front end to Excel.

I think you may be surprised at how easy it is to create a data entry front end with Visual Basic. The program presented here, FRONTEND.MAK, is designed for use with Excel, but the same principles can be applied to other applications as well. FRONTEND's data entry form is shown in Figure 5.3; it completes the following tasks:

*   Starts Excel.
*   Provides three Text Box controls for data entry.

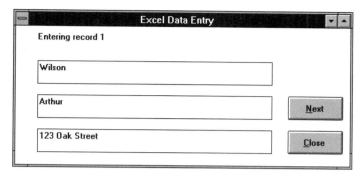

Figure 5.3 A data entry form that "pokes" data to an Excel spreadsheet.

- Pokes data in the Text Boxes to cells A1, B1, and C1 of the spreadsheet when the user selects Next. Subsequent entries are poked to rows 2, 3, and so on.

- Updates a label on the form to inform the user of the current record number.

- Prompts for a filename entry when the user selects Close. Commands are sent to Excel to save the file, then to terminate.

As written, FRONTEND lacks many of the niceties that should be included in any program for distribution. For example, if the user enters the name of an existing Excel file, an error will occur. Excel will not overwrite an existing file without confirmation, causing the Visual Basic program to time-out while waiting for an acknowledgment to the Save File As command it sent to Excel.

Using FRONTEND.MAK

This demonstration, presented in Listings 5.5 and 5.6, is stored on disk as FRONTEND.MAK andFRONTEND.FRM.

Listing 5.5 Objects and Properties in FRONTEND.FRM

```
Begin Form Form1
   Caption          =    "Excel Data Entry"
   Begin CommandButton cmdClose
      Caption        =    "&Close"
   End
   Begin CommandButton cmdNext
      Caption        =    "&Next"
   End
```

```
   Begin TextBox Text1
      Index            =    2
      Text             =    " "
   End
   Begin TextBox Text1
      Index            =    1
      Text             =    " "
   End
   Begin TextBox Text1
      Index            =    0
      Text             =    " "
   End
   Begin Label Label1
   End
End
```

Listing 5.6   Code in FRONTEND.FRM

```
Option Explicit

Sub cmdClose_Click ()

Dim Cmd As String, Filename As String
Dim Prompt As String

' Get the name for the Excel file.
Prompt = "Name for Excel file (no extension)"

Filename = InputBox(Prompt, "Filename", "")
Filename = Filename & ".XLS"

' Save the spreadsheet. CHR$(34) is the double quote character,
Cmd = "[SAVE.AS(" & Chr$(34) & Filename & Chr$(34) & ")]"
Text1(2).LinkExecute  Cmd

' Close Excel.
Text1(2).LinkExecute  "[Quit()]"

End

End Sub

Sub cmdNext_Click ()

Const NONE = 0, MANUAL = 2

Dim X As Integer, Item As String
Static Row As Integer
```

```
' Poke the data to the Excel spreadsheet. Loop once
' for each Text Box in the control array. We know that
' Excel always starts with the default spreadsheet name
' SHEET1.
Row = Row + 1

For X = 0 To 2
    Text1(X).LinkMode = NONE
    Text1(X).LinkTopic = "EXCEL|SHEET1"
    Item = "R" & Right$(Str$(Row), Len(Str$(Row)) - 1)
    Item = Item & "C" & Right$(Str$(X + 1), Len(Str$(X + 1)) - 1)
    Text1(X).LinkItem = Item
    Text1(X).LinkMode = MANUAL
    Text1(X).LinkPoke
Next X

' Clear the Text Boxes for the next entry.

For X = 0 To 2
    Text1(X).Text = ""
Next X

' Set the focus to the first Text Box.
Text1(0).SetFocus

' Update label.
Label1.Caption = "Entering record" & Str$(Row + 1)

End Sub

Sub Form_Load ()

Dim X As Integer

On Local Error GoTo Errorhandler

' Start Excel minimized without focus.
X = Shell("EXCEL", 6)

' Display record number.
Label1.Caption = "Entering record 1"

Exit Sub

Errorhandler:

MsgBox "Unable to start Excel"
Resume Next

End Sub
```

OLE Automation Replaces DDE

With the introduction of OLE 2.0, Microsoft will merge the functions of Dynamic Data Exchange into the Object Linking and Embedding System. As applications developers begin to support OLE 2.0, many may abandon, or at least curtail support for DDE. Microsoft has declared that OLE 2.0 represents the future of Windows computing.

For now, all Windows applications that support inter-application communications support DDE, and it is likely that such support will continue for the forseeable future. Even the brand new release of Lotus 123 4.0 for Windows adheres to the old tried-and-true standards. But as you develop new Visual Basic applications, in particular programs that talk to other programs, you'll want to keep in mind the coming changes, which we'll discuss in more detail in Chapter 13.

Object Linking and Embedding

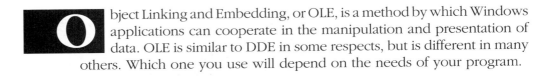

bject Linking and Embedding, or OLE, is a method by which Windows applications can cooperate in the manipulation and presentation of data. OLE is similar to DDE in some respects, but is different in many others. Which one you use will depend on the needs of your program.

OLE: The Basics

Imagine that you are writing a report that includes several charts. Any Windows word processor worth its salt can include charts that were created with other applications. But what if you needed to modify one of the charts? Wouldn't it be great if you could simply point at the chart in the document, double-click, and switch automatically to the application that created the chart, with the chart you want to modify already loaded? Wouldn't it be even better if, after making the necessary changes, you returned automatically to your word processing document with the modified chart already in place? Well, that's what OLE can do for you.

OLE is not really that complicated, but some explanations that you may read make it seem that way! In this chapter, I will present a clear and concise introduction to the fundamental concepts and terms of OLE. Once you have these concepts under your belt, you will be able to productively use OLE in your Visual Basic applications. Later, in Chapter 13, I'll explain the changes in terminology and the new capabilities of OLE 2 and the new OLE control for VB 3.0.

Clients and Servers

Like DDE, OLE interactions travel along a two- way street. The difference here is the OLE interactions involve a client and a server.

An OLE *server* is the application where the data object originates, such as a spreadsheet, word processor, or graphics application. An OLE *client* is the application that displays the data object. A Visual Basic program can be an OLE client, but not a server.

What Is an Object?

An OLE object is not the same thing as a Visual Basic object!

When dealing with OLE, the term *object* is nothing more than a fancy way of saying data. To be more specific, an OLE object is any chunk of data that can be displayed by an OLE client. An object can be a entire chart, a portion of a document, or just a single spreadsheet cell.

Every OLE object has a *class*. The class specifies the name of the application that created the data object—that is, the server. The class also specifies the object's data type. For example, a chart created within Excel has the class name "ExcelChart" and the data type, or display name "Microsoft Excel Chart."

Determining Class and Display Names

Visual Basic provides a sample program REGVIEW.MAK that shows how to read the class names of all the OLE server applications on your disk. The program is located in the \VB\SAMPLES\OLE directory.

Linking versus Embedding—What's the Difference?

Linking and embedding are two different ways of sharing data. Linking data means displaying the data in the client application, whereas embedding data means actually placing the data in the client application.

OLE might better stand for Object Linking *or* Embedding because linking and embedding are two different methods of sharing data. In other words, you do not link and embed an object—you either link it or embed it. The difference has to do with where the data is stored, and whether other applications have access to it.

Both linked and embedded objects are displayed in the client application. When an object is linked, the client application contains a place holder for the linked object. The actual data is stored elsewhere—in the original spreadsheet or word processor file, for example. When an object is embedded, the client application contains the actual data; the object's data is stored by the OLE client.

When the user selects an OLE object, the server application is automatically started, allowing the user to modify the object. When the user exits the server application, they are returned automatically to the client application which now displays the modified object. The difference between linking and embedding lies in the accessibility of the data object. A linked data object can be accessed and modified by multiple client applications. For example, an Excel spreadsheet could be linked to a Visual Basic client application and a Word for Windows client at the same time. Either of the clients (Visual Basic or Word for Windows) could access and modify the spreadsheet, and the changes would appear in the linked object in the other client the next time it was used.

In contrast, an embedded object is accessible only to the one client application — the one it's embedded in. No other applications can access or modify the object's data.

It's important to understand that an embedded object, like a linked object, originates in a data file belonging to the server application. To either link or embed, say, a range of cells in a spreadsheet, you start by selecting the cells. What happens next differs:

- If you link the object, the client becomes linked to the cells in the original server data file. If that original file is modified, the client reflects the changes.

- If you embed the object, a copy of the cells is passed to the client, which stores it separately from the original server data file. If that original data file is modified the client does not reflect the changes. The client can, however, use the server application to modify its own copy of the object.

The choice between linking and embedding obviously depends on your situation. Linking is similar to DDE in that data from a single source (the OLE server) can be automatically updated in one or more client applications that depend on it. OLE's advantage over DDE is that an OLE client has quick access to the server application when there is a need to modify the linked data. If, however, you simply need automatic data updating without access to the server, you probably should use DDE in preference to OLE because the latter technique is more demanding of system resources.

Embedding is not useful for automatic data updating, because only a single application has access to the data. Rather, embedding is used to provide a single application (the client) access to the data manipulation and presentation abilities of a variety of server applications.

Generally speaking, DDE is preferable when your program code needs access to the data, whereas OLE is preferable if you need only to display the data and edit it using the original application.

OLE in a Visual Basic Program

You implement OLE in a Visual Basic program using the OLE Client control.

To implement an OLE client in a Visual Basic program you use the OLE Client control. This is one of the two custom controls provided with both the Standard and Professional editions of Visual Basic. If it is not already part of your default project (see the Visual Basic Project window to determine if it is), you must use the Add File command to add OLECLIEN.VBX to your project. Once you have included this control in your project, an OLE Client button will display on the toolbar.

To create an OLE client, therefore, the first step is to add an OLE Client control to a form. This control shares many properties with other controls, such as those controlling its size, color, border, and visibility. It also has a number of specialized properties that relate specifically to OLE. We will deal with these properties in subsequent scenarios.

Using the Registration Database

You use the registration database to obtain information about the OLE servers that are available on a system.

In order for a Visual Basic program to function as an OLE client, it needs information about the OLE server applications that are available on the current system. Just because you have Excel on your system doesn't mean that everyone who will use your Visual Basic program does also! A potential OLE client must have accurate information about what servers are available on the system. A client cannot assume that a particular server application will be available. Information about OLE servers is maintained in the *registration database*, in a disk file named REG.DAT (located in the \WINDOWS directory).

The information in the registration database is maintained automatically. Whenever an OLE server application is installed on the system it stores certain data in the REG.DAT file. This data includes the server command line, the OLE protocols it supports, the class names of the objects it supports, and so on. This information is required by any program trying to establish itself as an OLE client to one of the server applications. By obtaining this information from the registration database, a client can insure that it will attempt to establish an OLE relationship only with servers that are available. A Visual Basic program accesses the registration database by means of the *server properties* of the OLE Client control.

Beware of Deleted Servers!

One possible source of OLE errors is the notorious "deleted server" problem. If a user installed a server application on their disk, then later deleted it because it wasn't needed, the server's data will still be present in the system's registration database. To a client obtaining information from the database, it will appear as if the server is present. Errors will occur if the client tries to access the deleted server.

Server Properties: Part 1

You use the server properties of an OLE Client control to obtain information and to control the OLE interaction.

An OLE Client control has quite a few server properties—in fact, I count 10! With so many properties involved in setting up an OLE Client control, it's no wonder that some people become confused and frustrated. I'll try my best to sort things out for you!

All of the server property names begin with "Server." They fall into two groups. One group is used by your program to obtain information from the registration database; these properties are all read-only. The other group of properties is used to control the way the OLE Client control operates; obviously, these properties can be modified at run time.

Perhaps the most fundamental of the "information" properties is ServerClasses. This is an indexed property that provides a list of all the OLE server classes available on the system. The ServerClasses property is used in conjunction with the ServerClassCount property, which specifies the number of classes in the ServerClasses list. You will most frequently use these properties to load a List Box control with the names of the available classes, from which the user selects. You'll see how to do this soon.

Another fundamental OLE Client control property is ServerClassesDisplay, which provides an indexed list of the class display names obtained from the registration database. Each server class has its own class display name, so the number of class display names is the same as the number of server classes—that is, the value of the ServerClassCount property. In addition, a given class name and its associated class display name always have the same index. For example, the class display name in ServerClassesDisplay(4) belongs to the server class in ServerClasses(4).

A program will usually display the available class display names in a List Box, along with the server classes in their own List Box (as explained in the previous paragraph). This permits the user to select an OLE server by class display name or by server class. The following code fragment shows how to load the List Boxes. (**Ole1** is an OLE Client control, and **ClassList** and **ClassDisplayList** are List Boxes.)

```
For X = 0 to Ole1.ServerClassCount - 1
        ClassList.AddItem  Ole1.ServerClasses(X)
        ClassDisplayList.AddItem  Ole1.ServerClassesDisplay(X)
Next X
```

In most cases, the first step in establishing an OLE relationship is to have the user select the proper OLE server class or class display name.

Once the user has selected a class, the next step involves another OLE Client property, ServerClass. The selected class must be assigned to the ServerClass property to inform the control of the type of server it will be dealing with. If the user has selected a class in the ClassList List Box control, then you can set the ServerClass property as follows:

```
Ole1.ServerClass = Ole1.ServerClasses(ClassList.ListIndex)
```

It's important to set the ServerClass property because it controls various aspects of how the OLE Client control operates, including the information returned by some of the other "informational" properties. We'll cover these other properties next.

The Protocol-Related Server Properties

Some of the OLE Client control's properties have to do with protocols, which control the interactions allowed between the client and the server.

The ServerProtocol property provides an indexed list of the OLE protocols supported by the selected server (the one that you assigned to the ServerClass property). The number of protocols in the list is specified by the ServerProtocolCount property. As you probably guessed, this information also comes from the registration database.

Why would you need to know the OLE protocols supported by a particular OLE server? The reason is that the OLE Client control has a Protocol property whose setting determines what can and cannot be done with the OLE object. You must know what protocols are available in order to select one to assign to the Protocol property.

In actuality, however, you will rarely need to access the ServerProtocol property. At the present time, almost all OLE servers support only a single protocol called StdFileEditing, which creates an OLE object that can be edited by the user and that can also send execution strings to the server application (you'll learn about execution strings later). And, since the default value of the OLE Client control's Protocol property is "StdFileEditing," there's rarely a need to change it.

As applications become more OLE-aware, support for other OLE protocols will become more common. Two other protocols you may see are:

- **StdExecute**, which creates an OLE object that can pass execution strings to the server application but cannot be edited.

• **Static**, which creates an OLE object that can be edited until the server application is closed. Once the server application has been closed, the OLE object cannot be re-edited, even if the server is opened again.

The Verb-Related Server Properties

These properties control the action that is taken when an OLE object is activated.

You learned in English class that verbs are action words—and that's the case in OLE too. The Verb property of an OLE Client control specifies the action to be taken by the server application when the OLE object is activated. The most common Verb property setting is Edit, which means that when the user selects the OLE object, the server application will be opened to edit the object. This is appropriate, of course, as most OLE objects consist of data such as a spreadsheet, chart, or document for which editing is the desired action. Some server applications also support the Play verb, which would allow an embedded object that represents recorded sounds to be played.

Available verbs can be obtained using the ServerVerbs and ServerVerbsCount properties, in the same manner as described for other indexed property lists. Note that the OLE Client control's Verb property takes an integer value specifying the position of the desired verb in the ServerVerbs list (remember that this is a zero-based list). Thus, if the verb Play is the second item in the ServerVerbs list (at index position 1), you would assign Play as the OLE Client control's verb by setting its Verb property to a value of 1. The default value of the Verb property is 0, corresponding to the first verb in the ServerVerbs list, which is almost always Edit.

The Action Property

By setting the Action property you determine the action, or operation, to be performed on the OLE object.

The Action property is, if you'll pardon the pun, where the action is. By setting the Action property to a particular value, the program in effect tells the OLE Client control to do something. This property can only be set in code at run time. Symbolic constants for Action property settings are defined the CONSTANT.TXT file. Table 6.1 lists these constants, gives their numerical values, and provides a brief description of the associated action. Following the table I present detailed explanations of each action.

Table 6.1 Available Settings for an OLE Client's Action Property

Constant	Value	Action
OLE_CREATE_NEW	0	Create new empty object
OLE_CREATE_FROM_FILE	1	Create object from existing file
OLE_COPY	4	Copy object to Clipboard
OLE_PASTE	5	Copy object from Clipboard
OLE_UPDATE	6	Retrieve data from server
OLE_ACTIVATE	7	Open object for exiting or other action
OLE_EXECUTE	8	Send command to server application
OLE_CLOSE	9	Closes an object
OLE_DELETE	10	Delete object
OLE_SAVE_TO_FILE	11	Save object data to file
OLE_READ_FROM_FILE	12	Load object data from file
OLE_CONVERT_TO_TYPE	13	Convert object to different type

OLE_CREATE_NEW creates a new instance of an embedded OLE object. Before using this action, you must set the Class property to specify the type of object to be created, the Protocol property to the desired protocol ("StdFileEditing" in most cases), and the ServerType property to 1 (Embedded). The OLE server application associated with the Class property must either be active or on the system's path. For example, the following code would create a new Word for Windows document as an OLE object embedded in the OLE Client control OLEClient1:

```
OLEClient1.Protocol = "StdFileEditing"
OLEClient1.ServerType = 1
OLEClient1.Class = "WordDocument"
OLEClient1.Action = OLE_CREATE_NEW
```

When the last line of this code fragment executes, here's what happens:

1. The Word for Windows server application is started, if it's not already running.

2. A new, blank document is opened and displayed for editing. The user can edit the document, and then save it to disk as a standard Word document file.

3. When the user closes the document or exits the application, Word responds with the prompt "Do you want to update object in OLEClient1?" Selecting Yes embeds the object (i.e., the Word document) in the OLE Client control.

4. Execution then returns to the Visual Basic program, where the embedded document is now displayed in the OLE Client control. As you'll learn in a later section, it is the Visual Basic program's responsibility to save the object.

OLE_CREATE_FROM_FILE creates a linked OLE object from the contents of a file. Before using this action, you must set the Class property to specify the type of object to be created, the Protocol property to the desired protocol ("StdFileEditing" in most cases), and the ServerType property to 0 (Linked). You must also set the SourceDoc property to specify the file from which the OLE object is to be created. If necessary, you can also set the SourceItem property (for example, to specify a row/ column range in an Excel worksheet). The server application associated with the class name must either be active or on the system's path. For example, the following code would create a linked OLE object consisting of cells A1..H10 (the first 10 rows and 8 columns) of the Excel worksheet SALES92.XLS:

```
OLEClient1.Class = "ExcelWorksheet"
OLEClient1.Protocol = "StdFileEditing"
OLEClient1.ServerType = 0
OLEClient1.SourceDoc = "C:\workshts\sales92.xls"
OLEClient1.SourceItem = "R1C1:R10C8"
OLEClient1.Action = OLE_CREATE_FROM_FILE
```

OLE_COPY places a copy of an OLE object on the Clipboard. You can copy both linked and embedded OLE objects to the Clipboard. In either case, all of the object's data and/or link information is placed on the Clipboard. You can use this action to implement an Edit Copy command.

OLE_PASTE copies data from the Clipboard to an OLE Client control. Before using this action you must set the OLE Client control's Protocol and ServerType properties, and then check the value of the PasteOK property. This property returns True only if the Clipboard contains an OLE object that can be pasted into the OLE Client control (based on the settings of its ServerType and Protocol properties). Set the Protocol property to "StdFileEditing" to paste a linked or embedded OLE object; set Protocol to "Static" to paste a static OLE object. You can use this action to support an Edit Paste command.

OLE_UPDATE retrieves the current data from the server application and displays it in the OLE Client control. This action applies to both linked (**ServerType = 0**) and embedded (**ServerType = 1**) OLE objects.

OLE_ACTIVATE opens an OLE object for an operation, such as editing. Before using this action you must set the OLE Client control's Verb property, which specifies the operation to occur when an object is activated (in most cases it is Edit, specified by setting the Verb property to 0). You should also set the ServerShow property to True if you want the server application displayed (usually the case), to False if you don't. If you set the ServerShow property to True, then the Focus property should be set to True (the default) if you want the server application to receive the focus, False otherwise.

In most programs, the **OLE_ACTIVATE** action is performed in response to double-clicking the OLE Client control, as shown in this code fragment:

```
Sub OleClient1_DblClick ()

OleClient1.Verb = 0
OleClient1.ShowServer = True
OleClient1.Focus = True
OleClient1.Action = OLE_ACTIVATE

End Sub
```

OLE_EXECUTE sends a command string to the server application for execution. You must first set the OLE Client control's Protocol property to StdExecute, and assign the string that you want executed to the Execute property. The command strings that are understood differ between the various server applications. The **OLE_EXECUTE** action is similar to the DDE **LinkExecute** method, except that server applications typically support different command strings for OLE objects than they do for DDE conversations.

OLE_CLOSE closes an OLE object and terminates the connection with the server application. This action is equivalent to the user selecting Close from the object's Control-menu box.

OLE_DELETE deletes the specified OLE object and frees the memory that it used. This action is required only when the programmer needs to explicitly delete an OLE object. Visual Basic automatically deletes objects when a form is closed or when the OLE Client control is updated to a new object.

OLE_SAVE_TO_FILE saves a client OLE object to a data file (see *Saving OLE Objects* later in this chapter for details).

OLE_READ_FROM_FILE loads a client OLE object from a data file (see *Loading OLE Objects from Disk* later in this chapter for details).

OLE_CONVERT_TO_TYPE converts the current OLE object to a different type of object. You must first assign the new type to the ServerType property. The only type conversion that OLE currently supports is from a linked or embedded OLE object to a static OLE object. To do this, first set **ServerType = 2** and **Protocol = "Static"**, then set **Action = 13**. The object will be converted to a static object (assuming that the server application supports the "Static" protocol).

Server Properties That You Can Ignore

There are a number of other properties that you probably don't need to worry about.

OLE is admittedly a very complex subject. It includes a number of advanced capabilities that are not frequently used. These advanced capabilities go beyond the most important—and, in my opinion, most useful—ability of OLE, which is to view a data object in the client application and have instant access to the server application for editing. Therefore, I will not be covering them in this chapter.

The OLE Client control has several properties that are used to access these advanced features. If you run across them you may wonder whether you need to be concerned about them. For basic OLE programming the answer is no. You can (and, in fact, should) leave them at their default values. These properties are Format, ServerGetFormats, ServerGetFormatsCount, ServerAcceptFormats, ServerAcceptFormatsCount, Data, and DataText.

How Are OLE Objects Displayed in an OLE Client Control?

What you see is not always what you get! You might be surprised at the way some OLE objects are displayed!

One of the main points of OLE is to display the server's data in the client application—right? Yes indeed, but the manner in which a linked data object is displayed in the client program is determined by the server application. Some objects are displayed as you would expect—a graph object is displayed as a graph, for example. This is not always the case, however. For example, if you embed or link a Word for Windows document, the OLE Client control displays the Word icon instead of the document text. You can still use the **OLE_ACTIVATE** action to start Word and edit the actual text, of course, but the client application won't display it.

Saving OLE Objects

It is the responsibility of the Visual Basic program to save OLE objects.

OLE objects do not automatically save themselves. When a form containing an OLE object is closed, the data associated with that object goes bye-bye. If you want an OLE object to be available the next time the program is run, you must explicitly save its data. Each OLE object is saved in its own Basic binary file. To do so, open a binary file and assign its file number to the OLE Client control's FileNumber property. Then, set the OLE Client control's Action property to **OLE_SAVE_TO_FILE** (value = 11). That's all there is to it! These steps are illustrated by this code fragment (assume the variable **FileName** holds the name for the file):

```
FileNum = FreeFile
Open FileName For Binary as #FileNum
OleClient1.FileNumber = FileNum
OleClient1.Action = OLE_SAVE_TO_FILE
Close #FileNum
```

The procedure for saving an OLE object is the same for linked and embedded OLE objects, but the nature of the data that is saved differs. For linked OLE objects, only the link information is saved to the file; the actual data in the object is maintained by the server application. For embedded OLE objects, the actual data is saved also.

Loading OLE Objects from Disk

A previously saved OLE object can be loaded into your Visual Basic program.

The procedure for loading an OLE object from disk is essentially the reverse of the procedure used to save it. Open the file in binary mode, assign the file number to the OLE Client control's FileNumber property, and set the Action property to **OLE_READ_FROM_FILE**.

Additional OLE Properties and Events

There are a few other miscellaneous properties and events you should know about.

As you learned in an earlier in this chapter, one method for updating an OLE object is to use the **OLE_UPDATE** action. This action may not be necessary for linked OLE objects, depending on the OLE Client control's UpdateOptions property setting. There are three possible settings for this property:

- 0 - Automatic (the default). The OLE Client control is updated whenever the linked data changes.

- 1 - Frozen. The OLE Client control is updated whenever the user saves the linked document from within the server application.

- 2 - Manual. The OLE Client control is updated only when the Action property is set to 6 - Update.

Remember that this property applies only to linked OLE objects (ServerType = 0 - Linked).

A Visual Basic program often needs to know when an OLE object has been updated by the server. You can accomplish this using the **Updated** event, which occurs each time the server application updates an OLE object. The syntax for this event is:

```
Sub OLEClient_Updated (Code As Integer)
```

The **Code** argument indicates how the OLE object was updated. Its possible values are listed here (the constant names in parentheses are located in the CONSTANT.TXT file):

- 0 (OLE_CHANGED)   Indicates that the object has been modified
- 1 (OLE_SAVED)   Indicates that the object has been saved by the server
- 2 (OLE_CLOSED)   Indicates that the object has been closed by the server
- 5 (OLE_RELEASE)   Indicates that the server has completed an operation and released the object to the client

This event is most commonly used to signal the program that the data in an embedded OLE object has been changed since it was last saved. To do this, use the **Update** event procedure to set a global variable indicating that the object needs to be saved. The code in the procedure that saves the object can reset the variable.

An OLE Demonstration

The material presented so far in this chapter is only an introduction to the most important aspects of OLE. There's plenty more, believe me! In fact, entire books have been written on OLE. If you want to become an OLE guru then by all means, you should seek out and study some more advanced sources of information. Yet, the information that you have learned here is enough to enable you to start doing useful things with OLE in your Visual Basic programs.

I have found that to be the best way to learn—actually writing and testing code. It's always best, it seems, if you have a model to work from, and that's the beauty of demonstration programs. This section presents a "bare-bones" OLE demonstration that will get you started.

The Demonstration Program

The program presented here shows how to create a new embedded object, how to edit an existing object, and how to save and retrieve objects on disk.

I suggest that you work with this demo until you are confident that you understand what is going on—and why! Then, you might want to look at the program OLEDEMO.MAK that is provided with Visual Basic. OLEDEMO is considerably more complex and full-featured, and makes a good second step in the learning process.

OLE1 presents you with a form containing a blank OLE Client control. Selecting Insert from the Object menu lets you select an OLE server from those available on your system (only those servers that support at least one protocol will be listed). When you select a server it will start, enabling you to create the object to be embedded. Exit the server, or select Update from its File menu (or the equivalent command), and the client (the Visual Basic program) will be updated and display the object.

Back in the Visual Basic program, you can delete the object by selecting Delete from the Object menu. You can also double-click the object to activate the server. Select File Save to save the object to disk (under the predefined filename OLE_DATA.XYZ). The program has safeguards that provide a warning if you try to delete the object before it's saved (you can, however, exit the program without saving the object).

When the program starts it checks the disk for the file OLE_DATA.XYZ. If the file is found you are given the option of loading the OLE Client control from the disk file (which contains a previously saved OLE object).

OLE1.MAK consists of two forms and one Basic module. The main form, OLE1.FRM, contains (in addition to a menu) only a single OLE Client control. Figure 6.1 shows this form displaying an embedded Paintbrush object. The form's objects and properties are given in Listing 6.1, and its code is in Listing 6.2.

The second form, INSERT.FRM, shown in Figure 6.2, permits the user to select a server application. The form's objects, properties, and code are in Listings 6.3 and 6.4. The Basic module, OLE1.BAS, contains global constant and variable definitions. Its code is presented in Listing 6.5.

Using OLE1.MAK

This demonstration, presented in Listings 6.1, 6.2, 6.3, 6.4, and 6.5, is stored on disk as OLE1.MAK, OLE1.FRM, INSERT.FRM, and OLE1.BAS.

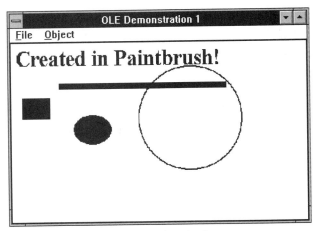

Figure 6.1 OLE1.FRM displaying a Paintbrush object.

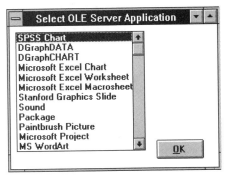

Figure 6.2 INSERT.FRM lets the user select a server application for the OLE object.

Listing 6.1 Objects and Properties in OLE1.FRM

```
Begin Form frmOle1
   Caption          =    "OLE Demonstration 1"
   Begin OleClient OleClient1
      BorderStyle   =   1  'Fixed Single
   End
   Begin Menu mnuFIle
      Caption       =    "&File"
      Begin Menu mnuFileSave
         Caption    =    "&Save"
      End
      Begin Menu mnuFileSep
         Caption    =    "-"
      End
      Begin Menu mnuFIleExit
```

```
        Caption          =    "E&xit"
    End
End
Begin Menu mnuObject
    Caption          =    "&Object"
    Begin Menu mnuInsert
        Caption          =    "&Insert"
    End
    Begin Menu mnuObjectDelete
        Caption          =    "&Delete"
    End
End
End
```

Listing 6.2   Code in OLE1.FRM

```
Option Explicit

Sub Form_Load ()

Dim FileNum As Integer, Reply As Integer

' If the OLE data file exists, give the user the option
' of loading the OLE object from it.
ObjectPresent = False
NotSaved = False

If Dir$(OLE_FILE_NAME) <> "" Then
    Reply = MsgBox("Load object from disk?", MB_YESNO + MB_ICONQUESTION,
        "Load Object")
    If Reply = IDYES Then
        Screen.MousePointer = 11
        FileNum = FreeFile
        Open OLE_FILE_NAME For Binary As #FileNum
        OleClient1.FileNumber = FileNum
        OleClient1.Action = OLE_READ_FROM_FILE
        ObjectPresent = True
        Close #FileNum
        Screen.MousePointer = 0
    End If
End If

End Sub

Sub Form_Resize ()

' Size and position the OLE Client control to
' fill the form.
```

```
OleClient1.Move 0, 0, frmOle1.ScaleWidth, frmOle1.ScaleHeight

End Sub

Sub mnuFile_Click ()

' Enable Save menu command only if an object exists.
If ObjectPresent Then
    mnuFileSave.Enabled = True
Else
    mnuFileSave.Enabled = False
End If

End Sub

Sub mnuFileExit_Click ()

End

End Sub

Sub mnuFileSave_Click ()

Call SaveObject

End Sub

Sub mnuInsert_Click ()

Dim Reply As Integer

' If an object is present, ask if it should be deleted. If
' user replies "no" exit sub.
If ObjectPresent Then
    Reply = MsgBox("Delete current object?", MB_YESNO And
      MB_ICONQUESTION, "Insert Object")

    If Reply = IDYES Then
        Call mnuObjectDelete_Click
    Else
        Exit Sub
    End If
End If

' Set the OLE Client control's ServerType property
' to specify an embedded object.
    OleClient1.ServerType = OLE_EMBEDDED

' Display the form to allow the user to select a
```

```
' server application.
frmInsert.Show 1

' Create the new object.
frmOle1.OleClient1.Action = OLE_CREATE_NEW

ObjectPresent = True
NotSaved = True
Screen.MousePointer = 0

End Sub

Sub mnuObject_Click ()

' Enable the Delete option only if an object is present.
If ObjectPresent Then
    mnuObjectDelete.Enabled = True
Else
    mnuObjectDelete.Enabled = False
End If

End Sub

Sub mnuObjectDelete_Click ()

Dim Reply As Integer

' If the object has not been saved, offer the option.
If NotSaved Then

    Reply = MsgBox("Save object before deleting?", MB_YESNOCANCEL +
      MB_ICONQUESTION, "Delete Object")

    If Reply = IDYES Then
        Call SaveObject
    ElseIf Reply = IDCANCEL Then
        Exit Sub
    End If

End If

' Now we can delete the object.
OleClient1.Action = OLE_DELETE
ObjectPresent = False
NotSaved = False

End Sub

Sub OleClient1_DblClick ()
```

```
' Activate the OLE object for editing.
OleClient1.Action = OLE_ACTIVATE
NotSaved = True

End Sub

Sub OleClient1_Updated (Code As Integer)

NotSaved = True

End Sub

Sub SaveObject ()

Dim FileNum As Integer

' Save the OLE object.
FileNum = FreeFile

Open OLE_FILE_NAME For Binary As #FileNum

OleClient1.FileNumber = FileNum
OleCliert1.Action = OLE_SAVE_TO_FILE
NotSaved = False

Close #FileNum

End Sub
```

Listing 6.3   Objects and Properties in INSERT.FRM

```
Begin Form frmInsert
    Caption          =    "Select OLE Server Application"
    Begin CommandButton cmdOK
        Caption        =    "&OK"
    End
    Begin ListBox lstServers
    End
End
```

Listing 6.4   Code in INSERT.FRM

```
Option Explicit

Dim DisplayClass As String

Sub cmdOK_Click ()

On Error Resume Next

Dim I As Integer
```

```
' Because the lstServers List Box may not include
' all class names (it omits those that don't have at least
' one protocol), we must find the class name that matches
' the selected server name.
DisplayClass = lstServers.List(lstServers.ListIndex)

For I = 0 To frmOle1.OleClient1.ServerClassCount - 1
    If frmOle1.OleClient1.ServerClassesDisplay(I) = DisplayClass Then
        frmOle1.OleClient1.Class = frmOle1.OleClient1.ServerClasses(I)
        Exit For
    End If
Next I

Screen.MousePointer = 11
Unload frmInsert

End Sub

Sub Form_Load ()

Dim I As Integer

' Display the names of the available server
' applications.
Screen.MousePointer = 11

For I = 0 To frmOle1.OleClient1.ServerClassCount - 1

    ' Add a server class to the List Box only if
    ' it supports at least one protocol.
    frmOle1.OleClient1.ServerClass = frmOle1.OleClient1.ServerClasses(I)

    If (frmOle1.OleClient1.ServerProtocolCount > 0) Then
        lstServers.AddItem frmOle1.OleClient1.ServerClassesDisplay(I)
    End If

Next I

lstServers.ListIndex = 0
Screen.MousePointer = 0

End Sub

Sub lstServers_DblClick ()

' Double-clicking an item in the List Box is the
' same as selecting OK.
Call cmdOK_Click

End Sub
```

Listing 6.5   Code in OLE1.BAS

```
Option Explicit

' Constants for OLE actions
Global Const OLE_CREATE_NEW = 0
Global Const OLE_ACTIVATE = 7
Global Const OLE_DELETE = 10
Global Const OLE_SAVE_TO_FILE = 11
Global Const OLE_READ_FROM_FILE = 12

' Constants for OLE server type
Global Const OLE_EMBEDDED = 1

' Constant for OLE filename
Global Const OLE_FILE_NAME = "OLE_DATA.XYZ"

' Constants for message box displays and replies
Global Const MB_YESNOCANCEL = 3
Global Const MB_YESNO = 4
Global Const MB_ICONQUESTION = 32
Global Const IDCANCEL = 2
Global Const IDYES = 6
Global Const IDNO = 7

' Global flags
Global NotSaved As Integer
Global ObjectPresent As Integer
```

Graphics

G raphics are one of Visual Basic's strong points—as you would certainly expect, since Windows is a graphical environment! Yet there's always room for improvement. A clever way of displaying images, a unique window design, or an unusual use of shapes can set your program apart from the competition. The techniques presented in this chapter show you some ways to extend the graphics capabilities of your Visual Basic programs.

Working with Images

Many Visual Basic programs work with images in one form or another. Whether the images are bitmaps, metafiles, or icons, Visual Basic and the Windows API provide a variety of tools for handling them. This section explores some of these tools.

Create a Scrollable Picture Viewer

You might think that creating a program that displays several graphic elements on screen at one time will limit you to smaller elements. Visual Basic provides a solution to this size limitation with a scrollable picture viewer, which allows the user to view large images a portion at a time.

Some graphic images are too large to be viewed in their entirety at one time, particularly if you don't want to devote the entire screen to the image. You can create a scrollable picture viewer that lets you view a portion of a large image at a time.

A Visual Basic program can display a graphics image on a form or in a Picture Box or Image control. The graphic can be loaded at design time or at run time, and can originate in a bitmap file, an icon file, or a Windows metafile. Displaying large images can sometimes be a problem, particularly if you want other program elements visible on the screen at the same time. The solution is a scrollable picture viewer that lets you scroll around the picture, viewing a portion at a time.

The scrollable picture viewer consists of a pair of Picture box controls in a parent-child relationship to each other. When one Picture Box control is a child of another Picture Box, the child cannot be moved out of the parent. More important for the present needs, any portions of the child Picture Box that fall outside the boundaries of the parent control are automatically clipped. If the child control contains a picture that is larger than the parent control, then the parent control will act as a window

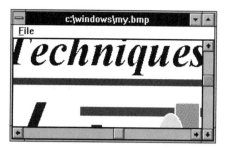

Figure 7.1   The scrollable picture viewer in operation.

through which a portion of the picture is visible—only the portion of the child control that can fit within the boundaries of the parent control will be visible a one time. By changing the relative positions of the two Picture Boxes you can scroll so that different portions of the picture are visible through the window. By adjusting the size of the parent Picture Box, you control the size of the viewing window.

To create this parent-child relationship, start by drawing the parent control. Then, draw the child Picture Box inside the parent Picture Box. You must draw the child Picture Box; you cannot add a child by double-clicking the Picture Box tool.

The program SCROLL.FRM implements a scrollable picture viewer that you can include in your own programs. You can add this form to your own projects with only minor changes. The only required change is in the **mnuFileExit_Click** event procedure; this code should be modified to return execution to the appropriate program location. As written, the procedure uses a simple Input Box to get the name of the image file from the user. You might want to add a more sophisticated File Open dialog box, or the calling program could pass the filename when loading the form.

Figure 7.1 shows the viewer in operation. Listing 7.1 gives the form's objects and properties; when creating the form, you don't have to worry about precise sizes and positions of the controls because they all will be sized and positioned in code, which is provided in Listing 7.2.

Listing 7.1   Objects and Properties in SCROLL.FRM

```
Begin Form frmScroll
   Caption          =    "Image scroller"
   ScaleMode        =    3  'Pixel
   Begin VScrollBar VScroll1
   End
   Begin HScrollBar HScroll1
   End
```

```
        Begin PictureBox pboxView
            AutoRedraw      =    -1  'True
            ScaleMode       =     3  'Pixel
            Begin PictureBox pboxHold
                AutoRedraw      =    -1   'True
                AutoSize        =    -1   'True
                ScaleMode       =     3   'Pixel
            End
        End
        Begin Menu mnuFile
            Caption         =     "&File"
            Begin Menu mnuFileLoad
                Caption         =     "&Load"
            End
            Begin Menu mnuFileExit
                Caption         =     "E&xit"
            End
        End
    End
End
```

Listing 7.2   Code in SCROLL.FRM

```
Option Explicit

' Global variable that specifies whether a picture is loaded.
Dim Picture_Loaded As Integer

Sub Form_Load ()

Picture_Loaded = False

End Sub

Sub Form_Resize ()

' This event procedure executes when the form is first
' displayed and anytime the user changes its size.
' Move the child Picture Box to the upper-left
' corner of the form.

pboxHold.Move 0, 0

' Move the parent Picture Box to the upper-left
' corner of the form, and size it to fill the form,
' leaving room for the scroll bars.
pboxView.Move 0, 0, ScaleWidth - VScroll1.Width, ScaleHeight -
    HScroll1.Height

' Position the scroll bars.
```

```
HScroll1.Left = 0
HScroll1.Top = pboxView.Height
HScroll1.Width = pboxView.Width

VScroll1.Top = 0
VScroll1.Left = pboxView.Width
VScroll1.Height = pboxView.Height + HScroll1.Height

' If a picture has not been loaded, exit the Sub.
If Picture_Loaded = False Then Exit Sub

' Set the scroll bars' Max property so that full travel of each
' bar represents scrolling the full width or height of the image.
HScroll1.Max = pboxHold.Width - pboxView.Width
VScroll1.Max = pboxHold.Height - pboxView.Height

' Set the scroll bars' Change properties so that a large change
' scrolls the width or height of the viewing window, and a small
' change scrolls 1/10 that distance.

HScroll1.LargeChange = HScroll1.Max \ (pboxHold.Width \ pboxView.Width)
VScroll1.LargeChange = VScroll1.Max \ (pboxHold.Height \ pboxView.Height)
HScroll1.SmallChange = HScroll1.LargeChange \ 10
VScroll1.SmallChange = VScroll1.LargeChange \ 10

' Enable each scroll bar only if the full extent of the
' picture is not already showing.
If (pboxView.Width < pboxHold.Width) Then
    HScroll1.Enabled = True
Else
    HScroll1.Enabled = False
End If

If (pboxView.Height < pboxHold.Height) Then
    VScroll1.Enabled = True
Else
    VScroll1.Enabled = False
End If

HScroll1.Refresh
VScroll1.Refresh

End Sub

Sub HScroll1_Change ()

' Move the parent Picture Box
pboxHold.Left = -(HScroll1.Value)
```

```
End Sub

Sub mnuFileExit_Click ()

End

End Sub

Sub mnuFileLoad_Click ()

Dim FileName As String, Msg As String

Const MB_ICONSTOP = &H10

On Local Error Resume Next

' Get a filename from the user.
FileName = InputBox("Name of file to load (may include path):", "File
  Load", "")

' Exit if user selected Cancel.
If FileName = "" Then Exit Sub

pboxHold.Picture = LoadPicture(FileName)

' Check for errors.
If Err Then
    If Err = 53 Then
        Msg = "File " + FileName + " not found."
        MsgBox Msg, MB_ICONSTOP
        Exit Sub
    Else
        Msg = "Error retrieving " + FileName
        MsgBox Msg, MB_ICONSTOP
        Exit Sub
    End If
End If

Picture_Loaded = True
frmScroll.Caption = FileName
Call Form_Resize

End Sub

Sub VScroll1_Change ()

' Move the parent Picture Box
pboxHold.Top = -(VScroll1.Value)

End Sub
```

Changing the Size of a Bitmap

The Windows API has a function that you can use to stretch or shrink a bitmap to the needed size.

The ability to view a small portion of a large picture is only one part of a versatile picture viewer. Sometimes you might also want to see a thumbnail sketch of the entire picture at the same time, enabling you to evaluate the relationship of the portion you are viewing to other elements of the picture. You already know that the picture is too large to view (otherwise you wouldn't need a scrollable viewer in the first place!), so how do we get a thumbnail sketch? The Windows API comes to the rescue with the **StretchBlt()** function. This function copies a bitmap from one location to another, stretching or shrinking it as needed to fit the size of the destination. The function declaration, which must be included in any program that uses it, is shown here:

```
Declare Function StretchBlt% Lib "GDI" (ByVal hDC%, ByVal X%,
    ByVal Y%, ByVal nWidth%, ByVal nHeight%, ByVal hSrcDC%, ByVal
    XSrc%, ByVal YSrc%, ByVal nSrcWidth%, ByVal nSrcHeight%,
    ByVal dwRop&)
```

The return value is non-zero if the function is successful. Otherwise, it is zero. The first five arguments define the destination for the copy operation:

- **hDC%** specifies the hDC property of the object to receive the bitmap.
- **X%** and **Y%** specify the logical X and Y coordinates in the destination object where the bitmap is to be placed.
- **nWidth%** and **nHeight%** specify the logical dimensions of the destination (the final size of the bitmap copy).

The second five arguments define the source for the copy operation:

- **hSrcDC%** specifies the hDC property of the bitmap source object.
- **XSrc%** and **YSrc%** specify the logical X and Y coordinates in the source object where the bitmap is to be copied from.
- **nSrcWidth%** and **nSrcHeight%** specify the logical dimensions of the source (the size of the bitmap to be copied).

The final argument, **dwRop&**, specifies the raster operation to be performed. In simple terms, *raster operation* means how the source bitmap is to be copied to the destination, and how it is to be combined with any bitmap already present in the destination.

Some options involve manipulation of the destination bitmap only—no source is involved. For those operations that involve a pattern, it is the pattern of the destination object's current brush that is used. Possible values for the **dwRop&** argument are given here, along with Windows global constants and their numerical values.

BLACKNESS (&H42): Turns all output black.

DSTINVERT (&H550009): Inverts the destination bitmap.

MERGECOPY (&HC000CA): Combines the pattern and the source bitmap by using the Boolean **AND** operator.

MERGEPAINT (&HBB0226): Inverts the source bitmap, then combines it with the destination bitmap by using the Boolean **OR** operator.

NOTSRCCOPY (&H330008): Inverts the source bitmap, then copies it to the destination.

NOTSRCERASE (&H1100A6): Combines the destination and source bitmaps by using the Boolean **OR** operator, then inverts the result.

PATCOPY (&HF00021): Copies the pattern to the destination bitmap.

PATINVERT (&H5A0049): Combines the destination bitmap with the pattern by using the Boolean **XOR** operator.

PATPAINT (&HFB0A09): Inverts the source bitmap and combines it with the pattern by using the Boolean **OR** operator. Then, combines the result of this operation with the destination bitmap by using the Boolean **OR** operator.

SRCAND (&H8800C6): Combines pixels of the destination and source bitmaps by using the Boolean **AND** operator.

SRCCOPY (&HCC0020): Copies the source bitmap to the destination bitmap.

SRCERASE (&H440328): Inverts the destination bitmap and combines the result with the source bitmap by using the Boolean **AND** operator.

SRCINVERT (&H660046): Combines pixels of the destination and source bitmaps by using the Boolean **XOR** operator.

SRCPAINT (&HEE0086): Combines pixels of the destination and source bitmaps by using the Boolean **OR** operator.

WHITENESS (&HFF0062): Turns all output white.

You can see that the **StretchBlt** API function offers you plenty of options. You may wish to experiment with the different raster operations to see what effects you can obtain. For the present purposes, however, all we want to do is to copy the source bitmap unchanged (except for size) to the destination. For this you use the **SRCCOPY** raster operation.

When a bitmap is compressed by **StretchBlt**, lines of pixels must be eliminated to make the image smaller. Of course you want to preserve as much detail as possible in the copy. Depending on the nature of the bitmap, different compression algorithms are best suited for preserving detail. You can set the compression algorithm used by **StretchBlt** with another Windows API function, **SetStretchBltMode**. Its declaration is:

```
Declare Function SetStretchBltMode% Lib "GDI" (ByVal hDC%, ByVal mode%)
```

The argument **hDC%** is the destination device context. The argument **mode%** specifies the one of the three compression algorithms shown here:

BLACKONWHITE (1): The eliminated lines are ANDed with preserved lines. This mode preserves black pixels at the expense of white pixels.

WHITEONBLACK (2): The eliminated lines are ORed with preserved lines. This mode preserves white pixels at the expense of black pixels.

COLORONCOLOR (3): The eliminated lines are deleted.

The **BLACKONWHITE** and **WHITEONBLACK** modes are used to preserve foreground pixels in monochrome bitmaps. The **COLORONCOLOR** mode is used to preserve the color in color bitmaps.

Now let's take a look at a demonstration. STRETCH.MAK is a single form that contains only two Picture Box controls; its objects, properties, and code are given in Listings 7.3 and 7.4. The source Picture Box, **pboxSource**, has its Visible property set to False, as we are not interested in viewing it. It functions only as a source for the **StretchBlt** function (which the program declares and uses as a **Sub**). The source Picture Box's AutoSize property is set to True so that the Picture Box automatically sizes to fit whatever picture is loaded into it. At design time, load a bitmap into **pboxSource**—for the demonstration I used WINLOGO.BMP, a bitmap of the Windows logo that can be found in your main Windows directory. This bitmap is shown stretched in Figure 7.2. The destination Picture Box control, **pboxDest**, is automatically sized in code so that it fills the form. The form's **Resize** event procedure also performs the bitmap resize operation. You can set the form to any size you like, and the bitmap will stretch or shrink to fit. Note that both Picture Box controls have their ScaleMode property set to 3-Pixel. This is required because the **StretchBlt** API call requires width and height arguments to be passed in terms of pixels.

Figure 7.2   The stretched bitmap WINLOGO.BMP.

Using STRETCH.MAK

This demonstration, presented in Listings 7.3 and 7.4, is stored on disk as STRETCH.MAK and STRETCH.FRM.

Listing 7.3   Objects and Properties in STRETCH.FRM

```
Begin Form Form1
   Caption         =    "Changing Bitmap Size"
   Begin PictureBox pboxSource
      AutoRedraw   =    -1   'True
      AutoSize     =    -1   'True
      Picture      =    (see text)
      ScaleMode    =    3    'Pixel
         Visible   =    0    'False
   End
   Begin PictureBox pboxDest
      AutoRedraw   =    -1   'True
      ScaleMode    =    3    'Pixel
   End
End
```

Listing 7.4   Code in STRETCH.FRM

```
Option Explicit

Const SRCCOPY = &HCC0020
Const COLORONCOLOR = 3
```

```
Declare Sub SetStretchBltMode Lib "GDI" (ByVal hDC As Integer,
   ByVal nStretchMode As Integer)

Declare Sub StretchBlt Lib "GDI" (ByVal hDC%, ByVal X%, ByVal Y%,
   ByVal nWidth%, ByVal nHeight%, ByVal hSrcDC%, ByVal XSrc%,
   ByVal YSrc%, ByVal nSrcWidth%, ByVal nSrcHeight%, ByVal dwRop&)

Sub Form_Resize ()

Dim XDst As Integer, YDst As Integer
Dim DstWidth As Integer, DstHeight As Integer
Dim XSrc As Integer, YSrc As Integer
Dim SrcHeight As Integer, SrcWidth As Integer

Screen.MousePointer = 11

' Set the Picture Box to fill the form.
pboxDest.Move 0, 0, Form1.ScaleWidth, Form1.ScaleHeight

' Set StretchBlt mode.
Call SetStretchBltMode(pboxDest.hDC, COLORONCOLOR)

' Copy the bitmap from source to destination.
XDst = 0
YDst = 0
XSrc = 0
YSrc = 0
SrcWidth = pboxSource.ScaleWidth
SrcHeight = pboxSource.ScaleHeight
DstWidth = pboxDest.ScaleWidth
DstHeight = pboxDest.ScaleHeight

Call StretchBlt(pboxDest.hDC, XDst, YDst, DstWidth, DstHeight,
   pboxSource.hDC, XSrc, YSrc, SrcWidth, SrcHeight, SRCCOPY)

pboxDest.Picture = pboxDest.Image

Screen.MousePointer = 0

End Sub
```

Previewing Wallpaper Styles and Icons

When you are programming for Windows, you use icons frequently. But what does that icon look like? Who can remember the appearances and/or names of dozens of icons? I know I can't, so I created a small program that lets you locate and preview icons and wallpaper images.

My utility lets me browse through the icon (*.ICO) and bitmap (*.BMP) files on my disk and preview the image each one contains. As an added feature, I provided the option to display a bitmap in "wallpaper" style—that is, as a repeated image. This can be helpful when selecting a bitmap to use as your Windows Program Manager wallpaper. Finally, the program can copy the filename of the file currently being viewed (including the full path) to the Clipboard. This can be very handy when, once you have found the desired image, you need to insert its filename into a program.

The project's form, PREVIEW.FRM, is shown displaying an icon in wallpaper style in Figure 7.3. If wallpaper style is not selected, the icon will appear in the center of the display area. Bitmaps that are too big to fit in the display area are clipped, with only the upper-left section displayed (this is usually enough to tell what the picture contains).

The program first loads the selected picture file into a hidden Picture Box control (Visible = False). The hidden Picture Box has its AutoSize property set to True so it will automatically size itself to fit whatever picture is loaded. We are now able to use the Picture Box's size properties to obtain information about the size of the image.

Next, the program copies the image from the hidden Picture Box to the visible display Picture Box (which has a fixed size). If the image is smaller than the destination Picture Box, it is either copied to the center of the Picture Box (if wallpaper mode is off), or it is copied repeatedly to fill the entire Picture Box (if wallpaper mode is on). If the image is larger than

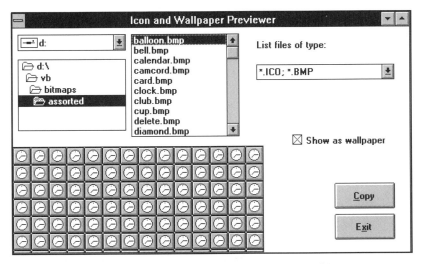

Figure 7.3   PREVIEW.FRM lets you preview icon and bitmap files.

the destination, then you need only to copy it once for either wallpaper mode setting.

You copy the image using the **BitBlt** API function, which copies a bitmap from a source device to a destination device. The function declaration is:

```
Declare Function BitBlt Lib "GDI" (ByVal hDestDC As Integer,
   ByVal X As Integer, ByVal Y As Integer, ByVal nWidth As
   Integer, ByVal nHeight As Integer, ByVal hSrcDC As Integer,
   ByVal XSrc As Integer, ByVal YSrc As Integer, ByVal dwRop As
   Long) As Integer
```

The function arguments are described here:

- **hDestDC** and **hSrcDC** specify the device context (hDC property) of the destination and source devices, respectively.

- **X** and **Y** specify the logical coordinates in the destination where the bitmap's upper-left corner is to be placed.

- **nWidth** and **nHeight** specify the logical dimensions of the bitmap.

- **XSrc** and **YSrc** specify the logical coordinates of the upper-left corner of the source bitmap.

- **dwRop** specifies the raster operation to perform—in other words, how the copy operation is to be done. There are over a dozen possible standard options for this argument. For our purpose, which is to simply copy a bitmap from one location to another without modification, we will use a **dwRop** argument of **&HCC0020**.

The **BitBlt** function returns a non-zero value on success, zero otherwise. Note that for **BitBlt** to work properly, the ScaleMode property of both the source and destination must be set to Pixel.

The program's objects, properties, and code are presented in Listings 7.5 and 7.6. I think you'll find this little utility to be very useful.

On Disk

Using PREVIEW.MAK

This demonstration, presented in Listings 7.5 and 7.6, is stored on disk as PREVIEW.MAK and PREVIEW.FRM.

Listing 7.5   Objects and Properties in PREVIEW.FRM

```
Begin Form Form1
   BorderStyle    =    1    'Fixed Single
```

```
      Caption         =    "Icon and Wallpaper Previewer"
      Begin CommandButton cmdCopy
          Caption       =     "&Copy"
      End
      Begin PictureBox Picture2
          AutoSize        =    -1  'True
          ScaleMode       =    3   'Pixel
          Visible         =    0   'False
      End
      Begin CheckBox chkTile
          Caption         =     "Show as wallpaper"
      End
      Begin PictureBox Picture1
          ScaleMode       =    3   'Pixel
      End
      Begin CommandButton cmdExit
          Caption         =     "E&xit"
      End
      Begin ComboBox Combo1
          Style           =    2   'Dropdown List
      End
      Begin FileListBox File1
          Pattern         =     "*.ICO;*.BMP"
      End
      Begin DirListBox Dir1
      End
      Begin DriveListBox Drive1
      End
      Begin Label Label1
          Caption         =     "List files of type:"
      End
  End
End
```

Listing 7.6   Code in PREVIEW.FRM

```
Option Explicit

Declare Function BitBlt Lib "GDI" (ByVal hDestDC As Integer,
  ByVal X As Integer, ByVal Y As Integer, ByVal nWidth As Integer,
  ByVal nHeight As Integer, ByVal hSrcDC As Integer, ByVal XSrc
  As Integer, ByVal YSrc As Integer, ByVal dwRop As Long)
  As Integer

Const MB_ICONSTOP = 16
Const SRCCOPY = &HCC0020

Dim FileName As String

Sub CenterPicture ()
```

```
Dim X As Integer
Dim XDest As Integer, YDest As Integer
Dim Hgt As Integer, Wdth As Integer

Screen.MousePointer = 11

' If the picture is smaller than the display Picture Box,
' center it. If it is larger, display as much as possible.
Picture2.AutoRedraw = True
Picture1.AutoRedraw = True
Hgt = Picture2.ScaleHeight
Wdth = Picture2.ScaleWidth

' If the source is smaller then the destination,
' calculate coordinates for centering.
If Picture2.Width < Picture1.Width Then
    XDest = (Picture1.ScaleWidth - Picture2.ScaleWidth) / 2
Else
    XDest = 0
End If

If Picture2.Height < Picture1.Height Then
    YDest = (Picture1.ScaleHeight - Picture2.ScaleHeight) / 2
Else
    YDest = 0
End If

Picture1.Cls
X = BitBlt(Picture1.hDC, XDest, YDest, Wdth, Hgt, Picture2.hDC, 0, 0,
  SRCCOPY)

Screen.MousePointer = 0

End Sub

Sub chkTile_Click ()

If chkTile.Value = 0 Then
    Call CenterPicture
Else
    Call WallPaperPicture
End If

End Sub

Sub cmdCopy_Click ()

' Copy the name of the currently displayed file
' to the Clipboard.
```

```
Clipboard.SetText  FileName
File1.SetFocus

End Sub

Sub cmdExit_Click ()

End

End Sub

Sub Combo1_Click ()

File1.Pattern = Combo1.Text

End Sub

Sub Dir1_Change ()

File1.Path = Dir1.Path

If File1.ListCount > 0 Then
    File1.ListIndex = 0
    cmdCopy.Enabled = True
    File1.SetFocus
Else
    Picture1.Cls
    cmdCopy.Enabled = False
End If

End Sub

Sub Drive1_Change ()

On Error GoTo DriveErrorhandler

Dir1.Path = Drive1.Drive
Exit Sub

' An error will occur if the user selects an invalid drive,
' such as a floppy drive with no diskette inserted.
DriveErrorhandler:

Drive1.Drive = Dir1.Path
Exit Sub

End Sub

Sub File1_Click ()
```

```
On Error GoTo LoadErrorhandler

FileName = Dir1.Path + "\" + File1.List(File1.ListIndex)

Picture2.Picture = LoadPicture(FileName)

If chkTile.Value = 0 Then
    Call CenterPicture
Else
    Call WallPaperPicture
End If

Exit Sub

LoadErrorhandler:

MsgBox "Error loading file", MB_ICONSTOP, "Error"
Resume Next

End Sub

Sub Form_Load ()

' Load choices into the Combo Box.
Combo1.Clear
Combo1.AddItem "*.ICO; *.BMP"
Combo1.AddItem "*.ICO"
Combo1.AddItem "*.BMP"
Combo1.ListIndex = 0

Form1.Show
File1.SetFocus
If File1.ListCount > 0 Then
    File1.ListIndex = 0
End If

End Sub

Sub WallPaperPicture ()

' If the Wallpaper option is selected. Display multiple
' copies of the picture, but only if it is smaller
' than the destination display area.
Dim Result As Integer, X As Integer, Y As Integer
Dim X1 As Integer, Y1 As Integer
Dim XDest As Integer, YDest As Integer
Dim Hgt As Integer, Wdth As Integer

Screen.MousePointer = 11
```

```
Picture2.AutoRedraw = True
Picture1.AutoRedraw = True
Hgt = Picture2.ScaleHeight
Wdth = Picture2.ScaleWidth

' If the source is larger then the destination,
' display as much as possible.
If Picture2.Width > Picture1.Width Or Picture2.Height > Picture1.Height Then
    XDest = 0
    YDest = 0
    Picture1.Cls
    Result = BitBlt(Picture1.hDC, XDest, YDest, Wdth, Hgt, Picture2.hDC,
      0, 0, SRCCOPY)
    Screen.MousePointer = 0
    Exit Sub
End If

' If we reach here the picture can be tiled.
Picture1.Cls

X1 = Picture1.ScaleWidth \ Picture2.ScaleWidth
Y1 = Picture1.ScaleHeight \ Picture2.ScaleHeight

For Y = 0 To Y1
    YDest = Y * Picture2.ScaleHeight
    For X = 0 To X1
        XDest = X * Picture2.ScaleWidth
        Result = BitBlt(Picture1.hDC, XDest, YDest, Wdth, Hgt,
          Picture2.hDC, 0, 0, SRCCOPY)
    Next X
Next Y

Screen.MousePointer = 0

End Sub
```

Drawing New Graphical Elements

Sometimes you want to give your program that something extra that will set it apart from the crowd. From a visual point of view, there's nothing quite as effective as adding some new graphical element to your program's display. In this section, I provide three approaches that I have found useful.

Creating a Gradated Color Form Background

You can give your forms a gradated, or faded, color background similar to that used by the Microsoft Windows Setup program.

It's easy to give your forms a color background, but how about something a little different? If you have used the Microsoft Setup program, you may remember the nifty screens that display a blue background that fades from light blue near the top of the form to dark blue or black at the bottom. You can use API calls to create the same background in your own programs.

The first API call you need is the function **CreateSolidBrush**. This function is used to create a brush for drawing a background. The declaration for this function is:

```
Declare Function CreateSolidBrush Lib "GDI" (ByVal crColor As
   Long) As Integer
```

The function returns the handle of a brush. In Windows graphics, the term *brush* refers to a type of object that is used for drawing on the screen. A "solid" brush is used to draw screen images that are or filled with a particular color. The argument **crColor** specifies the brush's color. For the present purposes we'll use the **RGB()** function to obtain color values corresponding to different shades of blue.

We will also use the **FillRect** API call. Its declaration is:

```
Declare Sub FillRect Lib "User" (ByVal hDC As Integer, lpRect
   As RECT, ByVal hBrush As Integer)
```

The arguments for this declaration are shown here:

- **hDC** is the device context of the form.
- **lpRect** is a type RECT structure that contains the logical coordinates of the rectangle to be filled. Note that this argument is not passed with the **ByVal** keyword.
- **hBrush** is the handle of the brush to be used to fill the rectangle.

The final API call, **DeleteObject,** is required to delete the brush object that was created; this step is advisable because it frees up memory. The procedure declaration is as follows; the argument **hObject** is the handle of the object being deleted.

```
Declare Sub DeleteObject Lib "GDI" (ByVal hObject As Integer)
```

Now we can outline the basic procedure that we'll use:

1. Divide the form into 64 narrow rectangular bands.
2. Create a brush using a light blue color.
3. Draw a filled rectangle in the topmost band.
4. Delete the brush.
5. Create a new brush using a slightly darker blue.
6. Draw a filled rectangle in the next band.
7. Return to step 4 and repeat until the entire form is filled.

The program FADEFORM.MAK shows how this is done. The form FADEFORM.FRM is for demonstration only; it consists of only a form with no controls and all properties left at their default values. The code for FADEFORM.FRM is presented in Listing 7.7. The meat of the program is in FADEFORM.BAS, in the procedure (what else?) **FadeForm**, presented in Listing 7.8. To fade your own forms, add the module FADEFORM.BAS to your project then call **FadeForm** as shown in the demonstration.

Using FADEFORM.MAK

This demonstration, presented in Listings 7.7 and 7.8, is stored on disk as FADEFORM.MAK, FADEFORM.FRM, and FADEFORM.BAS.

Listing 7.7   Code in FADEFORM.FRM

```
Option Explicit

Sub Form_Load ()

' Maximize the form.
WindowState = 2

End Sub

Sub Form_Paint ()

' Display gradated color whenever the form is painted.
Call FadeForm(Me)

End Sub
```

```
Sub Form_Resize ()

Call FadeForm(Me)

End Sub
```

Listing 7.8   Code in FADEFORM.BAS

```
Option Explicit

' Type used by FillRect API call.
Type RECT
    Left As Integer
    Top As Integer
    Right As Integer
    Bottom As Integer
End Type

' Number of steps in color fade (Max = 64).
Const STEPS = 64

Declare Function CreateSolidBrush Lib "GDI" (ByVal crColor As Long) As
  Integer
Declare Sub FillRect Lib "User" (ByVal hDC As Integer, lpRect As RECT,
  ByVal hBrush As Integer)
Declare Sub DeleteObject Lib "GDI" (ByVal hObject As Integer)

Sub FadeForm (Target As Form)

Dim FormY As Integer, Blue As Integer, DeltaY As Integer
Dim i As Integer, Result As Integer, OldMode As Integer
Dim hBrush As Integer
Dim Region As RECT

' Save old scale mode and switch to Pixel mode.
OldMode = Target.ScaleMode
Target.ScaleMode = 3   'Pixel

' Divide the form into STEPS regions.
FormY = Target.ScaleHeight
DeltaY = FormY \ STEPS

' Set coordinates of first region to fill.
Region.Left = 0
Region.Right = Target.ScaleWidth
Region.Top = 0
Region.Bottom = DeltaY

' Starting color
```

```
Blue = 255

For i = 1 To STEPS
    hBrush = CreateSolidBrush(RGB(0, 0, Blue))
    Call FillRect(Target.hDC, Region, hBrush)
    Call DeleteObject(hBrush)
    Region.Top = Region.Bottom
    Region.Bottom = Region.Bottom + DeltaY
    Blue = Blue - 4
Next i

' Fill the remainder of the form with black.
Region.Bottom = Region.Bottom + STEPS
hBrush = CreateSolidBrush(RGB(0, 0, 0))
Call FillRect(Target.hDC, Region, hBrush)
Call  DeleteObject(hBrush)

' Reset the original scale mode.
Target.ScaleMode = OldMode

End Sub
```

Displaying a Progress Gauge

Did you ever wonder how much longer you had to wait for an operation to complete? A progress gauge keeps the user informed of progress on program operations that take a significant amount of time. Here's how to create a progress gauge for your Visual Basic programs.

I'm sure that most of you have already seen a progress gauge, probably in a software installation program. When a lengthy program operation is in progress, this kind of gauge can be very useful, keeping the user informed of how much has been done and how much is left to do. Important decisions can be based on this information, such as "Do I have time to get a cup of coffee?"

You can display a progress gauge in your Visual Basic programs using the techniques described here. There are two parts to the gauge: a visual element displayed on the screen, which is the representation of the second part, the general procedure used to create it. The visual element contains only one control, a Picture Box. You create the graph element of the gauge by drawing a filled rectangle in the Picture Box; the percentage of the Picture Box filled by the rectangle represents the "percent done" status of whatever process is being monitored. The

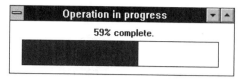

Figure 7.4 The progress gauge in operation.

progress gauge form also displays a text message indicating the percent done status. The progress gauge is shown in Figure 7.4.

The second part of the progress gauge is the general procedure **Progress_Gauge**. This procedure must be located in a Basic module so it can be accessed by all parts of the program. The calling program passes two arguments to **Progress_Gauge**: the first argument is an integer value indicating the current percent done to be displayed; the second argument is a string that is displayed in the title bar of the progress gauge form. Code in the procedure checks to see if the form **frmProgressGauge** is already displayed (using the Tag property); if not, it is loaded and displayed. If a negative value for percent done is passed, the progress gauge is closed.

Note that it is up to the calling program to monitor the operation and to determine the actual (or approximate) percent done. The progress gauge will be updated only when explicitly called by the main program. The calling program also must make a final call to **Progress_Gauge**, with a negative percent done argument, to close and unload the progress gauge.

The objects and properties of PROGRESS.FRM are given in Listing 7.9 and the code for PROGRESS.BAS is given in Listing 7.10. To use the progress gauge in your own programs, use the Add File command to add PROGRESS.FRM and PROGRESS.BAS to your project.

The demonstration program uses an additional form, PROGMAIN.FRM. Click the Start button to see the progress gauge in operation. The form contains only two Command Buttons; its code is given in Listing 7.11.

Using PROGRESS.MAK

This demonstration, presented in Listings 7.9, 7.10, and 7.11, is stored on disk as PROGRESS.MAK, PROGRESS.FRM, PROGMAIN.FRM, and PROGRESS.BAS.

Listing 7.9   Objects and Properties in PROGRESS.FRM

```
Begin Form frmProgressGauge
    BorderStyle    =    1 'Fixed Single
    Tag            =      "Progress gauge"
```

```
    Begin PictureBox Picture1
    End
End
```

Listing 7.10   Code in PROGRESS.BAS

```
Option Explicit

Sub Progress_Gauge (Percent As Integer, Title As String)

Dim x As Integer
Dim x2 As Single, y2 As Single, msg As String

' If a negative Percent was passed, unload the gauge
' and exit the Sub.
If Percent < 0 Then
    Unload frmProgressGauge
    Exit Sub
End If

' If the progress gauge form is not already displayed,
' display it.
If SCREEN.ActiveForm.Tag <> "Progress gauge" Then
    frmProgressGauge.Caption = Title
    frmProgressGauge.Show
End If

' Set coordinates for the right end of the rectangle
' that displays the progress bar.
y2 = frmProgressGauge.Picture1.ScaleHeight
x2 = Percent * frmProgressGauge.Picture1.ScaleWidth / 100

' Draw the rectangle. Use the QBColor function to
' obtain the color number for red. 4 is the "old"
' Quick Basic number for red.
frmProgressGauge.Picture1.Line (0, 0)-(x2, y2), QBColor(4), BF

' Clear the form of text.
frmProgressGauge.Cls

' Create the "percent complete" message and display it on the form.
msg = Str$(Percent) + "% complete."
x = (frmProgressGauge.Width - frmProgressGauge.TextWidth(msg)) / 2
frmProgressGauge.CurrentX = x
frmProgressGauge.CurrentY = 100
frmProgressGauge.Print  msg;

End Sub
```

Listing 7.11   Code in PROGMAIN.FRM

```
Option Explicit

Sub cmdExit_Click ()

End

End Sub

Sub cmdStart_Click ()

Dim Count1 As Integer, Count2 As Integer
Dim Title As String

Title = "Operation in progress"

For Count1 = 1 To 100 Step 2
    For Count2 = 1 To 6000
    Next Count2
    Call Progress_Gauge(Count1, Title)
Next Count1

Call Progress_Gauge(-1, "")

End Sub
```

Drawing and Filling Complex Shapes

An API call can be used to draw a variety of graphical objects in your Visual Basic programs.

Visual Basic's graphics methods are limited to drawing circles, lines, and rectangles. For more complex shapes you can turn to the **Polygon** API call. You can use this procedure to draw, and optionally fill, a variety of complex shapes. The declaration for this function is:

```
Declare Function Polygon Lib "GDI" (ByVal hDC As Integer,
    lpPoints As POINTAPI, ByVal nCount As Integer) As Integer
```

This function draws a polygon consisting of two or more points (vertices) connected by lines. If necessary, the function closes the polygon by drawing a line from the last vertex to the first. Polygons are surrounded by a frame drawn by using the current pen and filled by using the current brush.

The arguments for this function are described here:

- **hDC** specifies hDC property of the object (Form or Picture Box) on which the polygon is to be drawn.

- **lpPoints** is an array of user-defined structures that specifies the vertices of the polygon. (The Polygon procedure requires coordinates to be passed in terms of pixels.) Each structure contains two integers: one for the X coordinate and one for the Y coordinate. For example:

```
Type POINTS
        X As Integer
        Y As Integer
End Type
...
Dim V(10) as POINTS
```

- **nCount** specifies the number of vertices in the polygon. This value must be less than or equal to the number of elements in the array of vertices.

Another API call, **SetPolyFillMode**, can be used to control the fill mode used by **Polygon**. Its declaration is:

```
Declare Function SetPolyFillMode Lib "GDI" (ByVal hDC As Integer,
  ByVal nPolyFillMode As Integer) As Integer
```

Here, **hDC** specifies the device context of the object whose **Polygon** fill mode you are setting. The **nPolyFillMode** argument specifies one of two modes: ALTERNATE (the default; value = 1) fills every other enclosed surface. WINDING (value = 2) fills the entire polygon. **SetPolyFillMode** returns the previous fill mode on success, and zero on failure.

You can use the **Polygon** function to draw just about any weird shape that you can imagine. Remember that the term polygon means any closed shape with three or more sides—there's no requirement that the sides be equal in length, or the vertices be spaced evenly. You could generate 50 vertices using a random number generator and **Polygon** would draw the corresponding shape!

More useful, however, are polygons that are more-or-less symmetrical and that have a recognizable shape—triangles, squares, and so on. The **Polygon** function will be happy to draw these—all you need do is to determine the coordinates of the vertices and pass them to the function. To illustrate the use of the Polygon function, I have written a Basic subprocedure called **DrawPolygon** that uses the **Polygon** API function to draw any one of six "regular" shapes: triangle, inverted triangle, square, diamond, star, or cross. The program passes arguments to the procedure specifying the target to draw on, the shape to draw and its size, and the desired fill mode. The shape is drawn centered on the specified location coordinates.

As written, the procedure requires that the location coordinates be passed in terms of pixels (because the **Polygon** API function requires pixel arguments). If your application prefers using twips or some other measure, you can modify the procedure so that it converts the pixel coordinates before calling the **Polygon** API function.

Figure 7.5 illustrates the result of the demonstration program POLYGON.MAK—the six shapes that **DrawPolygon** can create. This program has a single form, whose objects, properties, and code are presented in Listings 7.12 and 7.13. The actual drawing function is contained in the Basic module POLYGON.BAS (Listing 7.14). You can use this function in your own programs by adding this module to your project.

Using POLYGON.MAK

This demonstration, presented in Listings 7.12, 7.13, and 7.14, is stored on disk as POLYGON.MAK, POLYGON.FRM, POLYGON.BAS.

Listing 7.12 Objects and Properties in POLYGON.FRM

```
Begin Form Form1
    Caption          =    "Drawing Polygons with API Calls"
    Begin PictureBox Picture1
    End
End
```

Figure 7.5 Polygons drawn by POLYGON.MAK.

Listing 7.13   Code in POLYGON.FRM

```
Option Explicit

Sub Form_Resize ()

'Size the Picture Box to fill the form.
Picture1.Move 0, 0, Form1.ScaleWidth, Form1.ScaleHeight

End Sub

Sub Picture1_Click ()

' Draw the six available shapes on the Picture Box.
Picture1.CurrentX = Picture1.ScaleWidth / 4
Picture1.CurrentY = Picture1.ScaleHeight / 3
Call DrawPolygon(Picture1, 30, PLY_TRIANGLE, WINDING)

Picture1.CurrentX = Picture1.ScaleWidth / 2
Call DrawPolygon(Picture1, 30, PLY_INVTRIANGLE, WINDING)

Picture1.CurrentX = Picture1.ScaleWidth * 3 / 4
Call DrawPolygon(Picture1, 30, PLY_SQUARE, WINDING)

Picture1.CurrentX = Picture1.ScaleWidth / 4
Picture1.CurrentY = Picture1.ScaleHeight * 2 / 3
Call DrawPolygon(Picture1, 30, PLY_DIAMOND, WINDING)

Picture1.CurrentX = Picture1.ScaleWidth / 2
Call DrawPolygon(Picture1, 30, PLY_STAR, WINDING)

Picture1.CurrentX = Picture1.ScaleWidth * 3 / 4
Call DrawPolygon(Picture1, 30, PLY_CROSS, WINDING)

End Sub
```

Listing 7.14   Code in POLYGON.BAS

```
Option Explicit

Type POINTAPI
    X As Integer
    Y As Integer
End Type

Declare Sub Polygon Lib "GDI" (ByVal hDC As Integer, lpPoints
    As POINTAPI, ByVal nCount As Integer)

Declare Sub SetPolyFillMode Lib "GDI" (ByVal hDC As Integer,
    ByVal nPolyFillMode As Integer)
```

```
' Constants for polygon types
Global Const PLY_TRIANGLE = 0
Global Const PLY_INVTRIANGLE = 1
Global Const PLY_SQUARE = 2
Global Const PLY_DIAMOND = 3
Global Const PLY_STAR = 4
Global Const PLY_CROSS = 5


' Constants for fill modes

Global Const ALTERNATE = 1
Global Const WINDING = 2


Sub DrawPolygon (Target As Control, Size As Integer, Shape As
   Integer, Fill As Integer)

' Draws a polygon on Target, centered at the object's
' current location. Other arguments are:
'
' Size is the center-to-edge size in pixels.
' Shape is one of the following constants (value):
'         PLY_TRIANGLE (1)
'         PLY_INVTRIANGLE (2)
'         PLY_SQUARE (3)
'         PLY_DIAMOND (4)
'         PLY_STAR (5)
'         PLY_CROSS (6)
'
' Fill is the polygon fill mode:
'         ALTERNATE (1)
'         WINDING (2)


' Create an array to hold vertices. Maximum number we will
' need is 12.
Static V(1 To 12) As POINTAPI

' Variables to hold old values.
Dim OldScaleMode As Integer, OldScaleLeft As Integer
Dim OldScaleTop As Integer, OldScaleWidth As Integer
Dim OldScaleHeight As Integer, OldFillStyle As Integer
Dim OldDrawWidth As Integer, numVertices As Integer
Dim xAdj As Integer, yAdj As Integer

' Save the control's current settings.
OldScaleMode = Target.ScaleMode
OldScaleLeft = Target.ScaleLeft
OldScaleTop = Target.ScaleTop
OldScaleWidth = Target.ScaleWidth
OldScaleHeight = Target.ScaleHeight
```

```
OldFillStyle  = Target.FillStyle
OldDrawWidth  = Target.DrawWidth

' Set as needed for drawing operation.
Target.ScaleMode = 3     ' pixel
Target.FillStyle = 0     ' solid
Target.DrawWidth = 1     ' one pixel border

' Load vertices array depending on the shape requested. The adjustment
' factors center each shape over the current X and Y coordinates.
xAdj = Target.CurrentX
yAdj = Target.CurrentY

Select Case Shape
Case PLY_TRIANGLE
    numVertices = 3
    V(1).X = xAdj
    V(1).Y = -Size + yAdj
    V(2).X = Size + xAdj
    V(2).Y = Size + yAdj
    V(3).X = -Size + xAdj
    V(3).Y = Size + yAdj
Case PLY_INVTRIANGLE
    numVertices = 3
    V(1).X = xAdj
    V(1).Y = Size + yAdj
    V(2).X = Size + xAdj
    V(2).Y = -Size + yAdj
    V(3).X = -Size + xAdj
    V(3).Y = -Size + yAdj
Case PLY_SQUARE
    numVertices = 4
    V(1).X = -Size + xAdj
    V(1).Y = -Size + yAdj
    V(2).X = Size + xAdj
    V(2).Y = -Size + yAdj
    V(3).X = Size + xAdj
    V(3).Y = Size + yAdj
    V(4).X = -Size + xAdj
    V(4).Y = Size + yAdj
Case PLY_DIAMOND
    numVertices = 4
    V(1).X = -Size + xAdj
    V(1).Y = yAdj
    V(2).X = xAdj
    V(2).Y = -Size + yAdj
    V(3).X = Size + xAdj
```

```
            V(3).Y = yAdj
            V(4).X = xAdj
            V(4).Y = Size + yAdj
        Case PLY_STAR
            numVertices = 5
            V(1).X = xAdj
            V(1).Y = -Size + yAdj
            V(2).X = Size * .666 + xAdj
            V(2).Y = Size + yAdj
            V(3).X = -Size + xAdj
            V(3).Y = -Size * .333 + yAdj
            V(4).X = Size + xAdj
            V(4).Y = V(3).Y
            V(5).X = -Size * .6 + xAdj
            V(5).Y = V(2).Y
        Case PLY_CROSS
            numVertices = 12
            V(1).X = -Size / 5 + xAdj
            V(1).Y = -Size + yAdj
            V(2).X = Size / 5 + xAdj
            V(2).Y = V(1).Y
            V(3).X = V(2).X
            V(3).Y = -Size / 5 + yAdj
            V(4).X = Size + xAdj
            V(4).Y = V(3).Y
            V(5).X = V(4).X
            V(5).Y = Size / 5 + yAdj
            V(6).X = V(3).X
            V(6).Y = V(5).Y
            V(7).X = V(6).X
            V(7).Y = Size + yAdj
            V(8).X = V(1).X
            V(8).Y = V(7).Y
            V(9).X = V(1).X
            V(9).Y = V(6).Y
            V(10).X = -Size + xAdj
            V(10).Y = V(9).Y
            V(11).X = V(10).X
            V(11).Y = V(3).Y
            V(12).X = V(1).X
            V(12).Y = V(11).Y
    End Select

    Call SetPolyFillMode(Target.hDC, Fill)
    Call Polygon(Target.hDC, V(1), numVertices)

End Sub
```

CHAPTER 8

Creating Your Own Dynamic Link Libraries

As powerful as Visual Basic is, there will always be some programmers who want to stretch it beyond its limits. And, since you're reading this book, you are probably one of them! Fortunately, Visual Basic is not limited to its built-in capabilities. As you have already seen, a Visual Basic program can make use of the wide variety of capabilities provided in the Windows API. If that's not enough, you can go even further by writing *custom* dynamic link libraries, which can provide almost any extension imaginable to Visual Basic

A Dynamic Link Library Primer

Before you get started writing your own DLLs, you need to know the basics: what they are and how a Visual Basic program uses them.

What Is a Custom DLL?

You already know that a DLL is a library of procedures that your programs can call. A custom DLL is simply a DLL that you write yourself to meet your specific needs.

DLLs are central to the Windows environment. If you browse through the files on the disk where Windows is installed you will find many DLLs. For example, KRNLx86.EXE, GDI.EXE, and USER.EXE are all DLLs, as are KEYBOARD.DRV and SYSTEM.DRV. Font files with the .FON extension are also DLLs. You'll also find plenty of files with the DLL extension—yes, these are DLLs too. As you may have guessed by now, a DLL file can have any extension, although the .DLL extension has become standard since the advent of Windows 3.0. The only practical difference is that dynamic link libraries with the .DLL extension are automatically loaded by Windows, whereas DLLs with other extensions must be explicitly loaded.

Many of the DLLs on your disk belong to Windows itself. In fact, Windows is largely comprised of several DLLs. The other DLLs belong to various Windows applications that you may have installed, such as Excel, Ami Pro, Micrografx Designer, and, of course, Visual Basic. DLLs fall into two general categories. The most common, which has no special name, is the type we have been discussing. It contains executable procedures that your programs can call. The other type, a *resource-only* library, doesn't contain any executable code. Rather, it contains resources, such as bitmaps or font definitions, that your programs can access. Font files (with the .FON extension) are an example of resource-only DLLs.

A custom DLL is no different from these other DLLs—except that *you* write it. And, since you write it, you can put anything you want in it (that's why it's called custom, of course!). Whether you need to display fractal images, calculate depreciation on undersea mining equipment, or model a hurricane, if you can write the code, you can put it in a DLL.

Why Use a DLL?

Putting a procedure in a DLL has certain advantages over including the procedure as part of the program.

You may be wondering why you should go to the trouble of putting a procedure in a DLL instead of simply including it as part of your Visual Basic program. DLLs have several advantages to offer.

For example, a procedure in a DLL is available to any and all programs executing under Windows. Once you have placed, say, your depreciation procedure in a DLL, any Visual Basic program can call the procedure (for that matter, programs written in other languages can call it too, but that's a subject for another book!).

Perhaps you are thinking that you can obtain the same result by writing the procedure in Basic, putting it in a Basic module, and adding that module to every Visual Basic project that needs to call the procedure. This will work, of course, but there will be a copy of the procedure's code in every Visual Basic program that uses it. Not only does this waste disk space, but it slows program compilation and loading. If the procedure were in a DLL, only a single copy would be present on disk (and in memory, while the DLL is in use) no matter how many different programs were accessing it.

Another advantage becomes apparent when you decide to modify the procedure. If you placed it in a Basic module, you would have to edit the module, then recompile every Visual Basic program that uses it (if you can remember them all!). With a DLL, on the other hand, you would have to modify and recompile only a single file, and the changes would automatically become available to all programs that call the procedure.

A final "advantage" is that you can use languages other than Basic to write DLLs. I put quotes around *advantage* because not everyone will think this is an advantage! In fact, you may feel that the need to learn and use another language is a distinct *disadvantage*. For the most part, DLLs are written in C or C++ because these languages are more suited for certain types of tasks than Basic. Yet, learning to program in C or C++ is no trivial matter!

How to Write and Use a DLL

Writing and using your own DLL may seem like advanced wizard/guru-type programming, but that's not necessarily true. Given the proper tools and some basic information, there's no reason why you shouldn't have your first working (and useful!) DLL in fairly short order. On the other hand, however, DLL programming is not a simple task that you can be careless about. C and C++ are powerful languages, but this power also makes them dangerous. A seemingly minor error in DLL code can cause all sorts of unexpected results, from errors in data to a system crash. So, use caution and keep backups of critical files!

What You'll Need

Here's what you need to get started writing your own DLLs.

There are two things you'll need to write a DLL. The first, of course, is the ability to program in C or C++. This is something that I can't teach you in a single chapter! You don't need to be a real expert, but you will need to know enough to get the language to do what you want it to do. There are plenty of good books on C and C++—and plenty of bad ones too! For C, I can modestly recommend *Teach Yourself C in 21 Days*, which I co-authored with Brad Jones, and for C++ you can't do better than Tom Swan's *C++ Primer* (both books are published by Howard W. Sams).

C and C++ Comments

Even if you don't know C or C++, you may be able to understand some of the listings in this chapter. It'll be a lot easier if you understand how C and C++ use comments! In C and C++, anything between /* and */ is a comment:

```
/* This is a comment. */
```

In C++, single lines beginning with // are also comments:

```
// This is a comment
```

The second thing you'll need is a C/C++ compiler with Windows DLL capability. There are several of these on the market, including Microsoft C++, Quick C for Windows, Borland C++, and Turbo C++ for Windows. While all of these products (plus many others) will create perfectly functional DLLs, they go about it in slightly different ways. For example, the way you set compiler options to specify that you're creating a DLL rather than a standard Windows executable program differs between products. There's really no choice except to read your compiler documentation to be sure you're doing things properly!

In the remainder of this chapter I'm going to take a "cookbook" approach to showing you how to create a DLL. In other words, I'm going to tell you what to do, but that's all. I will make little or no effort to explain why things are done a particular way, to point out alternate techniques that work equally well, or to go into the workings of C and C++. If I did all these things it would be a very long chapter indeed! If you want to get serious about C or C++, I suggest you get a good C/C++ book and spend some time reading it and your compiler documentation.

The Structure of a DLL

There are certain components that every DLL requires.

There are three things that every DLL must include: a Windows header file, a **LibMain()** function, and a Windows Exit Procedure, or **WEP**. When put together, these components form a sort of "template" that you can use as the starting point for your own DLLs. The first of these components, the Windows header file, is required for any Windows program. Thus, your DLL source code must contain the line:

```
#include <windows.h>
```

The second component, the **LibMain()** function, is analogous to the **main()** function that is required in every C and C++ executable program. When Windows loads the DLL it executes the code in **LibMain**, performing any initialization required by the DLL. For most DLLs, including the ones we'll write here, all you need are the following lines of code:

```
int FAR PASCAL LibMain( HINSTANCE hInstance, WORD
   wDataSegment, WORD wHeapSize, LPSTR lpszCmdLine )
{
if ( wHeapSize != 0 )
        UnlockData( 0 );
return 1;
}
```

The third and final component, the **WEP**, is called when the last program using the DLL terminates, freeing the DLL from memory, or when Windows itself shuts down. If the DLL has special "cleanup" requirements they can be taken care of by code in the WEP, but here I've provided only the minimum that is necessary:

```
int FAR PASCAL WEP ( int bSystemExit )
{
return 1;
}
```

Now we have the components for our DLL source code template, which is shown in Listing 8.1. You could actually compile this source code into a DLL, but of course it wouldn't be much good because it contains no procedures for your programs to call!

Listing 8.1   Tempate for C/C++ DLL Source Code File

```
#include <windows.h>
/* Other needed #include statements go here. */

/* Function prototypes go here (if they are not in
 their own include file). */

/* Actual DLL functions go either here or below. */

int FAR PASCAL LibMain( HINSTANCE hInstance, WORD wDataSegment, WORD
  HeapSize, LPSTR lpszCmdLine )
{
if ( wHeapSize != 0 )
        UnlockData( 0 );
return 1;
}

/* You may not need to include the WEP function in the
    source code because some compilers add it to the DLL
    automatically.
*/

int FAR PASCAL WEP ( int bSystemExit )
{
return 1;
}

/* DLL functions can go here. */
```

The Module Definition File

Your compiler may require a module definition file in order to create a DLL.

In addition to the C or C++ source file, you may also need a *module definition file* when creating a DLL. A module definition file is simply a small text file that provides the compiler with certain information about the current project (the concept of a *project* in C/C++ is similar to a Visual Basic project). To create a DLL called FINANCE.DLL, for example, your module definition file should look like this:

```
LIBRARY        Finance
DESCRIPTION    'Financial functions DLL'
EXETYPE        WINDOWS
CODE           PRELOAD MOVEABLE DISCARDABLE
DATA           PRELOAD MOVEABLE SINGLE
HEAPSIZE       1024
```

The only parts of this that you would need to change for other DLLs are the second sections of the first two lines. The name after LIBRARY specifies the DLL filename, and the string after DESCRIPTION describes the DLL.

You may have noticed that I said you *may* need a module definition file. Some compilers can create a DLL without a module definition file, providing you set the compiler options appropriately. For example, if you're using the Borland C++ Integrated Development Environment, you can use the Options Linker Settings Output command to specify that you are creating a DLL. Other compilers will have their own commands.

If you are using a module definition file, you must make it part of your DLL project. First, create the file using any text editor (giving the file a .DEF extension is traditional). Then, add it to the DLL project using your compiler's "Add to Project" command.

Data Types in Visual Basic and C/C++

If you are going to be passing data back and forth between a Visual Basic program and DLL procedures written in C/C++, you need to understand how the data types used by the two languages relate.

For the most part, Visual Basic and C/C++ work with the same kinds of data, but they don't always call it by the same names. Table 8.1 lists the numeric data name differences between Basic and C/C++.

Table 8.1   Visual Basic and C/C++ Numeric Data Names

Basic	C/C++
Integer	int
Long	long
Single	float
Double	double

C/C++ has no equivalent for Visual Basic's Currency data type. Conversely, Visual Basic has no data type corresponding to C/C++'s long double. With sophisticated programming techniques it is possible to pass data in these types back and forth between Visual Basic and C/C++, but that's a topic we won't tackle.

String arguments can be passed without problem. If a Visual Basic string is passed with the **ByVal** keyword in the declaration (as it must be), then it is automatically converted into the string format that C/C++ expects—a sequence of characters terminated by a null byte. A DLL procedure can modify a string passed in this way, as long as it does not try to extend the length of the string beyond its original length.

Your First DLL

Now its time to get started. In this section, you'll create and use your first DLL.

In the interest of starting out simple, this first DLL doesn't do anything really useful. It contains two functions, one that adds two numbers, the other that subtracts them. Not too exciting, and hardly the kind of thing you would really use a DLL for. Yet, it's a good place to start.

I created the DLL in two versions: one for Borland C++ version 3.1 and one for Microsoft Quick C for Windows version 1.0. The differences between the two versions are relatively minor, but it's often just this kind of minor difference that can cause lots of problems and be a real chore to track down! Although I have not tried it myself, I believe that the Borland version should work with Turbo C++ for Windows, and the Microsoft version should work with the "big" Microsoft C/C++ compiler (versions 6 and 7).

The Borland C++ version code for the DLL is presented in Listing 8.3, with the optional module definition file in Listing 8.2. The Quick C versions are in Listings 8.4 and 8.5. After a successful compilation, either FIRSTB.DLL or FIRSTM.DLL will be on your disk. The companion disk includes all of the source files as well as the compiled DLLs.

A DLL for Everyone

The Borland C++ version is on disk as FIRSTB.DEF, FIRSTB.CPP, and FIRSTB.DLL. The Quick C for Windows version is on disk as FIRSTM.DEF, FIRSTM.C, and FIRSTM.DLL.

Listing 8.2   FIRSTB.DEF

```
LIBRARY         FIRSTB
DESCRIPTION     'Your first DLL'
EXETYPE         WINDOWS
CODE            PRELOAD MOVEABLE DISCARDABLE
DATA            PRELOAD MOVEABLE SINGLE
HEAPSIZE        1024
```

Listing 8.3   Code in FIRSTB.CPP

```cpp
/* Demonstration DLL

        Compiler: Borland C++ version 3.1
        Output: Windows dynamic link library
        Caller: Visual Basic
*/

#include <windows.h>

// Function prototypes

extern "C" long FAR PASCAL _export SumOf(long x, long y);
extern "C" long FAR PASCAL _export Difference(long x, long y);

// The LibMain function. The #pragma argsused line is a Borland
// C++ switch that turns off warning messages that report
// unused arguments.

#pragma argsused
int FAR PASCAL LibMain( HANDLE hInstance, WORD wDataSegment,
  WORD wHeapSize, LPSTR lpszCmdLine )
{
        if ( wHeapSize != 0 )
        UnlockData( 0 );
        return 1;
}

#pragma argsused
int FAR PASCAL WEP ( int bSystemExit )
{
return 1;
}
```

```
long FAR PASCAL _export SumOf (long x, long y)
{
return (x + y);
}

long FAR PASCAL _export Difference (long x, long y)
{
return (x - y);
}
```

Listing 8.4   FIRSTM.DEF

```
LIBRARY        FIRSTM
DESCRIPTION    'Your first DLL'
EXETYPE        WINDOWS
CODE           PRELOAD MOVEABLE DISCARDABLE
DATA           PRELOAD MOVEABLE SINGLE
HEAPSIZE       1024
```

Listing 8.5   Code in FIRSTM.C.

```
/* DLL demonstration

        Compiler: Quick C for Windows v 1.0
        Output: Dynamic link library.
        Caller: Visual Basic
*/

#include <windows.h>

/* Function prototypes */

extern long FAR PASCAL _export SumOf(long x, long y);
extern long FAR PASCAL _export Difference(long x,
  long y);

/* The LibMain function */

int FAR PASCAL LibMain( HANDLE hInstance, WORD wDataSegment,
   WORD wHeapSize, LPSTR lpszCmdLine )
{
        if ( wHeapSize != 0 )
        UnlockData( 0 );
        return 1;
}


/*   The WEP function need not be included
     in source code because Quick C for Windows
     adds it automatically.
*/
```

```
long FAR PASCAL _export SumOf (long x, long y)
{
return (x + y);
}

long FAR PASCAL _export Difference (long x, long y)
{
return (x - y);
}
```

If you have any familiarity with C/C++, you may be puzzled about some of the keywords in the function headers. Here's a brief explanation:

- **FAR** specifies that the function will be accessed via a far call, one using a 32 bit address.
- **PASCAL** tells the compiler to use the PASCAL language's calling convention. This is the same convention used by Visual Basic, and different from C/C++'s usual calling convention.
- **_export** tells the linker to make the function callable from outside the DLL.

Next, we need a Visual Basic program that calls the DLL procedures. FIRSTDLL.MAK does just this, using the DLL procedures to calculate either the sum of or the difference between values in two Text Box controls. The program's form is shown in Figure 8.1, its objects and properties are provided in Listing 8.6, and its code is given in Listing 8.7. Note that in the two **Declare** statements for the DLL functions, you will need to change the DLL path to reflect the location of the DLL file on your disk. Remember also to reference the correct DLL (either FIRSTB.DLL or FIRSTM.DLL), depending upon which compiler you used.

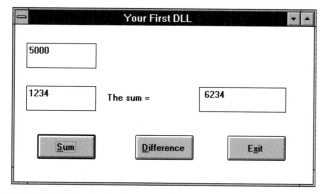

Figure 8.1   FIRSTDLL.FRM finds the sum of, or difference between two values.

Using FIRSTDLL.MAK

This demonstration, presented in Listings 8.6 and 8.7, is stored on disk as FIRSTDLL.MAK and FIRSTDLL.FRM.

Listing 8.6   Objects and Properties in FIRSTDLL.FRM

```
Begin Form frmDLL1
    Caption          =    "Your First DLL"
    Begin CommandButton Command1
        Caption        =    "E&xit"
        Index          =    2
    End
    Begin CommandButton Command1
        Caption        =    "&Difference"
        Index          =    1
    End
    Begin CommandButton Command1
        Caption        =    "&Sum"
        Index          =    0
    End
    Begin TextBox Text3
    End
    Begin TextBox Text2
    End
    Begin TextBox Text1
    End
    Begin Label Label1
    End
End
```

Listing 8.7   Code in FIRSTDLL.FRM

```
Option Explicit

Declare Function SumOf Lib "d:\borlandc\firstb.dll"
 (ByVal X As Long,  ByVal Y As Long) As Long
Declare Function Difference Lib "d:\borlandc\firstb.dll"
 (ByVal X As Long, ByVal Y As Long) As Long

Sub Command1_Click (Index As Integer)

Dim X As Long, Y As Long, Z As Long

Select Case Index
    Case 0
        X = Val(Text1.Text)
        Y = Val(Text2.Text)
```

```
        Z = SumOf(X, Y)
        Text3.Text = Str$(Z)
        Label1.Caption = "The sum ="
    Case 1
        X = Val(Text1.Text)
        Y = Val(Text2.Text)
        Z = Difference(X, Y)
        Text3.Text = Str$(Z)
        Label1.Caption = "The difference ="
    Case 2
        End
End Select

End Sub

Sub Form_Load ()

Text1.Text = "5000"
Text2.Text = "1234"

End Sub
```

Creating a DLL Using a Borland Compiler

Borland C and C++ compilers have their own way of returning floating point values to a calling program. You must take this into account when writing a DLL.

The *stack* is a region of temporary memory storage that a program uses for a variety of purposes. One of the main uses for the stack is to pass information between programs and procedures, including procedures in DLLs. When a program calls a DLL procedure, arguments that it passes to the procedure are placed on the stack, and the procedure retrieves the arguments from the stack. If the procedure is a function—that is, if it returns a value to the calling program—the return value is placed on the stack for retrieval by the calling program. All of this is taken care of automatically—all you need worry about is being sure that your program passes the correct number and type of arguments to each procedure.

Procedures compiled with a Borland C/C++ compiler handle arguments just as you would expect, using the stack. The same goes for integer return values (Basic types Integer and Long), which are returned on the stack. So far, so good. It's with floating point return values (Basic types Single and Double) that Borland strays from the norm. Floating point values are not returned on the stack, but by another method (which need not concern us here). And here's where the problem arises.

If a Visual Basic program calls a DLL function that is declared to return a type Double, Visual Basic expects to find that return value on the stack. If the function was compiled with a Borland compiler, however, the value will not be on the stack. Visual Basic notices that the stack is missing a value that should be there, and generates a "Bad DLL Calling Convention" error message.

For example, say that you wrote a DLL function to add two type DOUBLE values together and return the sum. (You wouldn't use a DLL for such a simple task, of course, but this is just an example!) Your C/C++ function would look like this:

```
double FAR PASCAL _export SumOf(double x, double y)
{
return (x + y);
}
```

Then, you would declare and call it from Visual Basic as follows:

```
Declare Function SumOf LIB "MY.DLL" (X As Double, Y As
  Double) As Double
...
X# = SumOf(Y#, Z#)
```

If the DLL had been compiled with Microsoft Quick C for Windows, there would be no problem. If, however, a Borland compiler had been used, a "Bad DLL Calling Convention" error will occur when execution reaches the function call.

Fortunately, there's a solution to this problem. The trick is to include code in the DLL function that places the return value on the stack where Visual Basic expects to find it. Here's how the function would be modified. First, include the header file dos.h in the DLL source file:

```
#include <dos.h>
```

Next, define a type that is a **FAR** pointer to type double:

```
typedef double FAR * lpDbl;
```

This is simply a convenience that allows you to type **lpDbl** as a synonym for **double FAR** *. Then, rewrite the function as follows:

```
lpDbl FAR PASCAL _export SumOf(double x, double y, WORD dummy)
{
        lpDbl result;
```

```
result = (lpDbl)MK_FP(_SS, dummy);
*result = x + y;
return (result);
}
```

Then, declare and call it from Visual Basic as follows:

```
Declare Function SumOf LIB "MY.DLL" (X As Double, Y As
    Double) As Double
...
X# = SumOf(Y#, Z#)
```

Note that the Visual Basic program ignores the new, third argument in the function. As the argument's name implies, it is a dummy argument whose sole purpose is to "trick" the Borland compiler into reserving an extra place on the stack. The code in the C/C++ function creates a pointer named "result" that points at that stack location, then assigns the return value x + y to that location. On return to the calling program, Visual Basic retrieves the return value from the stack where it "thinks" it should be. Note that the function uses the **return** statement to return the function's value in the normal Borland fashion. This statement is ignored by Visual Basic, but enables the function to be called by a Borland C/C++ program.

This is admittedly some rather advanced and complicated programming. You shouldn't worry if you don't understand it fully. There's really no need to, any more than you need to understand how fuel injection works in order to drive your car.

A Financial Functions DLL

Now let's put what we have learned to work, and create a DLL that can be useful for real programming tasks. The financial DLL presented in this section contains functions for a number of commonly needed financial calculations. You can use this DLL as the basis for a variety of programs, such as a home mortgage calculator, annuity comparisons, and car loan evaluator.

Note: The formulas used in these DLL functions were obtained from published financial references, and I have made every effort to ensure that they produce accurate results. I cannot, however, guarantee that I have considered every eventuality, so any use that you make of these functions is at your own risk. Visual Basic 3.0 now includes a set of financial functions that perform many of the same operations as the functions in this DLL. For VB 2.0 users, this library will provide most of the same features. VB 3.0 users will find this a useful example of a complete DLL.

The Library Functions

The financial DLL contains functions for seven commonly needed financial calculations.

In this section, I will describe the library functions and give an example of the type of problem each can be used for. The terms *present value* and *future value* relate to the fact that a sum of money received now has more value than the same sum received in the future, because of interest you might earn. *Annuity* is a general term for the situation where you receive or pay out a fixed sum of money at regular intervals. Additional terms are defined within the examples.

FVSum (Future Value of a Sum)
This function calculates the future value of a sum of money invested for a specified period at a specified rate of return. Its calling syntax is:

```
FutureValue = FVSum(Principal, Rate, Periods)
```

Principal is the amount being invested.

Rate is the periodic interest rate.

Periods is the number of periods the sum will be invested.

For example, you deposit $1000 in an account that pays 10% annual interest. The value in 10 years is calculated as:

```
FVSum(1000, 0.10, 10)
```

FVAnn (Future Value of an Annuity)
This function calculates the future value of a series of regular investments. Its calling syntax is:

```
FutureValue = FVAnn(Pmt, Rate, Periods)
```

Pmt is the amount being invested each period.

Rate is the periodic interest rate.

Periods is the number of periods.

For example, you deposit $600 per year in an account that pays 8% annual interest. The account value at the end of five years is calculated as

```
FVAnn(600, 0.08, 5)
```

As a second example, you deposit $50 per month in the same account for five years. In this case, the period is one month rather than one year, so the function arguments would be:

```
FVAnn(50, (0.08/12), 5*12)
```

PVSum (Present Value of a future Sum)

This function calculates the present value of a sum you would receive at a future date. The calling syntax is:

```
PresentValue = PVSum(Principal, Rate, Periods)
```

Principal is the amount to be received in the future.

Rate is the periodic interest rate.

Periods is the number of periods.

For example, suppose your employer offers you the option of taking a $1000 bonus now or a $1200 bonus to be paid 16 months from now. If you took the bonus now, you could invest it in an account paying 8% annual interest. To calculate the present value of $1200 paid 16 months from now:

```
PVSum(1200, (0.08 / 12), 16)
```

PVSum tells you that the present value is $1078.97. If you can wait, it is to your advantage to take the $1200 in 16 months rather than the $1000 now.

PVAnn (Present Value of an Annuity)

This function calculates the present value of a series of regular payments you would receive over a specified period. In other words, what lump sum would you need to deposit now in an interest-paying account to end up with the same final amount as a series of regular deposits to the same account. **PVAnn**'s calling calling syntax is:

```
PresentValue = PVAnn(Pmt, Rate, Periods)
```

Pmt is the amount of the periodic payment.

Rate is the periodic interest rate.

Periods is the number of periods for which you will receive payments.

For example, your boss offers you a $1500 cash bonus payable in a lump sum now, or $1800 payable $100 per month over the next 18 months. The lump sum or monthly payments could be invested in an account paying 7% annual interest. You would determine the present value of the 18 monthly payments as follows:

```
PVAnn(100, (0.07 / 12), 18)
```

PVAnn tells you that the present value of the payments is $1704.01. Clearly the monthly payment option is to your advantage.

Pmt (monthly payment on a loan)
    This function tells you the periodic payment on a regular, fixed-rate installment loan (such as a mortgage or an auto loan). The calling syntax is:

```
Pmt(Principal, Rate, Periods)
```

Principal is the loan amount.

Rate is the period interest rate.

Periods is the number of periods of the loan.

For example, to determine the monthly payment on a five year, $12,000 loan at 11.5% you would call the function as follows:

```
MonthlyPayment = Pmt(12000, (0.115 / 12), (5 * 12))
```

The answer is $263.91 per month.

Rate (interest rate necessary for a specified future value)
    This function calculates the periodic interest rate required for a given investment to grow to a specified future value over a specified number of periods. **Rate**'s calling syntax is:

```
Rate(Pv, Fv, Periods)
```

Pv is the present value (the initial investment amount).

Fv is the desired future value.

Periods in the number of interest compounding periods.

For example, you have $10,000 to invest and want it to grow to $15,000 after five years. What is the annual interest rate you must obtain? You would call the function as follows:

```
Rate(10000, 15000, 5)
```

The return value tells you that you must find an investment that pays at least 8.14% per year.

Term (number of periods required to reach a future value)

This function tells you how many regular, fixed payments into an account are required to reach a specified future value. The calling syntax is:

```
NumTerms = Term(Pmt, Fv, Rate)
```

Pmt is the periodic payment.

Fv is the desired future value.

Rate is the periodic interest rate.

For example, you are putting $100 a month into an account that pays 7.5% annual interest. How long will it take for the account to grow to $15,000? You would call the function as follows:

```
Term(1000, 15000, .075)
```

The answer is 106 months, or not quite 9 years.

The DLL Code

This section presents the source code for the financial functions DLL, for both Borland and Microsoft compilers.

Now we can get down to actually creating the DLLs. Once you know the format for a DLL source code file, it's not particularly difficult to do. Our financial functions library is intended to perform relatively simple tasks, so once you know the required formulas you're all set. Listings 8.8 and 8.9 present the module definition file and source code file for use with the Borland C++ compiler, and Listings 8.10 and 8.11 present the files for the Quick C for Windows compiler. If you're not interested in modifying the code, but just want to use the DLL in your Visual Basic program, the compiled DLLs are included on the listing diskette.

Using the Financial Functions DLL

The Borland version is on disk as FINANCEB.DEF, FINANCEB.CPP, and FINANCEB.DLL. The Microsoft version is on disk as: FINANCE-M.DEF, FINANCEM.C, and FINANCEM.DLL.

Listing 8.8   FINANCEB.DEF

```
LIBRARY          FINANCEB
DESCRIPTION      'Finance DLL'
EXETYPE          WINDOWS
CODE             PRELOAD MOVEABLE DISCARDABLE
DATA             PRELOAD MOVEABLE SINGLE
HEAPSIZE         1024
```

Listing 8.9   Code in FINANCEB.CPP

```cpp
/* Financial functions library

        Compiler: Borland C++ version 3.1
        Output: Windows dynamic link library
        Caller: Visual Basic
*/


#include <windows.h>
#include <dos.h>
#include <math.h>


typedef double FAR * lpDbl;

extern "C" lpDbl FAR PASCAL _export FVSum (double prin,
  double rate,  int periods, WORD npDbl);
extern "C" lpDbl FAR PASCAL _export FVAnn (double pmt,
  double rate,  int periods, WORD npDbl);
extern "C" lpDbl FAR PASCAL _export PVSum (double prin,
  double rate,  int periods, WORD npDbl);
extern "C" lpDbl FAR PASCAL _export PVAnn (double pmt,
  double rate,  int periods, WORD npDbl);
extern "C" lpDbl FAR PASCAL _export Pmt (double prin,
  double rate,  int periods, WORD npDbl);
extern "C" lpDbl FAR PASCAL _export Rate (double pv,
  double fv,  int periods, WORD npDbl);
extern "C" lpDbl FAR PASCAL _export Term (double pv,
  double fv,  double rate, WORD npDbl);

lpDbl FAR PASCAL _export FVSum (double prin, double
  rate, int periods, WORD npDbl)
{
/* Returns the future value of a sum.
        prin = principal
        rate = interest rate per period
        periods = number of periods
*/
        lpDbl Result;
        Result = (lpDbl)MK_FP(_SS, npDbl);
```

```
        *Result = prin * pow(rate + 1.0, periods);
        return (Result);
}


lpDbl FAR PASCAL _export FVAnn (double pmt, double
   rate, int periods, WORD npDbl)
{
/* Returns the future value of an annuity.
        pmt = periodic payment
        rate = periodic interest rate
        periods = number of periods
*/
        lpDbl Result;
        Result = (lpDbl)MK_FP(_SS, npDbl);
        *Result = pmt * ((pow(rate + 1.0, periods) - 1.0) / rate);
        return (Result);
}


lpDbl FAR PASCAL _export PVAnn (double pmt, double
   rate, int periods, WORD npDbl)
{
/* Returns the present value of an annuity.
        pmt = periodic payment
        rate = periodic interest rate
        periods = number of periods
*/
        lpDbl Result;
        Result = (lpDbl)MK_FP(_SS, npDbl);
        *Result = pmt * ((1.0 - (1.0 / (pow(rate + 1.0, periods)))))
           / rate;
        return (Result);
}


lpDbl FAR PASCAL _export PVSum (double prin, double
   rate, int periods, WORD npDbl)
{
/* Returns the present value of a future sum.
        prin = principal
        rate = interest rate per period
        periods = number of periods
*/
        lpDbl Result;
        Result = (lpDbl)MK_FP(_SS, npDbl);
        *Result = prin * (1.0 / (pow(rate + 1.0, periods)));
        return (Result);
}


lpDbl FAR PASCAL _export Pmt (double prin, double rate,
   int periods, WORD npDbl)
```

```c
{
/* Returns the periodic payment on a loan.
          prin = principal (amount borrowed)
          rate = interest rate per period
          periods = number of periods
*/
        lpDbl Result;
        Result = (lpDbl)MK_FP(_SS, npDbl);
        *Result = (prin * rate) / (1.0 - pow(rate + 1.0,
           (-periods)));
        return (Result);
}

lpDbl FAR PASCAL _export Rate (double pv, double fv,
  int periods, WORD npDbl)
{
/* Returns the periodic interest rate require for a
given sum (pv)to grow to a specified value (fv) over a certain period.
          pv = present value
          fv = future value
          periods = number of periods
*/
        lpDbl Result;
        Result = (lpDbl)MK_FP(_SS, npDbl);
        *Result = (pow(fv / pv, 1.0 / periods)) - 1;
        return (Result);
}

lpDbl FAR PASCAL _export Term (double pv, double fv,
  double rate, WORD npDbl)
{
/* Returns the number of periods required for a
periodicpayment (pmt) invested at a periodic rate (rate) to grow  to
  a specified value (fv).
          pmt = investment per period
          fv = desired future value
          rate = periodic interest rate
*/
        lpDbl Result;
        Result = (lpDbl)MK_FP(_SS, npDbl);
        fv = fv / (1.0 + rate);
        *Result = log(1.0 + fv * rate / pv) / log(1.0 + rate);
        return (Result);
}

#pragma argsused
int FAR PASCAL LibMain( HANDLE hInstance,
  WORD wDataSegment, WORD wHeapSize, LPSTR lpszCmdLine )
```

```
        {
                if ( wHeapSize != 0 )
                UnlockData( 0 );
                return 1;
        }


#pragma argsused
int FAR PASCAL WEP ( int bSystemExit )
{
return 1;
}
```

Listing 8.10   FINANCEM.DEF

```
LIBRARY          Financem
DESCRIPTION      'Finance DLL'
EXETYPE          WINDOWS
CODE             PRELOAD MOVEABLE DISCARDABLE
DATA             PRELOAD MOVEABLE SINGLE
HEAPSIZE         1024
```

Listing 8.11   Code in FINANCEM.C

```
/* Financial functions library

        Compiler:Microsoft Quick C for Windows v 1.0
        Output: Windows dynamic link library
        Caller: Visual Basic
*/


#include <windows.h>
#include <math.h>

extern double FAR PASCAL _export FVSum (double prin,
  double rate, int periods);
extern double FAR PASCAL _export FVAnn (double pmt,
  double rate, int periods);
extern double FAR PASCAL _export PVSum (double prin,
  double rate, int periods);
extern double FAR PASCAL _export PVAnn (double pmt,
  double rate, int periods);
extern double FAR PASCAL _export Pmt (double prin,
  double rate, int periods);
extern double FAR PASCAL _export Rate (double pv,
  double fv, int periods);
extern double FAR PASCAL _export Term (double pv,
  double fv, double rate);

double FAR PASCAL _export FVSum (double prin, double
```

```
  rate, int periods)
{
/* Returns the future value of a sum.
          prin = principal
          rate = interest rate per period
          periods = number of periods
*/
        double Result;
        Result = prin * pow(rate + 1.0, periods);
        return (Result);
}

double FAR PASCAL _export FVAnn (double pmt, double
  rate, int periods)
{
/* Returns the future value of an annuity.
          pmt = periodic payment
          rate = periodic interest rate
          periods = number of periods
*/
        double Result;
        Result = pmt * ((pow(rate + 1.0, periods) - 1.0) / rate);
        return (Result);
}

double FAR PASCAL _export PVAnn (double pmt, double
  rate, int periods)
{
/* Returns the present value of an annuity.
          pmt = periodic payment
          rate = periodic interest rate
          periods = number of periods
*/
        double Result;
        Result = pmt * ((1.0 - (1.0 / (pow(rate + 1.0, periods)))))
          / rate;
        return (Result);
}

double FAR PASCAL _export PVSum (double prin, double
  rate, int periods)
{
/* Returns the present value of a future sum.
          prin = principal
          rate = interest rate per period
          periods = number of periods
*/
        double Result;
        Result = prin * (1.0 / (pow(rate + 1.0, periods)));
```

```
        return (Result);
}


double FAR PASCAL _export Pmt (double prin, double
   rate, int periods)
{
/* Returns the periodic payment on a loan.
           prin = principal (amount borrowed)
           rate = interest rate per period
           periods = number of periods
*/
        double Result;
        Result = (prin * rate) / (1.0 - pow(rate + 1.0,
           (-periods)));
        return (Result);
}


double FAR PASCAL _export Rate (double pv, double fv,
   int periods)
{
/*      Returns the periodic interest rate require for a given sum (pv)
        to grow to a specified value (fv) over a certain period.
           pv = present value
           fv = future value
           periods = number of periods
*/
        double Result;
        Result = (pow(fv / pv, 1.0 / periods)) - 1;
        return (Result);
}


double FAR PASCAL _export Term (double pv, double fv,
   double rate)
{
/* Returns the number of periods required for a
periodic payment (pmt) invested at a periodic rate (rate) to grow to
a specified value (fv).
           pmt = investment per period
           fv = desired future value
           rate = periodic interest rate
*/
        double Result;
        fv = fv / (1.0 + rate);
        Result = log(1.0 + fv * rate / pv) / log(1.0 + rate);
        return (Result);
}


int FAR PASCAL LibMain( HANDLE hInstance, WORD
   wDataSegment, WORD wHeapSize, LPSTR lpszCmdLine )
```

```
{
        if ( wHeapSize != 0 )
        UnlockData( 0 );
        return 1;
}
```

Trying It Out

I just know that you are anxious to find out what the monthly payments on that new Porsche will be! What better excuse do you need for trying out the financial functions DLL?

I've created a simple "financial calculator" program that makes use of the financial functions DLL. The program's one form, shown in Figure 8.2, has a menu from which you select the type of calculation that you want to perform. There are three Text Box controls for entering the inputs to the calculation, and a fourth Text Box for displaying the answer. As it stands, it is pretty basic, so there's lots of room for improvement if you want to tinker! You will, however, probably need to change the **Declare** statements so the program looks for the proper DLL in the proper directory.

There's one aspect of FINANCE.FRM that deserves mention. This program is a good example of how you can make a single form serve multiple duties. Based on the user's selection of what calculation is desired, the form's title and labels are changed to accurately guide the user's entry of data. In addition, a global flag is set to control the way the data is handled and which DLL function is called. This is a much more efficient and flexible approach than creating a separate data input form for each of the seven financial calculations.

Note: Look for the use of "aliasing" in the **Declare** statements to prevent conflicts with equivalent VB 3.0 functions.

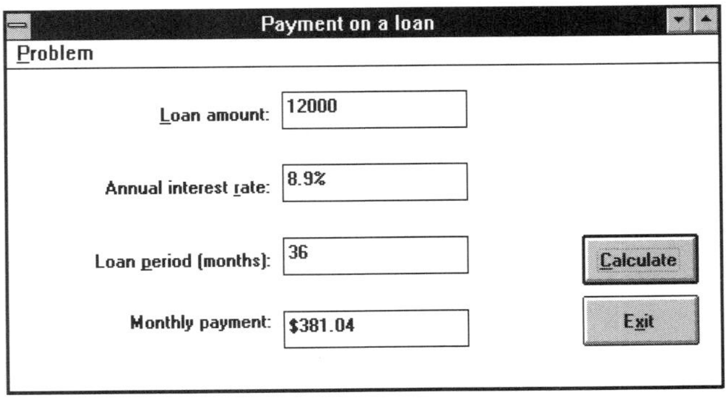

Figure 8.2   The financial calculator in action.

Using FINANCE.MAK

This demonstration, presented in Listings 8.12 and 8.13, is stored on disk as FINANCE.MAK and FINANCE.FRM.

Listing 8.12   Objects and Properties in FINANCE.FRM

```
Begin Form Form1
   BorderStyle       =    1  'Fixed Single
   Caption           =    "Financial Calculator"
   Begin CommandButton cmdExit
      Caption        =    "E&xit"
   End
   Begin CommandButton cmdCalculate
      Caption        =    "&Calculate"
   End
   Begin TextBox Text4
      TabIndex       =    8
   End
   Begin TextBox Text3
      TabIndex       =    5
   End
   Begin TextBox Text2
      TabIndex       =    3
   End
   Begin TextBox Text1
      TabIndex       =    1
   End
   Begin Label Label4
      Alignment      =    1  'Right Justify
      TabIndex       =    6
   End
   Begin Label Label3
      Alignment      =    1  'Right Justify
      TabIndex       =    4
   End
   Begin Label Label2
      Alignment      =    1  'Right Justify
      TabIndex       =    2
   End
   Begin Label Label1
      Alignment      =    1  'Right Justify
      TabIndex       =    0
   End
   Begin Menu mnuProblem
      Caption        =    "&Problem"
      Begin Menu mnuChoice
         Caption     =    "Present value of a sum"
```

```
                    Index           =    0
              End
              Begin Menu mnuChoice
                    Caption         =    "Future value of a sum"
                    Index           =    1
              End
              Begin Menu mnuChoice
                    Caption         =    "Present value of an annuity"
                    Index           =    2
              End
              Begin Menu mnuChoice
                    Caption         =    "Future value of an annuity"
                    Index           =    3
              End
              Begin Menu mnuChoice
                    Caption         =    "Payment on a loan"
                    Index           =    4
              End
              Begin Menu mnuChoice
                    Caption         =    "Interest rate required"
                    Index           =    5
              End
              Begin Menu mnuChoice
                    Caption         =    "Term required"
                    Index           =    6
              End
              Begin Menu mnuSep
                    Caption         =    "-"
              End
              Begin Menu mnuExit
                    Caption         =    "Exit"
              End
        End
End
```

Listing 8.13   Code in FINANCE.FRM

```
Option Explicit

Declare Function FVSum Lib "d:\borlandc\financeb.dll"
   (ByVal Prin#,  ByVal IntRate#, ByVal Periods%) As Double
Declare Function FVAnn Lib "d:\borlandc\financeb.dll"
   (ByVal Pmt#,  ByVal IntRate#, ByVal Periods%) As Double
Declare Function PVSum Lib "d:\borlandc\financeb.dll"
   (ByVal Prin#,  ByVal IntRate#, ByVal Periods%) As Double
Declare Function PVAnn Lib "d:\borlandc\financeb.dll"
   (ByVal Pmt#,  ByVal IntRate#, ByVal Periods%) As Double
Declare Function PmtAmt Lib "financeb.dll" Alias "Pmt"
   (ByVal Prin#,  ByVal IntRate#, ByVal Periods%) As Double
```

```
Declare Function IntRate Lib Alias "Rate" "d:\borlandc\financeb.dll"
   (ByVal ThePv#,  ByVal TheFv#, ByVal Periods%) As Double
Declare Function Term Lib "d:\borlandc\financeb.dll"
   (ByVal ThePv#,  ByVal TheFv#, ByVal IntRate#) As Double

Dim Choice As Integer

Const MB_ICONSTOP = 16

Sub cmdCalculate_Click ()

Dim A As Double, B As Double, C As Integer, D As Double
Dim Answer As Double

' Get values from data entry Text Boxes.
Select Case Choice
    Case 0 To 4
        A = Val(Text1.Text)

        ' See if user entered % sign - e.g. "9.5%"
        ' rather than "0.095".
        If Right$(Text2.Text, 1) = "%" Then
            B = Val(Left$(Text2.Text, Len(Text2.Text) - 1))
            B = B / 1200#
        Else
            B = Val(Text2.Text) / 12#
        End If
        C = Val(Text3.Text)
    Case 5
        A = Val(Text1.Text)
        B = Val(Text2.Text)
        C = Val(Text3.Text)
    Case 6
        A = Val(Text1.Text)
        B = Val(Text2.Text)

        If Right$(Text3.Text, 1) = "%" Then
            D = Val(Left$(Text3.Text, Len(Text3.Text) - 1))
            D = D / 1200#
        Else
            D = Val(Text3.Text) / 12#
        End If
End Select

' Verify that valid values have been entered.
If (A <= 0) Or (B <= 0) Or (C <= 0 And D <= 0) Then
    MsgBox "Invalid value(s) entered", MB_ICONSTOP, "Error"
    Text1.SetFocus
    Exit Sub
```

```vb
End If

' Call the proper DLL function.
Select Case Choice
    Case 0
        Answer = PVSum(A, B, C)
    Case 1
        Answer = FVSum(A, B, C)
    Case 2
        Answer = PVAnn(A, B, C)
    Case 3
        Answer = FVAnn(A, B, C)
    Case 4
        Answer = PmtAmt(A, B, C)
    Case 5
        Answer = 12 * IntRate(A, B, C)
    Case 6
        Answer = Term(A, B, D)
End Select

' Format the answer properly and display it.
Select Case Choice
    Case 0 To 4
        Text4.Text = Format$(Answer, "Currency")
    Case 5
        Text4.Text = Format$(Answer, "Percent")
    Case 6
        Text4.Text = Str$(Int(Answer) + 1) & " months"
End Select

End Sub

Sub cmdExit_Click ()

End

End Sub

Sub Form_Load ()

Text1.Text = ""
Text2.Text = ""
Text3.Text = ""
Text4.Text = ""
Show
Text1.SetFocus

End Sub
```

```
Sub mnuChoice_Click (Index As Integer)

' Put appropriate caption in the form's title bar.
Form1.Caption = mnuChoice(Index).Caption
Choice = Index

Text1.Text = ""
Text2.Text = ""
Text3.Text = ""
Text4.Text = ""


' Set up the form's labels for the selected calculation.
Select Case Index
    Case 0
        Label1.Caption = "&Future value:"
        Label2.Caption = "Annual interest &rate:"
        Label3.Caption = "Investment &period (months):"
        Label4.Caption = "Present value:"
    Case 1
        Label1.Caption = "&Initial investment:"
        Label2.Caption = "Annual interest &rate:"
        Label3.Caption = "Investment &period (months):"
        Label4.Caption = "Future value:"
    Case 2
        Label1.Caption = "&Monthly payment:"
        Label2.Caption = "Annual interest &rate:"
        Label3.Caption = "Investment &period (months):"
        Label4.Caption = "Present value:"
    Case 3
        Label1.Caption = "&Monthly payment:"
        Label2.Caption = "Annual interest &rate:"
        Label3.Caption = "Investment &period (months):"
        Label4.Caption = "Future value:"
    Case 4
        Label1.Caption = "&Loan amount:"
        Label2.Caption = "Annual interest &rate:"
        Label3.Caption = "Loan &period (months):"
        Label4.Caption = "Monthly payment:"
    Case 5
        Label1.Caption = "&Initial investment:"
        Label2.Caption = "Desired future &value:"
        Label3.Caption = "Investment &period (months):"
        Label4.Caption = "Required annual interest rate:"
    Case 6
        Label1.Caption = "Periodic &investment:"
        Label2.Caption = "Desired future &value"
        Label3.Caption = "Annual interest &rate:"
        Label4.Caption = "Required period (months):"
End Select
```

```
Text1.SetFocus

End Sub

Sub mnuExit_Click ()

End

End Sub
```

Working with Files

isual Basic provides a variety of tools for working with disk files. In particular, the Drive, Directory, and File List boxes are wonderfully convenient for creating any number of useful file utilities. In this chapter, I present three Visual Basic file utilities that I have found to be helpful in my day-to-day work. You may find these programs useful as-is, or you might use the programming techniques to develop your own specialized utilities. The chapter ends with a couple of less ambitious, but still useful, file techniques.

Find a File Anywhere on a Disk

Quick! Can you tell me how many copies of MOUSE.COM there are on your hard disk? Or, if you're a programmer, you may wonder how many outdated copies of LINK.EXE are lurking in dusty corners of your drive. A program that lets you search an entire disk or subdirectory branch for files can be extremely useful. You can buy one commercially, but why spend your hard-earned money when it's so easy to write your own in Visual Basic?

What Should the Program Do?

We'll start by deciding on the features that we want in a file find utility.

It goes without saying that we need to be able to specify the type of files to find (*.EXE, DATA.*, PROG??.FRM, etc.), and also the disk drive to search. We should also be able to specify a start directory for the search. In other words, the program will search a specified directory and all of its subdirectories. This gives the option of restricting the search to a portion of the disk. If it is necessary to search the entire disk, simply specify the root directory as the start directory.

A desirable feature is the option to list not only filenames, but also to include standard file information—the date and time it was last modified and its size in bytes. This is particularly valuable when searching for multiple versions of the same file, because it permits you to determine which version is most recent.

Finally, the user should have the ability to abort the search while it is in progress. Searching a large disk can take a while, and the user should not be forced to sit twiddling his or her fingers if they made an error entering the search parameters!

Using the Directory List Box Control

The Directory List Box control is at the heart of our File Find utility. You use it to find all subdirectories that exist under the starting directory.

To search a single subdirectory for matching files is no challenge, but how can you extend a search to all its subdirectories, their subdirectories, and so on until the entire tree has been searched? The answer lies in the abilities of the Directory List Box control. At run time, this control displays the disk's hierarchical directory structure. Each item in the display has an index number, and the index number sequence is based on the directories and subdirectories present when the control is created at run time. Here's how the index works:

- The currently expanded directory has index –1.

- Directories above the current directory are represented by negative indexes, with higher absolute values the further "above" you go. For example, the parent directory of the current directory has index –2, and the directory above that has index –3.

- The number of directories below the currently expanded directory (i.e., its subdirectories) is indicated by the ListCount property; these subdirectories have indexes ranging from 0 to ListCount –1.

It's this third characteristic of the index that we will use. It permits us to write code that will start in a specified directory, then "wind down" through all the subdirectories no matter how many levels there are. The process is iterative, and here's how you make it work.

1. Make the specified start directory current.
2. Search the current directory for matching files. If any are found, add them to the file list.
3. Are there any subdirectories? If not, we're done with this subdirectory. If so, use the ListCount and List() properties to create a list of all the subdirectories.
4. Make the first subdirectory in the list current.
5. Return to step 2.

This process may be clearer when you look at the program code in Listing 9.2.

The FileFind Utility

We are now ready to create a FileFind utility. I think you'll be surprised at how little code it takes!

The FileFind utility is shown in Figure 9.1, and its objects, properties, and code are in Listings 9.1 and 9.2. The form's controls include a Drive List Box and a Directory List Box that are used to select the drive and starting directory, and a Text Box for specifying the file search pattern; the default is *.*. A Check Box lets the user specify whether the list of matching files is to include time, date, and size information.

One important control not visible in the figure is a second Directory List Box with its Visible property set to false. This Directory List Box is used internally by the program to access the names of the disk's subdirectories. Note that even though the control is never visible, it is still fully functional.

You can use this program as a stand-alone utility, or incorporate it in a larger project. With minor modifications, the FileFind form could be used to delete selected files, or to allow the user to select a file for reading and writing.

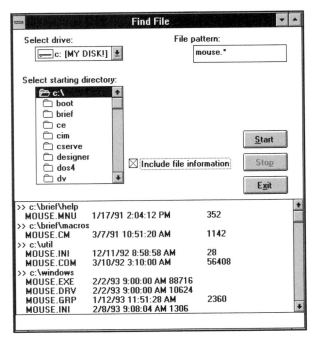

Figure 9.1   The FileFind utility in operation.

Using FILEFIND.MAK

This demonstration, presented in Listings 9.1 and 9.2, is stored on disk as FILEFIND.MAK and FILEFIND.FRM

Listing 9.1   Objects and Properties in FILEFIND.FRM

```
Begin Form Form1
   Caption          =   "Find Files"
   Begin ListBox lstFiles
   End
   Begin CheckBox chkFileInfo
      Caption       =   "Include file information"
   End
   Begin DirListBox dirHidden
      Visible       =   0   'False
   End
   Begin DirListBox dirStart
   End
   Begin DriveListBox Drive1
   End
   Begin CommandButton Command1
      Caption       =   "E&xit"
      Index         =   2
   End
   Begin CommandButton Command1
      Caption       =   "Sto&p"
      Index         =   1
   End
   Begin CommandButton Command1
      Caption       =   "&Start"
      Index         =   0
   End
   Begin TextBox txtPattern
   End
   Begin Label Label3
      Alignment     =   1   'Right Justify
      Caption       =   "File pattern:"
   End
   Begin Label Label2
      Alignment     =   1   'Right Justify
      Caption       =   "Select starting directory:"
   End
   Begin Label Label1
      Alignment     =   1   'Right Justify
      Caption       =   "Select drive:"
   End
End
```

Listing 9.2 Code in FILEFIND.FRM

```
Option Explicit

' Global variable to abort search.
Dim Stopp As Integer

Sub Command1_Click (Index As Integer)

Select Case Index
    Case 0    'Start
        Call StartSearch
    Case 1    'Stop
        Stopp = True
    Case 2 ' Exit
        End
End Select

End Sub

Sub dirHidden_Change ()

Dim Path As String, FileName As String
Dim FileName1 As String, Path1 As String, Entry As String
Dim NumDirs As Integer, X As Integer, Y As Integer
Dim DirAdded As Integer

' Here's where the actual search happens.

' Add a backslash at the end of Path if necessary.
Path = dirHidden.Path

If Right$(Path, 1) <> "\" Then
    Path = Path & "\"
End If

' The full search pattern is the current path plus the
' file pattern from the txtPattern Text Box.
Path1 = Path & txtPattern.Text

' The FileName function returns an empty string if
' a matching file is not found, and the filename if
' a matching file is found.
FileName = Dir$(Path1)

DirAdded = False

' Loop as long as a matching file is found.
Do Until FileName = ""
```

```
' If the directory name has not already been added to
' the List Box, add it now.
    If (DirAdded = False) Then
        lstFiles.AddItem ">> " & dirHidden.Path
        DirAdded = True
    End If


' Start building the next List Box entry.
    Entry = "      " & FileName

' If the FileInfo check box is checked, add the
' file's date, time, and length to the entry.
' Chr$(9) = Tab
    If chkFileInfo.Value Then
        FileName1 = Path & FileName
        Entry = Entry & Chr$(9) & Chr$(9) & FileDateTime(FileName1)
        Entry = Entry & Chr$(9) & FileLen(FileName1)
    End If

' Add the entry to the List Box.
    lstFiles.AddItem Entry

' Look for the next matching file.
    FileName = Dir$
Loop

' How many subdirectories are in the current directory?
NumDirs = dirHidden.ListCount

' Put the subdirectory names in an array.
ReDim DirList(NumDirs) As String

For X = 0 To NumDirs - 1
    DirList(X) = dirHidden.List(X)
Next X

' For each subdirectory, repeat the search process. Call DoEvents
' to enable user to abort the search by clicking the Stop
' Command Button.
For X = 0 To NumDirs - 1
    dirHidden.Path = DirList(X)
    Y = DoEvents()
    If Stopp Then
        Exit Sub
    End If
Next X

End Sub
```

```
Sub Drive1_Change ()

' If the user changes drives, pass the new path
' to the Directory List Box control.
dirStart.Path = Drive1.Drive

End Sub

Sub Form_Load ()

Stopp = False
txtPattern.Text = "*.EXE"
lstFiles.Clear

End Sub

Sub StartSearch ()

' Begin a search.

' Be sure Abort flag is not set.
Stopp = False

' Clear the List Box.
lstFiles.Clear

' Disable all controls except the Stop Command Button.
Command1(0).Enabled = False
Command1(1).Enabled = True
Command1(2).Enabled = False
Drive1.Enabled = False
dirStart.Enabled = False
txtPattern.Enabled = False

' If the invisible Directory List Box is already pointing to
' the same directory as the visible Directory List Box, we must
' trigger a Change event. If not, change its Path property,
' which will automatically trigger a Change event.

' It is the dirHidden.Change event that triggers
' the search process.
Screen.MousePointer = 11

If dirHidden.Path = dirStart.Path Then
    dirHidden_Change
Else
    dirHidden.Path = dirStart.Path
End If
```

```
' We reach here after the search is complete.
' Re-enable all controls except the Stop Command Button.
Screen.MousePointer = 0
Command1(0).Enabled = True
Command1(1).Enabled = False
Command1(2).Enabled = True
Drive1.Enabled = True
dirStart.Enabled = True
txtPattern.Enabled = True

End Sub


Sub txtPattern_GotFocus ()

' Highlight Text Box contents when Text Box gets the focus.
txtPattern.SelStart = 0
txtPattern.SelLength = Len(txtPattern.Text)

End Sub
```

Find Text in a File

Have you ever needed to locate all files that contain a particular section of text? It's a huge waste of time to open each file individually using a text editor or word processor and search for the text. Wouldn't you just love a neat little program that quickly scans a group of files and displays a list of those that contain the text you specified? Are you interested? Then read on!

What Features Do We Want?

There are many features that could be implemented in a text find utility.

The basic features that any text find utility must have are specifying the files to search, specifying the search text, and displaying a list of those files where the text was found. We might also want the option of performing a case-sensitive search, and the ability to cancel a search in progress. Finally, we want to be able to search files that are not pure text files. The most common example of this is word processing document files, which usually contain a lot of non-ASCII information that serves to specify formatting, fonts, and the like. Even so, the actual "text" in these files is in ASCII format, enabling us to use standard text comparison methods to find text strings.

This sounds like a good design specification for a useful program, but what other features can we dream up? Here's a few:

- Determine how many times the search text appears in each file.
- Display the section of the file where the search text is found.
- Find "whole word" matches only.
- Automatically search subdirectories as well as the selected directory.

I think you get the idea—there are plenty of other features that could be added to a text searching program. If you think any additional features would be useful to you, then it would be a good programming exercise to modify the program. For the demonstration, however, we'll stick to the basics.

How Does It Work?

The text find utility is remarkably simple to program.

Once the user has selected a directory and entered a file pattern and the search text, how does the program search each matching file? To maximize speed, and to ensure that the program can deal with non-text files, we will use binary mode to read the files. Using the **Get** statement, each file can be read, a block at a time, into a string variable that serves as a buffer. Then, the **Instr** function can be used to tell us if the target text is present in the buffer. In more precise terms:

1. Open the file.
2. Read 4096 bytes into a string variable.
3. Use **Instr** to determine if the target text is present. If so, add the file-name to the match list and go to step 5. If not, continue with step 4.
4. Has the entire file been checked? If not, return to step 2.
5. Close the file.
6. Is there another file to check? If so, return to step 1. If not, we're finished.

That sounds pretty straightforward, doesn't it? Now let's get to work.

The TextFind Utility

This section presents a basic but fully functional text finding utility.

FINDTEXT.MAK is a program for a text finding utility that meets all of the requirements that we developed above. The program is shown in operation

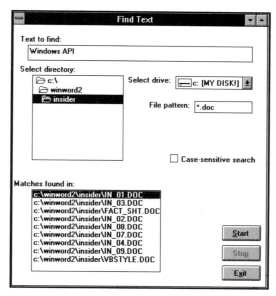

Figure 9.2 The FINDTEXT text finding utility.

is Figure 9.2. The form's objects and properties are given in Listing 9.3, and its code in Listing 9.4. You can use the program without modification as a stand-alone utility. It could also be readily modified to serve as a component of a larger program.

Using FINDTEXT.MAK

This demonstration, presented in Listings 9.3 and 9.4, is stored on disk as FINDTEXT.MAK and FINDTEXT.FRM.

Listing 9.3 Objects and Properties in FINDTEXT.FRM

```
Begin Form Form1
   Caption       =    "Find Text"
   Begin TextBox txtFind
   End
   Begin ListBox lstFiles
   End
   Begin CheckBox chkCaseSensitive
      Caption      =    "Case-sensitive search"
   End
   Begin DirListBox Dir1
   End
   Begin DriveListBox Drive1
```

```
    End
    Begin CommandButton Command1
        Caption         =    "E&xit"
    End
    Begin CommandButton Command1
        Caption         =    "Sto&p"
    End
    Begin CommandButton Command1
        Caption         =    "&Start"
    End
    Begin TextBox txtPattern
        Text            =    "*.*"
    End
    Begin Label Label5
        Alignment       =    1   'Right Justify
        Caption         =    "Matches found in:"
    End
    Begin Label Label4
        Alignment       =    1   'Right Justify
        Caption         =    "Text to find:"
    End
    Begin Label Label3
        Alignment       =    1   'Right Justify
        Caption         =    "File pattern:"
    End
    Begin Label Label2
        Alignment       =    1   'Right Justify
        Caption         =    "Select directory:"
    End
    Begin Label Label1
        Alignment       =    1   'Right Justify
        Caption         =    "Select drive:"
    End
End
```

Listing 9.4   Code in FINDTEXT.FRM

```
Option Explicit

' Global variable to abort search.
Dim Stopp As Integer

Const MB_ICONSTOP = 16
Const BUF_SIZE = 4096


Sub Command1_Click (Index As Integer)

Select Case Index
    Case 0 'Start
```

```
        Call StartSearch
    Case 1 'Stop
        Stopp = True
    Case 2        ' Exit
        End
End Select

End Sub

Sub Drive1_Change ()

' If the user changes drives, pass the new path
' to the Directory List Box control.
Dir1.Path = Drive1.Drive

End Sub

Sub Form_Load ()

Stopp = False
txtPattern.Text = "*.*"
lstFiles.Clear
Show
txtFind.SetFocus

End Sub

Sub StartSearch ()

Dim FileNum As Integer, FileName As String, Path As String
Dim FoundFile As String, Found As Integer, Buffer As String

' Begin a search.
lstFiles.Clear

' Create the filename.
Path = Dir1.Path

If Right$(Path, 1) <> "\" Then
    Path = Path & "\"
End If

FileName = Path & txtPattern.Text

FoundFile = Dir$(FileName)

' Be sure there is at least one matching file.
If FoundFile = "" Then
    MsgBox "No matching files.", MB_ICONSTOP, "File not found"
```

```
    Exit Sub
End If

' Be sure there is something entered in the "Text to find" box.
If txtFind.Text = "" Then
        MsgBox "No search text specified.", MB_ICONSTOP, "No search
text"
        Exit Sub
End If

' Clear the Abort flag.
Stopp = False

' Clear the List Box.
lstFiles.Clear

' Display an hourglass mouse pointer.
Screen.MousePointer = 11

' Disable all controls except the Stop Command Button.
Command1(0).Enabled = False
Command1(1).Enabled = True
Command1(2).Enabled = False
Drive1.Enabled = False
Dir1.Enabled = False
txtPattern.Enabled = False
txtFind.Enabled = False

Do While FoundFile <> ""
    FoundFile = Path & FoundFile
    Found = False
    FileNum = FreeFile
    Open FoundFile For Binary As #FileNum

' Read the file one buffer at a time until end
' of file is reached.
    Do While Not EOF(FileNum)
        Buffer = Space$(BUF_SIZE)
        Get #FileNum, , Buffer

' Call DoEvents to permit program to respond
' to user selecting the Stop Command Button.
        DoEvents

' See if the search text is present in the buffer.
        If TextFound(Buffer) Then Found = True
        If Found Then Exit Do
    Loop
```

```
       Close #FileNum

' If there was a match, add the filename to
' the List Box.
    If Found Then
        lstFiles.AddItem FoundFile
    End If

' Look for the next matching file.
    FoundFile = Dir$

' Exit if the user has selected the Stop Command Button.
    If Stopp Then
        lstFiles.AddItem "May be incomplete; user interrupt"
        Exit Do
    End If

Loop

' We reach here after the search is complete.
' Re-enable all controls except the Stop Command Button.
Screen.MousePointer = 0
Command1(0).Enabled = True
Command1(1).Enabled = False
Command1(2).Enabled = True
Drive1.Enabled = True
Dir1.Enabled = True
txtPattern.Enabled = True
txtFind.Enabled = True

' Set focus to the List Box.
lstFiles.SetFocus

If lstFiles.ListCount = 0 Then
    lstFiles.AddItem "No matches found"
End If

End Sub

Function TextFound (Buffer As String) As Integer

Dim Compare As Integer

' Did user request a case-sensitive search?
If chkCaseSensitive.Value = 1 Then
    Compare = 0
Else
    Compare = 1
End If
```

```
' Return True only if the text is found.
If InStr(1, Buffer, txtFind.Text, Compare) Then
    TextFound = True
Else
    TextFound = False
End If

End Function

Sub txtFind_GotFocus ()

' Highlight Text Box contents when Text Box gets the focus.
txtFind.SelStart = 0
txtFind.SelLength = Len(txtFind.Text)

End Sub

Sub txtPattern_GotFocus ()

' Highlight Text Box contents when Text Box gets the focus.
txtPattern.SelStart = 0
txtPattern.SelLength = Len(txtPattern.Text)

End Sub
```

Writing a Cross-Reference Utility

A cross-reference utility can be a very useful programmer's tool. In this section, we will use Visual Basic to write a program that can generate a cross-referenced listing of your Visual Basic programs.

What Is a Cross-Reference Utility?

A cross-reference utility generates a list of all the variable and procedure names in your programs, and identifies the lines on which they are used.

Every program's source code contains *identifiers*. An identifier is nothing more than a program item's name—a variable, a symbolic constant, a language keyword, a function name, and so on. For small Visual Basic programs, it's not too much of a problem to keep track of the identifiers being used—and you can always use the Find command to track them down if necessary. Once a program starts to grow in size, however, it will become more and more difficult to remember where in the source code each identifier appears. When debugging a program, or simply trying to keep track of its logical structure, you might find it very useful to know the exact locations of each identifier.

Here's where a cross-reference utility comes in handy. For any source code file, it can produce a listing of every identifier name and the numbers of all of the lines where that identifier appears. Part of a cross-reference list is shown here:

```
GetMenu:  68, 85
GetMenuItemID:  72, 92, 98, 104
GetSubMenu:  70, 86
hMenu:  70, 72, 74, 81, 85, 86, 93, 99, 105
hSubMenu:  81, 86, 92, 98, 104
hWnd:  68, 85
id:  81, 92, 93, 98, 99, 104, 105
Lib:  68, 70, 72, 74
lpString:  74
MF_BITMAP:  76, 93, 99, 105
MF_CHECKED:  77, 93
```

You can see in this example that the identifier GetMenu was used on lines 68 and 85, and so on. Using this type of information, you can quickly locate certain types of program bugs. A cross-reference list is particularly useful if you do not use the **Option Explicit** statement to require explicit variable declarations. A misspelled variable name, which is a frequent cause of bugs in programs without **Option Explicit**, will be obvious on the list.

Save Your Source Code as Text

A cross-reference utility can operate only on text files. Visual Basic's default is to save code in a special binary format. To save a program module for input into the cross-reference utility, you must use the Save File As command with the Save As Text option enabled to save to code in ASCII text format.

What Features Do We Want in the Program?

There are a number of features that our cross-reference utility should incorporate.

At its most basic, a cross-reference utility will read the specified source code file and generate the cross-referenced listing. What other features might be desirable? Here's what I came up with:

- The ability to cross-reference code in both form and Basic modules.
- Display the generated cross-reference in a scrollable on-screen list with the option of saving it to disk as well.
- The option of omitting or including Basic keywords (Print, Dim, Input, etc.).
- Can be modified to handle non-Basic source code without too much effort.

I imagine that you will be able to suggest additional features, but this list will do for a start!

How Can We Extract Identifier Names from Code?

The technique for locating and extracting identifiers is based on the fact that only certain characters are permitted in identifiers.

The name of a Visual Basic identifier must adhere to certain rules: It must begin with a letter and contain only letters, digits, and the underscore character. Since we would like object.property specifiers such as **Text1.Text** to be considered as identifiers, we will add the period to this list of "OK" characters. Given these rules, we can devise an algorithm for locating identifiers in source code, distinguishing them from non-identifier elements such as numbers, white space, and literal strings, and extracting them to the cross-referenced list.

The program reads the source code file one line at a time and passes each line to the parsing procedure. This procedure performs a variety of preprocessing functions that will be described shortly; the end result is that each line of code, trimmed of leading and trailing spaces, is passed to the procedure that extracts the identifiers.

The extraction procedure maintains two flags. The Mode flag specifies whether the procedure is processing code or is processing a literal string (characters enclosed in double quotation marks). The InIdentifier flag specifies whether the procedure is processing an identifier.

Each line of code is processed one character at a time, from left to right. At the start of each line the Mode flag is set to Code, and the InIdentifier flag is set to False. As each character is read it is examined and one of the following happens:

- If the character is a letter then it marks the start of an identifier. The program stores the position of the character in the line and sets the InIdentifier flag to True.
- If the character is a double quotation mark, it marks the start of a literal string. The Mode flag is set to "String."

- Any other character and we're not interested; no action is taken.

These rules apply, of course, only if Mode = "Code" and InIdentifier = False. If Mode = "String" then each character is interpreted by these rules:

- If the character is a double quotation mark, it marks the end of the literal string. Set Mode back to Code.
- Otherwise, the character is part of the literal string and we're not interested; no action is taken.

Likewise, there are different rules that apply when InIdentifier = True. They are as follows:

- If the character is a letter, digit, underscore, or period it is part of the identifier; no action is taken.
- Otherwise, the character marks the end of the identifier. Extract the identifier (using the start position stored earlier when the first character of the identifier was detected), and set InIdentifier to False.

There's one more thing. Anytime a single quotation mark character is encountered while Mode = Code, then it marks the beginning of a comment and the remainder of the line can be discarded.

That's all there is to it. If you look at the source code in Listing 9.6 it may be a bit confusing at first because there are, unavoidably, a lot of nested loops and **If** blocks. If you understand what the code does, however, it will be easier to pick it apart and see how it works!

The Cross-Reference Utility

This section presents the details of a fully functional cross-reference utility that is specifically designed for Visual Basic programs.

The actual extraction of the identifier names, as described in the previous section, may be the most challenging part of the cross-reference utility, but it is only part of the overall programming task. The user must be permitted to choose a file and select options, source file text must be preprocessed before being sent to the extraction routine, and the extracted identifier names must be organized and displayed along with their line numbers. Much of this is routine programming, but I will go over the basic outline of the code here.

The program includes a File Open dialog box that permits the user to select a source code file to process. Since we are interested in Visual Basic files, the dialog box is set to display only files ending with a .BAS or .FRM extension. Rather than create a File Open dialog box from scratch, I have used the one developed in the *Creating a Combined Drive/Directory List Box* section later in this chapter.

If the user selects a form file (*.FRM) for processing, two tasks are performed. The first, which is not absolutely necessary, is to verify that the file is in fact a valid form file. Form files saved directly from Visual Basic 2.0 have "Version 2.00" on the first line (remember, all program files must be saved as text to be processed by this utility). If the version line is missing (as it might be in a form definition file from another source) the first line will start with "Begin." The cross-reference utility checks to see that the first line of a .FRM file starts with either "Version" or "Begin." If it doesn't, a warning is displayed and the user is given the option of continuing or aborting.

The second .FRM file task is essential. In order for the cross-reference utility to process code, it must first get past the form and control definitions at the beginning of the file. The program does this by making use of the fact that the form and each of its controls is defined by a block that starts with a **Begin** line and ends with an **End** line. You can see this in any of the object and property listings in this book, which were taken directly from .FRM files.

Here's how it works. The program maintains a counter that starts at 0. Every time a line starting with **Begin** is encountered, the counter is incremented by 1. When a line beginning with **End** is encountered, the counter is decremented by 1. When the counter reaches 0, the last line of the form and control definitions has been reached and the program can start processing code lines.

For Basic files (*.BAS), the above steps are not necessary. There are no "non-code" lines to pass over, and since the first line of code in the file can be just about anything, there's no practical method of verifying that it is a valid Basic file.

After reading each line from the source code file, preprocessing code discards blank lines and comment lines (those beginning with ' or REM). Code lines are trimmed of leading and trailing spaces and then passed to the parsing procedure. As each identifier is extracted, it is compared against a list of identifiers already found and, if the user has selected the Omit Basic Keywords option, against a list of Basic keywords. The final cross-reference list that is constructed contains one line for each identifier, listing the identifier name and the line numbers where it occurs. The list is displayed in a sorted List Box and optionally written to disk. The cross-referenced listing file is given the same name as the source file with an .XRF extension.

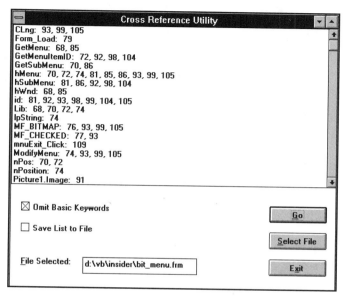

Figure 9.3 The cross-reference utility in action.

CROSSREF's main form is shown in Figure 9.3. The objects and properties for the project are in Listing 9.5, and its code is provided in Listing 9.6. Remember that the project also uses the File Open dialog box, FILEOPEN.FRM, that is presented in this chapter's final section.

Using CROSSREF.MAK

This demonstration, presented in Listings 9.5 and 9.6, is stored on disk as CROSSREF.MAK and CROSSREF.FRM.

Listing 9.5 Objects and Properties in CROSSREF.FRM

```
Begin Form frmXRef
   Caption        =   "Cross Reference Utility"
   Begin CheckBox chkSaveToFile
      Caption     =   "Save List to File"
   End
   Begin ListBox lstXref
      Height      =   3672
      Sorted      =   -1   'True
   End
   Begin CheckBox chkOmitBasicKeywords
      Caption     =   "Omit Basic Keywords"
```

```
        Value              =    1    'Checked
     End
     Begin TextBox txtFileName
     End
     Begin CommandButton cmdGo
        Caption            =    "&Go"
     End
     Begin CommandButton cmdExit
        Caption            =    "E&xit"
     End
     Begin CommandButton cmdSelect
        Caption            =    "&Select File"
     End
     Begin Label Label1
        Caption            =    "&File Selected:"
     End
End
```

Listing 9.6   Code in CROSSREF.FRM

```
Option Explicit

Dim Cancel As Integer
Dim CRLF As String

' String to hold Basic keywords.
Dim Keywords As String

' Array to store final listing. Increase its size if you
' will be working with large programs that may have more
' than 400 identifiers.
Dim Results(400) As String

' Variable to keep count of number of items in Results().
Dim Total As Integer

' Constants for message boxes.
Const MB_ICONSTOP = 16
Const MB_ICONQUESTION = 32
Const MB_YESNO = 4
Const MB_OKCANCEL = 1
Const MB_RETRYCANCEL = 5
Const IDYES = 6
Const IDNO = 7
Const IDOK = 1
Const IDCANCEL = 2

' Constants for scanning function.
Const CODE = 0
```

```
Const STRNG = 1

' Global variables to hold character sets.
Dim Letters As String
Dim Digits As String
Dim OKChars As String

Sub cmdExit_Click ()

Hide
End

End Sub

Sub cmdGo_Click ()

Dim FileNum As Integer, Temp As String
Dim LineNum As Integer, I As Integer
Dim Msg As String, Reply As Integer
Dim FileName As String, X As Integer

On Local Error Resume Next

Screen.MousePointer = 11
LineNum = 0
Cancel = False
Total = 0
lstXref.Clear

' Open the selected file.
FileNum = FreeFile

Open txtFileName.Text For Input As #FileNum

If Err Then
   Msg = "Unable to open " & txtFileName.Text
   Reply = MsgBox(Msg, MB_ICONSTOP + MB_RETRYCANCEL, "File Error")
   If Reply = IDCANCEL Then
     Screen.MousePointer = 0
     cmdGo.Enabled = False
     Exit Sub
   Else
     Resume
   End If
End If

' Read in each line of the file. Remove leading and
' trailing spaces and pass the line to the parse routine.
Do While Not EOF(FileNum)
```

```
        Line Input #FileNum, Temp
        LineNum = LineNum + 1
        Call Parse(Trim$(Temp), LineNum)
        If Cancel Then Exit Do
Loop

Close #FileNum

' Put the final listing into the List Box.
For I = 0 To Total - 1
   lstXref.AddItem Results(I)
Next I

' Save the list to a file, if the option is selected.
If chkSaveToFile.Value = 1 Then
   FileNum = FreeFile

' Create a filename identical to the source file
' but with the .XRF extension.
   X = InStr(txtFileName.Text, ".")

   If X > 0 Then
      FileName = Left$(txtFileName.Text, X - 1) & ".XRF"
   Else
      FileName = txtFileName.Text & ".XRF"
   End If

   Open FileName For Output As #FileNum

   For X = 0 To lstXref.ListCount - 1
      Print #FileNum, lstXref.List(X)
   Next X

   Close #FileNum

End If

Screen.MousePointer = 0

End Sub

Sub cmdSelect_Click ()

' Display the File Open dialog box, with
' .BAS and .FRM files.
frmFileOpen.File1.Pattern = "*.BAS;*.FRM"
frmFileOpen.Show 1

' Create a filename with full path.
```

```
    txtFileName.Text = frmFileOpen.Dir1.Path & "\" &
       frmFileOpen.txtFileName.Text

End Sub

Sub Form_Load ()

Dim FileNum As Integer, Temp As String
Dim Reply As Integer, Msg As String

On Local Error Resume Next

' Variable for carriage return-line feed combination.
CRLF = Chr$(13) & Chr$(10)

' Set up the strings that define character sets.
Letters = "abcdefghijklmnopqrstuvwxyz"
Letters = Letters & "ABCDEFGHIJKLMNOPQRSTUVWXYZ"
Digits = "0123456789_."
OKChars = Letters & Digits

' Read the keywords from the disk file.
FileNum = FreeFile

Open "keywords.txt" For Input As #FileNum

If Err Then
  Msg = "Unable to open Basic keyword file KEYWORDS.TXT" & CRLF
  Msg = Msg & "Select OK to continue, Cancel to Quit"
  Reply = MsgBox(Msg, MB_ICONSTOP + MB_OKCANCEL, "File Error")

  If Reply = IDCANCEL Then
    Hide
    End
  Else
    chkOmitBasicKeywords.Value = 2
    chkOmitBasicKeywords.Enabled = False
    Exit Sub
  End If
End If

Keywords = ";"

Do While Not EOF(FileNum)
  Line Input #FileNum, Temp
  Keywords = Keywords & UCase$(Trim$(Temp)) & ";"
Loop

Close #FileNum
```

```
' The Go Command Button is disabled until a file is selected.
cmdGo.Enabled = False

End Sub

Sub GetRef (S As String, LineNum As Integer)

Dim Mode As Integer, IDStart As Integer, Found As Integer
Dim InIdentifier As Integer, I As Integer
Dim J As Integer, K As Integer
Dim C As String * 1, Temp As String, CRLF As String
Static ID(1 To 40) As String, ID1(1 To 40) As String
Dim IdentCount As Integer, KWAdded As String

Mode = CODE
InIdentifier = False
IdentCount = 0

' Add a space at the end of S to ensure that the
' scanning routines pick out identifiers that
' end a line.
S = S & " "

' Loop once for each character in S.
For I = 1 To Len(S)

'Extract the Ith character.
  C = Mid$(S, I, 1)
  Select Case Mode
    Case CODE                    ' If in code mode.
      If C = Chr$(34) Then       ' Double quote

' Switch to string mode.
        Mode = STRNG

' If we were in an identifier, store it.
        If InIdentifier Then
          IdentCount = IdentCount + 1
          ID(IdentCount) = Mid$(S, IDStart, I - IDStart)
          InIdentifier = False
        End If

      ElseIf C = "'" Then        ' If starting a comment.

' If we were in an identifier, store it.
        If InIdentifier Then
          IdentCount = IdentCount + 1
          ID(IdentCount) = Mid$(S, IDStart, I - IDStart)
          InIdentifier = False
```

```
                End If

    ' Exit Sub since the rest of the line is a comment.
                Exit Sub

            Else          ' Neither string nor comment.

    ' Is the character in the "OK" list?
                If (InStr(OKChars, C)) Then

    ' If we are not already in an identifier, we are
    ' starting a new one only if it starts with a letter.
                    If (Not InIdentifier) And (InStr(Letters, C)) Then
                        IDStart = I
                        InIdentifier = True
                    End If
                Else

    ' If we were in an identifier and the character is not
    ' in the "OK" list, the identifier has ended.
                    If (InIdentifier) Then
                        IdentCount = IdentCount + 1
                        ID(IdentCount) = Mid$(S, IDStart, I - IDStart)
                        InIdentifier = False
                    End If
                End If

            End If

        End If

    Case STRNG

    ' If we're in string mode all we are interested is the
    ' closing double quotation mark
        If C = Chr$(34) Then Mode = CODE

    End Select

Next I      ' End of main loop.

' Exit the Sub if no keywords were found.
If IdentCount = 0 Then Exit Sub

' Go through the list of detected identifiers. Add each
' one to the ID1 array only if it hasn't been added
' already and, if the "Omit Basic Keywords" option is
' selected, if it is not a Basic keyword.
KWAdded = ";"
J = 0
```

```
For I = 1 To IdentCount
  Temp = ";" & ID(I) & ":"
  If (InStr(KWAdded, Temp) = 0) Then
    KWAdded = KWAdded & ID(I) & ";"
    If (chkOmitBasicKeywords.Value = 1) Then
      If InStr(Keywords, ";" & UCase$(ID(I)) & ";") = 0 Then
        J = J + 1
        ID1(J) = ID(I)
      End If
    Else
        J = J + 1
        ID1(J) = ID(I)
    End If
  End If
Next I

' Now the array ID1 contains one copy of each accepted
' identifier. If the array is empty, exit the Sub.
If J = 0 Then Exit Sub

' Put the accepted identifiers in the Results array. If the
' identifier is already in the Results array, add the new
' line number to the identifier's existing entry. Otherwise,
' create a new entry for the identifier.
For I = 1 To J
  Temp = ID1(I) & ": "
  Found = False

  If Total = 0 Then
    Results(Total) = Temp & Str$(LineNum)
    Total = Total + 1
  Else
    For K = 0 To Total - 1
      If (InStr(Results(K), Temp)) Then
          Results(K) = Results(K) & "," & Str$(LineNum)
          Found = True
          Exit For
      End If
    Next K

    If Not Found Then
      Results(Total) = Temp & Str$(LineNum)
      Total = Total + 1
    End If
  End If

Next I

End Sub
```

```
Sub Parse (S As String, LineNum As Integer)

Dim Reply As Integer, Msg As String
Static FormFile As Integer, ControlCount As Integer

' If it's a form file, verify that it's a valid one.
' The first line of form files starts with "Version"
' or "Begin". This is necessary only if we're looking at
' line 1 only. We will also set a flag indicating that
' it's a form file being processed.
If LineNum = 1 Then
    ControlCount = 0
    If UCase$(Right$(txtFileName.Text, 3)) = "FRM" Then
        FormFile = True
        If Left$(S, 7) <> "VERSION" And Left$(S, 5) <> "Begin" Then
            Msg = "This may not be a valid FRM file. Continue?"
            Reply = MsgBox(Msg, MB_ICONQUESTION + MB_YESNO, "")
            If Reply = IDNO Then
                Cancel = True
                Exit Sub
            End If
        End If
    Else
        FormFile = False
    End If
End If

' If we're dealing with a form file, we need to get
' past all the control listings before we reach the code.
If FormFile Then

    If Left$(S, 5) = "Begin" Then
        ControlCount = ControlCount + 1
    ElseIf Left$(S, 3) = "End" Then
        ControlCount = ControlCount - 1
    Else

' Do nothing - not the start or end of a
' control definition
    End If

' If we've reached at least the third line and the
' ControlCount is 0, then we have moved through all of
' the control definitions in the .FRM file.
    If LineNum > 2 And ControlCount = 0 Then
        FormFile = False
    End If

Exit Sub
```

```
End If

' We reach here only if we are processing code.
' If it's a blank line or a comment, return. Otherwise,
' send the line of code to the identifier extraction
' procedure.
If Len(S) = 0 Then
    Exit Sub
ElseIf Left$(S, 1) = "'" Then
    Exit Sub
ElseIf UCase$(Left$(S, 4)) = "REM " Then
    Exit Sub
Else
    Call GetRef(S, LineNum)
End If

End Sub

Sub txtFileName_Change ()

' Enable the Go Command Button only if there is a filename
' in the Text Box.
If txtFileName.Text <> "" Then
  cmdGo.Enabled = True
End If

End Sub
```

Other File-Related Techniques

The final part of this chapter presents two additional disk- and file-related programming examples.

Determining the Location of the Windows Directory

There may be times when you need to know the name of the directory where Windows is installed. You can't count on it always being C:\WINDOWS.

If you write Visual Basic programs for distribution, you may want to write an installation utility that automatically copies files from the distribution diskettes to the user's hard disk. You may need to place certain files, such as custom controls or dynamic link libraries, in the main Windows directory or in the Windows system directory. On most systems these are C:\WINDOWS and C:\WINDOWS\SYSTEM, but there is no guarantee that this is the case.

Figure 9.4 WIN_DIR displays the names of the Windows main and system directories.

Fortunately, the Windows API provides two functions that return the names of these directories. The two functions have similar declarations:

```
Declare Function GetWindowsDirectory Lib "Kernel" (ByVal lpBuffer
    As String, ByVal nSize As Integer) As Integer

Declare Function GetSystemDirectory Lib "Kernel" (ByVal lpBuffer
    As String, ByVal nSize As Integer) As Integer
```

For both functions, the argument **lpBuffer** is a string variable where the corresponding directory name is to be placed, and **nSize** is the size of the variable in characters. The string length should be a minimum of 144 characters, which is the maximum length permitted for the Windows or Windows system directory path. Both functions return non-zero on success, and zero on error.

The program WIN_DIR, shown in Figure 9.4, demonstrates how to use these API calls. The program's objects and properties are presented in Listing 9.7, and the code is presented in Listing 9.8. All that this demonstration does is to display the directory names on a form. For a real-world program, you could copy the API call declarations and the Basic functions **WindowsDirectory** and **WindowsSystemDirectory** into your own module.

ON
DISK

Using WIN_DIR.MAK

This demonstration, presented in Listings 9.7 and 9.8, is stored on disk as WIN_DIR.MAK and WIN_DIR.FRM.

Listing 9.7 Objects and Properties in WIN_DIR.FRM

```
Begin Form Form1
    Caption          =    "Determining Windows Directories"
    Begin CommandButton Command2
        Caption        =    "E&xit"
```

```
      End
      Begin CommandButton Command1
         Caption          =   "&Get"
      End
      Begin TextBox Text2
      End
      Begin TextBox Text1
      End
      Begin Label Label2
         Caption          =   "System directory:"
      End
      Begin Label Label1
         Caption          =   "Windows directory:"
      End
End
```

Listing 9.8   Code in WIN_DIR.FRM

```
Option Explicit

Declare Function GetWindowsDirectory Lib "Kernel" (ByVal
   lpBuffer As String, ByVal nSize As Integer) As Integer

Declare Function GetSystemDirectory Lib "Kernel" (ByVal
   lpBuffer As String, ByVal nSize As Integer) As Integer

Const MB_ICONSTOP = 16

Sub Command1_Click ()

Dim DirName As String

' Get the directory names.
DirName = WindowsDirectory()

If DirName = "" Then
    MsgBox "Error getting directory name", MB_ICONSTOP, "Error"
Else
    Text1.Text = DirName
End If

DirName = WindowsSystemDirectory()

If DirName = "" Then
    MsgBox "Error getting directory name", MB_ICONSTOP, "Error"
Else
```

```vb
        Text2.Text = DirName
    End If

End Sub

Sub Command2_Click ()

End

End Sub

Function WindowsDirectory ()

' Returns the Windows main directory, or an empty
' string on error.
Dim X As String, Y As Integer

X = Space$(144)

Y = GetWindowsDirectory(X, 144)

If Y <> 0 Then
    WindowsDirectory = X
Else
    WindowsDirectory = ""
End If

End Function

Function WindowsSystemDirectory ()

' Returns the Windows system directory, or an empty
' string on error.
Dim X As String, Y As Integer

X = Space$(144)

Y = GetSystemDirectory(X, 144)

If Y <> 0 Then
    WindowsSystemDirectory = X
Else
    WindowsSystemDirectory = ""
End If

End Function
```

Creating a Combined Drive/Directory List Box

Some users may prefer the old-style file dialog box where drives and directories are listed together in the same List Box. You can create this style of file dialog box in Visual Basic.

Visual Basic's Drive, Directory, and File List Box controls make it a snap to create dialog boxes that allow users to select files. Using these controls, the available disk drives are listed in a separate box from the directories. You may remember another style of file dialog box in which a single list presented both the available drives and directories. Here's how to create this type of list.

There's no trick here, no wonderful API procedure that we can call to do the work for us. The method is simply to use an invisible Drive List Box control to obtain drives, and an invisible Directory List Box control to obtain directories. By copying the drive and directory information into a regular List Box, we can obtain the combined drive/directory listing we desire.

The form FILEOPEN.FRM implements a File Open dialog box using this style, as shown in Figure 9.5.

The form's objects and properties are given in Listing 9.9, and its code is presented in Listing 9.10. Most of the code is quite straightforward, and there are only two parts that merit mention (these are the important parts, of course!). The procedure **UpdateAll** contains code that creates the combined drive/directory listing in the List Box. This procedure is called when the form loads, and whenever a user action changes the current drive or directory. There are three tasks required:

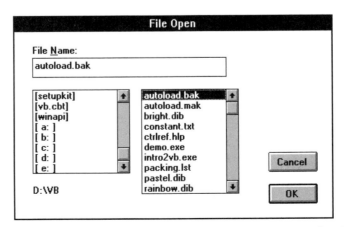

Figure 9.5   A File Open dialog box that uses a single combined list for drives and directories.

- If the current directory is a subdirectory, add "..", representing the parent directory, to the combined List Box.

- If the current directory contains any subdirectories, get their names from the invisible Directory List Box and copy them to the combined List Box.

- Copy the available drive letters from the invisible Drive List Box to the combined List Box.

The other important procedure is the double-click event procedure for the combined List Box. If the user double-clicks a drive or directory entry in this list, then the procedure must make the selected drive or directory current. Error-handling code is included to deal with the possibility that the user will select a drive that is not ready.

The form is designed to be incorporated directly into a program. The user can select a file by using the mouse or keyboard to highlight a file name in the Files List Box, then clicking on OK. Double-clicking on a filename has the same effect. The name of the selected file can be obtained by the calling program from the Text property of the txtFileName Text Box. If the user selects Cancel, this property will be set to an empty string to signal the calling program that no file was selected.

To use this File Open dialog box in your program, simply add the file FILEOPEN.FRM to your project (shown in Listings 9.9 and 9.10). You can try it out with the demonstration program FILE_OLD.MAK. The objects, properties, and code for the demonstration program's one form, MAIN1.FRM, are given in Listings 9.11 and 9.12.

Using FILE_OLD.MAK

This demonstration, presented in Listings 9.9, 9.10, 9.11, and 9.12, is stored on disk as FILE_OLD.MAK, MAIN1.FRM, and FILEOPEN.FRM.

Listing 9.9 Objects and Properties in FILEOPEN.FRM

```
Begin Form frmFileOpen
    BorderStyle      =    1  'Fixed Single
    Caption          =    "File Open"
    ControlBox       =    0  'False
    MaxButton        =    0  'False
    MinButton        =    0  'False
    Begin DirListBox Dir1
        Visible      =    0    'False
    End
```

```
    Begin DriveListBox Drive1
        Visible          =    0    'False
    End
    Begin FileListBox File1
    End
    Begin ListBox lstDirDrive
    End
    Begin TextBox txtFileName
        TabIndex         =    3
    End
    Begin CommandButton cmdCancel
        Cancel           =    -1   'True
        Caption          =    "Cancel"
    End
    Begin CommandButton cmdOK
        Caption          =    "OK"
        Default          =    -1   'True
    End
    Begin Label DirName
        Caption          =    "Label2"
    End
    Begin Label Label1
        Caption          =    "File &Name:"
        TabIndex         =    2
    End
End
```

Listing 9.10   Code in FILEOPEN.FRM

```
Option Explicit

Const MB_ICONEXCLAMATION = 48
Const MB_RETRYCANCEL = 5

Sub cmdCancel_Click ()

txtFileName.Text = ""
Hide

End Sub

Sub cmdOK_Click ()

txtFileName.Text = File1.FileName
Hide

End Sub

Sub File1_Click ()
```

```
' If the user single-clicks a filename,
' display it in the Text Box.
txtFileName.Text = File1.FileName

End Sub

Sub File1_DblClick ()

' Double clicking a filename in the File List Box is the
' same as selecting the OK button.
Call cmdOK_Click

End Sub

Sub File1_GotFocus ()

' If the Text Box gets the focus, select all
' of its text.
txtFileName.SelStart = 0
txtFileName.SelText = Len(txtFileName.Text)

End Sub

Sub Form_Load ()

Call UpdateAll

End Sub

Sub lstDirDrive_DblClick ()

' If the user double-clicks an entry in the combined
' drive/directory List Box.
On Local Error GoTo DriveError

Dim OldDir As String, NewDrive As String
Dim Reply As Integer, Junk As String

' If the user selected a different drive, change to that drive.
If Left$(lstDirDrive.Text, 2) = "[ " And Len(lstDirDrive.Text) = 6 Then
    OldDir = CurDir$
    NewDrive = Mid$(lstDirDrive.Text, 3, 1)
    ChDrive NewDrive

' Verify that the new drive is ready.
    Junk = CurDir$

' Else, user selected a new directory.
Else
```

```
        ChDir Mid$(lstDirDrive.Text, 2, Len(lstDirDrive.Text) - 2)
End If

On Local Error GoTo 0

Call UpdateAll

Exit Sub

DriveError:

' An error occurs if the system is unable to switch
' to the specified drive; for example, a diskette
' drive with the door left open.
Reply = MsgBox("Error switching to drive " & NewDrive,
    MB_ICONEXCLAMATION + MB_RETRYCANCEL, "Drive Error")

' If the user selects Cancel, reset to the old drive.
If Reply = 2 Then
    ChDrive Left$(OldDir, 1)
End If

Resume

End Sub

Sub txtFileName_GotFocus ()

' When the Text Box gets the focus, select
' all of its text.
txtFileName.SelStart = 0
txtFileName.SelLength = Len(txtFileName.Text)

End Sub

Sub UpdateAll ()

Dim X As Integer, Y As Integer, S As String

DirName.Caption = CurDir$
File1.Path = CurDir$
lstDirDrive.Clear

' Update the Path property of the invisible
' Directory List Box.
Dir1.Path = CurDir$
```

```
' If the current directory is a subdirectory, add ".." to
' the list to represent the parent directory.
If Right$(CurDir$, 1) <> "\" Then lstDirDrive.AddItem "[..]"

' Add to the list each directory in the invisible
' Directory List Box.
For X = 0 To Dir1.ListCount - 1
    S = Dir1.List(X)

' Extract the directory name from the full path name.
    For Y = Len(S) To 1 Step -1
        If Mid$(S, Y, 1) = "\" Then
            S = Mid$(S, Y + 1)
        End If
    Next Y

' Add the directory name in brackets to the list.
    lstDirDrive.AddItem "[" & S & "]"
Next X

' Add to the list the drives from
' the invisible Drive List Box.
For X = 0 To Drive1.ListCount - 1
    S = Mid$(Drive1.List(X), 1, 1)
    lstDirDrive.AddItem "[ " & S & ": ]"
Next X

End Sub
```

Listing 9.11   Objects and Properties in MAIN1.FRM

```
Begin Form Form1
    Caption        =    "Old Style File Dialog Demo"
    Begin Menu mnuFile
        Caption        =    "&File"
        Begin Menu mnuFileOpen
            Caption        =    "&Open"
        End
        Begin Menu mnuFileSeparator
            Caption        =    "-"
        End
        Begin Menu mnuFileExit
            Caption        =    "E&xit"
        End
    End
End
```

Listing 9.12 Code in MAIN1.FRM

```
Option Explicit

Sub mnuFileExit_Click ()

Hide
End

End Sub

Sub mnuFileOpen_Click ()

Dim Msg As String

frmFileOpen.Show 1

If frmFileOpen.txtFileName.Text = "" Then
    Msg = "You did not select a file."
Else
    Msg = "You selected " & frmFileOpen.txtFileName.Text
End If

MsgBox Msg

End Sub
```

Environment and System

All Visual Basic programs run under the Windows operating environment, which may also be running one or more other programs at the same time. Windows itself runs in cooperation with DOS. Together everything runs on a hardware platform that consists of a CPU, memory, and other components. This chapter shows you a variety of ways that Visual Basic can be used to obtain information about the environment and system it is running on, and to control certain aspects of the environment and system.

Who Was That Masked Window?

You may have noticed that the "Windows" in Microsoft Windows is definitely plural! If you're like me, you often find your screen cluttered with a multitude of windows, many of which you no longer recognize—which window belongs to which program? Until now, your only recourse was to activate the window and try to figure it out yourself. Wouldn't it be great to have a utility that would provide information about a window simply by pointing at it? That's what we'll develop in this section.

What Windows Information Is Available?

Every screen window has certain information associated with it.

What information about a window would be of use in our utility? Well, every window has a handle, a numerical value that uniquely identifies the window. The handle of a window may not seem like a particularly useful piece of information, but if you're programming or debugging a multiwindow application you may find it just what you need to keep track of all the program's windows!

Every windows also has a *class*. All windows that belong to the same class share a single Windows procedure. "So what's a Windows procedure?" you may ask. It's a section of code that processes Windows messages. Therefore, windows that have the same class have their messages processed by the same Windows procedure. For example, multiple document windows in a word processor will usually belong to the same class.

Many windows have a captioned title bar. This caption usually identifies the contents of the window or the program that created it. Being able to determine a window's caption without having to display the full window can be a time-saver when you are trying to sort out a complex screen.

Some windows also have a *parent window*, which is the governing window in a parent-child relationship. For example, when you create a Visual Basic program that uses an MDI form, the MDI form will be the parent window to all of the program's other windows. Knowing the identity of a window's parent window can be very helpful in determining the origin and purpose of a mysterious screen window! Like any other window, a parent window has a handle, a class, and (maybe) a caption.

Finally, a parent window may have its own parent. In fact, it is possible for there to be a chain of parent-child relationships that is many layers deep. Moving through the layers from child to parent you will eventually find the "ultimate parent," the parent window that is not itself the child of another window. For lack of a recognized term, I will call this the "ancestor" window. Knowing the handle, class, and caption of the ancestor of a given screen window can provide additional useful information.

Getting the Window Information

You can use API functions to retrieve information about any window.

The Windows API provides a variety of functions whose sole task is to retrieve certain information about a window. But first we need to identify the window that is currently under the mouse pointer—a task that takes two steps. First, use the API procedure **GetCursorPos** to obtain the mouse cursor's current screen position. The procedure's declaration is:

```
Declare Sub GetCursorPos Lib "User" (lpPoint As PointAPI)
```

The argument **lpPoint** is a user-defined type as shown here:

```
Type PointAPI
    Y As Integer
    X As Integer
End Type
```

GetCursorPos retrieves the screen coordinates of the cursor's current position, placing them in the **X** and **Y** members of the **PointAPI** structure. The cursor position is always specified in screen coordinates and is not affected by the mapping mode of the window that contains the cursor.

Once you know the current position of the mouse cursor, you use the **WindowFromPoint** API function to obtain the handle of the window that is under the cursor. The function declaration is:

```
Declare Function WindowFromPoint Lib "User" (ByVal X As Integer,
   ByVal Y As Integer) As Integer
```

This function returns the handle of the window that contains the specified point. Now, to obtain the handle of the window under the mouse cursor, pass **WindowFromPoint** the **X** and **Y** values returned by the **GetCursorPos** procedure. The return value is 0 if no window exists at the specified point. Be aware that the **WindowFromPoint** function will not retrieve the handle of a hidden, disabled, or transparent window, even if the point is within the window. This limitation is not a concern for our present needs, however.

Once you have the handle of the window under the mouse cursor, the real work begins. To obtain the class name of a window, you use the **GetClassName** function. The declaration for this function is:

```
Declare Function GetClassName Lib "User" (ByVal hWnd As Integer,
   ByVal lpClassName As String, ByVal nMaxCount As Integer) As
   Integer
```

The **GetClassName** arguments are defined here:

- **hWnd** is the handle of the window whose class name you want.
- **lpClassName** is a buffer where the function places the class name string.
- **nMaxCount** is the size of the buffer, in characters.

The function returns 0 if the window handle is invalid. On success it returns the length of the string placed in the buffer.

The next piece if information you want is the window's caption—that is, the text in its title bar. You obtain this with the **GetWindowText** function. The declaration for this function is:

```
Declare Function GetWindowText Lib "User" (ByVal hWnd As Integer,
   ByVal lpString As String, ByVal nMaxCount As Integer) As Integer
```

The arguments are similar to those for the previous function:

- **hWnd** is the window handle.
- **lpString** is a buffer for the result.
- **nMaxCount** is the size of the buffer.

The function's return value is 0 if the window handle is invalid, if the window has no title bar, or if there is no text in the title bar. Otherwise, it returns the length of the string placed in the buffer.

So far we have the handle, class, and caption of the window under the mouse cursor. The next step is to determine the window's parent. You use the **GetParent** function to do this. The declaration for this function is:

```
Declare Function GetParent Lib "User" (ByVal hWnd As Integer) As
   Integer
```

Here, the argument **hWnd** is the handle of the window. The function returns the handle of the parent window, or 0 if there is no parent window or if the window handle argument passed to the function is invalid.

Once you have the handle of the parent window (if any), then you use the **GetWindowClass** and **GetWindowText** functions to obtain the parent window's class and caption information. To find the ancestor, use **GetParent** in a loop to get the parent window's parent until there's no more parent—then you know you have reached the ancestor window. Use **GetWindowClass** and **GetWindowText** functions to obtain the ancestor window's class and caption information, and you're done.

Now let's add a couple of "bells and whistles." It might be nice to have the option of making the information form "float" on the screen, remaining on top of all screen windows even when it is not active. For this purpose, you can use the **FloatWindow** procedure that we developed in Chapter 2. You might also want to place a Check Box on the form to turn the float option on and off.

Another desirable option is the ability to disable the program. That is, while it is executing the user should be able to "suspend" it so that it remains loaded, but no longer obtains and displays information about windows. Normally the program will run in the background, continuously displaying information even when another window is active. This processing takes time, even if only a little bit! When maximum performance is required, suspending the program may be desirable.

You could place a Check Box control on the form for the user to select when they want the program suspended, but a more elegant solution would be to have the program monitor input for the occurrence of a particular keystroke combination, switching between suspended and active modes each time the combination is received. Perhaps we can get the mouse buttons in on the act as well.

Turning to the API as always, we find a function that will do just what we want. **GetAsynchKeyState** can not only return information on whether a specific key is pressed, but can also tell you whether a mouse button is pressed. The function declaration is:

```
Declare Function GetAsyncKeyState Lib "User" (ByVal vKey As
   Integer) As Integer
```

The **vKey** argument specifies the key or mouse button you are interested in. The function returns a non-zero value if the specified key/button is currently pressed or if it has been pressed since the last call to this function.

There are Windows global constants to specify the mouse button or key you are interested in. These constants and their values are given in Table 10.1. For example, the constant for the Shift key is **VK_SHIFT**, which has a value of &H10. To detect if the user has pressed the Shift key you would write:

```
If GetAsyncKeyState(VK_SHIFT) Then
        ' Shift was pressed.
Else
        ' Shift key wasn't pressed.
End If
```

Similarly, the constant for the right mouse button is **VK_RBUTTON**, with a value of &H02. To detect if the user has pressed both the Shift key and the right mouse button you would write:

```
If GetAsyncKeyState(VK_RBUTTON) And GetAsyncKeyState(VK_SHIFT) Then
        ' Right mouse button and Shift key pressed.
End If
```

This is the method we'll use in our program to toggle it between suspended and active modes. You should remember that the **GetAsynchKeyState** function only tells you that the specified key or button has been pressed, and not whether it has been released. If you want to be sure that both have been released before further processing is done, you could use the loop shown here:

```
Do Until (GetAsyncKeyState(VK_RBUTTON) And GetAsyncKeyState(VK_SHIFT))
    = False
Loop
```

We now have all the tools needed to put together our little "snooping" utility.

The INFO Utility

This section presents INFO, a program that displays information about the window under the mouse pointer.

INFO, which if I do say so myself, is a pretty neat little utility! I have found it to be very useful, and think that you may as well. When running, INFO

Table 10.1 Windows Global Constants for Use with the GetAsynchKeyState Function

Constant	Value	Constant	Value
VK_LBUTTON	&H01	VK_NUMPAD2	&H62
VK_RBUTTON	&H02	VK_NUMPAD3	&H63
VK_CANCEL	&H03	VK_NUMPAD4	&H64
VK_MBUTTON	&H04	VK_NUMPAD5	&H65
VK_BACK	&H08	VK_NUMPAD6	&H66
VK_TAB	&H09	VK_NUMPAD7	&H67
VK_CLEAR	&H0C	VK_NUMPAD8	&H68
VK_RETURN	&H0D	VK_NUMPAD9	&H69
VK_SHIFT	&H10	VK_MULTIPLY	&H6A
VK_CONTROL	&H11	VK_ADD	&H6B
VK_MENU	&H12	VK_SEPARATOR	&H6C
VK_PAUSE	&H13	VK_SUBTRACT	&H6D
VK_CAPITAL	&H14	VK_DECIMAL	&H6E
VK_ESCAPE	&H1B	VK_DIVIDE	&H6F
VK_SPACE	&H20	VK_F1	&H70
VK_PRIOR	&H21	VK_F2	&H71
VK_NEXT	&H22	VK_F3	&H72
VK_END	&H23	VK_F4	&H73
VK_HOME	&H24	VK_F5	&H74
VK_LEFT	&H25	VK_F6	&H75
VK_UP	&H26	VK_F7	&H76
VK_RIGHT	&H27	VK_F8	&H77
VK_DOWN	&H28	VK_F9	&H78
VK_SELECT	&H29	VK_F10	&H79
VK_PRINT	&H2A	VK_F11	&H7A
VK_EXECUTE	&H2B	VK_F12	&H7B
VK_SNAPSHOT	&H2C	VK_F13	&H7C
VK_INSERT	&H2D	VK_F14	&H7D
VK_DELETE	&H2E	VK_F15	&H7E
VK_HELP	&H2F	VK_F16	&H7F
VK_NUMPAD0	&H60	VK_NUMLOCK	&H90
VK_NUMPAD1	&H61	VK_SCROLL	&H91

displays a small window with the caption Window Information, as shown in Figure 10.1. This window displays the handle, class, and caption of the window under the mouse cursor, and of its parent and ancestor, if they exist. As you move the mouse cursor from window to window the display is automatically updated. You can click the Stay on Top Check Box to make the window float and always be visible, and pressing Shift and the right mouse button simultaneously will toggle INFO between active and suspended modes.

INFO's objects and properties are given in Listing 10.1, and its code is given in Listings 10.2 and 10.3.

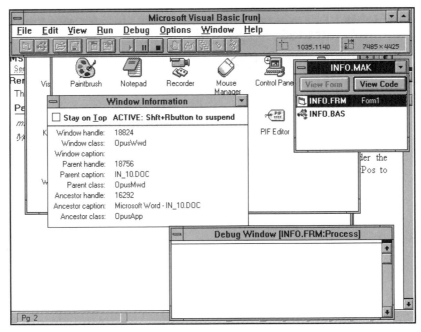

Figure 10.1   INFO displays a window containing the handle, class, and caption of the window under the mouse cursor, its parent, and its ancestor.

Using INFO.MAK

This demonstration, presented in Listings 10.1, 10.2, and 10.3, is stored on disk as INFO.MAK, INFO.FRM, and INFO.BAS.

Listing 10.1   Objects and Properties in INFO.FRM

```
Begin Form Form1
   BorderStyle     =   1   'Fixed Single
   Caption         =   "Window Information"
   MaxButton       =   0   'False
   Begin CheckBox chkOnTop
      Caption      =   "Stay on &Top"
   End
   Begin Line Line1
      BorderColor  =   &H00808080&
      BorderWidth  =   2
   End
   Begin Label Label1
   End
   Begin Label lblPClass
```

```
End
Begin Label lblAncestorClass
End
Begin Label lblPCaption
End
Begin Label lblAncestorCap
End
Begin Label lblAncestor
End
Begin Label lblParent
End
Begin Label lblCaption
End
Begin Label lblClassName
End
Begin Label lblWinHandle
End
Begin Label Label2
    Alignment        =    1   'Right Justify
    Caption          =    "Parent class:"
    Index            =    8
End
Begin Label Label2
    Alignment        =    1   'Right Justify
    Caption          =    "Ancestor class:"
    Index            =    7
End
Begin Label Label2
    Alignment        =    1   'Right Justify
    Caption          =    "Parent caption:"
    Index            =    6
End
Begin Label Label2
    Alignment        =    1   'Right Justify
    Caption          =    "Ancestor caption:"
    Index            =    5
End
Begin Label Label2
    Alignment        =    1   'Right Justify
    Caption          =    "Ancestor handle:"
    Index            =    4
End
Begin Label Label2
    Alignment        =    1   'Right Justify
    Caption          =    "Parent handle:"
    Index            =    3
End
Begin Label Label2
    Alignment        =    1   'Right Justify
```

```
        Caption          =    "Window caption:"
        Index            =    2
    End
    Begin Label Label2
        Alignment        =    1    'Right Justify
        Caption          =    "Window class:"
        Index            =    1
    End
    Begin Label Label2
        Alignment        =    1    'Right Justify
        Caption          =    "Window handle:"
        Index            =    0
    End
End
```

Listing 10.2   Code in INFO.FRM

```
Option Explicit

' Global variable

Dim wHnd As Integer

' Constants

Const VK_SHIFT = &H10
Const VK_RBUTTON = &H2
Const SWP_NOSIZE = &H1
Const SWP_NOMOVE = &H2
Const HWND_TOPMOST = -1
Const HWND_NOTOPMOST = -2
Const ACTIVE = -1
Const INACTIVE = 0


Sub chkOnTop_Click ()

Dim X As Integer

X = chkOnTop.Value
Call FloatWindow(wHnd, X)

End Sub

Sub FloatWindow (X As Integer, action As Integer)

' When called by a form:
'
' If action <> 0 makes the form float (always on top).
' If action = 0 "unfloats" the window.
```

```
Dim wFlags As Integer, result As Integer
wFlags = SWP_NOMOVE Or SWP_NOSIZE

If action <> 0 Then        ' Float
    Call SetWindowPos(X, HWND_TOPMOST, 0, 0, 0, 0, wFlags)
Else                       ' Sink
    Call SetWindowPos(X, HWND_NOTOPMOST, 0, 0, 0, 0, wFlags)
End If

End Sub

Sub Form_Load ()

Dim X As Integer
'Extend grey line across form.
Line1.X1 = 0
Line1.X2 = Form1.Width
' Store window handle.
wHnd = hWnd
Call Process

End Sub

Sub Process ()

Dim WHandle As Integer
Dim Z As Integer, ParentHandle As Integer
Dim Ancestor As Integer
Dim Buffer As String * 64
Dim Mode As Integer
Dim MousePos As PointAPI

Mode = ACTIVE     ' Begin in ACTIVE state
Form1.Show        ' Show form
Form1.Label1 = "ACTIVE: Shft+Rbutton to suspend"

Do While DoEvents()        ' Infinite loop

    ' If user pressed Shift+Rt button change mode.
    If GetAsyncKeyState(VK_RBUTTON) And GetAsyncKeyState(VK_SHIFT)
    Then

      If Mode = ACTIVE Then
          Mode = INACTIVE
      Else
          Mode = ACTIVE
      End If

        ' Wait until key/button released
```

```
        Do Until (GetAsyncKeyState(VK_RBUTTON) And
          GetAsyncKeyState(VK_SHIFT)) = False
        Loop

        ' Update label.
        If Mode = ACTIVE Then
            Form1.Label1 = "ACTIVE: Shft+Rbutton to suspend"
        Else
            Form1.Label1 = "INACTIVE: Shft+Rbutton to activate"
        End If
    End If

    ' If mode = ACTIVE then determine the cursor position
    ' and retrieve the ID of the window under the cursor.
    If Mode = ACTIVE Then

        ' Get the current mouse position.
        Call  GetCursorPos(MousePos)

        ' Get the handle of the window under the mouse.
        WHandle = WindowFromPoint(MousePos.X, MousePos.Y)
        Form1.lblWinHandle = WHandle

        ' Get the window's class name.
        Z = GetClassName(WHandle, Buffer, 63)
        Form1.lblClassName = Left$(Buffer, InStr(Buffer, Chr$(0)) - 1)

        ' Get the window's caption.
        Z = GetWindowText(WHandle, Buffer, 63)
        Form1.lblCaption = Trim(Left$(Buffer, InStr(Buffer, Chr$(0)) - 1))

        ' Get the handle and caption of the window's parent.
        ParentHandle = GetParent(WHandle)
        Form1.lblParent = ParentHandle
        Z = GetWindowText(ParentHandle, Buffer, 63)
        Form1.lblPCaption = Trim(Trim(Left$(Buffer, InStr(Buffer,
          Chr$(0)) - 1)))

        ' If there's a valid parent handle, get the parent class name.
        If ParentHandle Then
            Z = GetClassName(ParentHandle, Buffer, 63)
            Form1.lblPClass = Left$(Buffer, InStr(Buffer, Chr$(0)) - 1)
        Else
            Form1.lblPClass = ""
        End If

        ' Loop back as far as possible through "parents"
        ' to get the ancestor.
```

```
            Ancestor = ParentHandle
            Do While ParentHandle
                Ancestor = ParentHandle
                ParentHandle = GetParent(Ancestor)
            Loop

            ' Display ancestor handle.
            Form1.lblAncestor = Ancestor

            ' Get ancestor caption.
            Z = GetWindowText(Ancestor, Buffer, 63)
            Form1.lblAncestorCap = Trim(Left$(Buffer, InStr(Buffer,
                Chr$(0)) - 1))

            ' If there's a valid ancestor get its class name.
            If Ancestor Then
                Z = GetClassName(Ancestor, Buffer, 63)
                Form1.lblAncestorClass = Left$(Buffer, InStr(Buffer,
                Chr$(0)) - 1)
            Else
                Form1.lblAncestorClass = ""
            End If
        End If
    Loop
Loop

End Sub
```

Listing 10.3   Code in INFO.BAS

```
Option Explicit

' Data type used by GetCursorPos API call.
Type PointAPI
    Y As Integer
    X As Integer
End Type

' API Call declarations
Declare Sub GetCursorPos Lib "User" (P As PointAPI)

Declare Function WindowFromPoint Lib "User" (ByVal X As Integer,
    ByVal Y As Integer) As Integer

Declare Function GetParent Lib "User" (ByVal hWnd As Integer) As
    Integer

Declare Function GetClassName Lib "User" (ByVal hWnd As Integer,
    ByVal lpZ As String, ByVal nMaxCount As Integer) As Integer
```

```
Declare Function GetWindowText Lib "User" (ByVal hWnd As Integer,
   ByVal lpString As String, ByVal aint As Integer) As Integer

Declare Sub SetWindowPos Lib "User" (ByVal hWnd As Integer,
   ByVal hWndInsertAfter As Integer, ByVal X As Integer,
   ByVal Y As Integer, ByVal cx As Integer, ByVal cy As Integer,
   ByVal wFlags As Integer)

Declare Function GetAsyncKeyState Lib "User" (ByVal VKCODE As
   Integer) As Integer
```

Windows, DOS, and System Information

Every Visual Basic program runs within the Windows operating environment, and Windows runs in conjunction with the DOS operating system. Together, everything is running on a hardware system, that includes video hardware, memory, disk space, and other components. In this section we will look at a variety of methods that your Visual Basic programs can use to obtain information about the status of Windows, DOS, and the hardware.

Monitoring System Resources

You can monitor your system resources without having to continually open the About... dialog box in Program Manager or your application.

What exactly are *system resources*? First of all, they are something you definitely don't want to run out of! Second, you probably don't have as many as you think, so you may want to keep track of them as you work. But this doesn't answer the original question: what are they?

System resources are the memory that Windows has available at any given moment to perform certain tasks, such as creating windows and drawing graphical objects. You may be thinking "No problem—I jammed umpteen megabytes of RAM into my machine." Unfortunately, that's irrelevant—system resources are *not* the same as total memory. Windows sets aside three 64K sections of memory, 192K in all, for system resources. Unfortunately, that's often not enough, particularly when you are running multiple applications. It doesn't matter how much RAM you have, you are limited to the same puny system resources allocation as the rest of us!

You can check system resources by displaying the Program Manager's About... dialog box. (Select About Program Manager... from the Help menu.) Most applications programs have a similar dialog box. Sometimes available memory, disk space and math co-processor status are also displayed, but it's system resources that we're interested in. You can have a huge amount of free memory and still have very few resources left. If you run out of system resources, programs will not be able to perform certain tasks, such as creating new windows. Most applications are designed to recover gracefully from such a situation, but you can never be sure. Ideally, you would continually monitor system resources during a work session, and if they became alarmingly low (less than 20%, say) you could close down unneeded programs to free some resources. A resource monitoring program might even sound an alarm if resources fall below a set level.

There are actually three types of system resources to be concerned about: *User* resources, which are devoted primarily to managing windows and menus; *GDI* (Graphics Device Interface) resources, which are used for management of brushes, pens, regions, fonts, and bitmaps; and *General* resources, which are used for miscellaneous purposes.

The API has a function that returns information about free system resources of all three types. The function declaration is:

```
Declare Function GetFreeSystemResources Lib "User" (ByVal
  fuSysResource As Integer) As Integer
```

The function returns the percentage of system resources that are free. The argument **fuSysResource** specifies the type of resource to be checked. There are three possible values for this argument:

GFSR_SYSTEMRESOURCES (value = 0) Returns the percentage of general resources that are free.

GFSR_GDIRESOURCES (value = 1) Returns the percentage of GDI resources that are free.

GFSR_USERRESOURCES (value = 2) Returns the percentage of User resources that are free.

The return value specifies the percentage of free space for resources, if the function is successful. The return value is an integer. For example, a return value of 45 indicates 45 percent free resources.

You should be aware that the return value of this function does not guarantee that a Visual Basic program (or any other application) will be able to carry out any particular action, such as creating a new window or graphical object. However, by keeping an eye on resources, you'll soon get a feeling for what levels are too low, and take action accordingly. By

Figure 10.2   System resources displayed by RESRCES.MAK.

Figure 10.3   This form lets the user set an alarm that will sound if a resource falls below a specified value.

monitoring resources you can also see what effects certain actions have in terms of using or freeing resources.

The program RESRCES will continually monitor all three types of resources, displaying the percent free values in a screen window, as shown in Figure 10.2. Optionally, the program will sound an alarm if any of the resource values falls below a user-specified value. To display the alarm-setting form, shown in Figure 10.3, double-click the main program form. When the alarm is set, an asterisk displays on the main form. This program makes use of one of our favorite tricks to offer a Stay on Top option so the resource values will always be visible.

The objects and properties for the program's main form are provided in Listings 10.4 and its code is given in Listing 10.5; likewise, the objects, properties, and code for the alarm-setting form are given in Listings 10.6 and 10.7.

Using RESRCES.MAK

This demonstration, presented in Listings 10.4, 10.5, 10.6, and 10.7, is stored on disk as RESRCES.MAK, RESRCES.FRM, and ALARM.FRM.

Listing 10.4   Objects and Properties in RESRCES.FRM

```
Begin Form frmResources
    Caption          =   "Resources"
    MaxButton        =   0    'False
    Begin CheckBox chkOnTop
```

```
            Caption          =    "Stay on Top"
      End
      Begin TextBox Text3
         BorderStyle      =    0   'None
      End
      Begin TextBox Text2
         BorderStyle      =    0   'None
      End
      Begin TextBox Text1
         BorderStyle      =    0   'None
      End
      Begin Label Label3
         Alignment        =    1  'Right Justify
         Caption          =    "User:"
      End
      Begin Label Label2
         Alignment        =    1  'Right Justify
         Caption          =    "GDI:"
      End
      Begin Label Label1
         Alignment        =    1  'Right Justify
         Caption          =    "System:"
      End
   End
End
```

Listing 10.5   Code in RESRCES.FRM

```
Option Explicit

Declare Function GetFreeSystemResources Lib "User" (ByVal
   fuSysResource As Integer) As Integer
Declare Sub SetWindowPos Lib "User" (ByVal hWnd As Integer,
   ByVal hWndInsertAfter As Integer, ByVal X As Integer,
   ByVal Y As Integer, ByVal cx As Integer, ByVal cy As Integer,
   ByVal wFlags As Integer)

Const GFSR_SYSTEMRESOURCES = 0
Const GFSR_GDIRESOURCES = 1
Const GFSR_USERRESOURCES = 2
Const SWP_NOSIZE = &H1
Const SWP_NOMOVE = &H2
Const HWND_TOPMOST = -1
Const HWND_NOTOPMOST = -2

Dim wHandle As Integer

Sub chkOnTop_Click ()

Dim X As Integer
```

```
X = chkOnTop.Value
Call FloatWindow(wHandle, X)

End Sub

Sub FloatWindow (X As Integer, Action As Integer)

' When called by a form:
'
' If action <> 0 makes the form float (always on top).
' If action = 0 "unfloats" the window.
Dim wFlags As Integer, result As Integer
wFlags = SWP_NOMOVE Or SWP_NOSIZE

If Action <> 0 Then      ' Float
    Call SetWindowPos(X, HWND_TOPMOST, 0, 0, 0, 0, wFlags)
Else                     ' Sink
    Call SetWindowPos(X, HWND_NOTOPMOST, 0, 0, 0, 0, wFlags)
End If

End Sub

Sub Form_DblClick ()

Dim OldOnTop As Integer

' Disable "on top" if necessary so alarm form
' can be displayed.
OldOnTop = frmResources.chkOnTop.Value
frmResources.chkOnTop.Value = 0
Call chkOnTop_Click

' Display the alarm form.
frmAlarmSet.Show 1

' Reset "on top" setting to original value.
frmResources.chkOnTop.Value = OldOnTop
Call chkOnTop_Click

' If the alarm is set display * on form.
If frmAlarmSet.Check1.Value = 1 Then
    chkOnTop.Caption = "Stay on Top*"
Else
    chkOnTop.Caption = "Stay on Top"
End If

End Sub

Sub Form_Load ()
```

```
' Show the form and save its handle.
Show
wHandle = hWnd

' Start the main loop.
Call GetResources

End Sub

Sub GetResources ()

Dim X As Integer, Y As Integer, Z As Integer
Dim Q As Integer
Static Sounded As Integer

Do While DoEvents()

' Get and display the three resource percentages.
X = GetFreeSystemResources(GFSR_SYSTEMRESOURCES)
Text1.Text = Str$(X)

Y = GetFreeSystemResources(GFSR_GDIRESOURCES)
Text2.Text = Str$(Y)

Z = GetFreeSystemResources(GFSR_USERRESOURCES)
Text3.Text = Str$(Z)

' Sound the alarm?
If frmAlarmSet.Check1.Value = 1 Then
    Q = Val(frmAlarmSet.txtAlarmLevel.Text)
    If ((X < Q) Or (Y < Q) Or (Z < Q)) Then
        If Not Sounded Then
            Beep: Beep
            Sounded = True
        End If
    Else
        Sounded = False
    End If
End If

Loop

End Sub
```

Listing 10.6   Objects and Properties in ALARM.FRM

```
Begin Form frmAlarmSet
    Caption        =    "Set Alarm Level"
    Begin CommandButton cmdOK
```

```
    Caption         =    "&OK"
    Default         =    -1   'True
End
Begin TextBox txtAlarmLevel
    Text            =    ""
End
Begin CheckBox Check1
    Caption         =    "&Activate alarm"
End
Begin Label Label1
    AutoSize        =    -1   'True
    Caption         =    "Alarm level (any resource): "
End
End
End
```

Listing 10.7   Code in ALARM.FRM

```
Option Explicit

Const MB_ICONSTOP = 16

' Defaults for alarm level settings.
Const MAX_ALARMLEVEL = 95
Const MIN_ALARMLEVEL = 5
Const DEFAULT_ALARMLEVEL = 40


Sub cmdOK_Click ()


Dim Msg As String

' Ensure that a valid alarm level was entered.
If Val(txtAlarmLevel.Text) < MIN_ALARMLEVEL Or Val(txtAlarmLevel.Text)
  > MAX_ALARMLEVEL Then
    Msg = "Alarm level must be between"
    Msg = Msg & Str$(MIN_ALARMLEVEL) & " and"
    Msg = Msg & Str$(MAX_ALARMLEVEL)
    MsgBox Msg, MB_ICONSTOP, "Invalid entry"
    txtAlarmLevel.SelStart = 0
    txtAlarmLevel.SelLength = Len(txtAlarmLevel.Text)
    txtAlarmLevel.SetFocus
    Exit Sub
End If

Hide

End Sub

Sub Form_Activate ()

' When the form is activated set the focus
```

```
' to the Text Box and highlight its contents.
txtAlarmLevel.SetFocus
txtAlarmLevel.SelStart = 0
txtAlarmLevel.SelLength = Len(txtAlarmLevel.Text)

End Sub

Sub Form_Load ()

' Load the default alarm level into the Text Box.
txtAlarmLevel.Text = Str$(DEFAULT_ALARMLEVEL)

End Sub
```

Determining the Windows and DOS Version Numbers

To ensure compatibility with current and future versions of Windows, a program may need to know what version of Windows it is running on.

Everyone is running version 3.1 of Windows, right? Well, maybe not! How about DOS—versions 5.0 or 6.0 seem a good bet. However, there are probably some holdovers who are still using Windows 3.0 and DOS 4.x. In some remote corner of the world, a few copies of Windows 2.x may still be in use. What's more, there are sure to be future versions of DOS and Windows that add new features and API calls. If you're writing a Visual Basic program that is to be commercially distributed, you need to ensure that the program takes into account the differences between Windows versions. For example, the **GetFreeSystemResources** API function, used earlier in this chapter, was introduced with Windows 3.1. Anyone using an earlier version would not be able to run the resource monitoring program.

The Windows API comes to our rescue yet again. The **GetVersion** API function returns the versions of DOS and Windows that the calling program is running on. Its declaration is:

```
Declare Function GetVersion Lib "Kernel" () As Long
```

The function takes no arguments and returns a single value that codes both the Windows and DOS version numbers, both the major and minor parts. The major version number is the part to the left of the decimal point, and the minor version number is the part to the right of the decimal point. For example, for Windows 3.1 the major version number is 3 and the minor version number is 1. The version numbers are coded as follows (remember that the function returns a Long value):

High-order word: High-order byte codes DOS major version.
                          Low-order byte codes DOS minor version.
Low-order word: High-order byte codes Windows minor version.
                          Low order byte codes Windows major version.

The **GetVersion** function is demonstrated in the program SYSINFO, later in the chapter. Look there for details of how to extract the various version numbers from the value returned by the **GetVersion** function.

Determining the Amount of Free Memory

There's an API function that can tell you the total amount of free memory available to Windows.

You can use the **GetFreeSpace** API function to obtain the number of bytes of memory currently available. The function declaration is:

```
Declare Function GetFreeSpace Lib "Kernel" (ByVal wFlags As
   Integer) As Long
```

The argument **wFlags** is ignored in Windows 3.1, and is included only for compatibility with earlier versions. You can pass any value. The function's return value is the amount of available memory, in bytes. If Windows is running in standard mode, the value returned represents the number of bytes in the global heap that are not used and that are not reserved for code. In 386-enhanced mode, the return value is an estimate of the amount of memory available to an application. It does not account for memory held in reserve for non-Windows applications.

Remember that available memory is not related to available system resources. Clearly, there is no easy way to interpret the "free memory" value returned by this function. You cannot arbitrarily define free memory values that are "OK" and other values that are "not OK." However, the free memory value can provide a general picture of how much of the system's RAM is available for program code and data.

Using the **GetFreeSpace** function will be demonstrated in the SYSINFO program later in the chapter.

Accessing System Information

The API provides access to a variety of information about your system configuration.

You say you're curious about your system hardware and how Windows is running on it? There's no need to puzzle any longer—by using the

GetWinFlags API function you can determine all sorts of interesting information about your system. The function's declaration is:

```
Declare Function GetWinFlags Lib "Kernel" () As Long
```

Notice that **GetWinFlags** takes no arguments, and returns a value that specifies certain information about the Windows system and memory configuration. The value that is returned by the function consists of a number of flags, with each flag signaling yes/no, present/absent, or on/off for a particular system component or mode. The flag constants (these are Windows global constants, of course), their values, and meanings are shown in Table 10.2.

The way to extract items of information is to call **GetWinFlags**, and then perform an **AND** operation between the return value and each flag of interest. If the value is zero, the related item is not true; if the value if non-zero, the related item is true. For example,

```
Answer& = GetWinFlags()
If (Answer& And WF_CPU386) Then
        CPU= "80386"
Else If (Answer& And WF_CPU486) Then
        CPU = "80486"
End If
```

You'll see a demonstration of the **GetWinFlags** function in the SYSINFO program later in the chapter.

Table 10.2   The GetWinFlags Flag Constants

Constant	Value	Meaning
WF_PMODE	&H1	Windows is running in protected mode (always true in Windows 3.1)
WF_CPU286	&H2	An 80286 processor is present
WF_CPU386	&H4	An 80386 processor is present
WF_CPU486	&H8	An 80486 processor is present
WF_STANDARD	&H10	Windows is running in standard mode
WF_WIN286	&H10	Same as WF_STANDARD
WF_ENHANCED	&H20	Windows is running in 386 enhanced mode
WF_WIN386	&H20	Same as WF_ENHANCED
WF_LARGEFRAME	&H100	EMS memory is using a large frame
WF_SMALLFRAME	&H200	EMS memory is using a small frame
WF_80x87	&H400	A math co-processor is present

Determining Keyboard Type

A program may want to use the F11 and F12 function keys, but not all keyboards have them. How can a program determine the number of function keys?

The API includes a function called **GetKeyboardType** that retrieves information about the current keyboard. The function's declaration is:

```
Declare Function GetKeyboardType Lib "Keyboard" (ByVal FnKeybInfo
   As Integer) As Integer
```

The argument **fnKeybInfo** determines the type of keyboard information that the function returns. A value of 0 retrieves the keyboard type, 1 retrieves the keyboard subtype, and 2 retrieves the number of function keys on the keyboard. When retrieving keyboard type (**fnKeybInfo = 0**) the function's return value is interpreted as shown here:

Return Value	Keyboard Type
1	IBM PC/XT or compatible (83-key) keyboard
2	Olivetti "ICO" (102-key) keyboard
3	IBM AT (84-key) or similar keyboard
4	IBM Enhanced (101- or 102-key) keyboard
5	Nokia 1050 and similar keyboards
6	Nokia 9140 and similar keyboards
7	Japanese keyboard

The subtype is an OEM-dependent value, and is of no interest to us. When retrieving number of function keys (**fnKeybInfo = 2**) the return value is the number of function keys on the current keyboard.

Note that in many cases a program can determine the number of function keys on a keyboard from the keyboard type. The number of function keys for each keyboard type is shown here:

Type	Number of Function Keys
1	10
2	12 (sometimes 18)
3	10
4	12
5	10
6	24
7	OEM-dependent

It's safer, however, to use the **GetKeyboardType** function to retrieve the number of function keys directly rather than relying on this table.

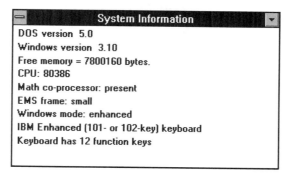

Figure 10.4 SYSINFO displays a variety of information about your system.

The SYSINFO Program

Now we can pull together everything we've learned about determining Windows, DOS, and system information to write a handy little utility.

SYSINFO, presented in Listings 10.8 and 10.9, illustrates the various methods of obtaining system information that we have been covering. As shown in Figure 10.4, the program displays the DOS and Windows version numbers, free memory, CPU type and math co-processor status, the EMS frame type, the Windows operating mode, and keyboard information. If the user clicks anywhere on the form, the information is updated. Updating really makes no sense for any of the information except the free memory (your CPU type or keyboard is hardly likely to change while the program is running!).

Using SYSINFO.MAK

This demonstration, presented in Listings 10.8 and 10.9, is stored on disk as SYSINFO.MAK and SYSINFO.FRM.

Listing 10.8 Objects and Properties in SYSINFO.FRM

```
Begin Form Form1
   BorderStyle     =   1   'Fixed Single
   Caption         =   "System Information"
   MaxButton       =   0   'False
   Begin Label Label1
      AutoSize      =   -1   'True
      Caption       =   "Label1"
      Index         =   0
   End
End
```

Listing 10.9   Code in SYSINFO.FRM

```
Option Explicit

Declare Function GetVersion Lib "Kernel" () As Long
Declare Function GetKeyboardType Lib "Keyboard" (ByVal nTypeFlag As
   Integer) As Integer
Declare Function GetWinFlags Lib "Kernel" () As Long
Declare Function GetFreeSpace Lib "Kernel" (ByVal wFlags As Integer)
   As Long

Const WF_CPU286 = &H2
Const WF_CPU386 = &H4
Const WF_CPU486 = &H8
Const WF_80x87 = &H400
Const WF_LARGEFRAME = &H100
Const WF_ENHANCED = &H20

Sub Form_Click ()

' Update display when form clicked.
Call ShowInfo

End Sub

Sub Form_Load ()

Const LABEL_HEIGHT = 200
Const LABEL_SPACING = 250
Const LABEL_LEFT = 100

Dim I As Integer

' Place the Labels on the form.
For I = 1 To 8
    Load Label1(I)
Next I

For I = 0 To 8
    Label1(I).Left = LABEL_LEFT
    Label1(I).Height = LABEL_HEIGHT
    Label1(I).Top = 50 + I * LABEL_SPACING
    Label1(I).Visible = True
Next I

' Display the information.
Call ShowInfo

End Sub
```

```
Sub Label1_Click (Index As Integer)

' Update display if any Label is clicked.
Call ShowInfo

End Sub

Sub ShowInfo ()

Dim X As Long, DOSVer As Long
Dim WinMajor As Integer, WinMinor As Integer
Dim DOSMajor As Integer, DOSMinor As Long
Dim I As Integer

' Get DOS and Windows versions.
X = GetVersion()

DOSVer = X \ &H10000

WinMajor = X And &HFF
WinMinor = (X And &HFFFF) \ 256

DOSMinor = DOSVer And &HFF
DOSMajor = DOSVer \ 256

Label1(0).Caption = "DOS version "
Label1(0).Caption = Label1(0).Caption & Str$(DOSMajor) & "."
Label1(0).Caption = Label1(0).Caption & Right$(Str$(DOSMinor),
   Len(Str$(DOSMinor)) - 1)

Label1(1).Caption = "Windows version "
Label1(1).Caption = Label1(1).Caption & Str$(WinMajor) & "."
Label1(1).Caption = Label1(1).Caption & Right$(Str$(WinMinor),
   Len(Str$(WinMinor)) - 1)

' Get free memory.
Label1(2) = "Free memory =" & Str$(GetFreeSpace(I)) & " bytes."

' Get the Windows status flags.
X = GetWinFlags()

' Get CPU type.
If X And WF_CPU286 Then
    Label1(3) = "CPU: 80286"
ElseIf X And WF_CPU386 Then
    Label1(3) = "CPU: 80386"
ElseIf X And WF_CPU486 Then
    Label1(3) = "CPU: 80486"
Else
```

```
        Label1(3) = "CPU: Unknown"
End If


' Co-processor present?
If X And WF_80x87 Then
        Label1(4).Caption = "Math co-processor: present"
Else
        Label1(4).Caption = "Math co-processor: not present"
End If


' EMS Frame type
If X And WF_LARGEFRAME Then
        Label1(5).Caption = "EMS frame: large"
Else
        Label1(5).Caption = "EMS frame: small"
End If


' Mode
If X And WF_ENHANCED Then
        Label1(6).Caption = "Windows mode: enhanced"
Else
        Label1(6).Caption = "Windows mode: standard"
End If


' Get keyboard type.
I = GetKeyboardType(0)

Select Case I
    Case 1
        Label1(7) = "IBM PC/XT, or compatible (83-key) keyboard"
    Case 2
        Label1(7).Caption = "Olivetti ICO (102-key) keyboard"
    Case 3
        Label1(7).Caption = "IBM AT (84-key) or similar keyboard"
    Case 4
        Label1(7).Caption = "IBM Enhanced (101- or 102-key) keyboard"
    Case 5
        Label1(7).Caption = "Nokia 1050 or similar keyboard"
    Case 6
        Label1(7).Caption = "Nokia 9140 or similar keyboard"
    Case 7
        Label1(7).Caption = "Japanese keyboard"
    Case Else
        Label1(7).Caption = "Unknown keyboard type"
End Select

' Number of function keys
I = GetKeyboardType(2)
```

```
Label1(8).Caption = "Keyboard has" & Str$(I) & " function keys"

End Sub
```

Program Execution

This section presents some techniques for controlling the execution of programs and of Windows itself. You'll learn how to prevent a Visual Basic program from loading more than once, how to run a DOS program and capture its output under Visual Basic control, and more.

Prevent Multiple Instances of a Visual Basic Program from Being Loaded

Windows will let you run two or more instances of the same application. While this can be a useful technique, there may sometimes be applications for which multiple instances should not be permitted. You can design a Visual Basic program to check the environment to see if it's already running.

The technique we will use to detect if another instance of a program is already loaded involves the *module handle*. Whenever a program, or module, is loaded, Windows assigns it a handle. If a second instance of the same program is loaded, Windows is smart enough to reuse the same code, assigning the same module handle. Therefore, a program can obtain its own module handle using the **GetModuleHandle** function, and then determine how many instances of that handle exist with the **GetModuleUsage** function. If the answer is more than one, then another instance of the program is already loaded.

The declaration for the **GetModuleHandle** function is:

```
Declare Function GetModuleHandle Lib "Kernel" (ByVal
    lpModuleName As String) As Integer
```

The argument **lpModuleName** is the name of the module whose handle you want—that is, the name of the .EXE file (for example, MYPROG.EXE). The function returns the module's handle, or zero on failure.

The declaration for **GetModuleUsage** is:

```
Declare Function GetModuleUsage Lib "Kernel" (ByVal hModule
    As Integer) As Integer
```

Figure 10.5 The program ONE_ONLY will not permit a second instance of itself to be loaded.

hModule is the handle you're interested in. The function returns the handle count, which tells you how many instances of the program are loaded.

The program ONE_ONLY demonstrates how to use these API functions to prevent a second instance of a program from loading. The program consists only of a single form with no controls; its code is given in Listing 10.10. To test the program you must create an .EXE file, then try to run it twice from the Program Manager. On the second try you'll get a message indicating that the program is already running, as shown in Figure 10.5.

Using ONE_ONLY.MAK

This demonstration, presented in Listing 10.10, is stored on disk as ONE_ONLY.MAK and ONE_ONLY.FRM.

Listing 10.10   Code in ONE_ONLY.FRM

```
Option Explicit

Declare Function GetModuleHandle Lib "Kernel" (ByVal
  lpModuleName As String) As Integer
Declare Function GetModuleUsage Lib "Kernel" (ByVal hModule
  As Integer) As Integer

Const MB_ICONSTOP = 16

Sub Form_Load ()

Dim Instances As Integer, Handle As Integer
Dim Msg As String

Handle = GetModuleHandle("ONE_ONLY.EXE")
Instances = GetModuleUsage(Handle)
If Instances > 1 Then
  Msg = "This program is already running." & Chr$(13) & Chr$(10)
  Msg = Msg & "Multiple instances are not permitted."
  MsgBox Msg, MB_ICONSTOP, "Error"
  End
```

```
Else
   Show
End If

End Sub
```

Execute a DOS Program, Capture its Output, and Determine When It's Done

A Visual Basic program can easily execute a DOS program using the Shell statement. It's more difficult, however, to determine when the DOS program is done and to capture its output for use in the Visual Basic program.

Despite the ever-increasing array of Windows programs, many of us still have DOS programs that we need to run. In some cases, we have no choice but to open a DOS screen and interact with the clunky DOS interface directly. At times, however, the DOS program can be hidden from the user by wrapping it, so to speak, in a Visual Basic shell. This is often true of DOS programs that can accept command-line arguments telling them what to do. The DOS program's output can be redirected to a disk file, then when it's finished the output file can be read into the Visual Basic program.

Several things are required for this sort of strategy to work. First of all, we'll use Visual Basic's **Shell** statement to execute the DOS program. However, when you want to redirect output to a file, using **Shell** directly doesn't work. Let's say you want to run the DOS DIR command and put its sorted output into a file for reading by Visual Basic. You might try the following:

```
X = Shell("DIR | SORT >> DIRFILE.TXT")
```

Unfortunately, this won't work. The DOS program runs, but its output is not redirected to the file as specified. In order to accomplish redirection into a file, you must create a DOS batch file containing the desired command, then run the batch file with **Shell**. For example, create a batch file named DO_DIR.BAT that contains the one line

```
DIR | SORT >> DIRFILE.TXT
```

Then execute the following **Shell** statement from Visual Basic:

```
Shell("DO_DIR.BAT")
```

We have solved one of our problems. This technique has a weakness, in that it is dependent on the existence of a particular batch file on disk. If the batch file is accidentally deleted or changed, the Visual Basic program will not work properly. To avoid being dependent on the batch file, we can create it "on the fly" from within the Visual Basic program. This not only avoids the possible problem of a missing batch file, but it lets the Visual Basic program customize the batch file as needed and delete it when it's no longer needed. Here's how you would do it:

```
FileNum = FreeFile
Open "DO_DIR.BAT" for output as #FileNum
Print #FileNum, "DIR | SORT >> DIRFILE.TXT"
Close #FileNum
Shell("DO_DIR.BAT")
Kill "DO_DIR.BAT"
```

Well, we have solved another problem. As you have probably noticed, however, running a DOS program using the **Shell** statement hands over the entire screen to the DOS program, even if only briefly. If the user doesn't need to interact with the DOS program, and doesn't need to see its output directly, there's no need for this. Wouldn't it be better to have the DOS program work quietly "behind the scenes?" It's possible to have the DOS session run in the background, minimized to an icon. This way it can do its work without intruding on the screen. The user may never even be aware that a DOS program was executed! To run a DOS program minimized in the background you must create a PIF file for it. Use the Windows PIF Editor for this purpose. Create a PIF file that has the same name as the DOS file you are running or, if you are using a batch file as explained above, the same name as the batch file (the PIF file has the .PIF extension, of course). In the PIF Editor set the Program Filename to the name of the file you'll be running (MYFILE.EXE or MYFILE.BAT, for example), and set the Start-up Directory to the program location. Set Display Usage to Windowed and Execution to Background. It's these last two setting that permit the DOS program to run in the background as an icon. Optionally, enter a name for Window Title; this is the name that will be displayed on the DOS program's icon while it's running.

Once you have created and saved the PIF file you're just about ready to go. This time, when you execute the batch file with the **Shell** statement, include an argument that tells **Shell** to run the program minimized. You can use an argument of **2** (minimized with focus) or **7** (minimized without focus):

```
Shell("DO_DIR.BAT", 2)
```

or

```
Shell("DO_DIR.BAT", 7)
```

The only practical difference between these two arguments is that if the Visual Basic program's form is overlapping the location where the DOS program icon will be displayed, then a **Shell** argument of **2** permits the icon to show through the Visual Basic form, whereas an argument of **7** does not.

Now you're all set. Well, almost! There's one more potential problem to deal with. The **Shell** statement runs programs *asynchronously*, which means that you cannot be sure that the program run by **Shell** will be finished executing before the next Basic statement, the one following the **Shell** statement, is executed. In some circumstances this will not be a problem. If, however, the Visual Basic program is dependent in some way on the DOS program's completion, there will most certainly be a problem. For example, if the DOS program's output is being redirected into a file that the Visual Basic program will open and read, you had better be sure that the DOS program is finished before trying to open and read the output file!

How can your Visual Basic program tell when a DOS program has terminated? There are at least two methods that can be used. One of these methods uses the **GetActiveWindow** and **IsWindow** API functions. The function declarations for these functions are:

```
Declare Function GetActiveWindow Lib "User" () As Integer

Declare Function IsWindow Lib "User" (ByVal hWnd As Integer)
   As Integer
```

The **GetActiveWindow** function returns the handle of the currently active window. The **IsWindow** function is passed a handle and returns True if the corresponding window exists. Here's how to use them for our current needs. Immediately after calling the **Shell** statement to run your DOS task, call **GetActiveWindow** to get the handle of the DOS window (it will be the active window since you just activated it). This only works, of course, if you give the DOS window the focus by calling **Shell** with the proper second argument, **2**:

```
Shell("DO_DIR.BAT", 2)
```

Then, execute a loop that uses the **IsWindow** function to determine if the DOS window is still open. If it is, then the DOS process has not ended. As soon as **IsWindow** returns False, you know the DOS process has ended, and you can terminate the loop and continue with processing the output of the DOS program. Here's the needed code:

```
ShellHandle = GetActiveWindow()
Do While IsWindow(ShellHandle)
  X = DoEvents()
Loop
```

The second method for pausing a Visual Basic program until a shelled DOS task has completed uses the **GetNumTasks** API function. The declaration for this function is:

```
Declare Function GetNumTasks Lib "Kernel" () As Integer
```

GetNumTasks returns the number of tasks that are currently active on the system. Here's how it works: call **GetNumTasks** just before the **Shell** statement; this will give you the number of current system tasks. While the shelled DOS task is running, the number of tasks will be increased by one. You can use a loop to repeatedly call **GetNumTasks**. When the number of tasks has returned to the value it had before **Shell** was called, you know the DOS task has completed. Your code would look like this:

```
X = Shell(TASK_NAME, 2)
Do While GetNumTasks() <> NumTasks
    X = DoEvents()
Loop
```

This method does not depend on the DOS task having the focus, so the **Shell** statement's second argument could be **7** (minimized without focus). Using the **GetNumTasks** function is reliable for monitoring DOS tasks that complete relatively quickly. If the task takes a while to run, however, there's always the chance that the user will start a new task or terminate an existing task, which will throw off your task count.

Be Sure to Call DoEvents in Your Loop

To prevent your Visual Basic application from hogging processor time, place a call to **DoEvents** inside the loop that waits for the DOS task to complete. Doing so ensures that processing time is made available for other Windows processes.

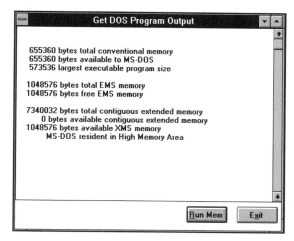

Figure 10.6 RUN_DOS executes a DOS program and displays its output in the Text Box.

The program RUN_DOS, provided in Listings 10.11 and 10.12, illustrates the techniques we have been discussing. The program creates a batch file containing the desired DOS command, then uses the **Shell** statement to execute the batch file. The batch file command directs the DOS program's output into a temporary file. Once the DOS task has completed, the program opens the temporary file and reads it into a Text Box. Finally, the batch file and temporary file are deleted.

As written, RUN_DOS executes the MS-DOS MEM utility to obtain a summary of the system's memory configuration. The output of MEM is shown in the program's Text Box in Figure 10.6. MEM was introduced with DOS 5; if you are still using an earlier DOS version you will need to substitute a DOS command that is available on your system, such as DIR or CHKDSK.

Remember to create a PIF file for the DOS process. The program will work without a PIF file, but the DOS process will run full screen, not as an icon.

Using RUN_DOS.MAK

This demonstration, presented in Listings 10.11 and 10.12, is stored on disk as RUN_DOS.MAK and RUN_DOS.FRM.

Listing 10.11   Objects and Properties in RUN_DOS.FRM

```
Begin Form Form1
   Caption          =    "Get DOS Program Output"
```

```
    Begin CommandButton cmdExit
        Caption          =    "E&xit"
    End
    Begin CommandButton cmdRunMem
        Caption          =    "&Run Mem"
    End
    Begin TextBox Text1
        MultiLine        =    -1 'True
        ScrollBars       =    2  'Vertical
    End
End
```

Listing 10.12   Code in RUN_DOS.FRM

```
Option Explicit

Declare Function GetNumTasks Lib "Kernel" () As Integer
Declare Function GetActiveWindow Lib "User" () As Integer
Declare Function IsWindow Lib "User" (ByVal hWnd As Integer)
  As Integer

Sub cmdExit_Click ()

End

End Sub

Sub cmdRunMem_Click ()

' Names for the batch and temporary files.
Const BATFILE_NAME = "MYBAT.BAT"
Const TEMPFILE_NAME = "MYTEMP.TXT"

Dim Cmd As String, Buffer As String
Dim FileNum As Integer, X As Integer
Dim ShellHandle As Integer, NumTasks As Integer

' Create the command and write it to a batch file.
Cmd = "MEM > " & TEMPFILE_NAME
FileNum = FreeFile
Open BATFILE_NAME For Output As #FileNum
Print #FileNum, Cmd
Close #FileNum

' Use Shell to run the batch file.
MousePointer = 11
NumTasks = GetNumTasks()
X = Shell(BATFILE_NAME, 2)
```

```
' Pause until the DOS Shell task has completed.
Do While GetNumTasks() <> NumTasks
    X = DoEvents()
Loop

' Commented code that follows is the alternate method
' of waiting until the DOS Shell process is completed.

'ShellHandle = GetActiveWindow()

'Do While IsWindow(ShellHandle)
'   X = DoEvents()
'Loop
MousePointer = 0

' Read DOS program output into a Text Box.
FileNum = FreeFile
Open TEMPFILE_NAME For Input As #FileNum
Text1.Text = ""
Cmd = ""

While Not EOF(FileNum)
   Line Input #FileNum, Buffer
   Cmd = Cmd & Buffer & Chr$(13) & Chr$(10)
Wend

Close #FileNum

Text1.Text = Cmd

' Delete the batch and temporary files.
Kill BATFILE_NAME
Kill TEMPFILE_NAME

End Sub
```

Preventing Data Loss When Windows Terminates

If the user tries to shut down Windows while a program is still running, there is always the chance of data loss. Here's how to prevent this from happening to your Visual Basic programs.

When the user tries to terminate the entire Windows session, Windows sends an "Is it OK to terminate?" message to all applications that are running. Each application can reply either "Yes" or "No." If Windows receives any "No" replies, it displays the "Application Still Active" message and does not terminate.

Unfortunately, Visual Basic programs do not have a built-in response to a pending Windows termination. If Windows is terminating, any executing Visual Basic programs can simply be shut down without warning. Clearly, the opportunity for data loss exists, and well written application should not permit this! What can you do?

It's fairly simple to include code in your programs that will prevent unexpected termination. The technique is based on the fact that whenever a Windows shutdown is imminent, the Visual Basic **Form_Unload** event is triggered. You can place code in the **Form_Unload** event procedure that automatically saves data before termination, or you can offer the user the choice of exiting after saving data, exiting without saving data, or canceling (not exiting). Your code might look something like this:

```
Sub Form_Unload (Cancel As Integer)

Const MB_YESNOCANCEL = 3
Const MB_ICONSTOP = 16
Const IDYES = 6
Const IDNO = 7
Const IDCANCEL = 2

Dim Reply As Integer

Reply = MsgBox("Save data before exiting?", MB_YESNOCANCEL +
   MB_ICONSTOP, "Termination")

Select Case Reply
    Case IDYES        ' Save data then exit.
        Call SaveData
    Case IDNO
        ' Take no action.
    Case IDCANCEL
        Cancel = True
End Select

End Sub
```

In addition to an imminent Windows shutdown, the **Form_Unload** event is also triggered by the **Unload** statement and by the user selecting Close from the form's Control menu. This makes it an ideal place for code that gives the user the chance to save data or cancel program termination.

Exit Windows under Program Control

A Visual Basic program can use an API call to exit Windows.

You may run across circumstances where you want to be able to terminate a Windows session under the control of a Visual Basic program. To do this, you use the **ExitWindows** API call. Its declaration is:

```
Declare Function ExitWindows Lib "User" (ByVal dwReserved As Long,
    ByVal wReturnCode As Integer) As Integer
```

The first argument, **dwReserved**, is reserved and must be 0. The second argument, **wReturnCode**, specifies the action to be taken. To terminate Windows and return to DOS, pass a value of 0 for the second argument.

When the **ExitWindows** function is called, Windows sends a message to all applications notifying them that a request has been made to terminate Windows. As I described in an earlier section, applications can either "agree" or "refuse" to terminate. The return value of the **ExitWindows** function is 0 if one or more applications refuse to terminate. The function returns a non-zero value if all applications agree to be terminated.

To exit Windows by issuing a command in a Visual Basic program, you would write something like this:

```
Sub cmdExitWindows_Click ()

Dim Reply As Integer

Reply = MsgBox("Exit Windows - are you sure?", MB_ICONSTOP +
    MB_OKCANCEL, "Exit Windows")

If Reply = IDCANCEL Then
    Exit Sub
End If

If ExitWindows(0, 0) = 0 Then
    MsgBox ("Cannot exit Windows")
End If

End Sub
```

Odds and Ends

T his is the "catch-all" chapter, the place where I put all the stuff that didn't seem to belong in one of the other chapters (there's one more chapter to come, but that's a "fun" chapter so I left it until last). You'll find techniques related to printing, fonts, data storage and manipulation, mouse programming, and more. Enjoy!

Obtaining Printer and Font Information from Windows

Visual Basic makes most aspects of producing printed output quite simple. The Printer object and its properties and methods provide most of the capabilities anyone will every need. Some potentially useful printer and font information, however, cannot be accessed via the Printer object's properties. Our old friend the Windows API can help us obtain this information.

Determining the Default Printer Name, Driver, and Port

Information about the default Windows printer, its driver, and the default printer port is stored in the WIN.INI file. You can retrieve this information with the GetProfileString API function.

Windows stores a lot of its configuration information in the WIN.INI file in the main Windows directory. The first part of Chapter 3 presented information about the format and contents of WIN.INI—you may wish to refer back to that chapter if you don't remember the details.

Among the many items of information stored in WIN.INI is the name of the default printer, the default printer driver, and the default printer port. This information is stored in the [windows] section of WIN.INI following the device= line. For example, in the [windows] section of my WIN.INI file there is the line

```
device=HP LaserJet III,hppcl5a,LPT1:
```

This line indicates that my default printer is the HP LaserJet III, the driver is named hppcl5a, and the LPT1: is the default port. A Visual Basic program can read this information from WIN.INI using the **GetProfileString** function. The declaration for this function is:

```
Declare Function GetProfileString Lib "Kernel" (ByVal
    lpAppName As String, ByVal lpKeyName As String, ByVal
```

```
lpDefault As String, ByVal lpReturnedString As
String, ByVal nSize As Integer) As Integer
```

GetProfileString returns the actual number of characters read from WIN.INI. (If you would like a more detailed explanation of the **GetProfileString** function, refer to Chapter 3.) The function's arguments are described here:

- **lpAppName** specifies which .INI file section contains the information to be read; for the present purposes, we'll set this argument to "windows."

- **lpKeyName** specifies the entry whose value is to be read; to obtain printer information set this argument to "device."

- **lpReturnedString** is the string variable where the data read from the file will be placed.

- **lpDefault** specifies the string that will be placed in **lpReturnedString** if **lpAppName** or **lpKeyName** cannot be found in the .INI file.

- **nSize** is the size, in characters, of **lpReturnedString**.

Using this function, you can obtain the string that follows the device= field in the [windows] section of WIN.INI. Knowing that this string contains the printer name, driver name, and port name separated by commas, you can easily parse it into its three components. You'll see how this is done in the program PR_INFO later in this chapter.

Getting Page Layout Information

You can use the GetDeviceCaps function to obtain certain printer information that allows you to create sophisticated page layouts.

If you want to have better control over the page layout in your printed pages, you need to know certain information about the printer. Most important is the number of dots, or pixels, per inch (why this is important will become clear soon). You can obtain this information using the **GetDeviceCaps** function. The declaration is:

```
Declare Function GetDeviceCaps Lib "GDI" (ByVal hDC As
    Integer, ByVal nIndex As Integer) As Integer
```

The argument **hDC** is the device context of the device whose capabilities you are querying. For printer information, use the **Printer.hDC** property. The **nIndex** argument identifies the specific capability you are querying (see below). The function returns the numerical value corresponding to the capability that was queried.

GetDeviceCaps can return a wide range of information about any device for which a valid context exists. A full discussion of this function is well beyond our current needs. It's sufficient for us to know how to obtain the pixels per inch information about the printer. There are actually two pieces of information needed: pixels per inch in the X (horizontal) direction, and pixels per inch in the Y (vertical) direction. You get this information by passing the appropriate **nIndex** argument to **GetDeviceCaps**; these arguments are best passed as Windows global constants—**LOGPIXELSX** (value = 88) to obtain horizontal pixels per inch and **LOGPIXELSY** (value = 90) to obtain vertical pixels per inch. For example,

```
XPixelsPerInch = GetDeviceCaps(Printer.hDc, LOGPIXELSX)
```

Determining a Printer's Color Capabilities

The GetDeviceCaps function can also be used to determine the color capabilities of the printer.

Printers with color capabilities are becoming more and more common. You can no longer assume that your program will run on a system that is limited to monochrome printing. If you want to be able to take advantage of a color printer when it is available, your program needs to be able to determine when a color-capable printer is installed and how many colors it can reproduce. You can use the **GetDeviceCaps** function to obtain this information (you can also use it to determine the color capabilities of the video display). The function's declaration was given in the previous section. To determine a device's color capabilities, pass one of the following values as the **nIndex** argument to **GetDeviceCaps**:

BITSPIXEL (value = 12) to determine the number of adjacent bits used to control the color of each pixel.

PLANES (value = 14) to determine the number of bit planes.

NUMCOLORS (value = 24) to obtain the total number of colors the device supports.

Most output devices that support color use either multiple bits per pixel or multiple bit planes, but not both, to represent color. In other words, either the number of adjacent bits or the number of bit planes will be 1 in almost all cases. However, we must take into account the rare case in which this is not true. To calculate a device's color capabilities from these values, use the following formula:

```
Colors = 2 ^ (AdjacentBits * BitPlanes)
```

Note that a result of 2 indicates a standard monochrome device. But what about **NUMCOLORS**? From the description above it seems that passing this argument is all you need to obtain a device's color capabilities. That is indeed true (usually)—the value returned by **GetDeviceCaps** when **NUMCOLORS** is passed as the **nIndex** argument is almost always the same as the value obtained by plugging the adjacent bits and bit planes values into the above formula. The values will, however, be different for some multiple pen plotters and for certain specialized video hardware.

Determining Page Size and Orientation

To further enhance your page layout, you will want to obtain the page size and orientation.

What other information do we need for working with the page layout? We need to know the size of the actual page, and also its *orientation*. By orientation I means is it in the standard *portrait* orientation, where lines of text run parallel to the short edge of the page, or in *landscape* orientation, where lines of text run parallel to the long edge of the page. This information can be obtained with the API **Escape** function. This function is used both for sending commands to, and retrieving information from, devices when the capabilities are not directly available through the Windows Graphics Device Interface (GDI). Calls to the **Escape** function are translated and sent directly to the device driver. The declaration for this function is:

```
Declare Function Escape Lib "GDI" (ByVal hDC As
   Integer, ByVal nEscape As Integer, ByVal nCount As
   Integer,  lpInData As Any, lpOutData As Any) As
   Integer
```

The function's arguments are described here:

- **hDC** is the device context of the device.
- **nEscape** identifies the specific **Escape** function to be performed.
- **nCount** is the size, in characters, of the input data buffer or structure.
- **lpInData** is the buffer or structure holding the input data.
- **lpOutData** is the buffer or structure where the output data is placed.

Error in Win 3.1 API Help

The declaration for the **Escape** function provided in the Win 3.1 API Help indicates that all five arguments should be declared with the **ByVal** keyword. This declaration is wrong. If you use it, you will get serious errors when the program is run. To correct this error, declare the last two arguments, **lpInData** and **lpOutData**, without the **ByVal** keyword, as shown above.

Notice that two of the arguments refer to input data. These arguments are necessary only when **Escape** is being used to send information or commands to a device—when using **Escape** to retrieve information from a device, as we want to do, both of these arguments should be set to 0.

The **hDC** argument is the device context; for the printer, this is the hDC property of the Printer object. The way that the **Escape** function returns information varies with the specific request being made:

- If the returned information is a single value, then it is passed back as the function's return value. The **lpOutData** argument is not needed and should be set to 0.

- If the returned information consists of more than one value, the values are returned in the data structure specified by the **lpOutData** argument.

The return value is positive on success. A return value of 0 indicates that the **Escape** function is not supported by the specified device, and a return value less than 0 indicates that an error has occurred.

If the above seems confusing, it's because it *is* confusing! The **Escape** function was deliberately made somewhat open-ended so that developers could adapt it for their own drivers. There is no set of general rules that you can follow that will always work to perform a certain task. Rather, there are specific implementations of **Escape** that you must, unavoidably, learn as you encounter them. You are, in fact, about to encounter your first two!

To determine the current setting of the printer orientation, pass an **nEscape** argument of **30** (we'll use a constant, of course); a return value of 1 or 2 indicates portrait or landscape orientation, respectively:

```
Const GETPAGEORIENT = 30
...
PageOrientation = Escape(Printer.hDC, GETPAGEORIENT, 0, 0, 0)
```

To determine the physical page size, pass an **nEscape** argument of **12**. The page size is returned in a type **PointAPI** structure that the program must define. For example:

```
Type PointAPI
        X As Integer
        Y As Integer
End Type

Const GETPAGESIZE = 12
...
Dim PageSize as PointAPI
X = Escape(Printer.hDC, GETPAGESIZE, 0, 0, PageSize)
```

Following the call, **PageSize.X** contains the page width and **PageSize.Y** contains the page length. Both values are expressed in terms of pixels, or dots. You can obtain the actual page dimensions, in inches, by dividing these values by the pixels-per-inch values obtained with the **GetDeviceCaps** function that we covered earlier in this chapter.

Obtaining Text Metric Information

Under most circumstances you can let Visual Basic and Windows handle all or most of the font details for you, and you'll get perfectly good results. At other times, however, you may want to control printing more closely yourself, in which case you need to have access to information about the font being used. You can use the GetTextMetric API function to obtain useful information about the current font.

As fonts have become more attractive and sophisticated, they have also become more complicated. The Windows API provides a convenient way to obtain most of the needed font information. The **GetTextMetrics** function returns a variety of information about the font that is current for a specified device. The function declaration is:

```
Declare Function GetTextMetrics Lib "GDI" (ByVal hDC As
    Integer, lpMetrics As TEXTMETRIC) As Integer
```

This function returns non-zero on success, zero otherwise. The argument **hDC** is the device context; for a printer font, you would use the hDC property of the Printer object. **lpMetrics** is a data structure of type

TEXTMETRIC where the function places the font information. Type **TEXTMETRIC** is defined as follows:

```
Type TEXTMETRIC
    tmHeight As Integer
    tmAscent As Integer
    tmDescent As Integer
    tmInternalLeading As Integer
    tmExternalLeading As Integer
    tmAveCharWidth As Integer
    tmMaxCharWidth As Integer
    tmWeight As Integer
    tmItalic As String * 1
    tmUnderlined As String * 1
    tmStruckOut As String * 1
    tmFirstChar As String * 1
    tmLastChar As String * 1
    tmDefaultChar As String * 1
    tmBreakChar As String * 1
    tmPitchAndFamily As String * 1
    tmCharSet As String * 1
    tmOverhang As Integer
    tmDigitizedAspectX As Integer
    tmDigitizedAspectY As Integer
End Type
```

The interpretation of the information in the various fields is explained in Table 11.1. Note that all measurement values are in pixels. This list does not include all of the **TEXTMETRIC** fields, but only those that a Visual Basic program is likely to have need for. For a visual representation of some of the measurements, see Figure 11.1.

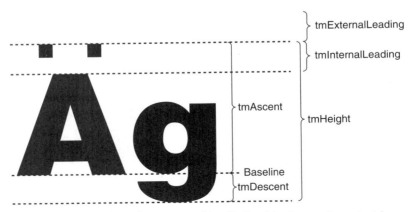

Figure 11.1 Five of the values returned by GetTextMetrics are important in determining a font's vertical height.

Table 11.1 TEXTMETRIC Fields

TEXTMETRIC Fields	*Description*
tmHeight	The overall character height (equal to the sum of **tmDescent** and **tmAscent**)
tmAscent	The character height above the baseline
tmDescent	The character height below the baseline
tmInternalLeading	The space for diacritical marks on uppercase letters This space is included in the **tmHeight** measurement. You can obtain actual font size by subtracting **tmInternalLeading** from **tmHeight**.
tmExternalLeading	The amount of space between lines of text recommended by the font designer
tmAveCharWidth	The average character width
tmMaxCharWidth	The width of the widest character
tmWeight	The weight of the current font, in the range 0-999 Values are 400 for a normal font, 700 for boldface
tmItalic	A non-zero value if the font is italic
tmUnderlined	A non-zero value if the font is underlined
tmStruckOut	A non-zero value if the font is a strike-through font
tmCharSet	A value of 0 for an ANSI character set, 2 for a symbol character set, and 255 for an OEM character set
tmFirstChar	The ASCII code of the first character in the character set. This is normally 32 (space) for ANSI character sets.
tmLastChar	The ASCII code of the last character in the character set. This is normally 255 for ANSI character sets.
tmDefaultChar	The ASCII code of the character used to display characters not available in the font. For ANSI character sets, normally 128.
tmBreakChar	The ASCII code of the character that should be used for breaking words when justifying text. Normally this is 32 (space).

You can see that there is *a lot* of font information available! This information has a variety of uses. For example, when you are creating printed output that spans multiple pages, you need to know how many lines of text wili print on a page in order to start new pages at the proper locations. The number of text lines that will fit on a page depends on a number of factors: the size of the page, the pixels-per-inch value for the printer, and the height, in pixels, of the current font. As you may already have realized, this information is all available using the techniques that have been covered above. You'll see how to put them all together in the demonstration program in the next section.

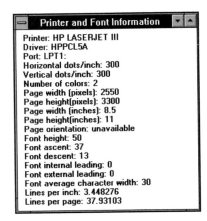

Figure 11.2   Printer and font information displayed by PR_INFO.

Obtaining Printer Information—a Demonstration

The program in this section uses these techniques to obtain information about the current printer and font.

PR_INFO shows how to use the techniques we have been discussing to obtain information about the current printer and font. The information is displayed in a window, as shown in Figure 11.2. The program's objects, properties, and code are given in Listings 11.1, 11.2, and 11.3.

Using PR_INFO.MAK

This demonstration, presented in Listings 11.1, 11.2, and 11.3, is stored on disk as PR_INFO.MAK, PR_INFO.FRM, and PR_INFO.BAS.

Listing 11.1   Objects and Properties in PR_INFO.FRM

```
Begin Form Form1
    Caption          =    "Printer and Font Information"
    Begin Label Label1
        AutoSize      =    -1   'True
        Index         =    0
    End
End
```

Listing 11.2   Code in PR_INFO.FRM

```
Option Explicit
```

```
' Number of labels needed to display information.
Const NUM_LABELS = 19

Const LABEL_HEIGHT = 120
Const LABEL_SEPARATION = 75
Const LABEL_LEFT = 150

Sub Form_Load ()

Const BUF_SIZE = 81

Dim Buffer As String, Temp1 As String, Temp2 As String
Dim x As Integer, I As Integer, L As Integer
Dim XPix As Integer, YPix As Integer
Dim PageSize As PointAPI, tm As TEXTMETRIC

L = 0

' Load the Label array and place the
' labels on the form.
For I = 1 To NUM_LABELS - 1
    Load Label1(I)
Next I

For I = 0 To NUM_LABELS - 1
    Label1(I).Left = LABEL_LEFT
    Label1(I).Height = LABEL_HEIGHT
    Label1(I).Top = LABEL_SEPARATION + (I *
      (LABEL_SEPARATION + LABEL_HEIGHT))
    Label1(I).Visible = True
Next I

' Size the form.
Form1.Height = Label1(NUM_LABELS - 1).Top + 5 * LABEL_HEIGHT
Form1.Width = Form1.Height

' Get the printer, driver, and port names from WIN.INI.
Buffer = Space$(BUF_SIZE)

x = GetProfileString("windows", "device", "", Buffer, BUF_SIZE)

Buffer = Trim$(Buffer)

Temp1 = Left$(Buffer, InStr(Buffer, ",") - 1)
Label1(L).Caption = "Printer: " & UCase$(Temp1)
L = L + 1
Buffer = Right$(Buffer, Len(Buffer) - InStr(Buffer, ","))
Temp1 = Left$(Buffer, InStr(Buffer, ",") - 1)
```

```
Label1(L).Caption = "Driver: " & UCase$(Temp1)
L = L + 1
Buffer = Right$(Buffer, Len(Buffer) - InStr(Buffer, ","))
Label1(L).Caption = "Port: " & UCase$(Buffer)
L = L + 1

' Get the pixels-per-inch values for the printer.
XPix = GetDeviceCaps(Printer.hDC, LOGPIXELSX)
Label1(L).Caption = "Horizontal dots/inch:" & Str$(XPix)
L = L + 1
YPix = GetDeviceCaps(Printer.hDC, LOGPIXELSY)
Label1(L).Caption = "Vertical dots/inch:" & Str$(YPix)
L = L + 1

' Get the color capabilities.
x = GetDeviceCaps(Printer.hDC, NUMCOLORS)
Label1(L).Caption = "Number of colors:" & Str$(x)
L = L + 1

' Get logical page size.
x = Escape(Printer.hDC, GETPAGESIZE, 0, 0, PageSize)

Label1(L).Caption = "Page width (pixels):" & Str$(PageSize.x)
L = L + 1
Label1(L).Caption = "Page height(pixels):" & Str$(PageSize.Y)
L = L + 1

' Calculate physical page size.
Label1(L).Caption = "Page width (inches):" & Str$(PageSize.x / XPix)
L = L + 1
Label1(L).Caption = "Page height(inches):" & Str$(PageSize.Y / YPix)
L = L + 1

' Get page orientation.
x = Escape(Printer.hDC, GETPAGEORIENT, 0, 0, 0)

Select Case x
    Case 1
        Label1(L).Caption = "Page orientation: portrait"
    Case 2
        Label1(L).Caption = "Page orientation: landscape"
    Case Else
        Label1(L).Caption = "Page orientation: unavailable"
End Select
L = L + 1

' Get text metric information.
x = GetTextMetrics(Printer.hDC, tm)
```

```
If x = 0 Then
    MsgBox ("Error getting text metric information.")
Else
    Label1(L).Caption = "Font height:" & Str$(tm.tmHeight)
    L = L + 1
    Label1(L).Caption = "Font ascent:" & Str$(tm.tmAscent)
    L = L + 1
    Label1(L).Caption = "Font descent:" & Str$(tm.tmDescent)
    L = L + 1
    Label1(L).Caption = "Font internal leading:" &
      Str$(tm.tmInternalLeading)
    L = L + 1
    Label1(L).Caption = "Font external leading:" &
      Str$(tm.tmExternalLeading)
    L = L + 1
    Label1(L).Caption = "Font average character width:" &
      Str$(tm.tmAveCharWidth)
    L = L + 1
End If

' Calculate lines per inch and lines per page.
Label1(L).Caption = "Lines per inch:" & Str$(YPix / (tm.tmHeight +
    tm.tmAscent))
L = L + 1
Label1(L).Caption = "Lines per page:" & Str$(PageSize.Y / (tm.tmHeight
    + tm.tmAscent))
L = L + 1

End Sub
```

Listing 11.3   Code in PR_INFO.BAS

```
Option Explicit

Type PointAPI
    X As Integer
    Y As Integer
End Type

Type TEXTMETRIC
    tmHeight As Integer
    tmAscent As Integer
    tmDescent As Integer
    tmInternalLeading As Integer
    tmExternalLeading As Integer
    tmAveCharWidth As Integer
    tmMaxCharWidth As Integer
    tmWeight As Integer
```

```
        tmItalic As String * 1
        tmUnderlined As String * 1
        tmStruckOut As String * 1
        tmFirstChar As String * 1
        tmLastChar As String * 1
        tmDefaultChar As String * 1
        tmBreakChar As String * 1
        tmPitchAndFamily As String * 1
        tmCharSet As String * 1
        tmOverhang As Integer
        tmDigitizedAspectX As Integer
        tmDigitizedAspectY As Integer
End Type

Declare Function GetProfileString Lib "Kernel" (ByVal
    lpAppName As String, ByVal lpKeyName As String, ByVal
    lpDefault As String, ByVal lpReturnedString As
    String,  ByVal nSize AsInteger) As Integer
Declare Function GetDeviceCaps Lib "GDI" (ByVal hDC As
    Integer, ByVal nIndex As Integer) As Integer
Declare Function Escape Lib "GDI" (ByVal hDC As
    Integer, ByVal nEscape As Integer, ByVal nCount As
    Integer, lpInData As Any, lpOutData As Any) As Integer
Declare Function GetTextMetrics Lib "GDI" (ByVal hDC As
    Integer, lpMetrics As TEXTMETRIC) As Integer

Global Const LOGPIXELSX = 88
Global Const LOGPIXELSY = 90
Global Const GETPAGESIZE = 12
Global Const GETPAGEORIENT = 30
Global Const NUMCOLORS = 24
```

Data Storage and Manipulation

It's a rare program indeed that doesn't need to store and manipulate data in one way or another! Here are a few techniques you may find useful.

Using Global Memory

You can directly access Windows global memory to store large quantities of data, bypassing the restrictions of Visual Basic's arrays.

If you need to store large amounts of data, an array is usually the best approach. While Visual Basic supports Huge arrays up to 64 Mb in size, each array dimension is still limited to indexes in the range -32,768 to

32,767. If you want to store more than 65,536 elements in the array, therefore, you are forced to use a multi-dimensional array. While this is no problem for some applications, there are other situations where having to manipulate two or more indexes to access the array data is a problem.

Fortunately there is a way around it. Windows maintains a pool of memory, called *global memory,* or the *global heap,* that is available for the data storage needs of the various applications executing at any one time. When you use Visual Basic arrays to store data, you are indirectly using global memory. You can also access global memory directly, using API calls.

There are three fundamental steps to using global memory:

1. Ask Windows to allocate a certain amount of memory. This step reserves a block of global memory for your program. Windows will not permit any other application to access the reserved memory.
2. Write data to, and read data from, specific locations in the allocated memory block.
3. When the program is finished, it should de-allocate the memory. This step frees the memory so that it is available for other applications.

Let's take a look at the API calls needed. You use the **GlobalAlloc** function to allocate global memory. The function declaration is:

```
Declare Function GlobalAlloc Lib "Kernel" (ByVal wFlags
   As Integer, ByVal dwBytes As Long) As Integer
```

The **wFlags** argument specifies how Windows should allocate the memory, and **dwBytes** specifies the number of bytes to allocate. Windows has a variety of methods it can use to allocate memory, which need not concern us. For our purposes we will use the Windows global constants **GMEM_MOVEABLE (value = &H2)** and **GMEM_ZEROINIT (value = &H40)**. The first of these tells Windows to allocate a block of memory that can be moved to any location in the global heap, and the second specifies that the entire block is to be initialized to zero. For example, to allocate a 10,000 byte block of global memory you would write:

```
X = GlobalAlloc(GMEM_MOVEABLE Or GMEM_INITZERO, 10000)
```

The function returns a handle to the allocated memory block. If the memory could not be allocated, the function returns 0.

The memory handle returned by **GlobalAlloc** cannot be used by Visual Basic; it is necessary to convert it into a *selector* first. You perform the conversion with the **GlobalHandleToSel** function. Its declaration is:

```
Declare Function GlobalHandleToSel Lib "Toolhelp.DLL"
   (ByVal Handle As Integer) As Integer
```

Handle is the global memory handle returned by the **GlobalAlloc** function. The function returns the selector, or 0 if it fails. You'll see what the selector is used for in a moment.

Once you have allocated your block of memory, what can you do with it? To write data to the memory, use the **MemoryWrite** function. Its declaration is:

```
Declare Function MemoryWrite Lib "Toolhelp.dll" (ByVal
   wSel As Integer, ByVal dwOffSet as Long, lpvBuf as
   Any, ByVal dwcb As Long) As Long
```

The function returns the number of bytes copied, or 0 on error. The function's arguments are described here:

- **wSel** is the selector that you obtained from the **GlobalHandleToSel** function.
- **dwOffSet** is the offset in the allocated memory block where the data is to be written (more on offsets below).
- **lpvBuf** is the data to be written. Note that this argument is not passed with the **ByVal** keyword.
- **dwcb** is the length, in bytes, of the data to be written.

What is this offset argument? It is analogous to the index of an array, specifying the location in the memory block were the data is to be written. Offset always refers to bytes. A memory block *n* bytes long has offsets ranging from 0 to *n-1*. To write data to the block starting at the 10th byte, for example, you would pass an offset of **9** to the **MemoryWrite** function.

You can use **MemoryWrite** to store any of Visual Basic's *fixed-length* data types in global memory. By fixed-length I mean data types whose size does not change during program execution. This includes fixed-length strings and all of the standard numerical types: Integer, Long, Single, Double, and Currency. It does not include variable length strings or type Variant.

When writing data to global memory, your program must keep track of what data is stored where. Different data items have different lengths, and with the exception of single-character, fixed-length strings, all occupy more than one byte of memory. For most applications, you will be using a block of global memory to store a large number of data elements of the same type, meaning that the length, in bytes, of each item is the same. It is possible to "mix and match" data types in global memory, but it's rarely worthwhile because there is so much overhead involved in keeping track of what is stored where.

For storing same-size items, calculating the offset is simple. For the *n*th item, the offset is calculated as:

```
Offset = (n - 1) * ItemSize
```

The size of a type Integer is 2 bytes, of types Single and Long is 4 bytes, and of types Double and Currency is 8 bytes. The length of a fixed-length string is its length in characters. For example, to store three type Double values at the first three locations in an allocated block of global memory you would write:

```
X = MemoryWrite (wSel, 0, Dbl1, 8)
X = MemoryWrite (wSel, 8, Dbl2, 8)
X = MemoryWrite (wSel, 16, Dbl3, 8)
```

Note that the item size must be taken into account when allocating the memory block. If you want space to store *n* items, you must allocate (*n* * ItemSize) bytes of global memory.

Storing data in global memory is not much use unless you can retrieve it! To read data from global memory, you use the **MemoryRead** function. Its declaration is:

```
Declare Function MemoryRead Lib "Toolhelp.dll" (ByVal
   wSel As Integer, ByVal dwOffSet as Long, lpvBuf as
   Any, ByVal dwcb As Long) As Long
```

You can see that the function's arguments are identical to the arguments for **MemoryWrite**, and they operate in the same way. **MemoryRead** copies **dwcb** bytes of data from offset **dwOffSet** in the global memory block, placing the data in **lpvBuf**.

The final step in using global memory is to free it once you are finished using it. To free global memory, use the **GlobalFree** function. Its declaration is:

```
Declare Function GlobalFree Lib "Kernel" (ByVal hMem As
   Integer) As Integer
```

The argument **hMem** is the handle (*not* the selector) of the memory block to free. The function returns 0 on success, and returns the memory block's handle if it cannot free the memory.

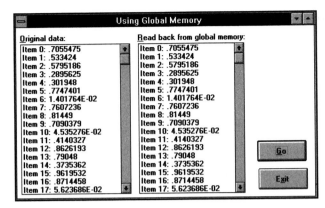

Figure 11.3 MEMALLOC demonstrates using global memory to store program data.

You can see that using global memory is not particularly complicated. As long as the program keeps track of what is stored where, and frees the allocated memory when finished, you should have no problems. Let's take a look at a simple example. The MEMALLOC program allocates a block of global memory and stores 1000 type Single values there. The values are then read back from global memory. Both the original values and the values read from global memory are displayed in List Boxes, so you can see that they are in fact the same.

MEMALLOC is shown executing in Figure 11.3, and its objects, properties, and code are presented in Listings 11.4 and 11.5.

Using MEMALLOC.MAK

This demonstration, presented in Listings 11.4 and 11.5, is stored on disk as MEMALLOC.MAK and MEMALLOC.FRM.

Listing 11.4   Objects and Properties in MEMALLOC.FRM

```
Begin Form Form1
   Caption        =    "Using Global Memory"
   Begin CommandButton cmdExit
     Caption       =    "E&xit"
   End
   Begin CommandButton cmdGo
     Caption       =    "&Go"
   End
   Begin ListBox List2
     TabIndex      =    3
```

```
   End
   Begin ListBox List1
      TabIndex        =    1
   End
   Begin Label Label2
      AutoSize        =    -1  'True
      Caption         =    "&Read back from global memory:"
      TabIndex        =    2
   End
   Begin Label Label1
      AutoSize        =    -1  'True
      Caption         =    "&Original data:"
      TabIndex        =    0
   End
End
```

Listing 11.5   Code in MEMALLOC.FRM

```
Option Explicit

Declare Function GlobalAlloc Lib "Kernel" (ByVal wFlags
   As Integer, ByVal dwBytes As Long) As Integer
Declare Function GlobalHandleToSel Lib "Toolhelp.DLL"
   (ByVal Handle As Integer) As Integer
Declare Function GlobalFree Lib "Kernel" (ByVal hMem As
   Integer) As Integer
Declare Function MemoryRead Lib "Toolhelp.dll" (ByVal
   wSel As Integer, ByVal dwOffSet As Long, lpvBuf As
   Any, ByVal dwcb As Long) As Long
Declare Function MemoryWrite Lib "Toolhelp.dll" (ByVal
   wSel As Integer, ByVal dwOffSet As Long, lpvBuf As
   Any, ByVal dwcb As Long) As Long

Const GMEM_MOVEABLE = &H2
Const GMEM_INITZERO = &H40
Const NUM_ELEMENTS = 1000
Const ELEMENT_SIZE = 4

Sub cmdExit_Click ()

End

End Sub

Sub cmdGo_Click ()

Dim Handle As Integer, Selector As Integer
```

```
Dim X As Integer, Z As Single, I As Integer
Dim OffSet As Long

' Display hourglass mouse pointer.
Screen.MousePointer = 11

' Allocate the needed memory.
Handle = GlobalAlloc(GMEM_MOVEABLE Or GMEM_INITZERO, (NUM_ELEMENTS *
   ELEMENT_SIZE))

' Display error message if allocation fails.
If Handle = 0 Then
    Screen.MousePointer = 0
    MsgBox "Could not allocate memory"
    Exit Sub
End If

' Get the selector.
Selector = GlobalHandleToSel(Handle)

' Write random values to global memory.
For I = 0 To NUM_ELEMENTS - 1
    Z = Rnd
    OffSet = I * ELEMENT_SIZE
    X = MemoryWrite(Selector, OffSet, Z, ELEMENT_SIZE)
    List1.AddItem "Item" & Str$(I) & ":" & Str$(Z)
Next I

' Read them back from global memory.
For I = 0 To NUM_ELEMENTS - 1
    OffSet = I * ELEMENT_SIZE
    X = MemoryRead(Selector, OffSet, Z, ELEMENT_SIZE)
    List2.AddItem "Item" & Str$(I) & ":" & Str$(Z)
Next I

Screen.MousePointer = 0

' Free the global memory.
X = GlobalFree(Handle)

End Sub

Sub Form_Load ()

List1.Clear
List2.Clear

End Sub
```

Setting Tabs in a List Box

A Visual Basic List Box can display snaking columns, but not parallel columns. It is possible to mimic parallel columns with careful use of tabs. You can use API calls to change the tab stops in a List Box.

List Box controls have default tab stop settings that work out to be, depending on the font in use, about every eight characters. If a Tab character (**Chr$(9)**) is encountered in a string in a List Box, subsequent text is "tabbed" over to the next tab stop. The default tab stop spacing is fine for some applications, but there are certainly times when it would be preferable to have a different spacing. You can change the tab stop settings by sending a message to the List Box.

You use the **SendMessage** procedure to send a message to a control. **SendMessage** is actually a function, but for the present purposes we can declare it as a procedure:

```
Declare Sub SendMessage Lib "User" (ByVal hWnd As
   Integer, ByVal wMsg  As Integer, ByVal wParam As
   Integer, lParam As Any)
```

The function's arguments are described here:

- **hWnd** is the handle of the object to which you are sending a message.

- **wMsg** is a numerical value that represents the specific message being sent. To change tab stops, you send the message **LB_SETTABSTOPS**, which is defined as being equal to the constant **WM_USER + 19**.

- **wParam** is the first parameter that accompanies the message. For setting tab stops, the parameter is the number of tab stops to set.

- **lParam** is the second parameter that accompanies the message. For setting tab stops, the parameter is the first element of an array that holds the desired tab stop settings.

So far, so good. But how does one specify tab stop positions? Unfortunately, it's not as easy as simply counting characters! Because Windows can use a variety of font sizes, using character positions for setting tab stops would not work. Rather, Windows uses what are called *dialog base units* to represent the width and height of text. To obtain this value, you use the **GetDialogBaseUnits** API function. Its declaration is:

```
Declare Function GetDialogBaseUnits Lib "User" () As
   Long
```

Stock #	Item	Price	On Hand
K1228	Ball-peen hammer	$10.98	8
J451	Hack saw	$12.49	12
M8879	Crescent wrench	$11.00	9
X1101	Soldering iron	$17.89	6
W909	Screw driver set	$15.49	14

Figure 11.4 By changing the tab stop settings, you can use a List Box to display columnar data.

This function returns the dialog box base units used by Windows when creating dialog boxes. This value, which is expressed in pixels, can be used by an application to calculate the average width of characters in the system font. The function returns a type Long that codes both the width and height values of dialog base units, with the width in the low-order word and the height in the high-order word.

To extract the low-order word, use the **Mod** operator to obtain the remainder when the function's return value is divided by 65536. To use this value for setting tab stops, divide it by 2 and multiply by the "character" position where you want the tab stop set. You'll see how this is done in the demonstration program.

LISTTABS.MAK shows you how to set tabs in a List Box. This program uses two other API calls that you have already been introduced to: **GetFocus** and **APISetFocus**. The program's form is shown in Figure 11.4; you can see that the tab stop spacing is quite different from the default eight characters per tab. The program's objects, properties, and code are presented in Listings 11.6 and 11.7.

Using LISTTABS.MAK

This demonstration, presented in Listings 11.6 and 11.7, is stored on disk as LISTTABS.MAK and LISTTABS.FRM.

Listing 11.6   Objects and Properties in LISTTABS.FRM

```
Begin Form Form1
   Caption          =    "Setting List Box Tab Stops"
   Begin ListBox List1
   End
End
```

Listing 11.7   Code in LISTTABS.FRM

```
Option Explicit
```

```
Declare Sub APISetFocus Lib "User" Alias "SetFocus"
  (ByVal hWnd As Integer)
Declare Sub SendMessage Lib "User" (ByVal hWnd As
  Integer, ByVal wMsg As Integer, ByVal wParam As
  Integer, lParam As Any)
Declare Function GetDialogBaseUnits Lib "User" () As
  Long
Declare Function GetFocus Lib "User" () As Integer

Const WM_USER = &H400
Const LB_SETTABSTOPS = WM_USER + 19

Sub Form_Load ()

Dim Tb As String * 1
Dim OldHandle As Integer, ListHandle As Integer
Dim DlgWidthUnits As Integer, I As Integer
ReDim TabStop(3) As Integer

' Define desired character locations for tab stops.
TabStop(0) = 10
TabStop(1) = 30
TabStop(2) = 45
TabStop(3) = 60

' The Tab character is Chr$(9).
Tb = Chr$(9)

' Show the form.
Show

' Save handle of object with focus.
OldHandle = GetFocus()

' Set focus to the List Box and get its handle.
List1.SetFocus
ListHandle = GetFocus()

' Get the width conversion units.
DlgWidthUnits = (GetDialogBaseUnits() Mod 65536) / 2

For I = 0 To 3
    TabStop(I) = TabStop(I) * DlgWidthUnits
Next I

Call SendMessage(ListHandle, LB_SETTABSTOPS, 4, TabStop(0))

' Return the focus to its original location.
Call APISetFocus(OldHandle)
```

```
' Put some text in the List Box.
List1.AddItem "Stock #" + Tb + "Item" + Tb + "Price" + Tb + "On Hand"
List1.AddItem "K1228" + Tb + "Ball-peen hammer" + Tb + "$10.98" + Tb +
   "8"
List1.AddItem "J451" + Tb + "Hack saw" + Tb + "$12.49" + Tb + "12"
List1.AddItem "M8879" + Tb + "Crescent wrench" + Tb + "$11.00" + Tb +
   "9"
List1.AddItem "X1101" + Tb + "Soldering iron" + Tb + "$17.89" + Tb + "6"
List1.AddItem "W909" + Tb + "Screw driver set" + Tb + "$15.49" + Tb +
   "14"

End Sub
```

Using API Functions to Classify Characters

The Windows API contains several functions that you can use to classify characters.

You will sometimes run across programming tasks that require you to examine an individual character and classify it—is it a letter, a numeral, a symbol, and so on. You can usually perform this sort of classification using Visual Basic alone. For example, to determine if a character is a letter you could use the following code:

```
Letters$ = "abcdefghijklmnopqrstuvwxyz"
If Instr(Letters$, Lcase$(TestChar$)) <> 0 Then
        ' TestChar$ is a letter.
Else
        ' TestChar$ is not a letter.
End If
```

You might find it more efficient, however, to use the functions provided in the API for this purpose. There are four character classification functions; their declarations are as follows:

```
Declare Function IsCharAlphaNumeric Lib "User" (ByVal
   cChar As Integer) As Integer

Declare Function IsCharAlpha Lib "User" (ByVal cChar As
   Integer) As Integer

Declare Function IsCharUpper Lib "User" (ByVal cChar As
   Integer) As Integer

Declare Function IsCharLower Lib "User" (ByVal cChar As
   Integer) As Integer
```

Each function takes a single type Integer argument that is the ASCII value of the character being tested. The function return value is non-zero if the character is in the specified category, zero if it is not. The sets are:

IsCharAlphanumeric (letters and numeric characters)

IsCharAlpha (letters)

IsCharUpper (uppercase letters)

IsCharLower (lowercase letters)

The language driver for the current language (the language the user selected at setup or by using the Windows Control Panel) determines whether the character is in the set. If no language driver is selected, Windows uses an internal function.

Remember that you don't pass the test character itself to these functions, but must pass the test character's ASCII value:

```
If (IsCharAlpha(Asc(TestChar$))) Then
        ' TestChar$ is a letter.
Else
        ' TestChar$ is not a letter.
End If
```

I won't bother providing a demonstration program, since using these functions is trivial. Note that you can combine two of these API functions to create additional character classification functions. For example, to test if a character is a numeric character you would create a Basic function like this:

```
Function IsCharNumeric(Ch as Integer) As Integer

If (IsCharAlpha(Ch) = False) And (IsCharAlphaNumeric(Ch) = True) Then
        IsCharNumeric = True
Else
        IsCharNumeric = False
End If

End Function
```

Using Hash Tables

A hash table is not something you'll find in a "greasy spoon" diner! Rather, it is a method of storing and indexing data that permits highly efficient searches.

In order to understand how hash tables work, and the advantages they offer, you need to understand some basics of other methods of database storage and indexing. In a database, every item, or *record*, consists of information that is stored and is capable of being retrieved. Each record also has an address, or *index*, that identifies its storage location. For example, in a database of names and phone numbers, you might have:

Address	Record
34	Smith, John, 919-555-1234
48	Jones, Mary, 212-555-9876
12	Wilson, William, 415-555-3456
7	O'Leary, Pat, 716-555-4321

and so on. In standard methods of database storage, the data in a record doesn't tell you anything about the address of that record. If you want to find a particular record, say William Wilson's, there is no alternative but to look through the list until you find it. While you can sort lists and use other sophisticated search strategies to speed up the process, the fact remains that you must search for the desired record.

A hash table is fundamentally different in that the address at which a record is stored is specified by the data in the record itself. To be more precise, a portion of the data in the record is converted by a mathematical formula, called a *hashing function*, into a numerical value that is used as the record's address. This process is performed when the record is initially stored. More important, the process is also performed when you are searching for a specific record. Let's say you are searching for the record with last name "Wilson." By putting "Wilson" through the hashing function you will obtain the proper address immediately—there is no need to search for it. Of course you must look at the address to be sure there is a record stored there—after all, maybe Wilson's data was never put into the table. Still, finding data in a hash table is much quicker than any other data retrieval method.

As Murphy's law requires, hash tables have some shortcomings. The size of the table must be decided on at the beginning, and you cannot expand the table later. The reason for this is that the hashing function must be designed to provide addresses in the proper range. In other words, for an n element hash table the hashing function must produce addresses ranging from 1 to n.

A second problem is that it is almost impossible to design a hashing function that produces a unique address from every string. Different strings could, therefore, produce the same address. When this occurs it is called *collision*. The chance of a collision depends on the hashing function, and also on how full the hash table is. The more of a table's addresses that are already taken, the higher the chance of collision.

Collisions can be dealt with by permitting a hash table to store more than one record at each address.

A record in a hash table is usually broken into two parts. The *key data string* is that part of the record used to generate the hash table address, and the *secondary data string* is the remainder of the record. This organization is accomplished by delimiting the data strings with special characters. The *record delimiter character* marks the beginning and end of each record, and the *key delimiter character* separates the key data string from the secondary data string. For example, if we use # as the record delimiter character and @ as the key delimiter character, records would be stored as follows:

```
#Smith@John,919-555-1234#
#Jones@Mary,212-555-9876#
#Wilson@William,415-555-3456#
#O'Leary@Pat,716-555-4321#
```

Obviously, it's important to select delimiter characters that would never appear in the data being stored. In a real application, you would probably not use # and @, but would instead use non-ASCII characters such as **Chr$(250)** and **Chr$(251)**.

In the above example, the key data string is last name. Some hash table implementations require that every record have a unique key data string, but this is not absolutely necessary. Of course, duplicate key data strings will generate the same hash table address, but this can be dealt with by storing more than one record at a given address:

```
#Smith@John,919-555-1234#Smith@Henry,203-555-8888#
```

The same technique is used for non-identical key data strings that cause a collision. Say that our hashing function returns the same address for "Smith" and "Smythe." The two records would be stored as shown here:

```
#Smith@John,919-555-1234#Smythe@Mildred,207-555-6677#
```

If your program allows more than one record to be stored at each address, then clearly the program must search records for specific data. For example, if you are searching for Mildred Smythe's record, it's not enough to generate the correct hash table address. The program must look through the record(s) stored at that address to determine if Mildred Smythe's record is actually stored there.

It is sometimes useful for each hash table record to store a count of how many records are stored there. When a hash table entry is initialized, it could contain the number:

#0000#

After the first record is stored at that address it would contain

#0001#Smith@John,919-555-1234#

and after the second record is stored:

#0002#Smith@John,919-555-1234#Smythe@Mildred,207-555-6677#

You can see that you have a good deal of flexibility in how data records are actually stored in the hash table. But now let's get back to the main topic and see how hash table addresses are generated. The goal, remember, is to generate a unique (or almost unique) numerical value for each string. The most common approach is based on a random number generator that uses the Modulo operator. For a single character Ch the function is:

```
X = N1 * Asc(Ch) Mod N2
```

where N1 and N2 are prime numbers. To generate an address from a string, apply the above formula to each of its characters in turn, summing the results. Finally, use the **Modulo** operator to find the remainder when the sum is divided by the number of entries in the hash table. This last step ensures that the address is in the acceptable range.

What's a Prime Number?

For those of you who are not familiar with prime numbers, it is an integer that cannot be evenly divided by any numbers except for 1 and itself. For example, 3, 5, 7, 11, 13, 17, 19, and 23 are all primes.

For example, here's a Basic function that uses the above mathematical technique to generate a hash table address from a string.

```
Function HashAddress (KeyString As String) As Integer

' Generates a hash table address from the argument.
' Address is in the range 0 to (NUM_RECORDS - 1)
Dim H As Integer, I As Integer

H = 0
For I = 1 To Len(KeyString)
    H = (H + 17 * Asc(Mid$(KeyString, I, 1)) Mod 23)
Next I
```

```
HashAddress = H Mod NUM_RECORDS

End Function
```

How can a Visual Basic program store a hash table? A variable-length string array is one approach, with the advantages that it uses memory efficiently and can be quickly and easily transferred to and from disk. Another possibility is a random-access disk file. There are other possibilities, and usually your decision will be based on the trade-off between speed and capacity that results from selecting disk-based versus memory-based storage.

Now let's look at a hash table demonstration. HASHTABL.MAK implements a simple hash table database for storing names and phone numbers. The last name is used as the key data string, and the first name and phone number are treated as secondary data. Although it probably wouldn't be a good idea in a real program, HASHTABL uses a List Box control to store the hash table, with the List Box index property serving as the address.

The List Box displays the hash table records in "raw" form, with the delimiter characters still in place, as shown in Figure 11.5. The program automatically stores the hash table in a disk file named HASH.DAT on exit. When the program is started, it looks for HASH.DAT and, if the file is found, loads the hash table from it. If the file is not found, the program initializes an empty hash table. The program has provisions for entering new records and locating existing records. I addressed the problem of duplicate key data strings and collisions by storing multiple records at the same address, as we discussed previously. When finding records, all the program does is highlight the matching record in the List Box.

The objects, properties, and code for the main form are given in Listings 11.8 and 11.9. The program also includes two secondary forms, ADD_DATA.FRM and FINDFORM.FRM. I have not shown screen shots of these forms since they are quite simple and you will be able to easily create them from the object and property descriptions in Listings 11.10 and 11.12. The code for these two secondary forms is given in Listings 11.11 and 11.13.

Using HASHTABL.MAK

This demonstration, presented in Listings 11.8, 11.9, 11.10, 11.11, 11.12, and 11.13, is stored on disk as HASHTABL.MAK, HASHTABL.FRM, ADD_DATA.FRM, and FINDFORM.FRM.

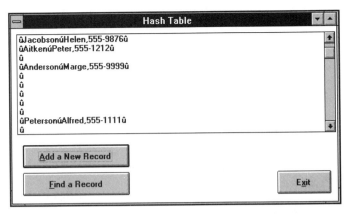

Figure 11.5   HASHTABL demonstrates a hash table kept in a List Box control.

Listing 11.8   Objects and Properties in HASHTABL.FRM

```
Begin Form Form1
   Caption          =   "Hash Table"
   Begin CommandButton cmdFind
      Caption        =   "&Find a Record"
   End
   Begin CommandButton cmdAdd
      Caption        =   "&Add a New Record"
   End
   Begin CommandButton cmdExit
      Caption        =   "E&xit"
   End
   Begin ListBox List1
   End
End
```

Listing 11.9   Code in HASHTABL.FRM

```
Option Explicit

Const NUM_RECORDS = 1000
Const FILE_NAME = "HASH.DAT"
Const KEY_DELIM = 250
Const REC_DELIM = 251

Sub cmdAdd_Click ()

' Add a new record to the hash table.
Dim Rdc As String * 1, Kdc As String * 1
Dim Address As Integer, Temp As String, Msg As String

Rdc = Chr$(REC_DELIM)
```

```
Kdc = Chr$(KEY_DELIM)

' Display the data entry form.
frmAdd.Show 1

' Be sure an entry was made in the Last name field.
If frmAdd.txtLname.Text = "" Then
    MsgBox "Cannot add a record without a Last Name"
    Exit Sub
End If

' Generate the hash address.
Temp = frmAdd.txtLname.Text
Address = HashAddress(Temp)

' Construct the record.
Temp = List1.List(Address)
Temp = Temp & frmAdd.txtLname.Text & Kdc
Temp = Temp & frmAdd.txtFname & "," & frmAdd.txtPhone
Temp = Temp & Rdc

'Delete the existing record and add the new one.
List1.RemoveItem Address
List1.AddItem Temp, Address

End Sub

Sub cmdExit_Click ()

Unload Form1
End

End Sub

Sub cmdFind_Click ()

' Locate a record in the hash table.
Dim Target As String, Msg As String
Dim Address As Integer, Temp As String
Dim Kdc As String * 1, Rdc As String * 1

Kdc = Chr$(KEY_DELIM)
Rdc = Chr$(REC_DELIM)

' Display the "find" form.
frmFind.Show 1

Target = frmFind.txtFind.Text
```

```
If Target = "" Then
    MsgBox "No search string entered."
    Exit Sub
End If

Address = HashAddress(Target)

' Bracket the target with delimiter characters
' to ensure that we don't find an embedded string.
Target = Rdc & Target & Kdc

' If not found, display a message.
Temp = List1.List(Address)
If InStr(Temp, Target) = 0 Then
    Msg = "No matching records could be found"
    MsgBox Msg
    Exit Sub
End If

' If found, make that List Box entry current.
List1.ListIndex = Address

End Sub

Sub Form_Load ()

' See if the hash table data file exists. If so, read the
' records into the List Box. If not, initialize the hash table.
Screen.MousePointer = 11

If Dir(FILE_NAME) = "" Then
    Call InitializeTable
Else
    Call ReadTable
End If

Screen.MousePointer = 0

End Sub

Sub Form_Unload (Cancel As Integer)

' Save the hash table to disk.
Dim FileNum As Integer, I As Integer

Screen.MousePointer = 11
```

```
FileNum = FreeFile

Open FILE_NAME For Output As #FileNum

For I = 0 To NUM_RECORDS - 1
    Print #FileNum, List1.List(I)
Next I

Close #FileNum

Screen.MousePointer = 0

End Sub

Function HashAddress (KeyString As String) As Integer

' Generate a hash table address from the argument.
' Address is in the range 0 to (NUM_RECORDS - 1)
Dim H As Integer, I As Integer

H = 0
For I = 1 To Len(KeyString)
   H = (H + 17 * Asc(Mid$(KeyString, I, 1)) Mod 23)
Next I

HashAddress = H Mod NUM_RECORDS

End Function

Sub InitializeTable ()

' Initialize the hash table.
Dim Rdc As String * 1, I As Integer

' Record the delimiter character.
Rdc = Chr$(REC_DELIM)

For I = 1 To NUM_RECORDS
    List1.AddItem Rdc
Next I

End Sub

Sub ReadTable ()

' Reads an existing data file from disk
' into the hash table.
Dim FileNum As Integer, Temp As String
```

```
FileNum = FreeFile

Open FILE_NAME For Input As #FileNum

While Not EOF(FileNum)
    Line Input #FileNum, Temp
    List1.AddItem Temp
Wend

Close #FileNum

End Sub
```

Listing 11.10   Objects and Properties in ADD_DATA.FRM

```
Begin Form frmAdd
    Caption         =   "Data Entry"
    Begin CommandButton cmdOK
        Caption         =   "&OK"
    End
    Begin TextBox txtPhone
        TabIndex        =   5
    End
    Begin TextBox txtFname
        TabIndex        =   4
    End
    Begin TextBox txtLname
        TabIndex        =   3
    End
    Begin Label Label3
        Alignment       =   1  'Right Justify
        Caption         =   "Phone number:"
    End
    Begin Label Label2
        Alignment       =   1  'Right Justify
        Caption         =   "First name:"
    End
    Begin Label Label1
        Alignment       =   1  'Right Justify
        Caption         =   "Last name:"
    End
End
```

Listing 11.11   Code in ADD_DATA.FRM

```
Option Explicit

Sub cmdOK_Click ()
```

```
Hide

End Sub

Sub Form_Paint ()

' Clear all Text Boxes and set focus to the
' first one.
txtLname = ""
txtFname = ""
txtPhone = ""
frmAdd.txtLname.SetFocus

End Sub
```

Listing 11.12   Objects and Properties in FINDFORM.FRM

```
Begin Form frmFind
   Caption          =    "Find a Record"
   Begin CommandButton cmdOK
      Caption       =    "&OK"
   End
   Begin TextBox txtFind
   End
   Begin Label Label1
      Caption       =    "Last name to find:"
   End
End
```

Listing 11.13   Code in FINDFORM.FRM

```
Option Explicit

Sub cmdOK_Click ()

Hide

End Sub

Sub Form_Paint ()

' Clear the Text Box and set the focus to it.
txtFind.Text = ""
txtFind.SetFocus

End Sub
```

Mouse Programming

This section presents a couple of techniques that you can use to enhance the use of the mouse in your programs.

Using Custom Cursors

You can display a custom mouse cursor over any Visual Basic control that can detect a MouseMove event.

Well planned use of mouse cursor designs can improve the appearance and usability of your Visual Basic programs. Most controls have a MousePointer property that lets the programmer specify one of twelve predefined cursor shapes to be displayed whenever the cursor is over the control. But what if you want to use something different, a design not included in the twelve predefined cursors? With the technique presented here, you can display a customized cursor over any control—Directory List Box, File List Box, Grid, Image, Label, List Box, OLE Client, and Picture Box controls—that detects the **MouseMove** event.

The technique for displaying a custom mouse cursor makes use of the DragIcon property, which lets you specify a custom icon to be displayed while a drag-and-drop operation is in progress for the object. At design time, simply specify the desired icon file that contains the custom cursor you want displayed. Then, place code in the control's **MouseMove** event procedure to activate the **Drag** method. The result is that as soon as the mouse cursor moves over the control, the custom cursor is displayed.

What about removing the custom cursor when the cursor leaves the control? We assume that when the cursor leaves the control it will be over the control's parent form. We can therefore use the form's **DragOver** event procedure to cancel to **Drag** method for the control.

There's one minor complication. While a **Drag** operation is in progress, **Click** events are treated differently than they are normally. If the user clicks on a control during a **Drag** operation, Visual Basic treats the action as a **DragDrop** event, not a **Click** event. Left to its own devices, Visual Basic will terminate the **Drag** operation, restoring the default cursor. To prevent the termination, and to permit the control to respond to clicks in the normal fashion, we place code in the control's **DragDrop** event procedure to restart the **Drag** operation and to call the **Click** event procedure.

One additional feature is desirable. To avoid unnecessary processor overhead, we should activate the **Drag** method only the when the cursor initially enters the control, and not every time it moves somewhere within the control. We can accomplish this by using the control's Tag property, as you'll see in the demonstration program.

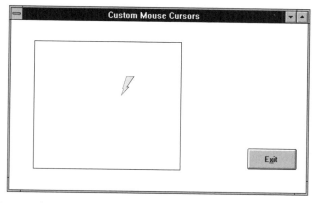

Figure 11.6 Displaying a custom mouse cursor over a control.

The program CSTMCRSR demonstrates the above techniques. For the custom cursor, I used one of the icon in the Visual Basic icon library: LITENING.ICO, located in the ICONS\ELEMENTS directory. The program, shown in Figure 11.6, displays the custom cursor over the Picture Box control. Objects, properties, and code for this program are presented in Listings 11.14 and 11.15.

Using CSTMCRSR.MAK

This demonstration, presented in Listings 11.14 and 11.15, is stored on disk as CSTMCRSR.MAK and CSTMCRSR.FRM.

Listing 11.14 Objects and Properties in CSTMCRSR.FRM

```
Begin Form Form1
   Caption          =   "Custom Mouse Cursors"
   Begin CommandButton cmdExit
     Caption        =   "E&xit"
   End
   Begin PictureBox Picture1
     DragIcon       =   (see text)
   End
End
```

Listing 11.15 Code in CSTMCRSR.FRM

```
Option Explicit

Sub cmdExit_Click ()

End
```

```
End Sub

Sub Form_DragOver (Source As Control, X As Single, Y As
   Single, State As Integer)

' This event procedure is executed when the mouse cursor
' leaves the Picture Box control and re-enters the form.
If Source.Tag = "Custom" Then
    Source.Drag 0
    Source.Tag = ""
End If

End Sub

Sub Picture1_Click ()

' Beep to indicate receipt of a Click event.
Beep

End Sub

Sub Picture1_DragDrop (Source As Control, X As Single,
   Y As Single)

' This code is necessary to enable the Picture Box to
' respond to Click events.
Picture1.Drag
Picture1_Click

End Sub

Sub Picture1_MouseMove (Button As Integer, Shift As
   Integer, X As Single, Y As Single)

' If the mouse cursor has just moved over the Picture Box,
' initiate the Drag method and set the Tag property. If the
' mouse cursor has already been over the Picture Box, do nothing.
If Picture1.Tag <> "Custom" Then
    Picture1.Drag
    Picture1.Tag = "Custom"
End If

End Sub
```

Drawing an Animated "Rubber Band" Box

An animated rubber band box is an effective way to let users select items with the mouse.

Many Windows programs, including the Visual Basic development environment, permit the user to select an area using the mouse and a "rubber-band" box. The user points at one corner of an area, presses and holds the mouse button, and drags to the opposite corner of the area. As the mouse moves, a rectangular outline, or box, stretches between the original point and the current mouse location. This box makes it easy for the user to see where the selection begins and ends. When the user releases the mouse button, the box stays in place to delineate the area that was selected.

An additional nice touch is to animate the rubber-band box. This means that after the mouse button is released, the box outline appears to rotate, providing an impressive visual effect as well as a clear indication of the selected area. The techniques presented here show you how to create an animated rubber-band box in Visual Basic.

Drawing the initial non-animated rubber-band box is fairly straightforward. The **MouseDown** event is used to record the starting location, which will serve as one corner of the box. Then, as the mouse is moved, the **MouseMove** event procedure is used to erase the previous box (at the old position) and draw the new box (at the current position). If all you want is a non-animated box, then that's all there is to it.

An animated box doesn't really move; the appearance of movement is accomplished with the same sort of trick used in animated cartoons. Here's how you create one:

1. Draw the box using the default DrawMode and DrawStyle = 2 (Dash).
2. Save the DrawMode and the DrawStyle.
3. Set the DrawMode to 6 (Invert) and the DrawStyle to 0 (Solid).
4. Draw the same box you drew in Step 1.
5. Reset the DrawMode and DrawStyle properties that you saved in Step 2.
6. Pause for some time interval.
7. Repeat the process, starting at Step 1.

These techniques are demonstrated in RUB_BAND.MAK, which consists of a form on which you can draw an animated rubber-band box. Figure 11.7 shows the box; of course, you cannot see the animation in the figure, but it really does work! The program's objects, properties, and code are presented in Listings 11.16 and 11.17.

Using RUB_BAND.MAK

This demonstration, presented in Listings 11.16 and 11.17, is stored on disk as RUB_BAND.MAK and RUB_BAND.FRM.

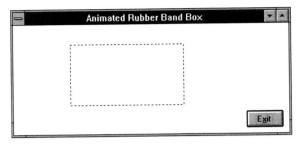

Figure 11.7   Using an animated rubber-band box to select an area on a form.

Listing 11.16   Objects and Properties in RUB_BAND.FRM

```
Begin Form Form1
    Caption           =    "Animated Rubber-Band Box"
    Begin CommandButton Command1
        Caption       =    "E&xit"
    End
    Begin Timer Timer1
        Interval      =    100
    End
End
```

Listing 11.17   Code in RUB_BAND.FRM

```
Option Explicit

Const INVERSE = 6
Const SOLID = 0
Const DASH = 2

Dim OldX As Single, OldY As Single
Dim StartX As Single, StartY As Single

Sub Command1_Click ()

End

End Sub

Sub DrawLine (X1 As Single, Y1 As Single, X2 As Single,
  Y2 As Single)

' Save the current DrawMode.
Dim OldDrawMode As Integer

OldDrawMode = DrawMode
```

```
' Set DrawMode to XOR.
DrawMode = INVERSE

' Draw a box.
Line (X1, Y1)-(X2, Y2), , B

' Reset DrawMode to original setting.
DrawMode = OldDrawMode

End Sub

Sub Form_Load ()

DrawStyle = DASH

End Sub

Sub Form_MouseDown (Button As Integer, Shift As
    Integer, X As Single, Y As Single)

' Disable timer while box is being drawn.
Timer1.Enabled = False

' Save the starting locations.
StartX = X
StartY = Y
OldX = X
OldY = Y

End Sub

Sub Form_MouseMove (Button As Integer, Shift As
    Integer, X As Single, Y As Single)

' Execute only if button is depressed.
If Button Then

' Restore the previous line's background.
Call DrawLine(StartX, StartY, OldX, OldY)

' Draw the new line.
Call DrawLine(StartX, StartY, X, Y)

' Save coordinates for the next call.
OldX = X
OldY = Y

End If
```

```
End Sub

Sub Form_MouseUp (Button As Integer, Shift As Integer,
  X As Single, Y As Single)

' When the mouse is released, start the "rotating" effect.
Timer1.Enabled = True

End Sub

Sub Timer1_Timer ()

Dim OldDrawStyle As Integer

OldDrawStyle = DrawStyle

' Solid is needed to create the inverse of the dashed line.
DrawStyle = SOLID

' Invert the dashed line.
Call DrawLine(StartX, StartY, OldX, OldY)
DrawStyle = OldDrawStyle

End Sub
```

Miscellaneous

Even in a chapter titled *Odds and Ends* there are some topics that don't seem to fit anywhere! You'll find them here.

Activating a Windows Screen Saver

You can activate a Windows screen saver from within a Visual Basic program.

Screen saver programs were created because the original IBM monochrome monitor had a phosphor that was sensitive to burn-in if the same image was left on the screen for an extended period of time. Screen savers sit quietly in memory, monitoring computer activity. If the keyboard and mouse are idle for some predefined length of time, the screen saver blanks the screen and displays a moving image, saving the monitor from permanent damage. As soon as the user touches the mouse or keyboard, the original program screen is restored.

With modern monitors, which are not subject to burn-in, screen savers are used more to protect sensitive data from prying eyes. When that snoopy co-worker from down the hall comes into your office and peers over your shoulder, you can pop up a screen saver to hide sensitive data that may be displayed on your screen. You can also invoke password protection to protect your system from unauthorized access while you are away from your desk.

With the **WinExec** API function, you can activate a screen saver from within a Visual Basic program. This function can actually be used to execute any Windows program. The function declaration is:

```
Declare Function WinExec Lib "Kernel" (ByVal lpCmdLine
    As String, ByVal nCmdShow As Integer) As Integer
```

The argument **lpCmdLine** is a string that contains the command line required to execute the program. The string must contain the program name, and can also contain optional command line parameters. The argument **nCmdShow** specifies how a Windows application window is to be shown.

The command-line argument can contain a path. If it does not, Windows searches for the program in this order:

1. The current directory.
2. The Windows directory (the directory containing WIN.COM).
3. The Windows system directory.
4. The directory containing the executable file for the current task.
5. The directories listed in the PATH environment variable.
6. The directories mapped in a network.

The value of the **nCmdShow** argument determines how a Windows application is displayed. (For a non-Windows application, the program-information file (PIF), if any, for the application determines the window state.) Possible values for this argument are:

SW_SHOWMAXIMIZED (**3**): Activates a window and displays it as a maximized window.

SW_SHOWMINIMIZED (**2**): Activates a window and displays it as an icon.

SW_SHOWMINNOACTIVE (**7**): Displays a window as an icon. The window that is currently active remains active.

Since we want the screen saver to cover the entire screen, we'll use **SW_SHOWMAXIMIZED**.

If the function is successful, its return value identifies the instance of the loaded program. Otherwise, the return value is an error value less than 32. Error codes and their meanings are Table 11.4.

Now let's get back to our original topic of screen savers. Windows version 3.1 comes with five screen savers:

- SSFLYWIN.SCR displays flying Windows logos (free advertising for Microsoft!).
- SSMARQUE.SCR displays a moving message.
- SSMYST.SCR displays changing geometric line drawings.
- SSSTARS.SCR displays an image of moving stars.
- SCRNSAVE.SCR displays a blank screen.

Table 11.4 WinExec Function Error Codes

Error Code	Meaning
0	The system was out of memory, executable file was corrupt, or relocation's were invalid
2	The file was not found
3	The path was not found
5	An attempt was made to dynamically link to a task, or there was a sharing or network-protection error
6	The library required separate data segments for each task
8	There was insufficient memory to start the application
10	The Windows version was incorrect
11	The executable file was invalid; either it was not a Windows application or there was an error in the .EXE image
12	The application was designed for a different operating system.
13	The application was designed for MS-DOS 4.0
14	The type of executable file was unknown
15	An attempt was made to load a real-mode application (developed for an earlier version of Windows)
16	An attempt was made to load a second instance of an executable file containing multiple data segments that were not marked read-only
19	An attempt was made to load a compressed executable file. A file must be decompressed before it can be loaded
20	The dynamic-link library (DLL) file was invalid, or one of the DLLs required to run this application was corrupt
21	The application requires Microsoft Windows 32-bit extensions

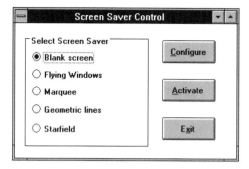

Figure 11.8 SCRNSAVE lets you configure and activate Windows screen savers.

You may be wondering how we can "execute" these screen savers. Despite the .SCR file extension, each screen saver is, in fact, an executable program that could also have the .EXE extension. Therefore, there is no problem using **WinExec** to execute them.

One final note: the screen saver programs accept command-line arguments that control their operation. The **-S** command-line switch activates the screen saver immediately, while the **-D** switch (or no switch) displays the screen saver's configuration dialog box. You use the configuration dialog box to control the appearance of the screen saver and also to enable password protection.

The program SCRNSAVR, shown in Figure 11.8, provides access to all five of the Windows screen savers. You can either configure or activate the selected screen saver program. The program's objects and properties are presented in Listing 11.18, and its code is in Listing 11.19. This form can be incorporated into your own programs. With some minor programming, you could arrange it so that the user could display the configuration screen or the screen saver itself from anywhere in the program by pressing a certain key combination.

Using SCRNSAVE.MAK

This demonstration, presented in Listings 11.18 and 11.19, is stored on disk as SCRNSAVE.MAK and SCRNSAVE.FRM.

Listing 11.18 Objects and Properties in SCRNSAVE.FRM

```
Begin Form Form1
   Caption          =   "Screen Saver Control"
   Begin CommandButton Command1
      Caption          =   "&Activate"
```

```
        Index           =    1
    End
    Begin CommandButton Command1
        Caption         =    "&Configure"
        Index           =    0
    End
    Begin CommandButton Command2
        Caption         =    "E&xit"
    End
    Begin Frame Frame1
        Caption         =    "Select Screen Saver"
        Begin OptionButton Option5
            Caption         =    "Starfield"
        End
        Begin OptionButton Option4
            Caption         =    "Geometric lines"
        End
        Begin OptionButton Option3
            Caption         =    "Marquee"
        End
        Begin OptionButton Option2
            Caption         =    "Flying Windows"
        End
        Begin OptionButton Option1
            Caption         =    "Blank screen"
        End
    End
End
```

Listing 11.19   Code in SCRNSAVE.FRM

```
Option Explicit

Declare Function WinExec Lib "Kernel" (ByVal lpCmdLine
  As String, ByVal nCmdShow As Integer) As Integer

Const SW_SHOWMAXIMIZED = 3

Sub Command1_Click (Index As Integer)

Dim CommandSwitch As String, Program As String
Dim Cmd As String, Result As Integer

' Set proper command-line switch for configure
' or activate.
If Index = 0 Then
    CommandSwitch = "-D"
Else
    CommandSwitch = "-S"
End If
```

```
If Option1.Value = True Then
    Program = "SCRNSAVE.SCR "
ElseIf Option2.Value = True Then
    Program = "SSFLYWIN.SCR "
ElseIf Option3.Value = True Then
    Program = "SSMARQUE.SCR "
ElseIf Option4.Value = True Then
    Program = "SSMYST.SCR "
ElseIf Option5.Value = True Then
    Program = "SSSTARS.SCR "
End If

Cmd = Program & CommandSwitch

Result = WinExec(Cmd, SW_SHOWMAXIMIZED)

If Result < 32 Then
    MsgBox "Error loading screen saver."
End If

End Sub

Sub Command2_Click ()

End

End Sub
```

Cleaning Up the Desktop

***You can use a simple API call to neatly arrange all of the icons on
your desktop.***

Windows uses icons—and sometimes it seems that it uses too many of
them! After working for a while, you may find that your desktop has
become cluttered with icons scattered here and there. Sure, you could
arrange the icons by dragging each one to a new location, but that seems
like unnecessary work. You could also use the Arrange Icons command,
or its equivalent, provided in the Program Manager, as well as in Program
Manager replacements, such as the Norton Desktop. A third option is
available, too: you can call an API function from your Visual Basic
program to arrange the desktop. The function declaration is:

```
Declare Function ArrangeIconicWindows Lib "User" (ByVal
  hWnd As Integer) As Integer
```

This function arranges all the minimized (iconic) child windows of the parent window that is identified by the **hWnd** argument. This window can be any window that has child windows, such as a Visual Basic MDI form. The return value is the height of one row of icons if the function is successful. Otherwise, it is 0.

To arrange the desktop icons, we need to first obtain the **hWnd** of the desktop. The **GetDesktopWindow** API function. does just that. The function declaration is:

```
Declare Function GetDesktopWindow Lib "User" () As Integer
```

The function returns the **hWnd** of the desktop window.

The program ARRANGE demonstrates how this works. It's a very simple little program, and the relevant lines of code can easily be incorporated into your own Visual Basic programs. Objects and properties are given in Listing 11.20, and the form's code is in Listing 11.21.

Using ARRANGE.MAK

This demonstration, presented in Listings 11.20 and 11.21, is stored on disk as ARRANGE.MAK and ARRANGE.FRM.

Listing 11.20 Objects and Properties in ARRANGE.FRM

```
Begin Form Form1
   Caption          =    "Arrange Desktop"
   Begin CommandButton cmdExit
     Caption         =    "E&xit"
   End
   Begin CommandButton cmdArrange
     Caption         =    "&Arrange"
   End
End
```

Listing 11.21 Code in ARRANGE.FRM

```
Option Explicit

Declare Function GetDesktopWindow Lib "User" () As Integer
Declare Function ArrangeIconicWindows Lib "User" (ByVal
  hWnd As Integer) As Integer

Sub cmdArrange_Click ()
```

```
Dim hWnd As Integer, H As Integer

hWnd = GetDesktopWindow()
H = ArrangeIconicWindows(hWnd)

End Sub

Sub cmdExit_Click ()

End

End Sub
```

CHAPTER 12

Fractal Fantasies

N ow we can move on and cover some fun stuff! In this chapter, we go beyond the work-a-day world of practical programming to the after-hours time, where your programming skills are put to work in the pursuit of enjoyment, entertainment, and possibly even a little intellectual exploration. We will take a look at the world of fractals, where mathematics and computer programming combine to create beautiful and fascinating images.

Fractal Images: Getting Started

Almost everyone has been exposed to fractals in one form or another. These complex, intriguing, and often colorful images have graced thousands of book covers, calendars, and posters ever since they became widely known about 15 years ago. The way that fractals are created and displayed lends itself perfectly to the use of personal computers. While the images may be complex, the programming required is not. Many PC users have found great enjoyment and challenge in exploring fractals, and you can too. In this section, I will provide an introduction to the theory and mathematics of fractals, and I will show you how to create fractal images using Visual Basic.

The field of fractals is large and complex, and I can only begin to scratch the surface here. If you're interested in exploring this topic further, I have listed several books that I have found very useful:

Fractals: Form, Chance, and Dimension, by Benoit B. Mandelbrot (W.H. Freeman and Co., San Francisco, CA, 1977)

The Science of Fractal Images, by M. F. Barnsley et al., (Springer-Verlag, New York, NY, 1989)

Fractal Creations, by Timothy Wegner and Mark Peterson (Waite Group Press, Mill Valley, CA, 1991)

Many people have seen fractal images without knowing exactly what they are, how they are created, or how they are different from other kinds of images. Many people have also heard that there is some connection between fractal images and certain natural objects without understanding just what that connection is. Before getting to the "how" of creating your own fractals, let's take a look at the "what" so you will have at least a basic idea of what you are working with.

Please remember that the low-resolution monochrome images reproduced in this book cannot do justice to the complexity and beauty of fractal images. If you have a high resolution color display (EGA, VGA, or better) they will look much better on your screen!

What Is a Fractal?

There are several characteristics that distinguish fractals from other kinds of shapes and images.

When someone says "images" or "shapes" to you, what do you think of? For most of us, the kinds of things that come to mind would include Euclidean geometrical shapes, such as circles, spheres, triangles, and cubes, and the objects of the everyday world, such as telephones, cars, basketballs, and earlobes. How are fractal images different? There are two partially related answers.

- Fractal images are *self-similar*. That is, if you look at a small portion of a fractal image under high magnification, it appears similar to the larger image. If you then magnify a still smaller portion, it too appears similar to the larger image. In other words, the whole image is similar to all of its parts, and vice versa. This is not true of Euclidean shapes or everyday objects! If you magnify a portion of a triangle or a car, you most certainly do not find smaller triangles or cars!

- Fractal images are independent of *scaling*. Everyday objects tend to have characteristic sizes, and Euclidean shapes have one or at most a few characteristic measurements (the diameter of a sphere or the size of a square, for example). In contrast, fractal images do not have a characteristic size or measurement.

Enough talk! It's time to look at a fractal image. Figure 12.1 shows the Mandelbrot set, certainly the most famous fractal. It was discovered (or

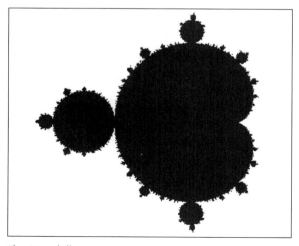

Figure 12.1   The Mandelbrot set.

Figure 12.2 A section of the Mandelbrot set magnified approximately 20 times.

perhaps invented—I'm not sure which term is more appropriate!) by Benoit Mandelbrot, the father of fractals.

We will look at the Mandelbrot set in more detail shortly. For now, let me point out a couple of interesting things. The black part of the image is the Mandelbrot set, and the white parts are those points that are not in the set. Clearly there are large areas of solid black and solid white—these areas are of relatively little interest. It is at the edges of the set where things are intriguing. Even in this low-resolution reproduction, you can see that the edges of the Mandelbrot set are very complex, with larger buds, or bays, giving off smaller buds which in turn have their own smaller buds.

Now what do you see if you magnify a part of the set? Figure 12.2 shows a portion of the edge of the Mandelbrot set magnified by approximately 20 times. There's still plenty of detail, and the general motif of the design is the same.

What happens if you continue to increase magnification? There's no limit to how much you can see, because there's no limit to the set—it is infinitely complex. If you start exploring the Mandelbrot set at high magnification there's a good chance that you'll see parts of it that no one has seen before. One intriguing fact is that at high magnifications you'll find, scattered here and there within the set, what look like "baby"

Mandelbrot sets. And that is just what they are—not exact copies of the entire set, but a close copy, buried way down inside the "parent" set. In fact, the Mandelbrot set contains many close copies of itself buried in various locations at different levels of magnification.

I hope you are suitably impressed with the incredible complexity of the Mandelbrot set. The set's complexity is, in fact, infinite. It has been proven mathematically that no matter how much you increase the magnification, there is always as much detail at the next magnification level as at the previous level. The Mandelbrot set has been called the most complex object in mathematics. And here is what may be the most intriguing part— the entire Mandelbrot set with its infinite detail and complexity is generated from the simple formula

```
Z² + c
```

Hard to believe? I can hardly blame you, but please read on.

How Are Fractals Created?

All fractals are generated by repeatedly evaluating a formula.

At the heart of fractal generation is the process of *iteration*, or repetition. An initial, or seed, value is plugged into a formula, and the formula is evaluated. The result is plugged back into the formula, and it is evaluated again. This process is repeated many times, with the result being examined after each iteration. The formula used, the number of iterations, and the criterion applied to the result all depend on the specific fractal being generated. The result of the iteration determines the contribution of the initial seed value to the fractal.

For example, consider the formula

```
X = Y²
```

If we start with the value 1.01 and iterate the formula, we get

```
1.01² = 1.0201
1.0201² = 1.04060401
```

And the next 13 terms in the series are:

```
1.08285670562808
1.1725786449237
1.3749406785311
1.89046186947956
```

```
3.57384607995613
12.7723758032178
163.133583658624
26612.5661173053
708228675.347948
5.01587856585109E+17
2.51590377873644E+35
6.32977182386031E+70
4.00660113421358E+141
```

Clearly, with a seed value of 1.01, the iterative process *diverges*, or heads off toward infinity. What if we try a seed of 0.99? Here are the first 15 terms of that series:

```
.9801
.96059601
.92274469442792
.851457771094875
.724980335957853
.525596487525562
.276251667699208
7.63149839065936E-02
5.82397676866365E-03
3.39187054019338E-05
1.15047857614318E-09
1.32360095416443E-18
1.75191948586499E-36
3.06922188495344E-72
9.42012297907717E-144
```

It's clear that with a seed value of 0.99, iteration of $X = Y^2$ does not head off toward infinity, but rather approaches 0. Now, this is a simple formula and all it takes is a little thought to realize that its iteration does not diverge for all seed values

```
-1 ≤ Y ≤ 1
```

and does diverge for all seed values

```
Y < -1, Y > 1
```

This may strike you as remarkably uninteresting, and I agree! It's a necessary introduction, however, and things rapidly become very interesting when this sort of iterative procedure is applied to special kind of number called a *complex number*. Fractals and complex numbers are intimately connected, and you'll learn about them later in the chapter.

Fractals and Nature

One reason that people find fractal images so interesting is that many parts of the natural world exhibit fractal structure.

You may wonder how a mathematically generated image can be related to the natural world. It's certainly true that you won't find any Mandelbrot sets floating about in nature, but it's equally true that fractal structure can be found almost anywhere in nature that you care to look.

What do I mean by "fractal structure?" You'll remember that the two fundamental characteristics of a fractal are self-similarity and independence of scale. And these characteristics are just what you find in nature.

For example, imagine that you are in the space shuttle looking down at the coastline of California from an altitude of 100 miles. You might be able to see a total length of 200 miles. The coastline has a typical shape, with large and small bays, promontories, peninsulas, and so on. It is easily identifiable as a coastline.

Next, imagine that you are flying in a jetliner over the same coastline at 30,000 feet. Because your altitude is lower, you can only see 20 miles of coastline. You see large and small bays, peninsulas, promontories—all the typical features of a coastline. While the specific details are different, the general plan is the same as you saw from the space shuttle.

Closer still, you are floating in a hot air balloon 1000 feet above the coastline. You can see only one mile in each direction, but you still see large and small bays, promontories, peninsulas, and so on.

Finally, you take a stroll along the water. You can see only a few dozen yards, and the edge contains small pools, inlets, rocks jutting into the water—the same general types of features that you saw from the balloon, airplane, and shuttle.

Now in this example you would always have other visual cues available to provide the proper sense of scale. From the shuttle you would see large cloud formations, from the airplane you might see cities and towns, from the balloon individual people and automobiles, and from the ground starfish and seaweed. If, however, you extract the shape of the coastline, the boundary between land and water, you will find that there are striking similarities between the four views. If you were shown just the coast's outline, it would be very difficult to tell what altitude it was viewed from. In other words, the coastline's structure is self-similar.

Fractal pattern is also found in trees. The pattern of the branching of limbs from the main trunk is echoed as branches sprout from the limbs, twigs from the branches, and leaves from the twigs. The shapes of mountains and clouds, the patterns of turbulence in flowing water, the branching of passageways in a lung, all of these exhibit fractal properties. In complex natural systems, fractals are more the rule than the exception. Fractals have become widely used in many areas for the analysis of complex shapes.

Fractals have also helped to explain how certain complex structures come into being, particularly in regard to living organisms. Many aspects of our bodies are extraordinarily complex. Take, for example, the circulatory system, with its tens of thousands of vessels of different sizes, branching repeatedly in a network of incredible complexity that has a definite fractal structure. How could the enormous amount of information required to create such a complex system be encoded in our genes and expressed during growth? The answer may well be that very little information is actually needed. Fractals have shown us how the simplest of formulas can generate structures of infinite complexity. Maybe that's how the body works: a very simple set of instructions executed repeatedly until every capillary is in place.

Complex Numbers

Complex numbers are not called that because they are complicated! In fact, they are not really complex at all. They are, however, required for many fractal calculations—for example, the Z in the formula for the Mandelbrot set represents a complex number. You need to know what complex numbers are and how to work with them before you can start computing and displaying fractal images.

What Is a Complex Number?

A complex number contains both a real part and an imaginary part.

A complex number is comprised of two parts: a *real* part and an *imaginary* part. "Real" numbers are the numbers that most of us are used to working with, such as 99, 1,000,000, –3, 0.45677, and –45.6; "imaginary" numbers are based on the concept of the square root of –1. Now this may sound silly, since we all know perfectly well that any number times itself results in a positive number, so how can a negative number have a square root? Well, that's why they are called imaginary! Despite the apparently nonsensical nature of this concept, mathematicians soon found that imaginary numbers, while having no direct correspondence with anything existing in the real world, were nonetheless extremely useful in many types of calculations.

In a complex number the square root of –1 is symbolized by *i*, with the entire complex number written simply as the sum of its real and imaginary parts. Expressed generally, therefore, a complex number is written as

```
a + bi
```

For example,

```
4 + 3i
-7 + 23i
1.7 - 0.6i
```

Of course, either the real or imaginary part can be 0, giving a "pure" imaginary or real number.

Calculations with Complex Numbers

To create fractals, you have to perform calculations with complex numbers.

Arithmetic calculations with complex numbers follow straightforward rules. Addition (or subtraction) of two complex numbers consists of adding (or subtracting) the two real parts to get a new real part, and adding (or subtracting) the two imaginary parts to get a new imaginary part:

```
  (12 + 3i)
+ (9 + 2i)
_____
  (21 + 5i)

  (2 - 8i)
+ (4 + 2i)
_____
  (6 - 6i)

  (-3 + 5i)
- (-4 - 6i)
_____
   1 + 11i
```

To multiply two complex numbers, you multiply each part of one number by each of the two parts of the other, then add the results. In general terms:

```
(a + bi)(c + di) = a(c + di) + bi(c + di)
                = ac + adi + bci + iibd
```

Since by definition, i^2 is equal to –1, we have

```
                = ac + adi + bci + (-bd)
                = (ac - bd) + (ad + bc)i
```

Here's a specific example of multiplication:

```
(3 + 2i) (2 + 2i)

2 * 3    = 6
2 * 2i   = 4i
2i * 3   = 6i
2i * 2i  = 4i²
```

Remembering that i^2 is equal to –1, $4i^2$ evaluates to -4. The final result is

```
((6) + (-4)) + (4i + 6i)
```

or

```
2 + 10i
```

Squaring a complex number is even simpler:

```
(a + bi)(a + bi) = (a² - b²) + 2abi
```

For example:

```
(3 + 2i)² = (3² - 2²) + 2(3)(2)i = (9 - 4) + 12i = 5 + 12i
```

Dividing complex numbers is a bit more involved, but doesn't present any real difficulties:

$$\frac{a + bi}{c + di} = \frac{(a + bi)(c - di)}{(c + di)(c - di)} = \frac{(ac + bd) + (bc - ad)i}{c^2 + d^2}$$

Here's a real example:

$$\frac{(3 + 2i)}{(1 + 4i)} = \frac{((3)(1) + (2)(4)) + ((2)(1) - (3)(4))i}{1^2 + 4^2} = \frac{11 - 10i}{17}$$

Giving a final result of

```
0.6471 - 0.5882i
```

We will develop Basic procedures to perform these calculations later in the chapter.

The Complex Plane

Most fractal images exist on the complex plane, which is a graphical method for representing complex numbers.

The term *plane* is used here to mean a flat, two-dimensional surface, such as a sheet of paper or a computer screen. Whether you realize it or not, you are already familiar with the use of a plane to represent numbers that come in pairs. I'm talking about the computer screen, of course—any position on the screen specifies two numbers, X for the horizontal position and Y for the vertical position. If we can imagine a computer screen without limits, then for every pair of numbers (X,Y) there is a single, unique corresponding point on the screen, and for every point on the screen there is a single, unique corresponding pair of numbers (X,Y).

You have probably already figured out how this idea can be extended to complex numbers. The complex number $a + bi$ has a real part a and an imaginary part b. If you take the example from the previous paragraph and substitute a for X and b for Y, you have the complex plane. Each point on the complex plane represents a complex number, with the horizontal position corresponding to the real part and the vertical position corresponding to the imaginary part. As shown in Figure 12.3, the complex plane is often represented with a set of axes, a real (horizontal) axis and an imaginary (vertical) axis.

There is one more calculation to consider. When representing points on a plane, it is sometimes necessary to calculate the distance between two points. Taking the simplest case, that of the distance of a point from the origin (where the real and imaginary axes cross), we have the situation shown in Figure 12.4.

Going back to high-school geometry, you probably recall that the Pythagorean theorem expresses the relationship between the lengths of the sides of a right triangle. If c is the length of the hypotenuse (the longest side) and a and b are the lengths of the other sides, then we know that

```
c² = a² + b²
```

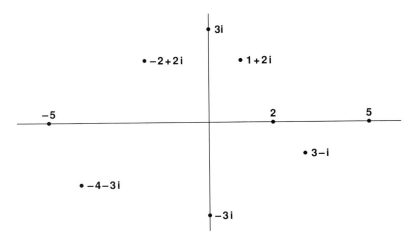

Figure 12.3   Every complex number has a unique position on the complex plane.

or

$$c = \sqrt{(a^2 + b^2)}$$

The distance of a complex point from the origin is referred to as the *modulus* of the complex number. The modulus is used in some of the fractal calculations. The modulus of a complex number Z is symbolized as $|Z|$. Thus, for complex number $Z = a + bi$ we have:

$$|Z| = \sqrt{(a^2 + b^2)}$$

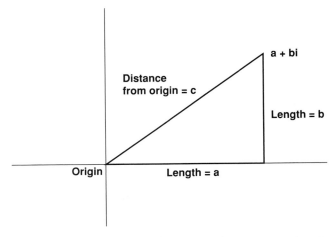

Figure 12.4   Calculating the distance of a point on the imaginary plane from the origin.

Basic Procedures for Complex Number Arithmetic

In this section, we will develop some Basic procedures that perform the fundamental arithmetic operations on complex numbers.

To work with complex numbers, it makes sense to create a user-defined type to hold the real and imaginary parts of the number.

```
Type COMPLEX
   a As Double
   b As Double
End Type
```

Ideally, we would create functions to perform the various arithmetic operations. However, Basic does not permit a function to return a user-defined type, so we must resort to using sub procedures that take an "extra" argument, that is then used to return the result. Thus, to calculate the sum of two complex numbers X and Y we can write:

```
Sub Add (X As COMPLEX, Y As COMPLEX, Z As COMPLEX)

' Adds complex numbers X and Y, assigning the
' sum to Z.
Z.a = X.a + Y.a
Z.b = X.b + Y.b

End Sub
```

To calculate the difference between two complex numbers, we can write:

```
Sub Subtract (X As COMPLEX, Y As COMPLEX, Z As COMPLEX)

' Subtracts complex number Y from complex number X,
' assigning the result to Z.
Z.a = X.a - Y.a
Z.b = X.b - Y.b

End Sub
```

To calculate the product of two complex numbers, we can write:

```
Sub Multiply (X As COMPLEX, Y As COMPLEX, Z As COMPLEX)

' Multiplies complex numbers X and Y, assigning
' the result to Z.
Z.a = (X.a * Y.a) - (X.b * Y.b)
```

```
Z.b = (X.a * Y.b) + (X.b * Y.a)

End Sub
```

To calculate the square of a complex number, we can write:

```
Sub Square (X As COMPLEX, Z As COMPLEX)

' Squares complex number X, assigning
' the result to Z.
Z.a = (X.a * X.a) - (X.b * X.b)
Z.b = 2 * X.a * X.b

End Sub
```

The one place where we can use a real function is to calculate the modulus:

```
Function Modulus (X As COMPLEX) As Double

' Returns the modulus of a complex number.
Modulus = Sqr(X.a * X.a + X.b * X.b)

End Function
```

The Speed of Fractal Calculations

This section might better be entitled "lack of speed" because the calculations required to generate a fractal can be rather lengthy.

By their very nature, the calculations required to create fractal images can be very time consuming. There are three factors that contribute to this:

- The calculations utilize type Double variables, and some involve multiplication. Such calculations are slow, particularly on systems that lack a math co-processor.
- The calculations are repetitive. For each point in a fractal image, the relevant formula may have to be iterated 20, 50, 100 or more times.
- There are lots of points. A full-screen fractal image in standard 640 x 480 VGA mode consists of 307,200 points. If you must iterate a formula 100 times for each point, you are talking about more than 30 million evaluations!

The bottom line is that many fractal calculations are rather slow, even on relatively fast hardware. If you don't want to mortgage your house to buy a Cray supercomputer, there are still a few things you can do. A faster system will help, of course, but that's impractical for most of us. The most cost-effective hardware enhancement is a math co-processor chip (8087, 80287, or 80387). For a relatively small expenditure, a co-processor chip can speed fractal calculation by as much as 10 times. As you are probably aware, when you add a math co-processor to your system, its speed rating must meet or exceed the speed rating of your main CPU.

There are also software approaches to the speed problem. One method takes advantage of the fact that the floating point calculations that are required during fractal generation are performed much more slowly than are calculations with integer or fixed point numbers. There are sophisticated programming algorithms that permit floating point calculations to be emulated using integer or fixed point calculations, speeding things up considerably. Another method examines the fractal image as it is being created, looking for sections that will be a solid color and filling them in immediately rather that performing the iterative calculation for each point. These specialized methods are, however, beyond the scope of the chapter; I am going to take the most direct, yet slowest, approach to fractal calculations. For a much more complete treatment of methods to speed fractal calculation, I suggest that you refer to the book by Wegner and Peterson mentioned earlier in this chapter.

The Mandelbrot Set

You were introduced to the Mandelbrot set earlier in the chapter. It is with good justification that it is considered to be the mother of all fractals, from both a historical and a mathematical point of view. In this section, I will explain the mathematics behind the Mandelbrot set and develop a Visual Basic program that can generate the entire set or a selected portion of it.

Generating the Mandelbrot Set

The Mandelbrot set may be infinitely complex, but it is generated from a very simple formula.

You saw the deceptively simple formula for the Mandelbrot set before:

```
z² + c
```

The calculation starts by taking a complex number, which is represented by the *c* in the equation. The first iteration is written as:

$$Z_{(next)} = (Z_{(previous)})^2 + c$$

Because this is the first iteration, there is no $(Z_{(previous)})$, so the equation becomes:

$$Z_{(next)} = c$$

With the second iteration there is a $(Z_{(previous)})$, so we have:

$$Z_{(next)} = c^2 + c$$

We continue plugging the result of each iteration back into the formula, giving us the following series:

$$Z_2 = Z_1^2 + c$$
$$Z_3 = Z_2^2 + c$$
$$Z_4 = Z_3^2 + c$$
$$\cdots$$
$$Z_{n+1} = Z_n^2 + c$$

In every iteration, c is always the original complex number, and Z is always the result of the previous iteration.

Now let's think about what can happen if you iterate the Mandelbrot formula over and over again for a given starting value c. With each successive iteration the value of Z is going to change, or course, but overall the series can do one of two things; which of these things occurs determines whether the starting value is in the Mandelbrot set:

- Z can continue to grow larger and larger, heading off toward infinity. The value is not in the Mandelbrot set.

- Z can remain finite no matter how many iterations are calculated. The value is in the Mandelbrot set.

It's a simple as that! Remembering that every complex number represents a point on the complex plane, you should be able to see how the Mandelbrot set is drawn:

1. Take a point on the complex plane.
2. Plug its value into the formula and iterate it a number of times.
3. If the series becomes infinite, color the point white. If the series remains finite, color the point black.
4. Move to the next point.

Alert readers may have noticed two areas of imprecision in the above steps. First of all, what does "becomes infinite" mean in practical terms? Do you have to continue iterating the formula until you obtain an infinite value? Fortunately, the answer to this question is no. It has been shown that if the iteration produces a complex value whose distance from the origin is greater than 2, then the series will always become infinite. Remember that the distance from the origin of a point on the complex plane is called its modulus, and I explained how to calculate it earlier in the chapter. Therefore, the procedure is to calculate the modulus of the value obtained after each iteration, and declare the original point to not be in the set as soon as a value with modulus > 2 appears.

The second area of imprecision involves the number of iterations to perform. Some initial points are no problem, because they produce a series that exceeds modulus = 2 very quickly, after only a dozen or so iterations. But what if a series is remaining "in-bounds" after 20 iterations, or 50, or 200? When can you say "OK, enough" and declare a point to be in the Mandelbrot set?

Strictly speaking, the answer is never. From a theoretical perspective, a point is in the Mandelbrot set only if the iterative series remains finite no matter how many times you iterate the calculation. Even if the modulus is less than 2 after 100, 500, or 1000 iterations, there's no way, other than actually performing the calculation, to be sure that it won't exceed 2 on the next calculation.

From a practical point of view, however, it's clear that you must set some upper limit on the number of iterations. This is an important decision because there's a direct relationship between the maximum number of iterations and the speed of processing. Twenty iterations is probably the minimum you should use, while values in the 50-100 range give a reasonable compromise between accuracy and speed.

Now we can rewrite our sequence of steps as follows:

1. Take a point on the complex plane.

2. Plug the value into the formula and evaluate it.

3. Does the result have modulus > 2?

    Yes: It's not in the set. Color it white and go to Step 5.

    No: Continue.

4. Have maximum iterations been reached?

    Yes: Point is in the set. Color it black and go to Step 5.

    No: Return to Step 2.

5. Take the next point on the complex plane and return to Step 2.

Let's look at a couple of examples. We'll start with the complex value 0.37 + 0.4i. Here are the results of the first 13 iterations of the Mandelbrot formula along with the corresponding modulus values:

Z(1) =	0.347 + 0.696i	|Z(1)|	=	0.778
Z(2) =	0.006 + 0.883i	|Z(2)|	=	0.883
Z(3) =	-0.409 + 0.410i	|Z(3)|	=	0.580
Z(4) =	0.369 + 0.064i	|Z(4)|	=	0.375
Z(5) =	0.502 + 0.447i	|Z(5)|	=	0.672
Z(6) =	0.422 + 0.849i	|Z(6)|	=	0.948
Z(7) =	-0.173 + 1.117i	|Z(7)|	=	1.130
Z(8) =	-0.848 + 0.014i	|Z(8)|	=	0.848
Z(9) =	1.089 + 0.376i	|Z(9)|	=	1.152
Z(10) =	1.415 + 1.219i	|Z(10)|	=	1.868
Z(11) =	0.885 + 3.850i	|Z(11)|	=	3.950
Z(12) =	-13.666 + 7.212i	|Z(12)|	=	15.452
Z(13) =	135.134 + -196.712i	|Z(13)|	=	238.656

You can see that on the 11th iteration the modulus exceeded 2, and continued to grow rapidly from there. I've only shown 13 iterations, but by the 15th iteration the modulus is over 3 billion! Not quite infinity, perhaps, but close enough for me! Clearly a program would be justified in stopping after the 11th iteration and declaring the point 0.37 + 0.4i to be outside the Mandelbrot set.

Now let's look at the value 0.37 + 0.2i. If we plug this value into the Mandelbrot formula and iterate it 200 times, we get (I've shown only the first and last 10 values in the series):

Z(1) =	0.467 + 0.348i	|Z(1)|	=	0.582
Z(2) =	0.467 + 0.525i	|Z(2)|	=	0.703
Z(3) =	0.312 + 0.690i	|Z(3)|	=	0.758
Z(4) =	-0.009 + 0.631i	|Z(4)|	=	0.631
Z(5) =	-0.028 + 0.189i	|Z(5)|	=	0.191
Z(6) =	0.335 + 0.189i	|Z(6)|	=	0.385
Z(7) =	0.446 + 0.327i	|Z(7)|	=	0.553
Z(8) =	0.463 + 0.492i	|Z(8)|	=	0.675
Z(9) =	0.342 + 0.655i	|Z(9)|	=	0.739
Z(10) =	0.058 + 0.648i	|Z(10)|	=	0.651
...				
Z(190) =	0.219 + 0.444i	|Z(190)|	=	0.495
Z(191) =	0.221 + 0.394i	|Z(191)|	=	0.452
Z(192) =	0.263 + 0.374i	|Z(192)|	=	0.457
Z(193) =	0.299 + 0.397i	|Z(193)|	=	0.497
Z(194) =	0.302 + 0.438i	|Z(194)|	=	0.532
Z(195) =	0.270 + 0.464i	|Z(195)|	=	0.537
Z(196) =	0.227 + 0.450i	|Z(196)|	=	0.504

```
Z(197) =    0.219 + 0.405i       |Z(197)| =    0.460
Z(198) =    0.254 + 0.377i       |Z(198)| =    0.455
Z(199) =    0.293 + 0.392i       |Z(199)| =    0.489
Z(200) =    0.302 + 0.429i       |Z(200)| =    0.525
```

This series shows no sign of diverging toward infinity. We are clearly justified in declaring it to be within the Mandelbrot set—in fact, we could have safely done so after only 100, 50, or even 20 iterations.

Color and the Mandelbrot Set

You may have seen pictures of the Mandelbrot set that are very colorful. This is not a property of the set itself, but rather of the way it is drawn.

The Mandelbrot set does not seem to lend itself to colorful reproduction. On the complex plane each point is either in the set or it is not, which seems most appropriately reproduced in black and white, as in the figures earlier. How then are the beautiful color images of the Mandelbrot set created?

The answer is that it's not the Mandelbrot set itself that is colored in these images, but rather the region outside the set. As you know, every point outside the set results in a divergence toward infinity when its value is iteratively calculated in the Mandelbrot formula. For a color image, each point outside the set is assigned a color based on how many iterations it took for it to diverge (that is, for its modulus to exceed 2). This results in a series of intricate and beautiful color bands surrounding the Mandelbrot set itself. Unfortunately we cannot include a color image in this book, but if you run the program presented later you'll see what I mean.

A Mandelbrot Set Display Program

This section presents a program that will generate and display the entire Mandelbrot set or a selected portion of it.

Now let's put all this theory to work. The program presented in this section, MBROT.MAK, shows how simple it is to create a fractal generation program in Visual Basic. The program's main form, MBT1.FRM, is shown in Figure 12.5 with the complete Mandelbrot set displayed (the figure is monochrome, but the program displays color).

The main form contains only a Picture Box control, where the image is drawn, and a menu. The Picture Box's BackColor property is set to Black, which permits us to explicitly draw only those points that are outside the set—points within the set are simply left at their default color.

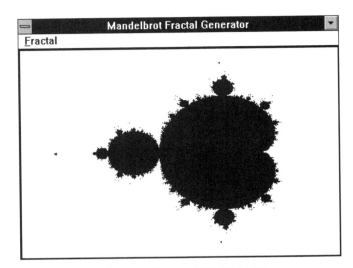

Figure 12.5 MBT1.FRM, the main form in MBROT.MAK.

The Form's BorderStyle property is set to 1–Fixed Single so the user cannot change its size during operation—because the calculations are based on pixel coordinates in the Picture Box, a change in size during calculation would obviously cause problems. You can, however, make the form any desired size at design-time, and the Picture Box will automatically resize to fit when the program begins execution.

All interaction with the program is done via the single menu. One of the menu choices, Evaluate Single Point, displays the form shown in Figure 12.6 (MBT2.FRM). This form is used to evaluate a single point on the complex plane. You enter values for the real and imaginary part of the complex number that you want to evaluate, and the desired number of iterations, and the program displays each iteration's result and its modulus. If the values become so large that an overflow error may occur (a number too large for the computer to handle) the code detects it, stops the calculations, and displays an error message.

The main part of the program is accessed by selecting Generate from the menu. You select Generate to display the dialog box shown in Figure 12.7. This dialog box is MBT_INFO.FRM, and you use it to enter the starting parameters for the Mandelbrot generation: the real and imaginary parts of the complex values that mark the diagonally opposite corners of the area that you want to generate, and the number of iterations to use. You can click the Reset Defaults Command Button to enter the default parameters, which will generate the entire set.

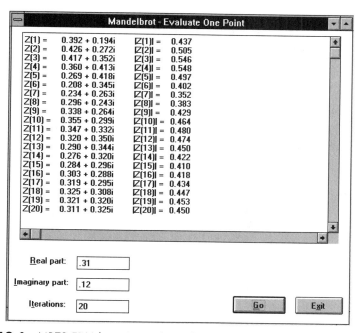

Figure 12.6 MBT2.FRM lets you evaluate the Mandelbrot expansion of a single point on the complex plane.

Once you have entered the desired parameters in this dialog box, select Go. The program will start generating the requested portion of the Mandelbrot set, displaying the set line-by-line in the Picture Box. While the program is running there's no way to pause it, although you can press Ctrl+Break if you are running it from within the Visual Basic environment.

When the fractal generation is complete, the program beeps. You can now quit, or select Generate again and enter new starting parameters. However, what most people want to do when the Mandelbrot set is displayed is to zoom in on a particularly interesting area to investigate details of the set at a greater magnification. To do this, point the mouse at one corner of the area that you want to enlarge, press and hold the button, and drag to the opposite corner of the area. When you release the mouse button a white box will be displayed on the form outlining the selected area, and the parameter dialog box (Figure 12.7) will be displayed with the coordinates of the selected area already entered, as shown in Figure 12.8.

While the program is running you can start your word processor or spreadsheet and do some "real" work, swapping back once in a while to see how things are coming. This swapping is made possible with the use of the **DoEvents** statement in processing loop. The **DoEvents** statement

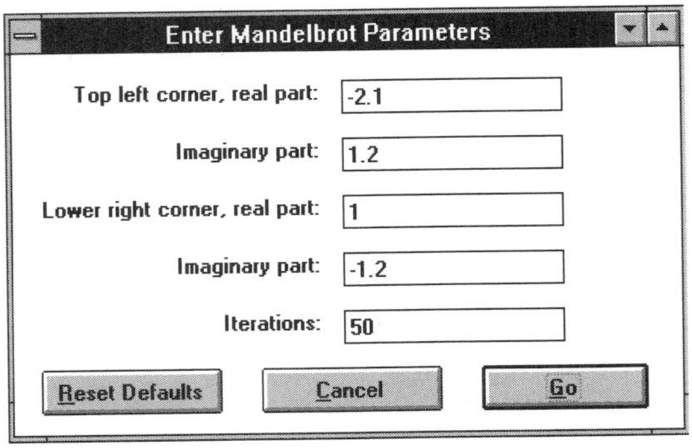

Figure 12.7 You use MBT_INFO.FRM to enter starting information for the Mandelbrot set generation.

is necessary to prevent the Mandelbrot set generator from completely monopolizing the system. Without **DoEvents** you would not be able to do anything else, such as switching to another window, while the program was in the process of generating the set. **DoEvents** permits Windows to work on other tasks during the generation. You can, in fact,

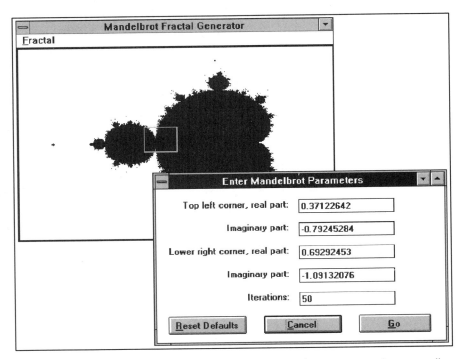

Figure 12.8 After generating an image you can use the mouse to select a smaller area to be magnified.

use another program and let the set be generated in the background—
a very handy option given that the computations take so long!

The placement of the **DoEvents** statement in the code has an effect on
performance. If **DoEvents** is executed more frequently, generation of the
Mandelbrot set will be slower, but any other Windows applications that
you run will be more responsive. The demonstration program places the
call to **DoEvents** in the middle loop, which gives reasonably fast
execution with acceptable performance of other Windows applications.
For faster Mandelbrot generation you can place **DoEvents** in the
outermost loop, but this results in other Windows applications executing
at what most people will find to be an unacceptably slow pace.

When writing a program that requires so much raw processing, it's
worth while to pay attention to the details of your code. Seemingly minor
changes can result in significant changes in overall processing speed. If
you can save a couple of milliseconds in a loop that executes tens of
thousands of times, the overall time savings will be significant.

One way that MBROT saves time is in the manner that it determines
whether the modulus of a complex number is greater than 2. You will
remember that the modulus of a complex number

```
a + bi
```

is calculated as

$$|Z| = \sqrt{(a^2 + b^2)}$$

Earlier in the chapter, I showed you a Basic function that takes a complex
number and returns its modulus. This function would certainly work, but
it performs a square root calculation, which is a relatively time-consuming
process. Note, however, that asking "Is the square root of a number
greater than 2?" is the same as asking "Is the number greater than 4?" For
a complex number a + bi, therefore, we can determine if its modulus is
greater than 2 by asking if $(a^2 + b^2)$ is greater than 4. We obtain the same
information without the time-consuming square root calculation.

Additional efficiency is gained by placing the code *inline*. This means
that the code is placed directly in the loop rather than being placed in a
function that is called by the loop. This speeds things up because the
overhead of calling a function and returning from it are eliminated. You
can try inlining the **Square** and **Add** procedures as well for additional
improvements.

The objects and properties of MBROT's three forms are given in Listings
12.1, 12.2, and 12.3, and the code in the forms is given in Listings 12.4,

12.5, and 12.6. The program also uses some of the procedures in FRACTAL.BAS; the listing for this module is given later in the chapter, in Listing 12.11.

Using MBROT.MAK

This demonstration, presented in Listings 12.1, 12.2, 12.3, 12.4, 12.5, and 12.6, is stored on disk as MBROT.MAK, MBT1.FRM, MBT2.FRM, MBT_INFO.FRM, and FRACTAL.BAS.

Listing 12.1 Objects and Properties in MBT1.FRM

```
Begin Form frmMBT1
    AutoRedraw       =    -1  'True
    BorderStyle      =    1   'Fixed Single
    Caption          =    "Mandelbrot Fractal Generator"
    MaxButton        =    0   'False
    Begin PictureBox Picture1
        AutoRedraw       =    -1  'True
        BackColor        =    &H00000000&
        ScaleMode        =    3   'Pixel
    End
    Begin Menu mnuFractal
        Caption          =    "&Fractal"
        Begin Menu mnuGenerate
            Caption          =    "&Generate"
        End
        Begin Menu mnuEvaluate
            Caption          =    "&Evaluate one point"
        End
        Begin Menu Sep
            Caption          =    "-"
        End
        Begin Menu mnuExit
            Caption          =    "E&xit"
        End
    End
End
```

Listing 12.2 Objects and Properties in MBT2.FRM

```
Begin Form frmMBT2
    Caption          =    "Mandelbrot - Evaluate One Point"
    Begin CommandButton cmgGo
        Caption          =    "&Go"
    End
    Begin CommandButton cmdExit
```

```
            Caption          =    "E&xit"
      End
      Begin TextBox txtIter
         TabIndex         =    6
      End
      Begin TextBox txtImag
         TabIndex         =    4
      End
      Begin TextBox txtReal
         TabIndex         =    2
      End
      Begin TextBox txtResult
         MultiLine        =    -1   'True
         ScrollBars       =    3    'Both
      End
      Begin Label Label3
         Alignment        =    1    'Right Justify
         Caption          =    "I&terations:"
         TabIndex         =    5
      End
      Begin Label Label2
         Alignment        =    1    'Right Justify
         AutoSize         =    -1   'True
         Caption          =    "&Imaginary part:"
         TabIndex         =    3
      End
      Begin Label Label1
         Alignment        =    1    'Right Justify
         Caption          =    "&Real part:"
         Height           =    255
         TabIndex         =    1
      End
End
```

Listing 12.3   Objects and Properties in MBT_INFO.FRM

```
Begin Form frmGetMBTInfo
   Caption           =    "Enter Mandelbrot Parameters"
   Begin TextBox txtIter
   End
   Begin TextBox txtLRImag
   End
   Begin TextBox txtLRReal
   End
   Begin TextBox txtTLImag
   End
   Begin TextBox txtTLReal
   End
   Begin CommandButton cmdCancel
```

```
            Cancel          =     -1   'True
            Caption         =     "&Cancel"
        End
        Begin CommandButton cmdGo
            Caption         =     "&Go"
            Default         =     -1   'True
        End
        Begin CommandButton cmdDefaults
            Caption         =     "&Reset Defaults"
        End
        Begin Label Label5
            Alignment       =     1    'Right Justify
            Caption         =     "Iterations:"
        End
        Begin Label Label4
            Alignment       =     1    'Right Justify
            Caption         =     "Imaginary part:"
        End
        Begin Label Label3
            Alignment       =     1    'Right Justify
            Caption         =     "Lower-right corner, real part:"
        End
        Begin Label Label2
            Alignment       =     1    'Right Justify
            Caption         =     "Imaginary part:"
        End
        Begin Label Label1
            Alignment       =     1    'Right Justify
            Caption         =     "Upper-left corner, real part:"
        End
End
```

Listing 12.4   Code in MBT1.FRM

```
Option Explicit

Dim EndX As Single, EndY As Single
Dim StartX As Single, StartY As Single
Dim DeltaI As Double, DeltaR As Double

Dim Done As Integer

Const INVERSE = 6


Sub DrawLine (X1 As Single, Y1 As Single, X2 As Single, Y2 As
    Single, C As Integer)

' Save the current DrawMode.
```

```
Dim OldDrawMode As Integer

OldDrawMode = DrawMode

' Set DrawMode to XOR
DrawMode = INVERSE

' Draw a box
Picture1.Line (X1, Y1)-(X2, Y2), QBColor(C), B

' Reset DrawMode to original setting.
DrawMode = OldDrawMode

End Sub

Sub Form_Load ()

' Set the location and size of the Picture Box to
' fill the form.
Picture1.Top = 0
Picture1.Left = 0
Picture1.Height = frmMBT1.ScaleHeight
Picture1.Width = frmMBT1.ScaleWidth

Done = False

End Sub

Sub Generate ()

' Generates the Mandelbrot set according to the parameters
' entered by the user.
Dim XPixels As Integer, Ypixels As Integer
Dim RealRange As Double, ImagRange As Double
Dim X As Integer, Y As Integer, I As Integer
Dim C As COMPLEX, Z As COMPLEX
Dim Z1 As COMPLEX, Z2 As COMPLEX
Dim NIter As Integer, InSet As Integer

Done = False
Picture1.Cls

Picture1.MousePointer = 11

' How many pixels are in the Picture Box vertically
' and horizontally?
XPixels = Picture1.ScaleWidth
Ypixels = Picture1.ScaleHeight
```

```
' Calculate the range of real and imaginary values (in other
' words, the dimensions of the image on the complex plane).
RealRange = Abs(Val(frmGetMBTInfo.txtTLReal.Text) -
   Val(frmGetMBTInfo.txtLRReal.Text))
ImagRange = Abs(Val(frmGetMBTInfo.txtTLImag.Text) -
   Val(frmGetMBTInfo.txtLRImag.Text))

' Calculate the amount of change represented by each
' row or column of pixels.
DeltaR = RealRange / XPixels
DeltaI = ImagRange / Ypixels

' What is the number of iterations.
NIter = Val(frmGetMBTInfo.txtIter.Text)

' What is the starting value at upper-left corner.
C.a = Val(frmGetMBTInfo.txtTLReal.Text)

' Begin the main processing loop.
For X = 1 To XPixels

    C.a = C.a + DeltaR
    C.b = Val(frmGetMBTInfo.txtTLImag.Text)

    For Y = 1 To Ypixels

        C.b = C.b - DeltaI
        Z = C
        InSet = True

        For I = 1 To NIter

            Call Square(Z, Z1)
            Call Add(C, Z1, Z2)

            If ((Z2.a) * (Z2.a) + (Z2.b) * (Z2.b)) > 4 Then
                InSet = False
                Exit For
            End If

            Z = Z2

        Next I

        ' If point is not in the set, color it.
        If Not InSet Then
            Picture1.PSet (X, Y), QBColor((I Mod 15) + 1)
        End If
```

```
        ' Call DoEvents to allow other processes some access
        ' to the system.
        DoEvents

    Next Y

        ' Refresh the picture.
        Picture1.Refresh

        ' Put the call to DoEvents here for faster Mandelbrot processing
        ' but slower response in other applications while the
        ' program is running.
Next X

Done = True
Picture1.MousePointer = 0
Beep

End Sub

Sub mnuEvaluate_Click ()

frmMBT2.Show

End Sub

Sub mnuExit_Click ()

End

End Sub

Sub mnuGenerate_Click ()

' Display the dialog box for the user to enter
' starting parameters.
frmGetMBTInfo.Show 1

If Cancel = False Then
    Call Generate
End If

End Sub

Sub Picture1_MouseDown (Button As Integer, Shift As Integer,
    X As Single, Y As Single)

' Save the coordinates where the user starts to drag.
StartX = X
```

```
StartY = Y

End Sub

Sub Picture1_MouseUp (Button As Integer, Shift As Integer,
  X As Single, Y As Single)

Dim Temp As Integer, X1 As Double
Dim X2 As Double, X3 As Double, X4 As Double

' If the program has completed generating the image,
' permit the user to select an area for magnification
' by dragging with the mouse.
If Done Then

    ' Save coordinates.

    EndX = X
    EndY = Y

    ' If necessary, swap Start and End values so that
    ' Start always refers to the upper-left corner
    ' of the area.
    If EndX < StartX Then
        Temp = StartX
        StartX = EndX
        EndX = Temp
    End If

    If EndY < StartY Then
        Temp = StartY
        StartY = EndY
        EndY = Temp
    End If

    ' Draw a box around the selected area.
    Call DrawLine(StartX, StartY, EndX, EndY, 7)

    ' Convert the mouse start and stop coordinates into
    ' complex plane coordinates and display them in the
    ' dialog box.
    X1 = Val(frmGetMBTInfo.txtTLReal.Text)
    X3 = X1
    X1 = X1 + (StartX * DeltaR)
    X3 = X3 + (EndX * DeltaR)

    X2 = Val(frmGetMBTInfo.txtTLImag.Text)
    X4 = X2
```

```
      X2 = X2 - (StartY * DeltaI)
      X4 = X4 - (EndY * DeltaI)

      frmGetMBTInfo.txtTLReal.Text = Format$(Str$(X1), "0.########")
      frmGetMBTInfo.txtTLImag.Text = Format$(Str$(X2), "0.########")
      frmGetMBTInfo.txtLRReal.Text = Format$(Str$(X3), "0.########")
      frmGetMBTInfo.txtLRImag.Text = Format$(Str$(X4), "0.########")

      frmGetMBTInfo.Show 1

      If Cancel = False Then
          Call Generate
      End If

  End If

End Sub
```

Listing 12.5   Code in MBT2.FRM

```
Option Explicit

Sub cmdExit_Click ()

Hide

End Sub

Sub cmgGo_Click ()

' Caculates a specified number of iterations of the
' Mandelbrot formula for a specified complex number.
Dim I As Integer, Iter As Integer
Dim C As COMPLEX, Z As COMPLEX, Z1 As COMPLEX
Dim Z2 As COMPLEX, Temp As String
Dim Msg As String

On Local Error GoTo Overflow

C.a = Val(txtReal)
C.b = Val(txtImag)
Iter = Val(txtIter)

Z.a = C.a
Z.b = C.b

Temp = ""
txtResult = ""
```

```
Screen.MousePointer = 11

For I = 1 To Iter
  Call Square(Z, Z1)
  Call Add(C, Z1, Z2)
  Temp = Temp & "Z(" & LTrim$(Str$(I)) & ") = "
  Temp = Temp & Chr$(9) & FormatComplex(Z2)
  Temp = Temp & Chr$(9) & "|Z(" & LTrim$(Str$(I)) & ")| =" & Chr$(9)
  Temp = Temp & Format$(Modulus(Z2), "#0.000") & Chr$(13) & Chr$(10)
  Z.a = Z2.a
  Z.b = Z2.b
Next I

OnError:

txtResult.Text = Temp

Screen.MousePointer = 0

Exit Sub

Overflow:

' Execution comes here if an overflow occurs.
Msg = "Arithmetic overflow occurred during calculations"
Msg = Msg & Chr$(13) & Chr$(10)
Msg = Msg & "Requested iterations were not completed."

MsgBox Msg

Resume OnError

End Sub

Sub Form_Paint ()

txtReal.SetFocus

End Sub
```

Listing 12.6   Code in MBT_INFO.FRM

```
Option Explicit

Sub cmdCancel_Click ()

Cancel = True
```

```
  Hide

  End Sub

  Sub cmdDefaults_Click ()

  ' Reset defaults for generation of complete Mandelbrot set.
  Dim Msg As String, Reply As Integer

  Msg = "Reset default parameters to generate complete set?"

  Reply = MsgBox(Msg, MB_ICONQUESTION + MB_OKCANCEL, "Reset")

  If Reply = IDCANCEL Then Exit Sub

  txtTLReal.Text = "-2.1"
  txtTLImag.Text = "1.2"
  txtLRReal.Text = "1"
  txtLRImag.Text = "-1.2"
  txtIter.Text = "20"

  End Sub

  Sub cmdGo_Click ()

  ' Be sure a valid value was entered for iterations.
  If Val(txtIter) < 5 Then
    Beep
    MsgBox "Iterations must be at least 5!"
    Exit Sub
  End If

  Cancel = False
  Hide

  End Sub
```

Julia Sets

Julia sets are named after their discoverer, the French mathematician Gaston Julia. While individual Julia sets are not as complex as the Mandelbrot set, there is an infinite number of them. This means that when you generate a particular Julia set, you may be the first person to ever see it! Julia sets come in a wide variety of shapes and patterns, and can be quite beautiful.

The Definition of a Julia Set

Julia sets are generated in a manner very similar to the Mandelbrot set.

To generate a Julia set, you plug a series of values into a formula and evaluate it iteratively. Values that "escape" to infinity are not in the set, while values that do not escape are in the set. This sounds very much like the technique for generating the Mandelbrot set, and in fact Julia sets use the same formula as the Mandelbrot set:

$$Z_{n+1} = Z_n^2 + c$$

The way the formula is applied, however, is different. For the Mandelbrot set, the value of c varies, taking on the value of each point on the complex plane. In contrast, the value of c remains fixed for each Julia set, and the value of Z varies. In fact, each Julia set is defined by a particular value of c.

Let's see how this works, using the Julia set defined by the complex point $0.43 + .26i$. To determine if the point $1 + 0.5i$ is in the Julia set, you would perform iterative calculation as shown here:

$$Z_1 = (1 + 0.5i)^2 + (0.43 + 0.26i)$$
$$Z_2 = (Z_1)^2 + (0.43 + 0.26i)$$
$$Z_3 = (Z_2)^2 + (0.43 + 0.26i)$$
$$\ldots$$
$$Z_{n+1} = (Z_n)^2 + (0.43 + 0.26i)$$

The rule for an "escape" is the same as before—if the modulus of Z exceeds 2, then the series is diverging to infinity and the point is not in the set.

As I mentioned earlier, there is an infinite number of Julia sets. This makes sense, of course, since there is an infinite number of points in the complex plane and each point defines a unique Julia set. Many of the sets are relatively uninteresting, while others are incredibly complicated and beautiful.

Julia Sets and the Mandelbrot Set

There is a fascinating relationship between Julia sets and the Mandelbrot set. In fact, the Mandelbrot set can be defined in terms of Julia sets.

Given that Julia sets are generated using the same formula as the Mandelbrot set, you might not be surprised to learn that there is a relationship between the two:

- Every point in the Mandelbrot set defines a *connected* Julia set. This means that the Julia set is contiguous, with every part connected to every other part.

- Every point outside the Mandelbrot set defines a *disconnected* Julia set that consists of a dust of infinitely many points.

Generally speaking, it is points near the edge of the Mandelbrot set that define the most interesting Julia sets. If you start within the Mandelbrot set and move toward the edge, the corresponding Julia sets become more and more convoluted. Just as you cross the edge the Julia set breaks apart. One way to define the Mandelbrot set is as the set of all points that define connected Julia sets.

By the way, the Mandelbrot set is a connected set. When you view the edges of the set at high magnification you will often see what appear to be small "islands" separate from the main set. It has been proven, however, that all such islands are actually connected to the main body.

A Julia Set Display Program

The program that I develop in this section can generate and display any Julia set.

The programming problems for generating Julia sets are not any different from those for the Mandelbrot set. In fact, the program JULIA was adapted with little trouble from the Mandelbrot generating program MBROT that was presented earlier in the chapter. The same advice about processing speed and use of the **DoEvents** statement apply here as well. The program functions in the same manner, including mouse selection of a small part of a generated set to be magnified. The primary exception is that the "Evaluate One Point" menu choice is not offered.

The program's main form, JULIA1.FRM, is visually identical to the form MBT1.FRM shown earlier in Figure 12.5. This form's objects and properties are given in Listing 12.7, and its code is presented in Listing 12.9.

The user enters starting parameters for the Julia set generation in JULIA2.FRM, shown in Figure 12.9. In addition to the number of iterations and the coordinates of the corners of the area to be shown, you must enter the real and imaginary parts of the point defining the Julia set. By choosing the Command Buttons Preset 1 through Preset 4 you can select parameters that produce four Julia sets that I think are particularly attractive. These sets are shown (in monochrome) in Figure 12.10. The objects, properties, and code in JULIA2.FRM are given in Listings 12.8 and 12.10.

The final program module is FRACTAL.BAS, which contains procedures for performing a variety of complex number calculations. Not all

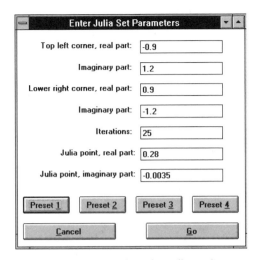

Figure 12.9   JULIA2.FRM is the dialog box that allows the user to enter parameters for Julia set generation and select one of four predefined sets of parameters.

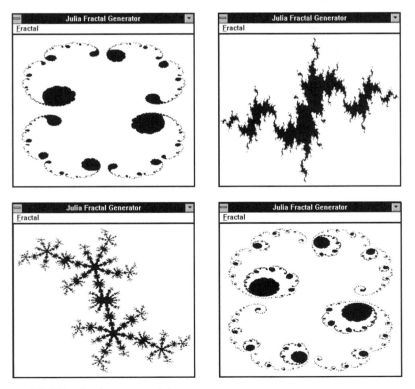

Figure 12.10   The four preset Julia sets.

of these procedures are used by the programs in this chapter, but you may find them useful if you go on to investigate other types of fractal images. FRACTAL.BAS will be found in Listing 12.11.

Using JULIA.MAK

This demonstration, presented in Listings 12.7, 12.8, 12.9, 12.10, and 12.11, is stored on disk as JULIA.MAK, JULIA1.FRM, JULIA2.FRM, and FRACTAL.BAS.

Listing 12.7   Objects and Properties in JULIA1.FRM

```
Begin Form frmJulia1
    AutoRedraw      =    -1   'True
    BorderStyle     =    1    'Fixed Single
    Caption         =    "Julia Fractal Generator"
    MaxButton       =    0    'False
    Begin PictureBox Picture1
        AutoRedraw      =    -1   'True
        BackColor       =    &H00000000&
        ScaleMode       =    3    'Pixel
    End
    Begin Menu mnuFractal
        Caption         =    "&Fractal"
        Begin Menu mnuGenerate
            Caption         =    "&Generate"
        End
        Begin Menu Sep
            Caption         =    "-"
        End
        Begin Menu mnuExit
            Caption         =    "E&xit"
        End
    End
End
```

Listing 12.8   Objects and Properties in JULIA2.FRM

```
Begin Form frmJulia2
    Caption         =    "Enter Julia Set Parameters"
    Begin CommandButton cmdDefaults
        Caption         =    "Preset &4"
        Index           =    3
    End
    Begin CommandButton cmdDefaults
        Caption         =    "Preset &3"
        Index           =    2
```

```
End
Begin CommandButton cmdDefaults
   Caption        =     "Preset &2"
   Index          =     1
End
Begin CommandButton cmdDefaults
   Caption        =     "Preset &1"
   Index          =     0
End
Begin TextBox txtStartImag
End
Begin TextBox txtStartReal
End
Begin TextBox txtIter
End
Begin TextBox txtLRImag
End
Begin TextBox txtLRReal
End
Begin TextBox txtTLImag
End
Begin TextBox txtTLReal
End
Begin CommandButton cmdCancel
   Cancel         =     -1   'True
   Caption        =     "&Cancel"
End
Begin CommandButton cmdGo
   Caption        =     "&Go"
   Default        =     -1   'True
End
Begin Label Label7
   Alignment      =     1  'Right Justify
   Caption        =     "Julia point, imaginary part:"
End
Begin Label Label6
   Alignment      =     1  'Right Justify
   Caption        =     "Julia point, real part:"
End
Begin Label Label5
   Alignment      =     1  'Right Justify
   Caption        =     "Iterations:"
End
Begin Label Label4
   Alignment      =     1  'Right Justify
   Caption        =     "Imaginary part:"
End
Begin Label Label3
   Alignment      =     1  'Right Justify
```

```
                 Caption        =    "Lower-right corner, real part:"
      End
      Begin Label Label2
         Alignment      =    1  'Right Justify
         Caption        =    "Imaginary part:"
      End
      Begin Label Label1
         Alignment      =    1  'Right Justify
         Caption        =    "Upper-left corner, real part:"
      End
End
```

Listing 12.9   Code in JULIA1.FRM

```
Option Explicit

Dim EndX As Single, EndY As Single
Dim StartX As Single, StartY As Single
Dim DeltaI As Double, DeltaR As Double

Dim Done As Integer

Const INVERSE = 6

Sub DrawLine (X1 As Single, Y1 As Single, X2 As Single,
   Y2 As Single, C As Integer)

' Save the current DrawMode.
Dim OldDrawMode As Integer

OldDrawMode = DrawMode

' Set DrawMode to XOR.
DrawMode = INVERSE

' Draw a box.
Picture1.Line (X1, Y1)-(X2, Y2), QBColor(C), B

' Reset DrawMode to original setting.
DrawMode = OldDrawMode

End Sub

Sub Form_Load ()

' Set the location and size of the Picture Box to
' fill the form.
Picture1.Top = 0
Picture1.Left = 0
```

```
Picture1.Height = frmJulia1.ScaleHeight
Picture1.Width = frmJulia1.ScaleWidth

Done = False

End Sub

Sub Generate ()

' Generates the Julia set according to the parameters
' entered by the user.
Dim XPixels As Integer, Ypixels As Integer
Dim RealRange As Double, ImagRange As Double
Dim X As Integer, Y As Integer, I As Integer
Dim C As COMPLEX, Z As COMPLEX
Dim Z1 As COMPLEX, Z2 As COMPLEX, Z3 As COMPLEX
Dim NIter As Integer, InSet As Integer

Done = False
Picture1.Cls

Picture1.MousePointer = 11

' How many pixels are in the Picture Box vertically
' and horizontally?

XPixels = Picture1.ScaleWidth
Ypixels = Picture1.ScaleHeight

' Calculate the range of real and imaginary values (in other
' words, the dimensions of the image on the complex plane).
RealRange = Abs(Val(frmJulia2.txtTLReal.Text) -
    Val(frmJulia2.txtLRReal.Text))
ImagRange = Abs(Val(frmJulia2.txtTLImag.Text) -
    Val(frmJulia2.txtLRImag.Text))

' Calculate the amount of change represented by each
' row or column of pixels.
DeltaR = RealRange / XPixels
DeltaI = ImagRange / Ypixels

' What is the number of iterations?
NIter = Val(frmJulia2.txtIter.Text)

' Starting value at upper-left corner.
C.a = Val(frmJulia2.txtStartReal.Text)
C.b = Val(frmJulia2.txtStartImag.Text)
Z.a = Val(frmJulia2.txtTLReal.Text)
```

```
' Begin the main processing loop.
For X = 1 To XPixels

    Z.a = Z.a + DeltaR
    Z.b = Val(frmJulia2.txtTLImag.Text)

    For Y = 1 To Ypixels

        Z.b = Z.b - DeltaI
        Z3 = Z
        InSet = True

        For I = 1 To NIter

            Call Square(Z3, Z1)
            Call Add(C, Z1, Z2)

            If ((Z2.a) * (Z2.a) + (Z2.b) * (Z2.b)) > 4 Then
                InSet = False
                Exit For
            End If

            Z3 = Z2

        Next I

        ' If point is not in the set, color it.
        If Not InSet Then
            Picture1.PSet (X, Y), QBColor((I Mod 15) + 1)
        End If

    ' Call DoEvents to allow other processes some access
    ' to the system.
    DoEvents

    Next Y

    ' Refresh the picture.
    Picture1.Refresh

    ' Put the call to DoEvents here for faster Julia processing
    ' but slower response in other applications while the
    ' program is running.
Next X

Done = True
Picture1.MousePointer = 0
Beep
```

```
End Sub

Sub mnuExit_Click ()

End

End Sub

Sub mnuGenerate_Click ()

' Display the dialog box for the user to enter
' starting parameters.
frmJulia2.Show  1

If Cancel = False Then
    Call Generate
End If

End Sub

Sub Picture1_MouseDown (Button As Integer, Shift As Integer,
  X As Single, Y As Single)

' Save the coordinates where the user starts to drag.
StartX = X
StartY = Y

End Sub

Sub Picture1_MouseUp (Button As Integer, Shift As Integer,
  X As Single, Y As Single)

Dim Temp As Integer, X1 As Double
Dim X2 As Double, X3 As Double, X4 As Double

' If the program has completed generating the image,
' permit the user to select an area for magnification
' by dragging with the mouse.
If Done Then

    ' Save coordinates.
    EndX = X
    EndY = Y

    ' If necessary, swap Start and End values so that
    ' Start always refers to the upper-left corner
    ' of the area.
    If EndX < StartX Then
        Temp = StartX
```

```
        StartX = EndX
        EndX = Temp
    End If

    If EndY < StartY Then
        Temp = StartY
        StartY = EndY
        EndY = Temp
    End If

    ' Draw a box around the selected area.
    Call DrawLine(StartX, StartY, EndX, EndY, 7)

    ' Convert the mouse start and stop coordinates into
    ' complex plane coordinates and display them in the
    ' dialog box.
    X1 = Val(frmJulia2.txtTLReal.Text)
    X3 = X1
    X1 = X1 + (StartX * DeltaR)
    X3 = X3 + (EndX * DeltaR)

    X2 = Val(frmJulia2.txtTLImag.Text)
    X4 = X2
    X2 = X2 - (StartY * DeltaI)
    X4 = X4 - (EndY * DeltaI)

    frmJulia2.txtTLReal.Text = Format$(Str$(X1), "0.########")
    frmJulia2.txtTLImag.Text = Format$(Str$(X2), "0.########")
    frmJulia2.txtLRReal.Text = Format$(Str$(X3), "0.########")
    frmJulia2.txtLRImag.Text = Format$(Str$(X4), "0.########")

    frmJulia2.Show 1

    If Cancel = False Then
        Call Generate
    End If

End If

End Sub
```

Listing 12.10   Code in JULIA2.FRM

```
Option Explicit

Sub cmdCancel_Click ()

Cancel = True
Hide
```

```
End Sub

Sub cmdDefaults_Click (Index As Integer)

' Reset parameters for generation of one of four
' preset Julia sets.
Select Case Index
    Case 0
        txtTLReal.Text = "-0.9"
        txtTLImag.Text = "1.2"
        txtLRReal.Text = "0.9"
        txtLRImag.Text = "-1.2"
        txtIter.Text = "25"
        txtStartReal = "0.28"
        txtStartImag = "-0.0035"
    Case 1
        txtTLReal.Text = "-1.65"
        txtTLImag.Text = "0.8"
        txtLRReal.Text = "1.65"
        txtLRImag.Text = "-0.8"
        txtIter.Text = "25"
        txtStartReal = "-1.03"
        txtStartImag = "-0.26"
    Case 2
        txtTLReal.Text = "-1.2"
        txtTLImag.Text = "1.2"
        txtLRReal.Text = "1.2"
        txtLRImag.Text = "-1.2"
        txtIter.Text = "35"
        txtStartReal = "0.14"
        txtStartImag = "0.65"
    Case 3
        txtTLReal.Text = "-0.9"
        txtTLImag.Text = "1.15"
        txtLRReal.Text = "0.9"
        txtLRImag.Text = "-1.15"
        txtIter.Text = "50"
        txtStartReal = "0.27"
        txtStartImag = "-0.0035"
End Select

End Sub

Sub cmdGo_Click ()

' Be sure a valid value was entered for iterations.
If Val(txtIter) < 5 Then
  Beep
  MsgBox "Iterations must be at least 5!"
```

```
   Exit Sub
End If

Cancel = False
Hide

End Sub
```

Listing 12.11   Code in FRACTAL.BAS

```
Option Explicit

Type COMPLEX
  a As Double
  b As Double
End Type

Global Const MB_ICONQUESTION = 32
Global Const MB_OKCANCEL = 1
Global Const IDOK = 1
Global Const IDCANCEL = 2

Global Cancel As Integer

Sub Add (X As COMPLEX, Y As COMPLEX, Z As COMPLEX)

' Adds complex numbers X and Y, assigning the
' sum to Z.
Z.a = X.a + Y.a
Z.b = X.b + Y.b

End Sub

Function FormatComplex (Z As COMPLEX) As String

' Returns a formatted string expressing
' the complex number argument.
Dim S As String

S = Format$(Z.a, "#0.000")
S = S & " + "
S = S & Format$(Z.b, "#0.000") & "i"

FormatComplex = S

End Function

Function Modulus (X As COMPLEX) As Double
```

```
' Returns the modulus of a complex number.
Modulus = Sqr(X.a * X.a + X.b * X.b)

End Function

Sub Multiply (X As COMPLEX, Y As COMPLEX, Z As COMPLEX)

' Multiplies complex numbers X and Y, assigning
' the result to Z.
Z.a = (X.a * Y.a) - (X.b * Y.b)
Z.b = (X.a * Y.b) + (X.b * Y.a)

End Sub

Sub Square (X As COMPLEX, Z As COMPLEX)

' Squares complex number X, assigning
' the result to Z.
Z.a = (X.a * X.a) - (X.b * X.b)
Z.b = 2 * X.a * X.b

End Sub

Sub Subtract (X As COMPLEX, Y As COMPLEX, Z As COMPLEX)

' Subtracts complex number Y from complex number X,
' assigning the result to Z.
Z.a = X.a - Y.a
Z.b = X.b - Y.b

End Sub
```

OLE 2.0

W ith the release of Visual Basic 3.0 in May 1993, Microsoft introduced support for OLE 2.0. This new *Object Linking and Embedding* system refines and expands the original concepts of OLE, which we discussed in Chapter 6. OLE 2.0 is the centerpiece of what is becoming known as *Component Software*, the software equivalent of interchangeable, standardized parts.

In the past, developers have been forced to implement their own versions of many major software subsystems. For example, almost every programmer has had to write a text editor at one time or another. Not only does this represent a true waste of time for programmers, it has also forced end-users to master the subtleties—and not-so-subtleties—of the various editors scattered among the programs they use.

Windows has provided some relief for end-users by providing interface standards for the most common software features, especially cursor positioning commands, menu selection methods, and the common dialogs (known formally with capital letters as Common Dialogs), such as file and color selection. But ironically, the simplicity and standards that users enjoy can mean even greater headaches for programmers. Windows applications may be easy to use, but often they make up for that by being terribly difficult to write, as anyone who's tried to write a Windows text editor with support for variably spaced fonts will confirm.

Wouldn't it be handy if we could just incorporate our favorite applications into our own—legally, without nefariously obtained source code? That would save programmers from continually re-inventing the wheel, and in some cases, it may enable end-users to choose their personal favorites as components of the parent application. Those who preferred Microsoft Word could edit documents in Word, those who favored Lotus Ami Pro could use Ami Pro.

That's what Microsoft hopes we'll do with OLE 2.0.

As Visual Basic programmers, we're already accustomed to the component software approach to software development. Each of the controls in our tool palette is a software component, and at the moment we can choose from among hundreds of commercial custom controls that do everything from dressing up our forms with 3-D effects to complete spreadsheet programs. But now, with OLE 2.0, any Windows application installed on your system can become a custom control—but only if it fully supports OLE 2.0.

What's New in OLE 2.0?

The changes to OLE come in two categories: The least significant of these is new terminology; the more significant is *OLE Automation*. Let's begin where we must, with semantics.

In the original OLE, which we'll call OLE 1, we referred to OLE applications as either *clients* or *servers* or both. In OLE 2.0, we refer to *OLE objects* and *container applications*. Beware of the analogies. These new terms are *not* synonymous with their predecessors.

A *server* in OLE 1 was an application that we called upon to manipulate embedded or linked data. In OLE 2.0, an *OLE object* is not the application, but the data element itself. In other words, it's the Word document object, or the Quattro Pro spreadsheet object, or the Lotus 123 graph object. Actually, if you look at the chapter on OLE in Microsoft's *Visual Basic Programmer's Guide*, you'll find that the term *object* has existed all along. Microsoft just wants us to stop calling the parent applications *servers*.

Microsoft now refers to the parent application of the embedded or linked data as the *Object Class*, a dubious application of terminology from the world of object-oriented programming. On the other hand, *container applications* perform much the same function as *clients* do in OLE 1, except that they have more control over OLE objects than OLE 1 clients had over OLE 1 servers, which brings us to *OLE Automation*.

OLE Automation

In OLE 2.0, the container application can not only invoke the parent application (in full parlance: the application identified by the OLE object's Object Class), it can also operate that application by sending it commands and requesting data elements, just like DDE. In fact, with one important exception, OLE 2.0 combines and replaces the functions of both OLE and DDE.

From our perspective as Visual Basic programmers, we can use applications that support OLE Automation like custom controls. The functions of those applications, at least all those that their creators offer through the OLE interface, become the methods of those controls, and we can set the properties of those embedded applications just as easily as we set the properties of Visual Basic's native objects.

And what's the important exception? While your Visual Basic program can act as either *source* or *destination* in a DDE conversation, it can act only as the *container application* under OLE, regardless of whether you're using linking and embedding or just OLE Automation. *Visual Basic programs cannot export OLE objects.*

Manipulating Objects

Instead of sending command strings to embedded or linked objects, OLE 2.0 permits us to execute methods on them.

While DDE enables us to send command strings to other applications by way of the LinkExecute property, OLE 2.0 treats commands as methods, just like the methods on any Visual Basic object.

Instead of telling Excel to save the current worksheet by sending it the command string

```
Text1.LinkExecute  "[SAVE()]"
```

we would just invoke the Save method on the embedded object:

```
OLE1.Object.Save
```

The methods available to any particular object will depend entirely on its Object Class (the "server application").

Don't worry too much about OLE Automation yet. Windows and Visual Basic still support DDE. In fact, at the moment, DDE is the only system supported by most Windows applications software, including Microsoft's own products. Compliance with DDE does not automatically enable the features of OLE Automation. Developers will have to modify their products to support this new inter-application communication system.

HOT TIP

Use the DDE Protocol

If your Visual Basic application needs to act as the *source* of dynamic data exchanges, you must use the DDE protocol. With Visual Basic we cannot yet create OLE Automation servers.

Since we can't use Visual Basic to create both ends of an OLE Automation link, and since no commercial applications support OLE Automation (as of this writing), we can't do much with it yet.

Linking and Embedding

The other function of OLE 2.0 is, of course, linking and embedding. For the most part, linking and embedding in OLE 2.0 behaves much the same as it did in OLE 1. The most significant enhancement is the introduction of *in-place editing*.

Under OLE 1, when a user activates an embedded object, the server application appears in its own window. To the user, it looks as if the embedded object has been temporarily lifted from its place in the client's document to be edited within the confines of the server's own window. If the server and container both support OLE 2.0, however, the server application can be used to edit the embedded object without removing it from its container. When the user clicks an OLE 2.0 spreadsheet object, for example, OLE replaces the menu of the container application with the menu of the server application, and the user can manipulate the embedded object as if they were running the server application directly.

As with OLE Automation, support for in-place editing requires changes at the application level. Besides this functional enhancement, some important details have changed in the implementation of OLE 2.0 within our Visual Basic programs. Fortunately, the update to OLE won't invalidate all your existing code. However, some important details have changed in the implementation.

Running Existing OLE 1 Applications

You don't have to change your existing applications until you need the new capabilities of OLE 2.0.

You can still run your OLE 1 applications under Visual Basic 3.0, as long as you have the original OLE control installed on your system (look for OLECLIEN.VBX, which Visual Basic 2.0 installed in your \WINDOWS \SYSTEM directory). If you upgraded from Visual Basic version 2.0 to version 3.0, you should be able to load and run the OLE1.MAK example from Chapter 6 without any modifications. When you load it, you'll notice that the old OLE control appears in the Toolbox.

Any OLE applications you've written with the old control will continue to work with Visual Basic 3.0 and Windows 3.1. You cannot, however, just substitute the new MSOLE2.VBX for the old OLECLIEN.VBX in your Visual Basic Project.

Note: The OLE controls are just like any other custom controls for Visual Basic. In fact, Visual Basic 2.0 itself contains no intrinsic support for OLE; those capabilities come from the OLE custom control. If your Windows system supports OLE 1 (a standard feature of Windows 3.1), then the original OLECLIEN.VBX will work with either Visual Basic version 2.0 or 3.0. If you've installed OLE 2.0 in your Windows system (which Visual Basic 3.0 does automatically during installation), then the MSOLE2.VBX will also work.

Migrating to OLE 2.0

Programs that incorporate the original Visual Basic OLE control, will not work unchanged with the new OLE 2.0 control.

To accommodate changes both in terminology and in function, the properties of the new OLE custom control differ significantly from those of its predecessor.

First of all, the control type has changed from *OleClient* to just plain *OLE*. When you add an OLE control to a form, instead of a default name of OleClient1 (or OleClient2, OleClient3, etc.) Visual Basic will give it the default name OLE1. This name does not indicate OLE version 1.0, it just means the first OLE control. The second one will receive the name OLE2, the third OLE3, and so on; that is, unless you substitute your own more meaningful names.

The most extensive changes have occurred among the properties: several property names have changed, new properties have been added, and some properties have been deleted. Review Tables 13.1, 13.2, and 13.3 for details.

Table 13.1   OLE 2.0 Property Name Changes

Old Name	New Name
ServerAcceptFormats()	ObjectAcceptFormat()
ServerAcceptFormatsCount	ObjectAcceptFormatsCount
ServerGetFormats()	ObjectGetFormats()
ServerGetFormatsCount	ObjectGetFormatsCount
ServerType	OLEType
ServerVerbs()	ObjectVerbs()
ServerVerbsCount	ObjectVerbsCount

Table 13.2 OLE 2.0 New Properties

New Properties	Use
AppIsRunning	Returns True or False to indicate whether the application that created the object in the OLE control is active.
AutoActivate	Determines how the OLE object is activated. It offers three choices: (1) programmatic activation by setting the Action property to OLE_ACTIVATE, (2) activation whenever the OLE control gets the focus, and (3) activation when double-clicked.
AutoVerbMenu	Displays a pop-up menu of the object's Verbs when the user presses the right mouse button.
DisplayType	Determines whether an object's contents appear in the OLE control, or just as an icon. Some applications will display only an icon, regardless of this setting (the Recorder for example).
Object	Provides an object reference for an OLE Automation method. The old method of manipulating an OLE object under program control was to assign a command string to the now obsolete Execute property (OleClient1.Execute = "Save"). In OLE 2.0, OLE objects work just like any other objects, such as Visual Basic Forms and Controls. That is, instead of assigning a command string to a property, you execute a method (OLE1.Object.Save). In this example, OLE1 is the control object, the Object property refers to the current OLE object contained by the control, and Save is a method of that object. This command would perform the same operation that a user would if they selected the Save command from the File menu of the server application.
ObjectVerbFlags()	A collection of flags that indicate whether a Verb is currently available. If you choose to build your own verb menu, instead of the pop-up menu provided by setting the AutoVerbMenu property to True, you must use these flags to set the menu's properties. For each element you find in the ObjectVerbs collection property, you will find one flag entry in ObjectVerbFlags. This integer value may contain five possible values:

MF_ENABLED	&H0000
MF_GRAYED	&H0001
MF_DISABLED	&H0002
MF_CHECKED	&H0008
MF_SEPARATOR	&H0800

Table 13.2   OLE 2.0 New Properties (Continued)

OLETypeAllowed	Determines whether the control can contain linked objects only (OLETypeAllowed = 0), embedded objects only (OLETypeAllowed = 1), or either type of object (OLETypeAllowed = 2).
SizeMode	Determines how the OLE control will display an object. A value of 0 means to display it actual size, and to clip it if it's too big. A value of 1 causes it to stretch the object to fit within the borders of the control. A value of 2 causes the control to resize itself to display the entire object, within the limits of the current window, of course. The old OLE control always stretched (which can also mean squashed) the object. The new default mode is 0, clip.

The Execute property has been replaced by OLE Automation, and the three Protocol properties no longer exist because they determined or indicated whether the server would respond to the Execute property.

The ServerClass properties were used, as you may recall, to determine what server applications were available to supply OLE objects. In the program OLE1.MAK we used these properties to build a List Box from which the user could select an OLE server. As you'll soon see, the OLE 2.0 control supports the new OLE Dialogs, which standardize this function. So the ServerClass properties are no longer needed.

Table 13.3   Eliminated Properties

Execute
Focus
Protocol
ServerClass
ServerClassCount
ServerClasses()
ServerClassesDisplay()
ServerProtocol
ServerProtocolCount
ServerShow
TimeOut

The Focus and ServerShow properties worked together to determine whether the server application should appear when an object was created, and if so, whether it should receive the input focus. These properties might have proven useful in cases where you wanted to manipulate an OLE object by sending commands to the server application with the Execute property. The new control instead offers the AutoActivate property (see Table 13.2), which performs a similar function.

Adapting the Demonstration Program

The OLE 2.0 version of the demonstration program we originally created in Chapter 6 is simpler than the original.

A few of the changes to the code in OLE2.FRM consist of changes in property names and the name of the OLE control itself. The control has been renamed from OleClient1 to OLE1. The OLE1 property ServerType has been renamed to OleType. I've also renamed the form itself from frmOle1 to frmOle2.

The most conspicuous change is the disappearance of the form frmInsert (in the file INSERT.FRM). frmInsert is a dialog box that enables the user to choose an OLE object. OLE 2.0 offers a pre-defined dialog box for that purpose, called the Insert Object Dialog. To activate the dialog box, you just set the Action property:

```
OLE1.Action = OLE_INSERT_OBJ_DLG
```

The Insert Object Dialog will set all the appropriate properties.

In the **mnuInsert_Click ()** event of OLE1.FRM, we set the ServerType property to specify an embedded object:

```
OleClient1.ServerType = OLE_EMBEDDED
```

The Type property of the new OLE2 control, however, is read-only at run-time and tells us what type of object has been selected. To specify what types of objects we'll allow in our programs we use the OleTypeAllowed property:

```
OLE1.OleTypeAllowed = OLE_EMBEDDED
```

Finally, I've added the global constant declaration for **OLE_INSERT _OBJ_DLG** to OLE2.BAS.

On Disk

Using OLE2.FRM

This demonstration program, presented in Listings 13.1, 13.2, and 13.3, is stored on disk as OLE2.FRM and OLE2.BAS.

Listing 13.1   Objects and Properties in OLE2.FRM

```
Begin Form frmOle2
    Caption           =    "OLE2 Demonstration "
    ClientHeight      =    4005
    ClientLeft        =    1110
    ClientTop         =    1740
    ClientWidth       =    7350
    Height            =    4695
    Left              =    1050
    LinkTopic         =    "Form1"
    ScaleHeight       =    4005
    ScaleWidth        =    7350
    Top               =    1110
    Width             =    7470
    Begin OLE OLE1
        fFFHk             =    -1    'True
        Height            =    3972
        Left              =    0
        TabIndex          =    0
        Top               =    0
        Width             =    4332
    End
    Begin Menu mnuFIle
        Caption           =    "&File"
        Begin Menu mnuFileSave
            Caption           =    "&Save"
        End
        Begin Menu mnuFileSep
            Caption           =    "-"
        End
        Begin Menu mnuFIleExit
            Caption           =    "E&xit"
        End
    End
    Begin Menu mnuObject
        Caption           =    "&Object"
        Begin Menu mnuInsert
            Caption           =    "&Insert"
        End
        Begin Menu mnuObjectDelete
            Caption           =    "&Delete"
        End
    End
End
```

Listing 13.2 Code in OLE2.FRM

```
Option Explicit

Sub Form_Load ()

Dim FileNum As Integer, Reply As Integer

' If the OLE data file exists, give the user the option
' of loading the OLE object from it.

ObjectPresent = False
NotSaved = False

If Dir$(OLE_FILE_NAME) <> "" Then
    Reply = MsgBox("Load object from disk?", MB_YESNO + MB_ICONQUESTION,
        "Load Object")
    If Reply = IDYES Then
        Screen.MousePointer = 11
        FileNum = FreeFile
        Open OLE_FILE_NAME For Binary As #FileNum
        OLE1.FileNumber = FileNum
        OLE1.Action = OLE_READ_FROM_FILE
        ObjectPresent = True
        Close #FileNum
        Screen.MousePointer = 0
    End If
End If

End Sub

Sub Form_Resize ()

' Sixe and position the OLE Client control to
' fill the form.

OLE1.Move 0, 0, frmOle2.ScaleWidth, frmOle2.ScaleHeight

End Sub

Sub mnuFile_Click ()

' Enable Save menu command only if an object exists.

If ObjectPresent Then
    mnuFileSave.Enabled = True
Else
    mnuFileSave.Enabled = False
End If
```

```
End Sub

Sub mnuFileExit_Click ()

End

End Sub

Sub mnuFileSave_Click ()

Call SaveObject

End Sub

Sub mnuInsert_Click ()

Dim Reply As Integer

' If an object is present, ask if it should be deleted. If
' user replies "no" exit sub.

If ObjectPresent Then
    Reply = MsgBox("Delete current object?", MB_YESNO And
        MB_ICONQUESTION, "Insert Object")

    If Reply = IDYES Then
        Call mnuObjectDelete_Click
    Else
        Exit Sub
    End If
End If

' In the first version of this program (OLE1), we set the
' OLE Client control's ServerType property to specify an
' embedded object:
'
'   OleClient1.ServerType = OLE_EMBEDDED
'
' The Type property of the new OLE2 control is read-only at
' run-time and tells us what type of Object has been selected.
' To specify what types of objects we'll allow in our programs
' we use the OLETypeAllowed property:

    OLE1.OleTypeAllowed = OLE_EMBEDDED

' In the previous version of this program we used a separate
' form to display a list box from which the user could select
' a server application.  We invoked that form with the line:
'
```

```
'    frmInsert.Show 1
'
' frmInsert set the ServerClass property.  We then set the
' Action property to create the new object:
'
'    frmOle2.OleClient1.Action = OLE_CREATE_NEW
'
' Now instead, we just invoke the new pre-defined
' OLE Insert Dialog:
'
     frmOle2.OLE1.Action = OLE_INSERT_OBJ_DLG

ObjectPresent = True
NotSaved = True
Screen.MousePointer = 0

End Sub

Sub mnuObject_Click ()

' Enable the Delete option only if an object is present.

If ObjectPresent Then
    mnuObjectDelete.Enabled = True
Else
    mnuObjectDelete.Enabled = False
End If

End Sub

Sub mnuObjectDelete_Click ()

Dim Reply As Integer

' If the object has not been saved, offer the option.

If NotSaved Then

    Reply = MsgBox("Save object before deleting?", MB_YESNOCANCEL +
        MB_ICONQUESTION, "Delete Object")

    If Reply = IDYES Then
        Call SaveObject
    ElseIf Reply = IDCANCEL Then
        Exit Sub
    End If

End If
```

```
' Now we can delete the object.

OLE1.Action = OLE_DELETE
ObjectPresent = False
NotSaved = False

End Sub

Sub OLE1_DblClick ()

' Activate the OLE object for editing.

OLE1.Action = OLE_ACTIVATE
NotSaved = True

End Sub

Sub OLE1_Updated (Code As Integer)

NotSaved = True

End Sub

Sub SaveObject ()

Dim FileNum As Integer

' Save the OLE object.

FileNum = FreeFile

Open OLE_FILE_NAME For Binary As #FileNum

OLE1.FileNumber = FileNum
OLE1.Action = OLE_SAVE_TO_FILE
NotSaved = False

Close #FileNum

End Sub
```

Listing 13.3   Code in OLE2.BAS

```
Option Explicit

' Constants for OLE actions.

Global Const OLE_CREATE_NEW = 0
Global Const OLE_ACTIVATE = 7
```

```
Global Const OLE_DELETE = 10
Global Const OLE_SAVE_TO_FILE = 11
Global Const OLE_READ_FROM_FILE = 12
Global Const OLE_INSERT_OBJ_DLG = 14

' Constants for OLE object type.

Global Const OLE_EMBEDDED = 1

' Constant for OLE file name.

Global Const OLE_FILE_NAME = "OLE_DATA.XYZ"

' COnstants for message box displays and replies.

Global Const MB_YESNOCANCEL = 3
Global Const MB_YESNO = 4
Global Const MB_ICONQUESTION = 32
Global Const IDCANCEL = 2
Global Const IDYES = 6
Global Const IDNO = 7

' Global variables and flags.

Global NotSaved As Integer
Global ObjectPresent As Integer
```

OLE Out of Control

Unlike Visual Basic 2.0, Visual Basic 3.0 provides intrinsic support for OLE. We can use OLE objects without embedding them or linking them to an OLE control.

The new Object variable type enables us to declare an object variable, to which we may then assign an OLE object:

```
Dim Doc As Object
Set Doc = CreateObject("MyWordprocessor.Document")
```

Once the object exists, you may set its properties and execute its methods as you wish (as long as it has some).

It's possible that as OLE 2.0 catches on, some software companies will offer objects—that is, they will "expose objects"—in addition to their basic data elements. For example, a word processor could offer its spelling checker, thesaurus and grammar checker as objects, which we could then use in our own applications. Or a spreadsheet may expose its expression parser, so we could build Visual Basic applications that accept mathematical expressions from the end user:

```
Dim Parser As Object
Dim AnyFormula, AnnualPmtTotal
AnyFormula = "Pmt(100000,0.08/12,360)*12"
Set Parser = CreateObject("ASpreadsheetProgram.ExpressionParser")
AnnualPmtTotal = Parser.Evaluate AnyFormula
Parser.Quit
```

Note that the function **CreateObject()** doesn't create the expression parser. The parser must exist in the program called ASpreadsheetProgram, and must be exposed by that program as an OLE object. **CreateObject()** creates an *instance* of that object type which we may then activate through its methods.

As support for OLE 2.0 expands, we'll gain more and more tools, or *software components*, with which to build our Visual Basic applications.

The Access Database Engine

When Microsoft simultaneously introduced Visual Basic 2.0 and Access, their new database system, many of us assumed that the new ODBC (Open Database Connectivity) manager would enable us to easily read and write Access files from our Visual Basic programs. But, despite our optimistic wishes, Microsoft provided no ODBC driver for VB 2.0, so the only way to integrate these two systems was to call upon the services of DDE.

Anyone who has followed the traffic on the Compuserve Microsoft Basic Forum since the release of Visual Basic 2.0 knows that questions about integrating Visual Basic and Access abound. Apparently Microsoft noticed this too. If you look at the overall scope of differences between Visual Basic 2.0 and Visual Basic 3.0, it's clear that the main reason Microsoft introduced version 3.0 was to fill this void.

For version 3.0, Microsoft added a new Data control, and enhanced several of the existing controls to make them "data aware." But they didn't stop there. In the Professional Edition, you'll find a set of eight objects with methods and properties that enable us to directly manipulate Access databases at the "programmatic layer."

The methods you choose to manipulate your database files will depend on several factors, including the ultimate size of the database, its complexity in terms of the number of tables it contains, and the average number of fields in each table. You'll also need to consider the sophistication of the end-user and the amount of time you have to get the application working.

Building Database Applications

We most often use the word *database* to refer to collections of *records*. Records contain collections of data elements, or *fields*. A database may consist of a single collection of a single type of record, or it may contain several collections of records, each with its own record structure.

Most modern programming languages provide support for record-structured data files. In Visual Basic, we can create a record definition with a **Type** statement:

```
Type InvoiceRecord
    Number As Integer
    Clerk As Integer
    Date As String * 8
```

```
      LastName As String * 35
      FirstName As String * 15
      Total As Single
End Type
```

We can then open a file for Random Access based on that structure:

```
Dim Invoice As InvoiceRecord
Open "INVOICE.DAT" For Random As #1 Len = Len(Invoice)
```

And we can read and write records from and to that file with **Get** and **Put** statements:

```
For RecordNumber = 1 To (LOF(1) / Len(Invoice))
Get #1, RecordNumber, Invoice
Form1.Print Invoice.Number
Next Record-Number
```

With that simple model, we can build a variety of sophisticated applications, limited only by the capacities of the computers on which they need to run, and by the amount of time we have in which to create them.

It so happens that database applications, as varied as they may be, share many common operations. So, whether you're tracking an auto parts inventory or storing patient medical records, you'll need to fulfill a handful of key requirements:

- Add Records
- Edit Records
- Delete Records
- Browse Records
- Generate Reports of Records

The difference between a standard system for file input and output, or *file I/O*, and a database management system is that the database management system makes it easy to store, search, retrieve and order records without building complex contraptions. The database system itself provides most of those contraptions.

Database Management with Standard File I/O

You can build database applications without the Access engine, if you dare.

In the first sample application in this chapter, I've used the basic data storage tools to create a simple database system that places records in two files (actually, as you'll see, I've created three files, but the third contains only one record). Once we've examined this program, I'll discuss the advantages of the new database management features and demonstrate them by revising the sample program to store its data in an Access database.

DATABAS1.MAK

The sample program DATABAS1.MAK includes three program files: DATABAS1.FRM, DETAILF1.FRM, and DATABAS1.BAS. You'll also need GRID.VBX.

The sample program DATABAS1 stores invoices and their detail line items in two separate files, also known in the database world as *tables*, named INVOICE1.DAT and DETAILS1.DAT. A third file, called INVSTAT1.DAT holds a single record that contains two counters, which indicate the current number of record positions in each of the two data tables.

The main form, stored in the file DATABAS1.FRM and named with default name Form1, accepts the general invoice information, the fields that we'll store in INVOICE1.DAT, and displays the detail records for each invoice in a Grid control. This form is shown in Figure 14.1.

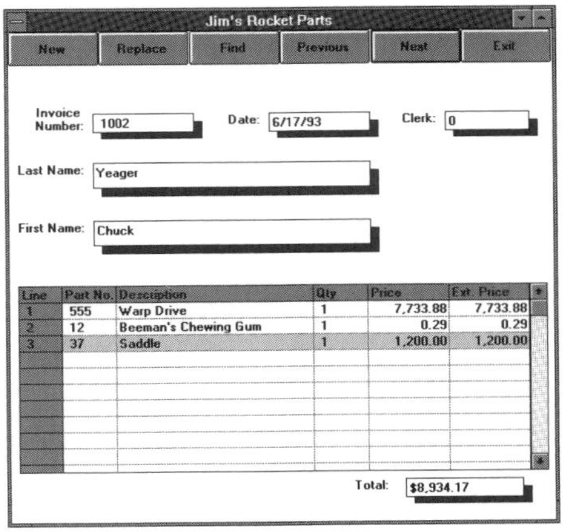

Figure 14.1   DATABAS1.FRM, the main form of DATABAS1.MAK.

Since the Grid control cannot be edited by the user at runtime, we'll use a second form, Form2, shown in Figure 14.2, which is stored in DETAILF1.FRM and collects or edits each detail item.

To find an existing invoice you can either step through the file one record at a time with the Next button, or you can enter an invoice number and press the Find button. To add a new detail to an invoice, double-click on the Grid control anywhere. To edit an existing detail, click on the corresponding line number. The rest of the controls are self explanatory.

Aside from the machinations of the Grid control, much of the code in this program manages the placement and replacement of records in the two main data files. To retrieve an existing invoice requires the services of these three procedures: **FindButton_Click**, **FindInvoice()**, and **GetInvoice()**.

This program is only as simple as it is because I've made no effort to store the records in any particular order. Each time the user adds an invoice or a detail record, we store it in the first available location—either by appending it to the end of the file, or by re-using a location vacated by a deleted record. You'll also notice that although I've enabled the **SaveInvoice** and **SaveDetails()** procedures to re-use empty records, for the sake of simplicity I've provided no delete functions. Because the records fall where they may, when it comes time to retrieve one, the program has to search the file from the beginning, record-by-record. This linear search continues until it either finds a record with the requested invoice number or bumps into the end of the file.

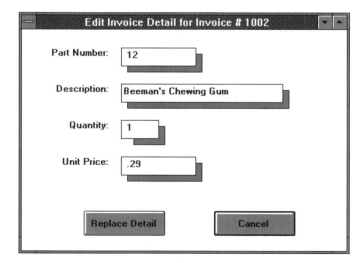

Figure 14.2 The user enters new details or edits existing details on DETAILF1.FRM.

```
Function FindInvoice (InvoiceNumberToFind As Integer) As Integer
    Dim Invoice As InvoiceRecord
    Dim InvoiceFound As Integer
    Dim Counter As Integer
    Dim FileStatus As DBStatusRecord
    Dim DetailRecordsFound As Integer
    Dim Detail As DetailRecord

    InvoiceFound = False
    If InvoiceNumberToFind > 0 Then
        Get StatusFile, 1, FileStatus
        Counter = 0
        Do Until (Counter = FileStatus.NumberOfInvoices) Or InvoiceFound
            Counter = Counter + 1
            Get InvoiceFile, Counter, Invoice
            InvoiceFound = (Invoice.Number = InvoiceNumberToFind)
            DoEvents
            Loop
        If InvoiceFound Then
            FindInvoice = Counter
        Else
            FindInvoice = 0
        End If
    Else
        FindInvoice = 0
    End If
End Function
```

Linear searches work fine for small files, but when your database grows to several thousand records, they can, and usually do, become far too slow. The picture changes when you can arrange the records in order, according to the value of one or more of its fields.

The most natural way to arrange invoices would be by invoice number. Then you could perform a more efficient search that would take into account that order. You could get the records into order by sorting them, but that means you can only retrieve them according to that particular ordering scheme. What if you wanted to search for invoices by customer name, or print a list of invoices in order by sales clerk and invoice data? You wouldn't want to re-sort the entire file each time you printed a report with different order requirements.

Another more efficient way to order the records is to create a separate *index*. The simplest kind of index is a separate file that contains a list of records consisting of a *key field* and the record position of the actual data record within its own file. Instead of sorting the records, we sort the records in the key file. We can maintain as many separate key files as we need.

We can manage our key files more efficiently if we do away with sorting altogether, and find a way to link the key records in such as way that we can insert new keys into their proper positions and remove old keys without rearranging the entire key file. In fact, these techniques are common. The hashing system discussed in an earlier chapter is one kind of indexing scheme.

As you might imagine, the code to maintain an index, or worse, multiple indices on multiple files, can become quite complex, much more so than the code to perform a bunch of linear searches. Fortunately, the need for ordered data files is so common that systems have been created that can perform these tasks for us. We call them database managers or *database engines.*

The Access Database Engine

Microsoft's Access database system, a stand-alone data management tool, uses an underlying engine to manage data. The database management features of Visual Basic 3.0 call the same database engine. With Visual Basic we can build our own user interfaces to Access databases.

The second sample database program, DATABAS2.MAK, uses the same forms as the previous example, but I've replaced the flat file data storage scheme with an Access database, and modified the corresponding code. In some procedures, the code shrinks substantially:

```
Function FindInvoice (InvoiceNumberToFind As Integer) As String

    Invoices.Index = "InvoiceNumber"
    Invoices.Seek "=", InvoiceNumberToFind
    If Invoices.NoMatch Then
        FindInvoice = ""
      Else
        FindInvoice = Invoices.Bookmark
      End If
End Function
```

In other procedures, the amount of code doesn't change much at all. The new **GetInvoice** procedure, for example, though different in its details, is just about the same length as the old one. Listings 14.1 and 14.2 show both versions of the procedure.

Listing 14.1 The GetInvoice Procedure from DATABAS1.BAS

```
Sub GetInvoice (RecordNumber As Integer)
    Dim Invoice As InvoiceRecord
    Dim Counter As Integer
    Dim FileStatus As DBStatusRecord
    Dim DetailRecordsFound As Integer
    Dim Detail As DetailRecord

    Get InvoiceFile, RecordNumber, Invoice
    Form1.InvClerkText.Text = Invoice.Clerk
    Form1.InvNumberText.Text = Str$(Invoice.Number)
    Form1.InvDateText.Text = Format$(Invoice.Date, "ddddd")
    Form1.InvLastNameText.Text = Invoice.LastName
    Form1.InvFirstNameText.Text = Invoice.FirstName
    Invoice.Total = 0

    Get StatusFile, 1, FileStatus
    DetailRecordsFound = 0
    Form1.Grid1.Row = 1
    ClearGrid Form1.Grid1
    For Counter = 1 To FileStatus.NumberOfDetails
        Get DetailFile, Counter, Detail
        If Detail.InvoiceNumber = Invoice.Number Then
            DetailRecordsFound = DetailRecordsFound + 1
            ReDim Preserve DetailArray(DetailRecordsFound)
            DetailArray(DetailRecordsFound).Detail = Detail
            DetailArray(DetailRecordsFound).RecordPosition = Counter
            AddDetailToGrid DetailArray(DetailRecordsFound).Detail,
                Form1.Grid1, DetailRecordsFound
            Invoice.Total = Invoice.Total + Detail.Price * Detail.Quantity
        End If
        DoEvents
    Next Counter
    Form1.InvTotalText.Text = Format$(Invoice.Total, "$#,##0.00")
    OldInvoiceNumber = Invoice.Number
    CurrentInvoiceRecordPosition = RecordNumber

End Sub
```

Listing 14.2 The GetInvoice Procedure from DATABAS2.BAS

```
Sub GetInvoice ()
    Dim DetailRecordsFound As Integer
    Dim TempInvoiceNumber As Long
    Dim StillOnCurrentInvoice As Integer

    Form1.InvNumberText.Text = Invoices!Number
    Form1.InvDateText.Text = Invoices!Date
```

```
Form1.InvClerkText.Text = Invoices!Clerk
Form1.InvLastNameText.Text = Invoices![Last Name]
Form1.InvFirstNameText.Text = Invoices![First Name]
InvoiceTotal = 0

DetailRecordsFound = 0
Form1.Grid1.Row = 1
ClearGrid Form1.Grid1
Details.Index = "InvoiceNumber_SerialNumber"
TempInvoiceNumber = Invoices!Number
Details.Seek ">=", TempInvoiceNumber, 1
If Not Details.NoMatch Then
    StillOnCurrentInvoice = True
    Do While (Not Details.EOF) And StillOnCurrentInvoice
        If (Details![Invoice Number] = Invoices!Number) Then
            StillOnCurrentInvoice = True
            DetailRecordsFound = DetailRecordsFound + 1
            ReDim Preserve DetailArray(DetailRecordsFound)
            DetailArray(DetailRecordsFound).InvoiceNumber =
                Details![Invoice Number]
            DetailArray(DetailRecordsFound).Number = Details!
                [Part Number]
            DetailArray(DetailRecordsFound).Description =
                Details!Description
            DetailArray(DetailRecordsFound).Quantity =
                Details!Quantity
            DetailArray(DetailRecordsFound).Price = Details!Price
            DetailArray(DetailRecordsFound).RecordPosition =
                Details.Bookmark
            AddDetailToGrid DetailArray(DetailRecordsFound),
                Form1.Grid1, DetailRecordsFound
            InvoiceTotal = InvoiceTotal + Details!Price *
                Details!Quantity
        Else
            StillOnCurrentInvoice = False
        End If
        Details.MoveNext
    Loop
End If
Form1.InvTotalText.Text = Format$(InvoiceTotal, "$#,##0.00")
OldInvoiceNumber = Invoices!Number
CurrentInvoiceRecordPosition = Invoices.Bookmark

End Sub
```

But comparisons like these don't take into account the added functionality of a database engine. Consider one major difference between the two
sample programs. The invoices in DATABAS1 appear in the data-entry

order, until some records are deleted and others are entered, in which case their order becomes less and less predictable. In DATABAS2, the invoices records are indexed by number, so no matter how many records we add or delete, or what invoice numbers we assign them, they always appear in numerical order. Furthermore, we can add indices on other fields just by declaring them and adding them to the database definition. The Access engine will automatically construct the new index for us.

We use the data Access object types and the **Append** method to modify a database. In fact, we use **Append** and the Access objects to contruct the original database.

Visual Basic/Access Databases Are Objects

All the elements of an Access database are objects, including the database itself.

The code in Listing 14.3, derived from the function **OpenTheDatabase( )** in DATABAS2.BAS, shows how to build a new database from its constituent objects.

Listing 14.3   Modified Partial Listing Derived from the OpenTheDatabase() Function in DATABAS2.BAS

```
Dim InvcData As Database ' In the actual program this is a global
                         ' declaration
Dim InvoiceTableDef As New TableDef
ReDim InvoiceField(6) As New Field
Dim InvoiceMainIndex As New Index
Dim DetailTableDef As New TableDef
ReDim DetailField(6) As New Field
Dim DetailMainIndex As New Index

    Set InvcData = CreateDatabase("InvcData.MDB", DB_LANG_GENERAL)

    ' Create fields of Invoice table
    InvoiceTableDef.Name = "Invoices"
    InvoiceField(1).Name = "Number"
    InvoiceField(1).Type = DB_LONG
     InvoiceTableDef.Fields.Append InvoiceField(1)
    InvoiceField(2).Name = "Date"
    InvoiceField(2).Type = DB_DATE
     InvoiceTableDef.Fields.Append InvoiceField(2)
    InvoiceField(3).Name = "Clerk"
    InvoiceField(3).Type = DB_INTEGER
     InvoiceTableDef.Fields.Append InvoiceField(3)
    InvoiceField(4).Name = "Last Name"
```

```
InvoiceField(4).Type = DB_TEXT
InvoiceField(4).Size = 35
InvoiceTableDef.Fields.Append  InvoiceField(4)
InvoiceField(5).Name = "First Name"
InvoiceField(5).Type = DB_TEXT
InvoiceField(5).Size = 15
InvoiceTableDef.Fields.Append  InvoiceField(5)
InvoiceField(6).Name = "Total"
InvoiceField(6).Type = DB_SINGLE
InvoiceTableDef.Fields.Append  InvoiceField(6)
' Create index on invoice Number
InvoiceMainIndex.Name = "InvoiceNumber"
InvoiceMainIndex.Unique = True
InvoiceMainIndex.Primary = True
InvoiceMainIndex.Fields = "Number"
InvoiceTableDef.Indexes.Append  InvoiceMainIndex
' Add Invoice table to database
InvcData.TableDefs.Append  InvoiceTableDef

' Create fields of Detail table
DetailTableDef.Name = "Details"
DetailField(1).Name = "Invoice Number"
DetailField(1).Type = DB_LONG
DetailTableDef.Fields.Append  DetailField(1)
DetailField(2).Name = "Part Number"
DetailField(2).Type = DB_LONG
DetailTableDef.Fields.Append  DetailField(2)
DetailField(3).Name = "Description"
DetailField(3).Type = DB_TEXT
DetailField(3).Size = 40
DetailTableDef.Fields.Append  DetailField(3)
DetailField(4).Name = "Quantity"
DetailField(4).Type = DB_INTEGER
DetailTableDef.Fields.Append  DetailField(4)
DetailField(5).Name = "Price"
DetailField(5).Type = DB_SINGLE
DetailTableDef.Fields.Append  DetailField(5)
DetailField(6).Name = "Serial Number"
DetailField(6).Type = DB_LONG
DetailField(6).Attributes = DB_AUTOINCRFIELD
DetailTableDef.Fields.Append  DetailField(6)
' Create index on [Invoice Number] + [Serial Number]
DetailMainIndex.Name = "InvoiceNumber_SerialNumber"
DetailMainIndex.Unique = True
DetailMainIndex.Primary = True
DetailMainIndex.Fields = "[Invoice Number];[Serial Number]"
DetailTableDef.Indexes.Append  DetailMainIndex
' Add Detail Table to database
InvcData.TableDefs.Append  DetailTableDef
```

```
' Must close and re-open to enable multi-user access
' to a newly created database.
InvcData.Close
```

To build this database I'm using four types of objects: *Database*, *TableDef*, *Index*, and *Field*. The Database object is the main container. A Database object has a property called its *TableDefs collection*. When we use the **Append** method to add a TableDef object, the new table definition is added to the TableDefs collection.

Similarly, each TableDef has two collection properties, the *Fields collection* and the *Indexes collection*. To define a table we declare a TableDef object and append Field objects to its Fields collection. We can also optionally append Index objects to its Indexes collection. The square brackets around the field names in the statement that sets the Index's Fields property enables the field names to include spaces.

```
DetailMainIndex.Fields = "[Invoice Number];[Serial Number]"
```

Note: Do not confuse the Fields collection property of a TableDef object with the Fields property of an Index object. The Fields collection is a collection of Field objects, each with its own properties. The Fields property of an Index object is a string that defines the fields on which to build an index for the table.

Visual Basic Access stores all the definition objects and all data in the database file you create and assigns them to the Database object with the **CreateDatabase( )** function. In DATABAS1, we stored each table as a separate disk file. In DATABAS2, the Invoices and Details tables reside within the file INVCDATA.MDB. Visual Basic will permit you to open more than one database simultaneously, but you should try to place related tables in the same database.

This may seem like a lot of work compared to declaring a couple of record types and executing three **Open** statements, but the effort will repay you in many ways.

Defining Keys and Indices

It's easier to manage a data table when each record has a Unique Key.

The Details table includes one special field:

```
DetailField(6).Name = "Serial Number"
DetailField(6).Type = DB_LONG
DetailField(6).Attributes = DB_AUTOINCRFIELD
DetailTableDef.Fields.Append  DetailField(6)
```

In our flat file database we can uniquely identify each record by its position in the file. But in a database table we can't rely on fixed record positions. In fact, Visual Basic doesn't even offer the record position. To ensure that every record has a unique identifier, we add an AutoIncrement field to the TableDef object. Each time we add a new record to the table, the database engine will automatically increment this counter and assign its new value to the field. With this field we can index the table so records appear in order not only by Invoice Number, but also in the order they were entered within each invoice—something we couldn't accomplish with record numbers. The Serial Number field is an internal field we create just for the index. The user never sees it.

Indices have two other important properties, *primary* and *unique*. By declaring in index unique (by setting this property to True), you instruct the database engine not to accept two records with identical keys into the table. A key is unique if the combination of all its field elements produces a unique value. In the index of the Details table, for example, the key comprises two fields, Invoice Number and Serial Number. Obviously, many records can share the same Invoice Number. But no two records can share the same combination of Invoice Number and Serial Number. In this table, the Serial Number alone would guarantee uniqueness, but it wouldn't help us fish out details for a particular invoice, so we use a combined index. If you try to add a record with a duplicate key to a table with one or more unique indices, the **Update** operation will generate a trappable error.

The primary index is a special index with a unique key (by default) that the database engine depends on to create recordsets from joined tables. You can use this index for all the other purposes of an index as well. Visual Basic Access won't perform a joined query unless you have declared at least one primary index for each of the tables you reference.

Although I haven't done so in this example, you may also use the **CreateQueryDef** method to store QueryDef objects in a database. QueryDefs are stored in the TableDefs collection.

Modify the Structure of an Existing Database

You use the same methods and objects you used to create a database to later change its structure. And, because you do use methods and objects to describe and create a database, you can also write programs that enable end-users to build or change their own databases.

We can actually modify the database in several ways that would require data conversion if we were using flat files. We can, for example, add a new data field whenever we need to just by declaring it, setting its properties, and appending it to the TableDef.

```
Dim InvcData As Database
Dim NewField As New Field

Set InvcData = OpenDatabase("INVCDATA.MDB", True)
NewField.Name = "Cost"
NewField.Type = DB_SINGLE
InvcData.TabledDefs!Details.Fields.Append  NewField
InvcData.Close
```

This code fragment above would add the new field called Cost, a single precision real number, to the record definition of the Details table. The Access engine would initialize this field in each existing record to a value of 0.

Note the space between **Append** and **NewField**. **Append** is a method; **NewField** is its parameter. Also note the **New** reserved word in the dimension statement for **NewField**. This qualifier has nothing to do with the fact that we're adding a new field. It means that the object we are declaring is an object, and that we would like a useable instance of that object. If we omit the word **New** in the declaration, as we do when we declare **InvcData**, we get a kind of non-object object; that is, an object with a special value of **Nothing**. Objects of **Nothing** have no properties or methods, so we can't use them for much of anything until we instantiate them. We do that for **InvcData** with the **Set** command and the **OpenDatabase()** function. But no analagous function exists for fields so we use **New** to create an empty field object rather than an object of **Nothing**.

Storing and Changing Records

Once you've created a database, you can add records even more easily than you could add them to a flat file.

The **AddNew** method establishes a freshly initialized record buffer. If you look in Listing 14.4, you'll notice that I'm not performing any data type conversion—such as **Val()** conversion—as I assign the values from the Text Box control Text properties to the Invoice Table's fields. The Access engine performs those conversions automatically, based on the Type property of each field object.

Listing 14.4 Code Fragment from the SaveInvoice Procedure in DATABAS2.BAS, Illustrating the AddNew Method

```
Invoices.AddNew
Invoices!Number  =  Form1.InvNumberText.Text
Invoices!Date  =  Form1.InvDateText.Text
Invoices!Clerk  =  Form1.InvClerkText.Text
Invoices![Last  Name]  =  Form1.InvLastNameText.Text
Invoices![First  Name]  =  Form1.InvFirstNameText.Text
Invoices!Total  =  InvoiceTotal
Invoices.Update
Invoices.Seek  "=",  Form1.InvNumberText.Text
```

Once the field values are set, use the **Update** method to insert the new record into the table and update the indices. If you change your position in the table without first invoking **Update**, you'll lose your new record.

Note: When you perform an AddNew operation, which consists of both the AddNew and the Update methods, Visual Basic Access will save your current record position, insert the new record, then return you to your starting position. After an AddNew, you will *not* find yourself positioned on the new record. You'll need to use the **Seek** method to locate it.

To change an existing record, you first use any of the positioning methods, such as **Seek**, **MoveFirst**, **MoveLast**, **MoveNext**, **MovePrevious**, or you can use the Bookmark property to locate the record and make it the current record. Then you invoke the **Edit** method, which is illustrated in Listing 14.5, make your changes, and invoke the **Update** method.

Listing 14.5 Code Fragment from the SaveInvoice Procedure in DATABAS2.BAS, Illustrating the Edit Method

```
Invoices.Bookmark  =  CurrentInvoiceRecordPosition
Invoices.Edit
Invoices!Number  =  Form1.InvNumberText.Text
Invoices!Date  =  Form1.InvDateText.Text
Invoices!Clerk  =  Form1.InvClerkText.Text
Invoices![Last  Name]  =  Form1.InvLastNameText.Text
Invoices![First  Name]  =  Form1.InvFirstNameText.Text
Invoices!Total  =  InvoiceTotal
Invoices.Update
```

The Access engine also provides a **Delete** method, which I have not used in the sample program (although a complete application would require this capability). When you use the **Delete** method you don't follow it with **Update**, but you must reposition yourself within the recordset, because the **Delete** method leaves you positioned on an invalid record. Ironically, the database engine doesn't actually remove the record from the table until you change your position.

Bookmarks

By saving a Bookmark we can return to a record without searching for it again.

In the first sample program, I saved the positions of the detail records in the **DetailArray()**. If the user chooses to replace an existing detail record, I can then use its position to return to the record without searching for it again. Access, however, doesn't provide physical position information for its records. The data fields you can see at any given time depend on your current virtual position in the recordset.

Fortunately, you can obtain a handle from the database that uniquely identifies your current position. The Bookmark property of your recordset (table, dynaset, or snapshot object) contains a uniqe binary key that you can use to relocate a record during your current session. Bookmarks are binary values, not integers or long integers. To store them, we assign them to either a string variable or a variant. Do not attempt to navigate the recordset by manipulating the value of a Bookmark; it won't work. You cannot, for example, move to the next record by incrementing the Bookmark value:

```
NewPosition = Val(Details.Bookmark) + 1        ' DON'T TRY THIS!
Details.Bookmark = Str$(NewPosition)           ' NOR THIS!
```

Often these statements will produce a runtime error, either because the **Val()** function can't convert the string, or because the resulting Bookmark doesn't exist in the recordset. If it does somehow manage to produce a valid Bookmark, it probably will not be the one you expect.

Protecting Data Integrity

Encapsulating database updates helps to protect databases from corruption during system failures, such as power outages and accidental resets.

Some of the complexity of the sample application reflects my attempts to encapsulate updates to the Details table. When you load an invoice by entering an invoice number and pressing the Find button, the program first locates and loads the invoice record from the Invoices table. The program then searches the Details table for detail records that belong to the invoice. As it finds the details, they are loadede into two data structures, the Grid control, and an array of ordinary Visual Basic structures declared with the **Type** statement.

The Grid displays just those fields from the record that would interest the user. The array records, though, contain the fields from the record that the user can modify, along with the position of the record in the table, as provided by the Bookmark property. As the user edits the details, or adds new ones, the changes are recorded in the Grid and the array. When the user selects the Replace button, the **SaveInvoice** procedure replaces all the existing records and adds the new details, all in one fell swoop.

By performing modifications to working copies of the records rather than to the actual records themselves we enable the user to abandon the whole process and leave the data unchanged. We also gain the opportunity to use *database transactions*, which you can see in Listing 14.6.

Listing 14.6 Code Fragment Based on the SaveInvoice Procedure in DATABAS2.BAS, Illustrating Transactional Updates

```
On Error Resume Next
BeginTrans
Invoices.Bookmark = CurrentInvoiceRecordPosition
Invoices.Edit
Invoices!Number = Form1.InvNumberText.Text
Invoices!Date = Form1.InvDateText.Text
Invoices!Clerk = Form1.InvClerkText.Text
Invoices![Last Name] = Form1.InvLastNameText.Text
Invoices![First Name] = Form1.InvFirstNameText.Text
Invoices!Total = InvoiceTotal
Invoices.Update
TempInvoiceNumber = Invoices!Number
SaveDetails TempInvoiceNumber
OldInvoiceNumber = Invoices!Number
If Err Then
   RollBack
Else
  CommitTrans
End If
```

When a database transaction is in effect, the database engine logs all the changes you make to the database, that is, any part of the database or any part of any other open database. Once all the related operations are complete, you issue a **CommitTrans** to tell the engine that all is well and it may dispose of the log. If any operation fails, you issue the

RollBack command, and the engine will use the log to restore the database (or databases) to its state prior to the **BeginTrans**.

While some database systems don't update the database until the commit has been issued, the Access engine appears to work in the opposite fashion, updating the database and recording those changes as it goes.

Unfortunately, this method doesn't provide protection from system failures, such as power loss or disk drive crashes, because in such as catastrophe we never get the chance to issue the **RollBack** command.

DATABAS2

Here are the listings for the Access-based version of the sample application.

Most of this program is contained in two form files and one main code module. I've also loaded the file DATACONS.TXT into the declarations section of a code module called DATACONS.BAS. The only other file you'll need is GRID.VBX, which the Visual Basic setup program hould have installed in your \WINDOWS\SYSTEM directory.

ON DISK

DATABAS2.MAK

This demonstration program, presented in Listings 14.7, 14.8, 14.9, 14.10, and 14.11 is stored on disk as DATABAS2.MAK, DATABAS2.FRM, DETAILF2.FRM, and DATABAS2.BAS.

Listing 14.7 Objects and Properties in DATABAS2.FRM

```
Begin Form Form1
    Caption          =   "Jim's Rocket Parts"
    ClientHeight     =   7230
    ClientLeft       =   945
    ClientTop        =   1440
    ClientWidth      =   7785
    Height           =   7635
    Left             =   885
    LinkTopic        =   "Form1"
    ScaleHeight      =   7230
    ScaleWidth       =   7785
    Top              =   1095
    Width            =   7905
    Begin TextBox InvClerkText
        Height           =      285
```

```
      Left            =    6240
      TabIndex        =    5
      Top             =    1200
      Width           =    1215
   End
   Begin CommandButton ExitButton
      Caption         =    "Exit"
      Height          =    495
      Left            =    6000
      TabIndex        =    18
      Top             =    0
      Width           =    1215
   End
   Begin CommandButton NextButton
      Caption         =    "Next"
      Height          =    495
      Left            =    4800
      TabIndex        =    17
      Top             =    0
      Width           =    1215
   End
   Begin CommandButton PrevButton
      Caption         =    "Previous"
      Height          =    495
      Left            =    3600
      TabIndex        =    16
      Top             =    0
      Width           =    1215
   End
   Begin CommandButton FindButton
      Caption         =    "Find"
      Default         =    -1    'True
      Height          =    495
      Left            =    2400
      TabIndex        =    15
      Top             =    0
      Width           =    1215
   End
   Begin CommandButton SaveButton
      Caption         =    "Save New"
      Height          =    495
      Left            =    1200
      TabIndex        =    14
      Top             =    0
      Width           =    1215
   End
   Begin CommandButton NewButton
      Caption         =    "New"
```

```
         Height            =     495
         Left              =     0
         TabIndex          =     13
         Top               =     0
         Width             =     1215
      End
      Begin TextBox InvDateText
         Height            =     285
         Left              =     3720
         TabIndex          =     3
         Top               =     1200
         Width             =     1455
      End
      Begin TextBox InvTotalText
         Alignment         =     1    'Right Justify
         Height            =     285
         Left              =     5640
         TabIndex          =     12
         TabStop           =     0    'False
         Top               =     6600
         Width             =     1695
      End
      Begin Grid Grid1
         Cols              =     6
         Height            =     2775
         Left              =     120
         Rows              =     12
         ScrollBars        =     2    'Vertical
         TabIndex          =     10
         Top               =     3720
         Width             =     7575
      End
      Begin TextBox InvFirstNameText
         Height            =     375
         Left              =     1200
         TabIndex          =     9
         Top               =     2760
         Width             =     3975
      End
      Begin TextBox InvLastNameText
         Height            =     375
         Left              =     1200
         TabIndex          =     7
         Top               =     1920
         Width             =     3975
      End
      Begin TextBox InvNumberText
         Height            =     285
         Left              =     1200
```

```
         TabIndex        =    1
         Top             =    1200
         Width           =    1455
      End
      Begin Shape Shape6
         BackColor       =    &H00FF0000&
         FillColor       =    &H00FF0000&
         FillStyle       =    0    'Solid
         Height          =    255
         Left            =    6360
         Top             =    1320
         Width           =    1215
      End
      Begin Label Label6
         Alignment       =    1    'Right Justify
         Caption         =    "Clerk:"
         Height          =    375
         Left            =    5520
         TabIndex        =    4
         Top             =    1200
         Width           =    615
      End
      Begin Label Label5
         Alignment       =    1    'Right Justify
         Caption         =    "Date:"
         Height          =    375
         Left            =    3000
         TabIndex        =    2
         Top             =    1200
         Width           =    615
      End
      Begin Shape Shape5
         FillColor       =    &H00FF0000&
         FillStyle       =    0    'Solid
         Height          =    255
         Left            =    3840
         Top             =    1320
         Width           =    1455
      End
      Begin Shape Shape4
         FillColor       =    &H00FF0000&
         FillStyle       =    0    'Solid
         Height          =    255
         Left            =    5760
         Top             =    6720
         Width           =    1695
      End
      Begin Label Label4
         Alignment       =    1    'Right Justify
```

```
         Caption        =    "Total:"
         Height         =    375
         Left           =    4680
         TabIndex       =    11
         Top            =    6600
         Width          =    735
      End
      Begin Shape Shape3
         FillColor      =    &H00FF0000&
         FillStyle      =    0   'Solid
         Height         =    375
         Left           =    1320
         Top            =    2880
         Width          =    3975
      End
      Begin Shape Shape2
         FillColor      =    &H00FF0000&
         FillStyle      =    0   'Solid
         Height         =    375
         Left           =    1320
         Top            =    2040
         Width          =    3975
      End
      Begin Shape Shape1
         FillColor      =    &H00FF0000&
         FillStyle      =    0   'Solid
         Height         =    255
         Left           =    1320
         Top            =    1320
         Width          =    1455
      End
      Begin Label Label3
         Alignment      =    1   'Right Justify
         Caption        =    "First Name:"
         Height         =    255
         Left           =    0
         TabIndex       =    8
         Top            =    2760
         Width          =    1095
      End
      Begin Label Label2
         Alignment      =    1   'Right Justify
         Caption        =    "Last Name:"
         Height         =    375
         Left           =    120
         TabIndex       =    6
         Top            =    1920
         Width          =    975
      End
```

```
      Begin Label Label1
         Alignment        =     1   'Right Justify
         Caption          =     "Invoice Number:"
         Height           =     495
         Left             =     120
         TabIndex         =     0
         Top              =     1080
         Width            =     975
      End
   End
End
```

Listing 14.8 Code in DATABAS2.FRM

```
Option Explicit

Sub ExitButton_Click ()
    Form_Unload (0)
    End
End Sub


Sub FindButton_Click ()
    Dim InvoiceRecordPosition As String
    Dim TempInvoiceNumber As String

    If Val(Form1.InvNumberText.Text) = 0 Then
        MsgBox "Please Enter an Invoice Number", 48, "Entry Error"
        Form1.InvNumberText.SetFocus
      Else
         InvoiceRecordPosition = FindInvoice(Val(InvNumberText.Text))
         If InvoiceRecordPosition <> "" Then
            SaveButton.Caption = "Replace"
            SaveButton.Enabled = True
            ReDim DetailArray(0)
            ClearGrid Grid1
            GetInvoice
          Else
            MsgBox "That Invoice Number Does Not Exist", 48, "Not Found"
            TempInvoiceNumber = InvNumberText.Text
            NewButton_Click
            InvNumberText.Text = TempInvoiceNumber
         End If
      End If
    InvNumberText.SetFocus
End Sub


Sub Form_Load ()
    Dim ButtonWidth As Integer

    Grid1.FixedRows = 0
```

```
    Grid1.FixedCols = 0
    Grid1.SelStartRow = 0
    Grid1.SelEndRow = 0
    Grid1.SelStartCol = 0
    Grid1.SelEndCol = 5
    Grid1.Clip = "Line" & Chr$(9) & "Part No." & Chr$(9) &
                "Description" & Chr$(9)
        & "Qty" & Chr$(9) & "Price" & Chr$(9) & "Ext. Price"
    Grid1.FixedRows = 1
    Grid1.FixedCols = 1
    Grid1.ColWidth(0) = Grid1.Width * .08
    Grid1.ColWidth(1) = Grid1.Width * .1
    Grid1.ColWidth(2) = (Grid1.Width * .37)
    Grid1.ColWidth(3) = Grid1.Width * .1
    Grid1.ColWidth(4) = Grid1.Width * .15
    Grid1.ColWidth(5) = Grid1.Width * .15
    Grid1.ColAlignment(4) = 1
    Grid1.ColAlignment(5) = 1

    ButtonWidth = Form1.ScaleWidth \ 6
    NewButton.Width = ButtonWidth
    NewButton.Left = 0
    SaveButton.Width = ButtonWidth
    SaveButton.Left = NewButton.Left + NewButton.Width
    FindButton.Width = ButtonWidth
    FindButton.Left = SaveButton.Left + SaveButton.Width
    PrevButton.Width = ButtonWidth
    PrevButton.Left = FindButton.Left + FindButton.Width
    NextButton.Width = ButtonWidth
    NextButton.Left = PrevButton.Left + PrevButton.Width
    ExitButton.Width = ButtonWidth
    ExitButton.Left = NextButton.Left + NextButton.Width
    InvDateText.Text = Format(Now, "ddddd")
    ReDim DetailArray(0)
    CurrentInvoiceRecordPosition = ""
    DatabaseOpen = OpenTheDatabase()
    If Not Invoices.BOF Then
        GetInvoice
        OldInvoiceNumber = Invoices!Number
        SaveButton.Caption = "Replace"
      Else
        OldInvoiceNumber = 0
        SaveButton.Caption = "Save New"
      End If
End Sub

Sub Form_Unload (Cancel As Integer)
    If DatabaseOpen Then
```

```
            Invoices.Close
            Details.Close
            InvcData.Close
        End If
    End Sub


Sub Grid1_Click ()

    AddingNewDetail = False
    If (Grid1.SelStartCol = 1) And (Grid1.SelEndCol = 5) And
        (Form1.Grid1.Text <> "") Then
        Form2.Caption = "Edit Invoice Detail for Invoice #" &
            Form1.InvNumberText.Text
        Form2.DetNumberText.Text = Str$(DetailArray(Grid1.Row).Number)
        Form2.DetDescriptionText.Text = DetailArray(Grid1.Row).Description
        Form2.DetQuantityText.Text = Str$(DetailArray(Grid1.Row).Quantity)
        Form2.DetPriceText.Text = Str$(DetailArray(Grid1.Row).Price)
        Form2.AddButton.Caption = "Replace Detail"
        Form2.Show
    End If
End Sub


Sub Grid1_DblClick ()

    If Not ((Grid1.SelStartCol = 1) And (Grid1.SelEndCol = 5) And
        (Val(Form1.Grid1.Text) = 0)) Then
        AddingNewDetail = True
        Form2.Caption = "Enter New Invoice Detail for Invoice #" &
            Form1.InvNumberText.Text
        Form2.DetNumberText.Text = ""
        Form2.DetDescriptionText.Text = ""
        Form2.DetQuantityText.Text = ""
        Form2.DetPriceText.Text = ""
        Form2.AddButton.Caption = "Add to Invoice"
        Form2.Show
    End If

End Sub


Sub InvNumberText_LostFocus ()
    If Val(InvNumberText.Text) > 32000 Then
        MsgBox "Please Enter a Number Less Than 32767", 16, "Data
            Entry Error"
        InvNumberText.SelStart = 0
        InvNumberText.SelLength = Len(InvNumberText.Text)
        InvNumberText.SetFocus
    End If
End Sub
```

```
Sub NewButton_Click ()

    InvNumberText.Text = ""
    InvDateText.Text = ""
    InvLastNameText.Text = ""
    InvFirstNameText.Text = ""
    InvTotalText.Text = ""
    ReDim DetailArray(0)
    ClearGrid Grid1
    InvDateText.Text = Format(Now, "ddddd")
    SaveButton.Caption = "Save New"
    SaveButton.Enabled = True
    CurrentInvoiceRecordPosition = ""
    OldInvoiceNumber = 0
    InvNumberText.SetFocus
End Sub


Sub NextButton_Click ()
    GetNextInvoice
    End Sub

Sub PrevButton_Click ()
    GetPreviousInvoice
End Sub

Sub SaveButton_Click ()
    SaveInvoice
    SaveButton.Caption = "Replace"
    InvNumberText.SetFocus
End Sub
```

Listing 14.9   Objects and Properties in DETAILF2.FRM

```
Begin Form Form2
    Caption         =   "Enter Invoice Detail"
    ClientHeight    =   4395
    ClientLeft      =   1425
    ClientTop       =   1485
    ClientWidth     =   6285
    Height          =   4800
    Left            =   1365
    LinkTopic       =   "Form2"
    ScaleHeight     =   4395
    ScaleWidth      =   6285
    Top             =   1140
    Width           =   6405
    Begin CommandButton CancelButton
```

```
      Caption          =    "Cancel"
      Height           =    495
      Left             =    3720
      TabIndex         =    9
      Top              =    3600
      Width            =    1575
   End
   Begin CommandButton AddButton
      Caption          =    "Add to Invoice"
      Default          =    -1   'True
      Height           =    495
      Left             =    1200
      TabIndex         =    8
      Top              =    3600
      Width            =    1575
   End
   Begin TextBox DetPriceText
      Height           =    375
      Left             =    1920
      TabIndex         =    3
      Top              =    2520
      Width            =    1455
   End
   Begin TextBox DetQuantityText
      Height           =    375
      Left             =    1920
      TabIndex         =    2
      Top              =    1800
      Width            =    735
   End
   Begin TextBox DetDescriptionText
      Height           =    375
      Left             =    1920
      TabIndex         =    1
      Top              =    1080
      Width            =    3135
   End
   Begin TextBox DetNumberText
      Height           =    375
      Left             =    1920
      TabIndex         =    0
      Top              =    360
      Width            =    1455
   End
   Begin Shape Shape4
      FillColor        =    &H00FF00FF&
      FillStyle        =    0   'Solid
      Height           =    375
```

```
        Left           =    2040
        Top            =    2640
        Width          =    1455
     End
     Begin Shape Shape3
        FillColor      =    &H00FF00FF&
        FillStyle      =    0    'Solid
        Height         =    375
        Left           =    2160
        Top            =    1920
        Width          =    615
     End
     Begin Shape Shape2
        FillColor      =    &H00FF00FF&
        FillStyle      =    0    'Solid
        Height         =    375
        Left           =    2040
        Top            =    1200
        Width          =    3135
     End
     Begin Shape Shape1
        FillColor      =    &H00FF00FF&
        FillStyle      =    0    'Solid
        Height         =    375
        Left           =    2040
        Top            =    480
        Width          =    1455
     End
     Begin Label Label5
        Alignment      =    1    'Right Justify
        Caption        =    "Unit Price:"
        Height         =    375
        Left           =    720
        TabIndex       =    7
        Top            =    2520
        Width          =    975
     End
     Begin Label Label4
        Alignment      =    1    'Right Justify
        Caption        =    "Quantity:"
        Height         =    375
        Left           =    720
        TabIndex       =    6
        Top            =    1800
        Width          =    975
     End
     Begin Label Label3
        Alignment      =    1    'Right Justify
```

```
         Caption          =     "Description:"
         Height           =     375
         Left             =     360
         TabIndex         =     5
         Top              =     1080
         Width            =     1335
      End
      Begin Label Label2
         Alignment        =     1   'Right Justify
         Caption          =     "Part Number:"
         Height           =     375
         Left             =     360
         TabIndex         =     4
         Top              =     360
         Width            =     1335
      End
   End
End
```

Listing 14.10 Code in DETAILF2.FRM

```
Option Explicit

Sub AddButton_Click ()
    Dim LineNumber As Integer

    If AddingNewDetail Then
       AddOrChangeDetail 0
     Else
       LineNumber = Form1.Grid1.Row
       AddOrChangeDetail LineNumber
     End If
    Form2.Hide
End Sub

Sub CancelButton_Click ()
    Form2.Hide
End Sub

Sub Form_Load ()
    Show
     Form2.DetNumberText.SetFocus
End Sub
```

Listing 14.11   DATABAS2.BAS

```
Option Explicit

Type DetailArrayRecord
    RecordPosition As Variant
```

```
        InvoiceNumber As Integer
        Number As Integer
        Description As String * 40
        Quantity As Integer
        Price As Single
End Type


' Access object declarations
Global InvcData As Database
Global Invoices As Table
Global Details As Table

Global InvoiceTotal As Single
Global DatabaseOpen As Integer
Global DetailArray() As DetailArrayRecord
Global AddingNewDetail As Integer
Global CurrentInvoiceRecordPosition As String
Global OldInvoiceNumber As Integer


Sub AddDetailToGrid (Detail As DetailArrayRecord, TheGrid As Grid,
        DetailLineNumber As Integer)
    Dim TempString As String

    If DetailLineNumber > TheGrid.Rows Then
        TheGrid.Rows = DetailLineNumber + 1
      End If
    TheGrid.FixedCols = 0
    TheGrid.SelStartRow = DetailLineNumber
    TheGrid.SelEndRow = DetailLineNumber
    TheGrid.SelStartCol = 0
    TheGrid.SelEndCol = 5
    TempString = Str$(DetailLineNumber)
    TempString = TempString & Chr$(9) & Str$(Detail.Number)
    TempString = TempString & Chr$(9) & Detail.Description
    TempString = TempString & Chr$(9) & Str$(Detail.Quantity)
    TempString = TempString & Chr$(9) & Format$(Detail.Price, "#,##0.00")
    TempString = TempString & Chr$(9) & Format$(Detail.Quantity *
        Detail.Price, "#,##0.00")
    TheGrid.Clip = TempString
    TheGrid.FixedCols = 1
End Sub

Sub AddOrChangeDetail (ArrayIndex As Integer)

    If ArrayIndex = 0 Then
        ArrayIndex = UBound(DetailArray, 1)
        ReDim Preserve DetailArray(ArrayIndex + 1)
        ArrayIndex = UBound(DetailArray, 1)
```

```
                DetailArray(ArrayIndex).RecordPosition = ""
             End If
          DetailArray(ArrayIndex).InvoiceNumber = Val(Form1.InvNumberText.Text)
          DetailArray(ArrayIndex).Number = Val(Form2.DetNumberText.Text)
          DetailArray(ArrayIndex).Description = Form2.DetDescriptionText
          DetailArray(ArrayIndex).Quantity = Val(Form2.DetQuantityText.Text)
          DetailArray(ArrayIndex).Price = Val(Form2.DetPriceText.Text)
          AddDetailToGrid DetailArray(ArrayIndex), Form1.Grid1, ArrayIndex

End Sub

Sub ClearGrid (TheGrid As Grid)

    TheGrid.FixedCols = 0
    TheGrid.SelStartCol = 0
    TheGrid.SelStartRow = 1
    TheGrid.SelEndRow = TheGrid.Rows - 1
    TheGrid.SelEndCol = TheGrid.Cols - 1
    TheGrid.FillStyle = 1
    TheGrid.Text = ""
    TheGrid.FillStyle = 0
    TheGrid.SelEndRow = 1
    TheGrid.SelEndCol = 1
    TheGrid.FixedCols = 1
End Sub

Function FindInvoice (InvoiceNumberToFind As Integer) As String

    Invoices.Index = "InvoiceNumber"
    Invoices.Seek "=", InvoiceNumberToFind
    If Invoices.NoMatch Then
        FindInvoice = ""
      Else
        FindInvoice = Invoices.Bookmark
      End If
    End Function

Sub GetInvoice ()
    Dim DetailRecordsFound As Integer
    Dim TempInvoiceNumber As Long
    Dim StillOnCurrentInvoice As Integer

    Form1.InvNumberText.Text = Invoices!Number
    Form1.InvDateText.Text = Invoices!Date
    Form1.InvClerkText.Text = Invoices!Clerk
    Form1.InvLastNameText.Text = Invoices![Last Name]
    Form1.InvFirstNameText.Text = Invoices![First Name]
    InvoiceTotal = 0
```

```
        DetailRecordsFound = 0
        Form1.Grid1.Row = 1
        ClearGrid Form1.Grid1
        Details.Index = "InvoiceNumber_SerialNumber"
        TempInvoiceNumber = Invoices!Number
        Details.Seek ">=", TempInvoiceNumber, 1
        If Not Details.NoMatch Then
            StillOnCurrentInvoice = True
            Do While (Not Details.EOF) And StillOnCurrentInvoice
                If (Details![Invoice Number] = Invoices!Number) Then
                    StillOnCurrentInvoice = True
                    DetailRecordsFound = DetailRecordsFound + 1
                    ReDim Preserve DetailArray(DetailRecordsFound)
                    DetailArray(DetailRecordsFound).InvoiceNumber =
                        Details![Invoice Number]
                    DetailArray(DetailRecordsFound).Number =
                        Details![Part Number]
                    DetailArray(DetailRecordsFound).Description =
                        Details!Description
                    DetailArray(DetailRecordsFound).Quantity =
                        Details!Quantity
                    DetailArray(DetailRecordsFound).Price = Details!Price
                    DetailArray(DetailRecordsFound).RecordPosition =
                        Details.Bookmark
                    AddDetailToGrid DetailArray(DetailRecordsFound),
                        Form1.Grid1,
                  DetailRecordsFound
                    InvoiceTotal = InvoiceTotal + Details!Price *
                        Details!Quantity
                Else
                    StillOnCurrentInvoice = False
                End If
              Details.MoveNext
            Loop
        End If
    Form1.InvTotalText.Text = Format$(InvoiceTotal, "$#,##0.00")
    OldInvoiceNumber = Invoices!Number
    CurrentInvoiceRecordPosition = Invoices.Bookmark

End Sub

Sub GetNextInvoice ()
    Dim PositionMarker As Variant

    PositionMarker = Invoices.Bookmark
    Invoices.MoveNext
    If Invoices.EOF Then
        MsgBox "No More Records in File", 48, "File Access Error"
        Invoices.Bookmark = PositionMarker
```

```
          Else
              Form1.SaveButton.Caption = "Replace"
              Form1.SaveButton.Enabled = True
              ReDim DetailArray(0)
              ClearGrid Form1.Grid1
              GetInvoice
          End If

      End Sub

      Sub GetPreviousInvoice ()
          Dim PositionMarker As Variant

          PositionMarker = Invoices.Bookmark
          Invoices.MovePrevious
          If Invoices.BOF Then
              MsgBox "Already On First Record", 48, "File Access Error"
              Invoices.Bookmark = PositionMarker
          Else
              Form1.SaveButton.Caption = "Replace"
              Form1.SaveButton.Enabled = True
              ReDim DetailArray(0)
              ClearGrid Form1.Grid1
              GetInvoice
          End If

      End Sub

      Function OpenTheDatabase () As Integer
          Dim InvoiceTableDef As New TableDef
          ReDim InvoiceField(6) As New Field
          Dim InvoiceMainIndex As New Index
          Dim DetailTableDef As New TableDef
          ReDim DetailField(6) As New Field
          Dim DetailMainIndex As New Index

          If Len(Dir$("InvcData.MDB")) = 0 Then
              ' Create and open database
              Set InvcData = CreateDatabase("InvcData.MDB", DB_LANG_GENERAL)

              ' Create fields of Invoice table
              InvoiceTableDef.Name = "Invoices"
              InvoiceField(1).Name = "Number"
              InvoiceField(1).Type = DB_LONG
              InvoiceTableDef.Fields.Append InvoiceField(1)
              InvoiceField(2).Name = "Date"
              InvoiceField(2).Type = DB_DATE
              InvoiceTableDef.Fields.Append InvoiceField(2)
              InvoiceField(3).Name = "Clerk"
```

```
InvoiceField(3).Type = DB_INTEGER
InvoiceTableDef.Fields.Append InvoiceField(3)
InvoiceField(4).Name = "Last Name"
InvoiceField(4).Type = DB_TEXT
InvoiceField(4).Size = 35
InvoiceTableDef.Fields.Append InvoiceField(4)
InvoiceField(5).Name = "First Name"
InvoiceField(5).Type = DB_TEXT
InvoiceField(5).Size = 15
InvoiceTableDef.Fields.Append InvoiceField(5)
InvoiceField(6).Name = "Total"
InvoiceField(6).Type = DB_SINGLE
InvoiceTableDef.Fields.Append InvoiceField(6)
' Create index on invoice Number
InvoiceMainIndex.Name = "InvoiceNumber"
InvoiceMainIndex.Unique = True
InvoiceMainIndex.Primary = True
InvoiceMainIndex.Fields = "Number"
InvoiceTableDef.Indexes.Append InvoiceMainIndex
' Add Invoice table to database
InvcData.TableDefs.Append InvoiceTableDef

' Create fields of Detail table
DetailTableDef.Name = "Details"
DetailField(1).Name = "Invoice Number"
DetailField(1).Type = DB_LONG
DetailTableDef.Fields.Append DetailField(1)
DetailField(2).Name = "Part Number"
DetailField(2).Type = DB_LONG
DetailTableDef.Fields.Append DetailField(2)
DetailField(3).Name = "Description"
DetailField(3).Type = DB_TEXT
DetailField(3).Size = 40
DetailTableDef.Fields.Append DetailField(3)
DetailField(4).Name = "Quantity"
DetailField(4).Type = DB_INTEGER
DetailTableDef.Fields.Append DetailField(4)
DetailField(5).Name = "Price"
DetailField(5).Type = DB_SINGLE
DetailTableDef.Fields.Append DetailField(5)
DetailField(6).Name = "Serial Number"
DetailField(6).Type = DB_LONG
DetailField(6).Attributes = DB_AUTOINCRFIELD
DetailTableDef.Fields.Append DetailField(6)
' Create index on [Invoice Number] + [Serial Number]
DetailMainIndex.Name = "InvoiceNumber_SerialNumber"
DetailMainIndex.Unique = True
DetailMainIndex.Primary = True
```

```
        DetailMainIndex.Fields = "[Invoice Number];[Serial Number]"
        DetailTableDef.Indexes.Append DetailMainIndex
        ' Add Detail Table to database
        InvcData.TableDefs.Append DetailTableDef

        ' Must close and re-open to enable multi-user access
        ' to a newly created database
        InvcData.Close
    End If
    Set InvcData = OpenDatabase("InvcData.MDB")
    Set Invoices = InvcData.OpenTable("Invoices")
    Set Details = InvcData.OpenTable("Details")
    OpenTheDatabase = True
End Function


Sub SaveDetails (CurrentInvoiceNumber As Long)
    Dim ArrayIndex As Integer

    For ArrayIndex = 1 To UBound(DetailArray, 1)
        If DetailArray(ArrayIndex).InvoiceNumber > 0 Then
            ' Just in case Invoice Number has changed
            DetailArray(ArrayIndex).InvoiceNumber =
                CurrentInvoiceNumber
        End If
        If DetailArray(ArrayIndex).RecordPosition <> "" Then
            ' Replacing an existing detail record
            Details.Bookmark = DetailArray(ArrayIndex).RecordPosition
            Details.Edit
            Details![Invoice Number] =
                DetailArray(ArrayIndex).InvoiceNumber
            Details![Part Number] = DetailArray(ArrayIndex).Number
            Details!Description = DetailArray(ArrayIndex).Description
            Details!Quantity = DetailArray(ArrayIndex).Quantity
            Details!Price = DetailArray(ArrayIndex).Price
            Details.Update
        ElseIf DetailArray(ArrayIndex).InvoiceNumber > 0 Then
            ' Add a new detail record
            Details.AddNew
            Details![Invoice Number] =
                DetailArray(ArrayIndex).InvoiceNumber
            Details![Part Number] = DetailArray(ArrayIndex).Number
            Details!Description = DetailArray(ArrayIndex).Description
            Details!Quantity = DetailArray(ArrayIndex).Quantity
            Details!Price = DetailArray(ArrayIndex).Price
            Details.Update
        End If
    Next ArrayIndex
End Sub
```

```
Sub SaveInvoice ()
    Dim TempInvoiceNumber As Long
    Dim OkayToReplace As Integer

    If Val(Form1.InvNumberText.Text) = 0 Then
        MsgBox "Please Enter an Invoice Number", 48, "Entry Error"
    ElseIf OldInvoiceNumber = 0 Then
        ' Attempting to add new invoice
        Invoices.Index = "InvoiceNumber"
        Invoices.Seek "=", Val(Form1.InvNumberText.Text)
        If (Not Invoices.NoMatch) Then
            MsgBox "That Invoice Number Already Exists." & Chr$(13) &
            "Please Try Another.", 16, "Data Entry Error"
        Else
            ' Add new invoice
            BeginTrans
            Invoices.AddNew
            Invoices!Number = Form1.InvNumberText.Text
            Invoices!Date = Form1.InvDateText.Text
            Invoices!Clerk = Form1.InvClerkText.Text
            Invoices![Last Name] = Form1.InvLastNameText.Text
            Invoices![First Name] = Form1.InvFirstNameText.Text
            Invoices!Total = InvoiceTotal
            Invoices.Update
            Invoices.Seek "=", Form1.InvNumberText.Text
            TempInvoiceNumber = Invoices!Number
            SaveDetails TempInvoiceNumber
            OldInvoiceNumber = Invoices!Number
            CommitTrans
        End If
    Else
        ' Attempting to replace existing invoice
        OkayToReplace = True
        If OldInvoiceNumber <> Val(Form1.InvNumberText.Text) Then
            Invoices.Seek "=", Val(Form1.InvNumberText.Text)
            If (Not Invoices.NoMatch) Then
                If (CurrentInvoiceRecordPosition <> Invoices.Bookmark)
                    Then
                    MsgBox "That Invoice Number Already Exists." &
                        Chr$(13) &
                "Please Try Another.", 16, "Data Entry Error"
                    OkayToReplace = False
                End If
            End If
        End If
        If OkayToReplace Then
            ' Replace Existing invoice
            BeginTrans
            Invoices.Bookmark = CurrentInvoiceRecordPosition
```

```
        Invoices.Edit
         Invoices!Number = Form1.InvNumberText.Text
         Invoices!Date = Form1.InvDateText.Text
         Invoices!Clerk = Form1.InvClerkText.Text
         Invoices![Last Name] = Form1.InvLastNameText.Text
         Invoices![First Name] = Form1.InvFirstNameText.Text
         Invoices!Total = InvoiceTotal
         Invoices.Update
         TempInvoiceNumber = Invoices!Number
         SaveDetails TempInvoiceNumber
         OldInvoiceNumber = Invoices!Number
        CommitTrans
      End If
    End If
End Sub
```

The Data Access Control

Along with all the advanced features that enable us to write complex database systems with magnificent and beautiful user interfaces, Visual Basic also provides some powerful tools with which we can assemble applications quickly, and sometimes with no program code at all.

The Data Control

By dropping a few controls on a form and setting their properties, we can browse and edit our files without writing code.

Open a new project in Visual Basic and place a Data control on the form. Set the control's DatabaseName property to InvcData.MDB (be sure to include the proper path information, or use the File Dialog by double-clicking the property), set its RecordSource property to Invoices, and change its Name property to InvoiceData.

Now place five Text Box controls on the form. On each of them, set the DataSource property to InvoiceData, and delete the default text by clearing the **Text** property. For each Text Box, you'll need to set the DataField property to one of the field names from the **Invoices TableDef**. That's easy because when you select the DataField property in the Properties window and click the down arrow on the List Box, Visual Basic will provide a list of all the fields. Choose a different one for each Text Box.

Run the program. You should end up with something resembling the program in Figure 14.3.

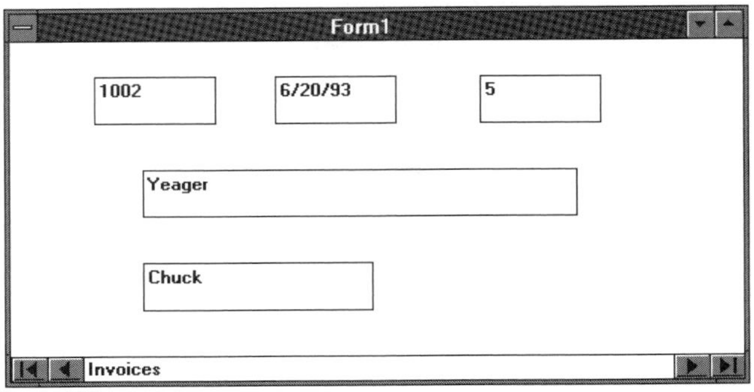

Figure 14.3 A codeless invoice program.

By clicking on the arrow buttons of the Data control you can step through, or leap to the ends of the records in the Invoice table. The Data control and the "data-aware" standard controls (like the Text Box) pave the quickest path to a functional database application. But not without limitations.

Any change you make to a field in one of the data-aware controls will be saved to the file as soon as you change record positions, so you may edit records to your heart's content. But to add or delete records you have to write some code—not too much code, but code nonetheless.

A Simplified Invoice Database

Use the Data controls and a dynaset to enter and edit invoices.

In this final sample program, I've used the Data control and data-aware Text Boxes to provide most of the same functions as the previous example, but with a somewhat stripped-down user interface. The forms for this program are shown in Figures 14.4 and 14.5.

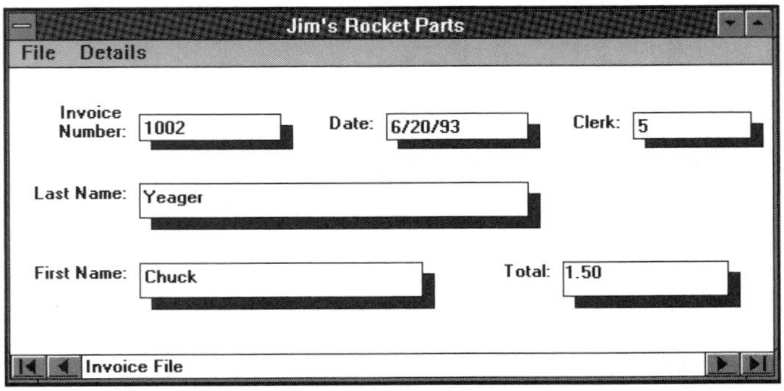

Figure 14.4 Form1 from DATABAS3.MAK, stored in the file DATABAS3.FRM.

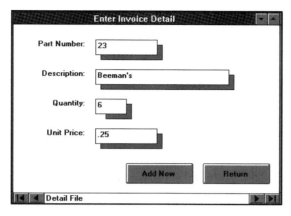

Figure 14.5 Form2 from DATABAS3.MAK, stored in the file DETAILF3.FRM.

Relational Techniques

Build a dynaset by querying the detail table.

Instead of grabbing the related detail records by searching for them with the **Seek** method and holding them in an array, we can build a recordset of just records that belong to the current invoice, which we can then attach to the Data control on Form2 by assigning the *query statement* to the control's RecordSource property:

```
Form2.DetailData.RecordSource =
        "SELECT * From Details WHERE Details![Invoice Number] = " &
            Form1.InvNumberText.Text
Form2.DetailData.Refresh
```

You interpret the query statement as "Select all fields (*) from the table Details where the Invoice Number of the detail record matches the invoice number currently displayed in the Text control InvNumberText on Form1." The **Refresh** method executes the query and updates the current recordset.

One of the major features of any relational database system is the ability to combine, or *join* data from multiple tables into a working table. Some systems physically copy the selected data from the source tables into the new joined table, which usually means that the combined table cannot be changed. An Access dynaset, however, simply references the original source tables, so any changes you make to a record in the dynaset will "write through" to the source table(s).

I could have used a dynaset to manage the detail records in the sample program DATABAS2, but that would have made it more difficult to hold back all the changes until the user pressed the Replace button. You *could* use database transactions to accomplish that, but it's not a good idea to allow user activity between **BeginTrans** and either **CommitTrans** or **Rollback**, because in a multi-user environment the transaction could leave a large number of locked pages scattered around in the tables. So instead of a dynaset, I chose to keep my own sub-table in a conventional array.

Queries, which create dynasets, and their lesser cousins *snapshots*, make it possible to generate complex relational inqueries and reports without writing complex nested search routines. But you must use them with care. On very large tables—on the order of several thousand, or tens of thousands of records, for example—a complex query could run for hours or days before it returns a result.

Because query statements are character strings, you can write applications that enable your end-users to generate their own dynasets at runtime. If you do, be sure they understand the pitfalls.

DATABAS3.MAK

This demonstration program, presented in Listings 14.12, 14.13, 14.14, and 14.15, is stored on disk as DATABAS3.MAK, DATABAS3.FRM, and DETAILF3.FRM.

Listing 14.12   Objects and Properties from DATABAS3.FRM

```
Begin Form Form1
    Caption          =   "Jim's Rocket Parts"
    ClientHeight     =   3255
    ClientLeft       =   420
    ClientTop        =   3765
    ClientWidth      =   7785
    Height           =   3945
    Left             =   360
    LinkTopic        =   "Form1"
    ScaleHeight      =   3255
    ScaleWidth       =   7785
    Top              =   3135
    Width            =   7905
    Begin Data InvoiceData
        Caption          =   "Invoice File"
        Connect          =   ""
```

```
      DatabaseName    =    "C:\VB3\INVCDATA.MDB"
      Exclusive       =    0    'False
      Height          =    270
      Left            =    0
      Options         =    0
      ReadOnly        =    0    'False
      RecordSource    =    "Invoices"
      Top             =    3000
      Width           =    7815
   End
   Begin TextBox InvClerkText
      DataField       =    "Clerk"
      DataSource      =    "InvoiceData"
      Height          =    285
      Left            =    6360
      TabIndex        =    5
      Top             =    480
      Width           =    1215
   End
   Begin TextBox InvDateText
      DataField       =    "Date"
      DataSource      =    "InvoiceData"
      Height          =    285
      Left            =    3840
      TabIndex        =    3
      Top             =    480
      Width           =    1455
   End
   Begin TextBox InvFirstNameText
      DataField       =    "First Name"
      DataSource      =    "InvoiceData"
      Height          =    375
      Left            =    1320
      TabIndex        =    9
      Top             =    2040
      Width           =    2895
   End
   Begin TextBox InvLastNameText
      DataField       =    "Last Name"
      DataSource      =    "InvoiceData"
      Height          =    375
      Left            =    1320
      TabIndex        =    7
      Top             =    1200
      Width           =    3975
   End
   Begin TextBox InvNumberText
      DataField       =    "Number"
```

```
        DataSource     =     "InvoiceData"
        Height         =     285
        Left           =     1320
        TabIndex       =     1
        Top            =     480
        Width          =     1455
     End
     Begin Label InvTotalText
        BorderStyle    =     1   'Fixed Single
        DataField      =     "Total"
        DataSource     =     "InvoiceData"
        Height         =     375
        Left           =     5640
        TabIndex       =     11
        Top            =     2040
        Width          =     1695
     End
     Begin Shape Shape6
        BackColor      =     &H00FF0000&
        FillColor      =     &H00FF0000&
        FillStyle      =     0   'Solid
        Height         =     255
        Left           =     6480
        Top            =     600
        Width          =     1215
     End
     Begin Label Label6
        Alignment      =     1   'Right Justify
        Caption        =     "Clerk:"
        Height         =     375
        Left           =     5640
        TabIndex       =     4
        Top            =     480
        Width          =     615
     End
     Begin Label Label5
        Alignment      =     1   'Right Justify
        Caption        =     "Date:"
        Height         =     375
        Left           =     3120
        TabIndex       =     2
        Top            =     480
        Width          =     615
     End
     Begin Shape Shape5
        FillColor      =     &H00FF0000&
        FillStyle      =     0   'Solid
        Height         =     255
```

```
      Left            =    3960
      Top             =    600
      Width           =    1455
   End
   Begin Shape Shape4
      FillColor       =    &H00FF0000&
      FillStyle       =    0    'Solid
      Height          =    375
      Left            =    5760
      Top             =    2160
      Width           =    1695
   End
   Begin Label Label4
      Alignment       =    1    'Right Justify
      Caption         =    "Total:"
      Height          =    375
      Left            =    4800
      TabIndex        =    10
      Top             =    2040
      Width           =    735
   End
   Begin Shape Shape3
      FillColor       =    &H00FF0000&
      FillStyle       =    0    'Solid
      Height          =    375
      Left            =    1440
      Top             =    2160
      Width           =    2895
   End
   Begin Shape Shape2
      FillColor       =    &H00FF0000&
      FillStyle       =    0    'Solid
      Height          =    375
      Left            =    1440
      Top             =    1320
      Width           =    3975
   End
   Begin Shape Shape1
      FillColor       =    &H00FF0000&
      FillStyle       =    0    'Solid
      Height          =    255
      Left            =    1440
      Top             =    600
      Width           =    1455
   End
   Begin Label Label3
      Alignment       =    1    'Right Justify
      Caption         =    "First Name:"
```

```
        Height          =    255
        Left            =    120
        TabIndex        =    8
        Top             =    2040
        Width           =    1095
     End
     Begin Label Label2
        Alignment       =    1  'Right Justify
        Caption         =    "Last Name:"
        Height          =    375
        Left            =    240
        TabIndex        =    6
        Top             =    1200
        Width           =    975
     End
     Begin Label Label1
        Alignment       =    1  'Right Justify
        Caption         =    "Invoice Number:"
        Height          =    495
        Left            =    240
        TabIndex        =    0
        Top             =    360
        Width           =    975
     End
     Begin Menu MenuFile
        Caption         =    "File"
        Begin Menu MenuNewRecord
           Caption         =    "New Record"
        End
        Begin Menu MenuExit
           Caption         =    "Exit"
        End
     End
     Begin Menu MenuDetails
        Caption         =    "Details"
     End
End
```

Listing 14.13   Code from DATABAS3.FRM

```
Option Explicit

Sub Form_Load ()
    Load Form2
    Form2.Hide
End Sub

Sub InvNumberText_LostFocus ()
```

```
        If Val(InvNumberText.Text) > 32000 Then
            MsgBox "Please Enter a Number Less Than 32767", 16,
                "Data Entry Error"
            InvNumberText.SelStart = 0
            InvNumberText.SelLength = Len(InvNumberText.Text)
            InvNumberText.SetFocus
        End If
    End Sub

Sub InvoiceData_RePosition ()
    InvTotalText.Caption = Format$(Val(InvTotalText.Caption), "#,##0.00")
End Sub

Sub MenuDetails_Click ()
    Dim Response As Integer

    Load Form2
    Form2.DetailData.RecordSource = "SELECT * From Details WHERE
        Details![Invoice Number] = " & Form1.InvNumberText.Text
    Form2.DetailData.Refresh
    If Form2.DetailData.RecordSet.BOF And
       Form2.DetailData.RecordSet.EOF Then
        Response = MsgBox("No Details Found." & Chr$(13) &
            "Do You Wish to Add One?", 36, "Detail Status")
        If Response = 6 Then
            Form2.Show
             Form2.DetailData.RecordSet.AddNew
              Form2.DetailData.RecordSet.Fields![Invoice Number] =
                  Form1.InvoiceData.RecordSet.Fields!Number
            Form2.SetFocus
          Else
            Form1.SetFocus
          End If
      Else
        Form2.Show
      End If

End Sub

Sub MenuExit_Click ()
    End
End Sub

Sub MenuNewRecord_Click ()
    InvoiceData.RecordSet.AddNew
    InvDateText.Text = Format(Now, "ddddd")
    InvNumberText.SetFocus
End Sub
```

Listing 14.14 Objects and Properties from DETAILF3.FRM

```
Begin Form Form2
    Caption          =    "Enter Invoice Detail"
    ClientHeight     =    4335
    ClientLeft       =    1365
    ClientTop        =    1530
    ClientWidth      =    6225
    ControlBox       =    0    'False
    Height           =    4740
    Left             =    1305
    LinkTopic        =    "Form2"
    ScaleHeight      =    4335
    ScaleWidth       =    6225
    Top              =    1185
    Width            =    6345
    Begin CommandButton AddNewButton
        Caption      =    "Add New"
        Height       =    495
        Left         =    2640
        TabIndex     =    9
        Top          =    3360
        Width        =    1575
    End
    Begin Data DetailData
        Caption      =    "Detail File"
        Connect      =    ""
        DatabaseName =    "C:\VB3\INVCDATA.MDB"
        Exclusive    =    0    'False
        Height       =    270
        Left         =    0
        Options      =    0
        ReadOnly     =    0    'False
        RecordSource =    "Details"
        Top          =    4080
        Width        =    6255
    End
    Begin CommandButton ReturnButton
        Caption      =    "Return"
        Height       =    495
        Left         =    4440
        TabIndex     =    8
        Top          =    3360
        Width        =    1575
    End
    Begin TextBox DetPriceText
        DataField    =    "Price"
        DataSource   =    "DetailData"
```

```
         Height          =     375
         Left            =     1920
         TabIndex        =     3
         Top             =     2520
         Width           =     1455
      End
      Begin TextBox DetQuantityText
         DataField       =     "Quantity"
         DataSource      =     "DetailData"
         Height          =     375
         Left            =     1920
         TabIndex        =     2
         Top             =     1800
         Width           =     735
      End
      Begin TextBox DetDescriptionText
         DataField       =     "Description"
         DataSource      =     "DetailData"
         Height          =     375
         Left            =     1920
         TabIndex        =     1
         Top             =     1080
         Width           =     3135
      End
      Begin TextBox DetNumberText
         DataField       =     "Part Number"
         DataSource      =     "DetailData"
         Height          =     375
         Left            =     1920
         TabIndex        =     0
         Top             =     360
         Width           =     1455
      End
      Begin Shape Shape4
         FillColor       =     &H00FF00FF&
         FillStyle       =     0    'Solid
         Height          =     375
         Left            =     2040
         Top             =     2640
         Width           =     1455
      End
      Begin Shape Shape3
         FillColor       =     &H00FF00FF&
         FillStyle       =     0    'Solid
         Height          =     375
         Left            =     2160
         Top             =     1920
         Width           =     615
```

```
End
Begin Shape Shape2
    FillColor        =    &H00FF00FF&
    FillStyle        =    0   'Solid
    Height           =    375
    Left             =    2040
    Top              =    1200
    Width            =    3135
End
Begin Shape Shape1
    FillColor        =    &H00FF00FF&
    FillStyle        =    0   'Solid
    Height           =    375
    Left             =    2040
    Top              =    480
    Width            =    1455
End
Begin Label Label5
    Alignment        =    1   'Right Justify
    Caption          =    "Unit Price:"
    Height           =    375
    Left             =    720
    TabIndex         =    7
    Top              =    2520
    Width            =    975
End
Begin Label Label4
    Alignment        =    1   'Right Justify
    Caption          =    "Quantity:"
    Height           =    375
    Left             =    720
    TabIndex         =    6
    Top              =    1800
    Width            =    975
End
Begin Label Label3
    Alignment        =    1   'Right Justify
    Caption          =    "Description:"
    Height           =    375
    Left             =    360
    TabIndex         =    5
    Top              =    1080
    Width            =    1335
End
Begin Label Label2
    Alignment        =    1   'Right Justify
    Caption          =    "Part Number:"
```

```
            Height          =    375
            Left            =    360
            TabIndex        =    4
            Top             =    360
            Width           =    1335
        End
    End
End
```

Listing 14.15 Code from DETAILF3.FRM

```
Option Explicit

Sub AddNewButton_Click ()
    DetailData.RecordSet.AddNew
    DetailData.RecordSet.Fields![Invoice Number] =
        Form1.InvoiceData.RecordSet.Fields!Number
    DetNumberText.Enabled = True
    DetNumberText.SetFocus
End Sub

Sub Form_Load ()
    Show
    DetNumberText.SetFocus
End Sub

Sub Form_Unload (Cancel As Integer)
    If Not (DetailData.RecordSet.EOF Or DetailData.RecordSet.BOF) Then
        DetailData.RecordSet.Update
    End If
End Sub

Sub ReturnButton_Click ()
    Dim TempTotal As Single

    If Not (DetailData.RecordSet.EOF Or DetailData.RecordSet.BOF) Then
        DetailData.RecordSet.Update
    End If
    DetailData.RecordSet.MoveFirst
    Do While Not DetailData.RecordSet.EOF
        TempTotal = TempTotal + (DetailData.RecordSet.Fields!Quantity *
            DetailData.RecordSet.Fields!Price)
        DetailData.RecordSet.MoveNext
    Loop
    Form1.InvTotalText.Caption = Format$(TempTotal, "#,##0.00")
    Form2.Hide
    Form1.SetFocus

End Sub
```

Exploring Visual Basic's Data Access Features

In a single book chapter I can hardly touch on all the features of this powerful database engine and Visual Basic's elegant interface to its many capabilities. A complete exploration of Visual Basic Access could easily fill a book. For now, I suggest that you study the manuals and try to get at least a basic understanding of all the Access engine's features. You'll find that such rich resources often yield surprising solutions—an observation we could well apply to Visual Basic as a whole.

Appendix: API Procedure Reference

This appendix contains information on all of the API procedures mentioned in this book. The API procedures are listed in alphabetical order and include each procedure's declaration syntax and a brief description of its purpose, arguments, and return value.

Please note that this appendix is not intended to be a complete reference. I do not try to provide a detailed explanation of each procedure, nor do I include information on each procedure's associated Windows global constants and data structures. This information can be found in the book's main text, or in a variety of printed and online sources.

API functions that were used in the book as subprocedures (that is, not returning a value) are listed here the same way.

API Procedures

ArrangeIconicWindows

Purpose:
Arranges all the minimized (iconic) child windows of a parent window.

Declaration:
```
Declare Function ArrangeIconicWindows Lib "User" (ByVal hWnd
  As Integer) As Integer
```

Arguments:
hWnd is the handle of the parent window.

Return value:
On success, the height of one row of icons; on failure, 0

Notes:
To arrange desktop icons pass the handle of the Desktop (obtained with the **GetDesktopWindow** function).

BitBlt

Purpose:
Copies a bitmap from one device context to a destination device context.

Declaration:

```
Declare Function BitBlt Lib "GDI" (ByVal hDestDC As Integer,
   ByVal X As Integer, ByVal Y As Integer, ByVal nWidth As Integer,
   ByVal nHeight As Integer, ByVal hSrcDC As Integer, ByVal XSrc
   As Integer, ByVal YSrc As Integer, ByVal dwRop As Long) As Integer
```

Arguments:

hDest identifies the destination device context.

X specifies the logical X coordinate of the upper-left corner of the destination rectangle.

Y specifies the logical Y coordinate of the upper-left corner of the destination rectangle.

nWidth specifies the width, in logical units, of the destination rectangle and source bitmap.

nHeight specifies the height, in logical units, of the destination rectangle and source bitmap.

hSrcDC identifies the device context from which the bitmap will be copied. This parameter must be NULL if the **dwRop** parameter specifies a raster operation that does not include a source. This parameter can specify a memory device context.

XSrc specifies the logical X coordinate of the upper-left corner of the source bitmap.

YSrc specifies the logical Y coordinate of the upper-left corner of the source bitmap.

dwRop specifies the raster operation to be performed.

Return value:

Non-zero on success, zero otherwise.

Notes:

Please refer to the text for information on the various raster operations.

CreateSolidBrush

Purpose:

Creates a brush that has a specified solid color. The brush can subsequently be selected as the current brush for any device.

Declaration:

```
Declare Function CreateSolidBrush Lib "GDI" (ByVal crColor
   As Long) As Integer
```

Arguments:

crColor specifies the color of the brush.

Return value:

The return value is the handle of the brush if the function is successful, 0 otherwise.

DeleteMenu

Purpose:

Deletes an item from a menu. If the menu item has a pop-up menu associated with it, **DeleteMenu** destroys the handle of the pop-up menu and frees its memory.

Declaration:

```
Declare Function DeleteMenu Lib "User" (ByVal hMenu As
   Integer, ByVal nPosition As Integer, ByVal wFlags As
   Integer) As Integer
```

Arguments:

hMenu identifies the menu to be deleted.

nPosition specifies the menu item to be deleted, as determined by the **wFlags** parameter.

wFlags specifies how the **idItem** parameter is interpreted.

Return value:

Non-zero if the function is successful, zero otherwise.

Notes:

See the text for information on the **wFlags** parameter.

DeleteObject

Purpose:

Deletes an object from memory.

Declaration:

```
Declare Sub DeleteObject Lib "GDI" (ByVal hObject As
   Integer)
```

Arguments:

hObject is the handle of the object to be deleted.

Return value:

Non-zero if the function is successful, zero otherwise.

Escape

Purpose:

Allows applications to access capabilities of a particular device that are not directly available through the graphics device interface (GDI). Escape calls made by an application are translated and sent to the driver.

Declaration:

```
Declare Function Escape Lib "GDI" (ByVal hDC As
   Integer,  ByVal nEscape As Integer, ByVal nCount As
```

```
Integer, lpInData As Any, lpOutData As Any) As
Integer
```

Arguments:

hDC identifies the device context.

nEscape specifies the escape function to be performed.

NCount specifies the size, in bytes, of the **lpInData** structure.

lpInData is the input structure containing data required for the specified escape command.

lpOutData is the structure that receives output from the escape. This parameter should be NULL if no data is returned.

Return value:

On success, an implementation-specific code greater than 0. An error code less than 0 on error. 0 if the escape command is not supported by the device.

Notes:

The commands you can send with the **Escape** function are dependent on the device.

ExitWindows

Purpose:

This function can restart Windows, terminate Windows and return control to MS-DOS, or terminate Windows and restart the system.

Declaration:

```
Declare Function ExitWindows Lib "User" (ByVal
  dwReserved As Long, ByVal dwReturnCode As Integer) As
  Integer
```

Arguments:

dwReserved is reserved and must be 0.

dwReturnCode specifies whether Windows should restart, terminate and return control to MS-DOS, or terminate and restart the system.

Return value:

0 if one or more applications refuse to terminate. The function does not return a value if all applications agree to be terminated.

Notes:

The high-order word of **dwReturnCode** should be 0. The low-order word specifies the return value to be passed to MS-DOS when Windows terminates. The low-order word can be one of the following values:

EW_REBOOTSYSTEM causes Windows to terminate and the system to restart.

EW_RESTARTWINDOWS causes Windows to restart.

FillRect

Purpose:

Fills a given rectangle using the specified brush.

Declaration:

```
Declare Sub FillRect Lib "User" (ByVal hDC As Integer,
  pRect As RECT, ByVal hBrush As Integer)
```

Arguments:

hDC identifies the device context.

pRect points to a **RECT** structure that contains the logical coordinates of the rectangle to be filled.

hBrush identifies the brush used to fill the rectangle.

Return value:

The return value is not used and has no meaning.

Notes:

The **FillRect** function fills the complete rectangle, including the left and top borders, but does not fill the right and bottom borders.

FlashWindow

Purpose:

Flashes the title bar of the given window once.

Declaration:

```
Declare Sub FlashWindow Lib "User" (ByVal hWnd As
  Integer, ByVal Invert As Integer)
```

Arguments:

hWnd identifies the window to be flashed.

Invert specifies whether to flash the window or return it to its original state. If **Invert** is True, the window is flashed from one state to the other. If **Invert** is False, the window is returned to its original state (either active or inactive).

Return value:

Non-zero if the window was active before the call to the **FlashWindow** function. Otherwise, it is zero.

Notes:

Flashing a window means changing the appearance of its title bar as if the window were changing from inactive to active status or vice versa. The window can be either open or minimized.

GetActiveWindow

Purpose:

Retrieves the window handle of the active window.

Declaration:

```
Declare Function GetActiveWindow Lib "User" () As
   Integer
```

Arguments:

(None)

Return value:

The handle of the active window, or 0 if no window is active.

Notes:

The active window is either the top-level window that has the input focus or the window explicitly made active by the **SetActiveWindow** function.

GetAsyncKeyState

Purpose:

Determines whether a key and/or mouse button is up or down at the time the function is called and whether the key or button has been pressed after a previous call to this function.

Declaration:

```
Declare Function GetAsyncKeyState Lib "User" (ByVal
   vKey As Integer) As Integer
```

Arguments:

vKey specifies the key and/or mouse button to check.

Return value:

The return value specifies whether the key/button was pressed since the last call to the **GetAsyncKeyState** function and whether the key/button is currently up or down. If the most significant bit of the return value is set the key/button is down; if the least significant bit is set, the key/button has been pressed since the preceding **GetAsyncKeyState** call.

Notes:

See the text for information on values of **vKey**.

GetClassName

Purpose:

Retrieves the class name of a window.

Declaration:

```
Declare Function GetClassName Lib "User" (ByVal hWnd As
   Integer, ByVal lpClassName As String, ByVal nMaxCount
   As Integer) As Integer
```

Arguments:

hWnd identifies the window.

lpClassName is a buffer that receives the null-terminated class name string.

nMaxCount specifies the length of the buffer pointed to by the **lpClassName** parameter.

Return value:

The length, in bytes, of the returned class name, not including the terminating NULL character. The return value is 0 if the specified window handle is invalid.

Notes:

 The class name string is truncated if it is longer than the buffer.

GetCursorPos

Purpose:

Retrieves the screen coordinates of the cursor's current position.

Declaration:

```
Declare Sub GetCursorPos Lib "User" (lpPoint As
   PointAPI)
```

Arguments:

lpPoint is the **POINT** structure that receives the cursor position.

Return value:

(None)

Notes:

The cursor position is always in screen coordinates; it is not affected by the mapping mode of the window that contains the cursor.

GetDC

Purpose:

Retrieves the handle of a device context for the given window's client area. The device context can be used in subsequent graphics device interface (GDI) functions to draw in the client area.

Declaration:

```
Declare Function GetDC Lib "User" (ByVal hWnd As
   Integer) As Integer
```

Arguments:

hWnd identifies the window. If this parameter is NULL, the function returns a device context for the screen.

Return value:

On success, the handle of the device context for the given window's client area, 0 otherwise.

GetDesktopWindow

Purpose:

Retrieves the handle of the desktop window.

Declaration:

```
Declare Function GetDesktopWindow Lib "User" () As
   Integer
```

Arguments:

(None)

Return value:

The handle of the desktop window.

Notes:

The desktop window covers the entire screen and is the area on top of which all icons and other windows are painted.

GetDeviceCaps

Purpose:

Retrieves device-specific information about a display device.

Declaration:

```
Declare Function GetDeviceCaps Lib "GDI" (ByVal hDC As
   Integer, ByVal nIndex As Integer) As Integer
```

Arguments:

hDC identifies the device.

nIndex specifies the type of information to be retrieved.

Return value:

The value of the specified capability.

Notes:

See the text for details on the types of device information that can be retrieved.

GetDialogBaseUnits

Purpose:

Retrieves the dialog base units used by Windows for the active window. These values are used by an application to calculate the average width of characters when displayed in a window.

Declaration:

```
Declare Function GetDialogBaseUnits Lib "User" () As
  Long
```

Arguments:

(None)

Return value:

The dialog base units value for the current window.

Notes:

See the text for information on interpreting the value returned by this function.

GetFocus

Purpose:

Retrieves the handle of the window that has the focus.

Declaration:

```
Declare Function GetFocus Lib "User" () As Integer
```

Arguments:

(None)

Return value:

The handle of the window with the focus, or 0 if no window has the focus.

GetFreeSpace

Purpose:

Retrieves the amount of free memory in the global heap.

Declaration:

```
Declare Function GetFreeSpace Lib "Kernel" (ByVal
  wFlags As Integer) As Long
```

Arguments:

wFlags is ignored in Windows 3.1.

Return value:

The amount of free memory, in bytes.

GetFreeSystemResources

Purpose:

Retrieves the percentage of system resources that are free.

Declaration:

```
Declare Function GetFreeSystemResources Lib "User"
  (ByVal fuSysResource As Integer) As Integer
```

Arguments:

fuSysResource specifies the type of system resource to be queried.

Return value:

The percentage of the specified system resource that is free.

Notes:

See the text for information on the three different types of system resources and their interpretation.

GetKeyboardType

Purpose:

Retrieves information about the current keyboard.

Declaration:

```
Declare Function GetKeyboardType Lib "Keyboard" (ByVal
  nTypeFlag As Integer) As Integer
```

Arguments:

nTypeFlag specifies the type of keyboard information to be retrieved. A value of 0 retrieves the keyboard type, 1 retrieves the keyboard subtype, and 2 retrieves the number of function keys on the keyboard.

Return value:

The return value specifies the requested information if the function is successful. Otherwise, the value is 0.

Notes:

See the text for information on interpreting the values returned by this function.

GetMenu

Purpose:

Retrieves the handle of the menu associated with the given window.

Declaration:

```
Declare Function GetMenu Lib "User" (ByVal hWnd As
  Integer) As Integer
```

Arguments:

hWnd identifies the window.

Return value:

On success, the handle of the window's menu. The return value is 0 if the given window has no menu, and is undefined if the window is a child window.

GetMenuItemID

Purpose:

Retrieves the identifier for a menu item located at the given position.

Declaration:

```
Declare Function GetMenuItemID Lib "User" (ByVal hMenu
   As Integer, ByVal nPos As Integer) As Integer
```

Arguments:

hMenu is the handle of the menu that contains the item whose identifier is to be retrieved.

nPosition specifies the zero-based position of the menu item whose identifier is to be retrieved.

Return value:

On success, the identifier of the pop-up menu item and -1 if the specified item is a pop-up menu (as opposed to an item within a pop-up menu). If **nPosition** specifies a Separator menu item, the return value is 0.

GetModuleHandle

Purpose:

Retrieves the handle of the specified module.

Declaration:

```
Declare Function GetModuleHandle Lib "Kernel" (ByVal
   lpModuleName As String) As Integer
```

Arguments:

lpModuleName is a string that specifies the name of the module.

Return value:

On success, the module handle, 0 otherwise.

GetModuleUsage

Purpose:

Retrieves the reference count of a specified module.

Declaration:

```
Declare Function GetModuleUsage Lib "Kernel" (ByVal
  hModule  As Integer) As Integer
```

Arguments:

hModule is the handle of the module.

Return value:

The reference count of the specified module.

Notes:

The reference count is equivalent to the number of instances of a module (program) that are loaded.

GetNumTasks

Purpose:

Retrieves the number of currently running tasks.

Declaration:

```
Declare Function GetNumTasks Lib "Kernel" () As Integer
```

Arguments:

(None)

Return value:

The number of tasks that are currently running.

GetParent

Purpose:

Retrieves the handle of the given window's parent window (if any).

Declaration:

```
Declare Function GetParent Lib "User" (ByVal hWnd As
  Integer) As Integer
```

Arguments:

hWnd identifies the window.

Return value:

The handle of the parent window, or 0 if there is no parent window or an error occurs.

GetPrivateProfileString

Purpose:

Retrieves a character string from the specified section in the specified initialization file.

Declaration:

```
Declare Function GetPrivateProfileString Lib "Kernel"
  (ByVal lpAppName As String, ByVal lpKeyName As
  String, ByVal lpDefault As String, ByVal
  lpReturnedString As String, ByVal nSize As Integer,
  ByVal lpFileName As String) As Integer
```

Arguments:

lpAppName specifies the .INI file section containing the entry.

lpKeyName specifies the .INI file entry whose associated string is to be retrieved. If this value is NULL, all entries in the section specified by the **lpAppName** parameter are retrieved.

lpDefault specifies the default value to be returned if the specified file, section, or entry cannot be found.

lpReturnedString is a buffer that receives the character string.

nSize is the size, in bytes, of the buffer **lpReturnedString**.

lpFileName names the initialization file. If this parameter does not contain a full path, Windows searches for the file in the Windows directory.

Return value:

The number of bytes copied to the specified buffer.

GetProfileString

Purpose:

Retrieves a character string from the specified section in the WIN.INI initialization file.

Declaration:

```
Declare Function GetProfileString Lib "Kernel" (ByVal
  lpAppName As String, ByVal lpKeyName As String,
  ByVal lpDefault As String, ByVal lpReturnedString
  As String, ByVal nSize As Integer) As Integer
```

Arguments:

lpAppName specifies the .INI file section containing the entry.

lpKeyName specifies the .INI file entry whose associated string is to be retrieved. If this value is NULL, all entries in the section specified by the **lpAppName** parameter are retrieved.

lpDefault specifies the default value to be returned if the specified section or entry cannot be found in WIN.INI.

lpReturnedString is a buffer that receives the character string.

nSize is the size, in bytes, of the buffer **lpReturnedString**.

Return value:

The number of bytes copied to the specified buffer.

GetSubMenu

Purpose:

Retrieves the handle of a pop-up menu.

Declaration:

```
Declare Function GetSubMenu Lib "User" (ByVal hMenu As
    Integer, ByVal nPos As Integer) As Integer
```

Arguments:

hMenu identifies the menu with the pop-up menu whose handle is to be retrieved.

nPos specifies the zero-based position in the given menu of the pop-up menu.

Return value:

On success, the handle of the popup menu, and 0 if no pop-up menu exists at the specified position.

GetSystemDirectory

Purpose:

Retrieves the path of the Windows system directory.

Declaration:

```
Declare Function GetSystemDirectory Lib "Kernel" (ByVal
    lpBuffer As String, ByVal nSize As Integer) As
    Integer
```

Arguments:

lpBuffer is a buffer where the system directory string will be placed.

nSize is the size, in bytes, of **lpBuffer**.

Return value:

On success, the length of the string retrieved, and 0 on failure.

Notes:

The Windows system directory contains such files as Windows libraries, drivers, and fonts. It is distinct from the main Windows directory.

GetSystemMenu

Purpose:

To retrieve a handle to a copy of the system menu.

Declaration:

```
Declare Function GetSystemMenu Lib "User" (ByVal hWnd
   As Integer, ByVal bRevert As Integer) As Integer
```

Arguments:

hWnd identifies the window that will own a copy of the System menu.

bRevert specifies the action to be taken. If this parameter is False, the function returns a handle of a copy of the System menu currently in use. This copy is initially identical to the System menu, but can be modified. If **bRevert** is True, **GetSystemMenu** resets the System menu back to the Windows default state. The previous System menu, if any, is destroyed. The return value is undefined in this case.

Return value:

If **bRevert** is False the return value is the handle of a copy of the System menu. If **bRevert** is True the return value is undefined.

Notes:

The **GetSystemMenu** function allows the application to access a copy of the System menu for copying and modification.

GetTextMetrics

Purpose:

Retrieves the metrics for the current font on a specified device.

Declaration:

```
Declare Function GetTextMetrics Lib "GDI" (ByVal hDC As
   Integer, lpMetrics As TEXTMETRIC) As Integer
```

Arguments:

hDC identifies the device context.

lpMetrics is a type **TEXTMETRIC** structure that receives the information.

Return value:

The return value is non-zero if the function is successful, otherwise, it is zero.

Notes:

See the text for more details on the information returned by this function.

GetVersion

Purpose:

Retrieves the version numbers of the Windows and MS-DOS operating systems that are in use.

Declaration:
```
Declare Function GetVersion Lib "Kernel" () As Long
```

Arguments:
(None)

Return value:
A value specifying the major and minor version numbers of Windows and of MS-DOS.

Notes:
The low-order word of the return value contains the version of Windows, with the major and minor version numbers contained in the low- and high-order bytes, respectively. The high-order word contains the version of MS-DOS, with the major and minor version numbers contained in the high- and low order bytes, respectively. See the text for details on extracting the major and minor version numbers.

GetWindowsDirectory

Purpose:
Retrieves the path of the Windows directory.

Declaration:
```
Declare Function GetWindowsDirectory Lib "Kernel"
  (ByVal lpBuffer As String, ByVal nSize As Integer)
  As Integer
```

Arguments:
lpBuffer is a buffer where the system directory string will be placed.
nSize is the size, in bytes, of **lpBuffer**.

Return value:
On success, the length of the string retrieved, and 0 on failure.

Notes:
This directory contains such files as Windows applications, initialization files, and help files.

GetWindowRect

Purpose:
Retrieves the dimensions of the bounding rectangle of a given window.

Declaration:
```
Declare Sub GetWindowRect Lib "User" (ByVal hWnd As
  Integer, lpRect As RECT)
```

Arguments:

hWnd identifies the window.

lpRect is a a type **RECT** structure that receives the screen coordinates of the upper-left and lower-right corners of the window.

Return value:

(None)

GetWindowText

Purpose:

Retrieves the text from the given window's title bar (if it has one).

Declaration:

```
Declare Function GetWindowText Lib "User" (ByVal hWnd
   As Integer, ByVal lpString As String, ByVal nMaxCount
   As Integer) As Integer
```

Arguments:

hWnd identifies the window.

lpString is a buffer where the text is to be placed.

nMaxCount is the size of **lpString**, in characters

Return value:

On success, the length of the retrieved text. the return value is 0 if the window has no title bar, the title bar is empty, or the **hWnd** parameter is invalid.

GetWinFlags

Purpose:

Retrieves the current Windows system and memory configuration.

Declaration:

```
Declare Function GetWinFlags Lib "Kernel" () As Long
```

Arguments:

(None)

Return value:

A value that specifies the current system and memory configuration.

Notes:

See the text for information on interpreting the value returned by this function.

GlobalAlloc

Purpose:

Allocates the specified number of bytes from the global heap.

Declaration:

```
Declare Function GlobalAlloc Lib "Kernel" (ByVal wFlags
  As Integer, ByVal dwBytes As Long) As Integer
```

Arguments:

wFlags specifies how the memory is to be allocated.

dwBytes specifies how many bytes of memory are to be allocated.

Return value:

On success, a handle to the allocated memory object, and 0 on failure.

GlobalFree

Purpose:

Frees the given global memory object (if the object is not locked) and invalidates its handle.

Declaration:

```
Declare Function GlobalFree Lib "Kernel" (ByVal hMem As
  Integer) As Integer
```

Arguments:

hMem is the handle of the memory object to be freed.

Return value:

0 on success, **hMem** on failure.

GlobalHandleToSel

Purpose:

Converts the given handle to a selector.

Declaration:

```
Declare Function GlobalHandleToSel Lib "Toolhelp.DLL"
  (ByVal Handle As Integer) As Integer
```

Arguments:

Handle is the handle to be converted to a selector.

Return value:

On success, a selector to the specified object, 0 is returned on failure.

Notes:

Visual Basic requires that a memory handle be converted to a selector before the memory can be accessed.

IsCharAlpha

Purpose:

Determines whether a character is in the set of language-defined alphabetic characters.

Declaration:

```
Declare Function IsCharAlpha Lib "User" (ByVal cChar As
    Integer) As Integer
```

Arguments:

cChar is the ASCII code of the character to be tested.

Return value:

Non-zero if the character is in the set of alphabetic characters, zero otherwise.

IsCharAlphaNumeric

Purpose:

Determines whether a character is in the set of language-defined alphabetic and numeric characters.

Declaration:

```
Declare Function IsCharAlphaNumeric Lib "User" (ByVal
    cChar As Integer) As Integer
```

Arguments:

cChar is the ASCII code of the character to be tested.

Return value:

Non-zero if the character is in the set of alphabetic and numeric characters, zero otherwise.

IsCharLower

Purpose:
Determines if a character is lowercase.

Declaration:

```
Declare Function IsCharLower Lib "User" (ByVal cChar As
    Integer) As Integer
```

Arguments:

cChar is the ASCII code of the character to be tested.

Return value:

Non-zero if the character is lowercase, zero otherwise.

IsCharUpper

Purpose:

Determines if a character is uppercase.

Declaration:

```
Declare Function IsCharUpper Lib "User" (ByVal cChar As Integer) As
Integer
```

Arguments:

cChar is the ASCII value of the character to be tested.

Return value:

Non-zero if the character is uppercase, zero otherwise.

IsWindow

Purpose:

Determines whether the given window handle is valid.

Declaration:

```
Declare Function IsWindow Lib "User" (ByVal hWnd As
  Integer) As Integer
```

Arguments:

hWnd identifies a window.

Return value:

Non-zero if the window handle is valid, zero otherwise.

MemoryRead

Purpose:

Copies data from the specified global heap object to the specified buffer.

Declaration:

```
Declare Function MemoryRead Lib "Toolhelp.dll" (ByVal
  wSel As Integer, ByVal dwOffSet as Long, lpvBuf as
  Any, ByVal dwcb As Long) As Long
```

Arguments:

wSel is the selector of the memory object.

dwOffSet specifies the offset in the memory object at which to begin reading. This value may point anywhere within the object.

lpvBuf is the buffer in which **MemoryRead** will place the data copied from the memory object. This buffer must be large enough to contain the entire amount of memory copied to it.

dwcb specifies the number of bytes to copy.

Return value:

On success, the number of bytes copied. If **wSel** is invalid or if **dwOffset** is out of the selector's range, the return value is 0.

MemoryWrite

Purpose:

Copies data from the specified buffer to the specified global heap object.

Declaration:

```
Declare Function MemoryWrite Lib "Toolhelp.dll" (ByVal
   wSel As Integer, ByVal dwOffSet as Long, lpvBuf as
   Any, ByVal dwcb As Long) As Long
```

Arguments:

wSel is the selector of the memory object.

dwOffSet specifies the offset in the memory object at which to begin writing. This value may point anywhere within the object.

lpvBuf is the buffer from which **MemoryWrite** will take the data copied to the memory object.

dwcb specifies the number of bytes to copy.

Return value:

On success, the number of bytes copied. If **wSel** is invalid or if **dwOffset** is out of the selector's range, the return value is 0.

ModifyMenu

Purpose:

Changes an existing menu item.

Declaration:

```
Declare Function ModifyMenu Lib "User" (ByVal hMenu As
   Integer, ByVal nPosition As Integer, ByVal wFlags As
   Integer, ByVal wIDNewItem As Integer, ByVal lpString
   As Any) As Integer
```

Arguments:

hMenu identifies the menu containing the item to change.

nPosition specifies the menu item to change, as determined by the **wFlags** parameter. When the **wFlags** parameter is **MF_BYCOMMAND**, this argument specifies the menu-item identifier. When the **wFlags** parameter is **MF_BYPOSITION**, this argument specifies the zero-based position of the menu item.

wFlags specifies how the **nPosition** argument is interpreted.

wIDNewItem specifies either the identifier of the modified menu item or, if **wFlags** is set to **MF_POPUP**, the menu handle of the pop-up menu.

lpString specifies the content of the changed menu item.

Return value:

Non-zero if the function is successful, zero otherwise.

Notes:

Refer to the text for more information on how to use this function.

Polygon

Purpose:

Draws a polygon consisting of two or more points connected by lines.

Declaration:

```
Declare Function Polygon Lib "GDI" (ByVal hDC As
   Integer, lpPoints As POINTAPI, ByVal nCount As
   Integer) As Integer
```

Arguments:

hDC is the device context.

lpPoints is an array of type **APIPOINT** structures that specify the vertices of the polygon. Each structure in the array specifies a vertex.

nCount specifies the number of vertices in the polygon.

Return value:

Non-zero on success, zero otherwise.

Notes:

The polygon is closed automatically, if necessary, with a line from the last vertex to the first. Polygons are surrounded by a frame drawn by using the current pen and filled by using the current brush. See the text for further information on using this function.

Rectangle

Purpose:

Draws a rectangle.

Declaration:

```
Declare Sub Rectangle Lib "GDI" (ByVal hDC As Integer,
   ByVal X1 As Integer, ByVal Y1 As Integer, ByVal X2 As
   Integer, ByVal Y2 As Integer)
```

Arguments:

hDC specifies the device context.

X1 and **Y1** specify the logical coordinates of the upper-left corner of the rectangle.

X2 and **Y2** specify the logical coordinates of the lower-right corner of the rectangle.

Return value:

Non-zero on success, zero otherwise.

Notes:

The rectangle is drawn using the current pen. The interior of the rectangle is filled by using the current brush.

ReleaseDC

Purpose:

Releases the specified device context, freeing it for use by other applications.

Declaration:

```
Declare Sub ReleaseDC Lib "User" (ByVal hWnd As
   Integer, ByVal hDC As Integer)
```

Arguments:

hWnd identifies the window whose device context is to be released.

hDC identifies the device context to be released.

Return value:

1 on success, 0 otherwise.

SelectObject

Purpose:

Selects an object in a given device context.

Declaration:

```
Declare Sub SelectObject Lib "GDI" (ByVal hDC As
   Integer, ByVal hObject As Integer)
```

Arguments:

hDC identifies the device context.

hObject specifies the object to be selected.

Return value:

On success, the handle of the object previously selected; on failure, 0.

SendMessage

Purpose:

Sends the specified message to the given window or windows.

Declaration:

```
Declare Function SendMessage Lib "User" (ByVal hWnd As
    Integer, ByVal wMsg As Integer, ByVal wParam As
    Integer, lParam As Any) As Long
```

Arguments:

hWnd specifies the window to receive the message. If this argument is **HWND_BROADCAST**, the message will be sent to all top-level windows, including disabled or invisible, unowned windows.

wMsg is the message to be sent.

wParam is 16 bits of additional message-dependent information.

lParam is 32 bits of additional message-dependent information.

Return value:

A value indicating the result of message processing, which is dependent on the message sent.

SetFocusAPI

Purpose:

Sets the input focus to the given window.

Declaration:

```
Declare Sub SetFocusAPI Lib "User" Alias "SetFocus"
    (ByVal hWnd As Integer)
```

Arguments:

hWnd identifies the window to receive the focus.

Return value:

On success, identifies the window that previously had the input focus. It is NULL if there is no such window or if the specified handle is invalid.

Notes:

In the API, this function is named **SetFocus**. Visual Basic programs must refer to it as **SetFocusAPI**, using the **Alias** keyword in the declaration, to avoid conflict with the **SetFocus** method.

SetPolyFillMode

Purpose:

Sets the specified polygon-filling mode.

Declaration:

```
Declare Function SetPolyFillMode Lib "GDI" (ByVal hDC
    As Integer, ByVal nPolyFillMode As Integer) As
    Integer
```

Arguments:

hDC identifies the device context.

nPolyFillMode specifies the new polygon fill mode.

Return value:

On success, the previous polygon fill mode; on failure, 0.

Notes:

Refer to the text for information on the available fill modes.

SetStretchBltMode

Purpose:

Sets the bitmap-stretching mode used by the **StretchBlt** function.

Declaration:

```
Declare Function SetStretchBltMode Lib "GDI" (ByVal hDC
  As Integer, ByVal mode As Integer) As Integer
```

Arguments:

hDC identifies the device context.

mode is the bitmap-stretching mode.

Return value:

On success, the previous stretching mode; on failure, 0.

Notes:

Refer to the text for information on the various stretching modes.

SetTextAlign

Purpose:

Sets the text-alignment flags for the given device context.

Declaration:

```
Declare Sub SetTextAlign Lib "GDI" (ByVal hDC As
  Integer, ByVal wFlags As Integer)
```

Arguments:

hDC specifies the device context.

wFlags specifies the text alignment flags.

Return value:

(None)

Notes:

Refer to the text for details on the possible settings of the alignment flags.

SetWindowPos

Purpose:

Changes the size, position, and Z order of child, pop-up, and top-level windows.

Declaration:

```
Declare Function SetWindowPos Lib "User" (ByVal hWnd As
   Integer, ByVal hWndInsertAfter As Integer, ByVal X As
   Integer, ByVal Y As Integer, ByVal Cx As Integer,
   ByVal Cy As Integer, ByVal wFlags As Integer) As
   Integer
```

Arguments:

hWnd identifies the window to be modified.

hWndInsertAfter specifies the window's position in the Z order. This argument can be the handle of the window that the current window is to follow, or one of the following: **HWND_BOTTOM** places the window at the bottom of the Z order, **HWND_TOP** places the window at the top of the Z order, and **HWND_TOPMOST** places the window above all non-topmost windows.

X and **Y** specify the position of the upper-left window corner.

Cx and **Cy** identify the width and height of the window.

wFlags specifies the window sizing and positioning options.

Return value:

Non-zero on success, zero otherwise.

Notes:

Refer to the text for information on the available window sizing and positioning options.

StretchBlt

Purpose:

Copies a bitmap from a source rectangle into a destination rectangle, stretching or compressing the bitmap if necessary to fit the dimensions of the destination rectangle.

Declaration:

```
Declare Function StretchBlt Lib "GDI" (ByVal hDC As
   Integer, ByVal X As Integer, ByVal Y As Integer,
   ByVal nWidth As Integer, ByVal nHeight As Integer,
   ByVal hSrcDC As Integer, ByVal XSrc As Integer,
   ByVal YSrc As Integer, ByVal nSrcWidth As Integer,
   ByVal nSrcHeight As Integer, ByVal dwRop As Long)
   As Integer
```

Arguments:

hDC identifies the destination context.

X and **Y** specify the logical coordinates of the destination rectangle.

nWidth and **nHeight** specify the logical width and height of the destination rectangle.

hSrcDC specifies the source context.

XSrc and **YSrc** specify the logical coordinates of the source rectangle.

nSrcWidth and **nSrcHeight** specify the logical width and height of the source rectangle.

dwRop specifies the raster operation to be performed.

Return value:

Non-zero on success, zero otherwise.

Notes:

Refer to the text for further information on the use of this function.

TrackPopupMenu

Purpose:

Displays the given floating pop-up menu at the specified location and tracks the selection of items on the pop-up menu.

Declaration:

```
Declare Function TrackPopupMenu Lib "User" (ByVal hMenu
  As Integer, ByVal wFlags As Integer, ByVal X As
  Integer, ByVal Y As Integer, ByVal nReserved As
  Integer, ByVal hWnd As Integer, lpReserved As Any)
  As Integer
```

Arguments:

hMenu identifies the pop-up menu to be displayed.

wFlags specifies the screen-position and mouse-button flags for the menu.

X and **Y** specify the screen coordinates of the top-left corner of the menu.

nReserved is reserved and must be 0.

hWnd identifies the window that owns the pop-up menu.

lpReserved is a type **RECT** structure that contains the screen coordinates of a rectangle in which the user can click without dismissing the pop-up menu. If this parameter is NULL, the pop-up menu is dismissed if the user clicks outside the pop-up menu.

Return value:

Non-zero on success, zero otherwise.

Notes:

Refer to the text for further information on using this function.

WindowFromPoint

Purpose:

Retrieves the handle of the window that contains the specified point.

Declaration:

```
Declare Function WindowFromPoint Lib "User" (ByVal X As
   Integer, ByVal Y As Integer) As Integer
```

Arguments:

X and **Y** are the screen coordinates of the point to be checked.

Return value:

The handle of the window containing the specified point, or 0 if no window exists at that point.

WinExec

Purpose:

Runs the specified application.

Declaration:

```
Declare Function WinExec Lib "Kernel" (ByVal lpCmdLine
   As String, ByVal nCmdShow As Integer) As Integer
```

Arguments:

lpCmdLine is the command line (filename plus optional parameters) needed to run the application.

nCmdShow specifies how the application is to be shown.

Return value:

On success, the instance of the loaded module. Otherwise, the return value is an error value less than 32.

Notes:

Refer to the notes for information on the **nCmdShow** options and the error codes.

WritePrivateProfileString

Purpose:

Copies a character string into the specified section of the specified initialization file.

Declaration:

```
Declare Function WritePrivateProfileString Lib "Kernel"
  (ByVal lpAppName As String, ByVal lpKeyName As
  String, ByVal lpString As String, ByVal lpFileName As
  String) As Integer
```

Arguments:

lpAppName specifies the .INI file section where the entry is to be placed.

lpKeyName specifies the entry to be associated with the string. If this value is NULL, all of the entries in the section specified by the **lpAppName** parameter are deleted.

lpString is a buffer that contains the character string to be written.

lpFileName names the initialization file. If this parameter does not contain a full path, Windows searches for the file in the Windows directory.

Return value:

Non-zero on success, zero otherwise.

WriteProfileString

Purpose:

Copies a character string into the specified section of the WIN.INI initialization file.

Declaration:

```
Declare Function WriteProfileString Lib "Kernel" (ByVal
   lpAppName As String, ByVal lpKeyName As String, ByVal
   lpString As String) As Integer
```

Arguments:

lpAppName specifies the .INI file section where the entry is to be placed.

lpKeyName specifies the entry to be associated with the string. If this value is NULL, all of the entries in the section specified by the **lpAppName** parameter are deleted.

lpString is a buffer that contains the character string to be written.

Return value:

Non-zero on success, zero otherwise.

Index

Italic page numbers refer to API procedure definitions.

READ THE MAGAZINE
OF TECHNICAL EXPERTISE!

Published by The Coriolis Group

For years, Jeff Duntemann has been known for his crystal-clear, slightly-be-mused explanations of programming technology. He's one of the few in computer publishing who has never forgotten that English is the one language we all have in common. Now he's teamed up with author Keith Weiskamp and created a magazine that brings you a selection of readable, practical technical articles six times a year, written by himself and a crew of the very best technical writers working today. Michael Abrash, Tom Swan, Jim Mischel, Keith Weiskamp, David Gerrold, Brett Glass, Michael Covington, Peter Aitken, Marty Franz, Jim Kyle, and many others will perform their magic before your eyes, and then explain how *you* can do it too, in language that you can understand.

If you program under DOS or Windows in C, C++, Pascal, Visual Basic, or assembly language, you'll find code you can use in every issue. You'll also find essential debugging and optimization techniques, programming tricks and tips, detailed product reviews, and practical advice on how to get your programming product finished, polished and ready to roll.

Don't miss another issue—subscribe today!

▢ 1 Year $21.95 ▢ 2 Years $37.95

▢ $29.95 Canada; $39.95 Foreign ▢ $53.95 Canada; $73.95 Foreign

Total for subscription _____
Arizona orders please add 6% sales tax _____
Total due, in US funds _____

Send to:
PC TECHNIQUES
7721 E. Gray Road, #204
Scottsdale AZ 85260

Name _____
Company_____
Address _____
City/State/ZIP _____
Phone _____

Phone (602) 483-0192
Fax   (602) 483-0193

VISA/MC # _____ Expires _____

Signature for charge orders _____

**THE
CORIOLIS
GROUP**

(John Wiley & Sons, Inc., is not responsible for orders placed with The Coriolis Group)

BC012